D1714449

Global Issues Series

General Editor: Jim Whitman

This exciting new series encompasses three principal themes: the interaction of human and natural systems; cooperation and conflict; and the enactment of values. The series as a whole places an emphasis on the examination of complex systems and causal relations in political decision-making; problems of knowledge; authority, control and accountability in issues of scale; and the reconciliation of conflicting values and competing claims. Throughout the series the concentration is on an integration of existing disciplines towards the clarification of political possibility as well as impending crises.

Titles include:

Berhanykun Andemicael and John Mathiason
ELIMINATING WEAPONS OF MASS DESTRUCTION
Prospects for Effective International Verification

Mike Bourne
ARMING CONFLICT
The Proliferation of Small Arms

Roy Carr-Hill and John Lintott
CONSUMPTION, JOBS AND THE ENVIRONMENT
A Fourth Way?

John N. Clarke and Geoffrey R. Edwards (*editors*)
GLOBAL GOVERNANCE IN THE TWENTY-FIRST CENTURY

Malcolm Dando
PREVENTING BIOLOGICAL WARFARE
The Failure of American Leadership

Neil Davison
'NON-LETHAL' WEAPONS

Toni Erskine (*editor*)
CAN INSTITUTIONS HAVE RESPONSIBILITIES?
Collective Moral Agency and International Relations

Brendan Gleeson and Nicholas Low (*editors*)
GOVERNING FOR THE ENVIRONMENT
Global Problems, Ethics and Democracy

Beth K. Greener
THE NEW INTERNATIONAL POLICING

Roger Jeffery and Bhaskar Vira (*editors*)
CONFLICT AND COOPERATION IN PARTICIPATORY NATURAL RESOURCE MANAGEMENT

Ho-Won Jeong (*editor*)
GLOBAL ENVIRONMENTAL POLICIES
Institutions and Procedures

APPROACHES TO PEACEBUILDING

Alexander Kelle, Kathryn Nixdorff and Malcolm Dando
CONTROLLING BIOCHEMICAL WEAPONS
Adapting Multilateral Arms Control for the 21st Century

W. Andy Knight
A CHANGING UNITED NATIONS
Multilateral Evolution and the Quest for Global Governance

Global Issues Series
Series Standing Order ISBN 978-0-333-79483-8
(*outside North America only*)

You can receive future titles in this series as they are published by placing a standing order. Please contact your bookseller or, in case of difficulty, write to us at the address below with your name and address, the title of the series and the ISBN quoted above.

Customer Services Department, Macmillan Distribution Ltd, Houndmills, Basingstoke, Hampshire RG21 6XS, England

'Non-Lethal' Weapons

Neil Davison

palgrave
macmillan

First published 2009 by
PALGRAVE MACMILLAN

Palgrave Macmillan in the UK is an imprint of Macmillan Publishers Limited,
registered in England, company number 785998, of Houndmills, Basingstoke,
Hampshire RG21 6XS.

Palgrave Macmillan in the US is a division of St Martin's Press LLC,
175 Fifth Avenue, New York, NY 10010.

Palgrave Macmillan is the global academic imprint of the above companies
and has companies and representatives throughout the world.

Palgrave® and Macmillan® are registered trademarks in the United States,
the United Kingdom, Europe and other countries.

ISBN-13: 978-0-230-22106-2   hardback
ISBN-10: 0-230-22106-8   hardback

This book is printed on paper suitable for recycling and made from fully
managed and sustained forest sources. Logging, pulping and manufacturing
processes are expected to conform to the environmental regulations of the
country of origin.

A catalogue record for this book is available from the British Library.

A catalog record for this book is available from the Library of Congress.

Printed and bound in Great Britain by
CPI Antony Rowe, Chippenham and Eastbourne

For Hannah

Contents

Tables

Foreword

Paul Rogers
Professor of Peace Studies, Department of Peace Studies, University of Bradford, UK

When coalition forces began the operation to terminate the Saddam Hussein regime in Iraq in March 2003 there was an expectation that the massive military superiority encapsulated in a 'shock and awe' approach would lead to a rapid conclusion to the conflict. This initially seemed to be the case, with the regime in Baghdad collapsing within three weeks. There was also an expectation that there would be few civilian casualties, due to the use of precision-guided munitions that would be targeted primarily on military forces with great accuracy, thereby minimising civilian casualties. This ability to wage 'war against real estate' appeared to have been demonstrated in the first war with Iraq in 1991, when cruise missiles could fly up city streets and explode precisely inside the structures being targeted.

Within six weeks of the start of the 2003 war, there were already some indications that there had actually been substantial numbers of civilian casualties. Many of them were due to the use of conventional firepower by coalition forces in a manner that did not appear to embody the ideals of precision that had previously been expected. The rising numbers of civilian casualties were recorded primarily by independent researchers and activists, with the attitude of coalition military leaders being 'we don't do body counts'.

Six years after the start of the Iraq War, attempts at direct counting of civilian casualties suggest a figure of about 100,000 people killed, with casualty surveys indicating even higher numbers. Many of the people have been killed as a result of intercommunal conflict within a complex and deeply unstable conflict, but what has resulted from the Iraq War has been a more general emphasis on the counting of civilian casualties in modern-day armed conflicts.

In its most demanding form, the casualty-counting movement is insisting that all parties to violent conflict have a responsibility to acknowledge the deaths and injuries resulting from their actions. The ultimate aim of the movement, which is still in the early stages of development, would be to codify such a process into an international agreement, perhaps related in some way to an extension of the Geneva Conventions.

This move towards casualty counting has coincided with a sharp rise in the proportion of major conflicts that have less to do with direct interstate warfare and much more to do with insurgencies, terrorism, and failed states. It also follows the response by the US and its coalition partners to the 9/11 attacks, that response being primarily focused on the use of military force.

So far that response has involved extensive conflicts in Iraq and Afghanistan as well as smaller scale military actions in Pakistan, Somalia, and Yemen.

While the new Obama administration may ultimately embrace a rather different approach, the response in the first few years since 9/11 has clearly been to change the Western military focus from interstate warfare to the control of irregular warfare. This has frequently been a matter of considerable controversy, especially when issues such as torture, prisoner abuse, and rendition are included, and the overall effect has been to damage the standing of the US and its closest coalition partners.

Nevertheless there are many indications that the control of irregular warfare is seen as a key role for Western military forces in the years ahead, yet this is coming at a time when such an approach inevitably results in civilian casualties, even if these are commonly termed 'collateral damage'. The overall effect of this dynamic is to make it more important that the control of irregular warfare is conducted in a manner that minimises civilian casualties, and it is therefore highly likely that military planners will look to the new forms of 'non-lethal' weapons that have become available in recent years. Thus, if it is possible to demonstrate that irregular threats to Western security can be handled in a forceful manner while avoiding most civilian casualties, then a forceful security posture has more chance of gaining domestic support.

The problem with this is that the very issue of 'non-lethal' weapons is itself deeply controversial, especially when there are urgent reasons for wanting to demonstrate their capabilities. It is all too easy for advocates of the more general use of 'non-lethal' weapons, whether they be motivated by political, military, or supply-side factors, to exaggerate the value of such weapons, which makes it all the more important to provide critical and robust analysis of the subject.

The development of 'non-lethal' weapons has involved two broad areas of application – policing and military – and it has also involved an extraordinarily wide range of technologies and applications. This book seeks to provide a broad historical perspective, analysing the many claims of efficacy for new systems, often made before there has been any substantive experience gained.

What is particularly valuable about this analysis is the combination of an independent perspective with timing. Because of the aftermath of 9/11 and the consequent 'war on terror', together with greater demands for minimising civilian casualties, there is a real danger that 'non-lethal' weapons will be seen as the easy way out. Given the evidence discussed in Neil Davison's book, this will be a highly dangerous simplification. Hopefully it is one that this book will help to avoid.

December 2008

Acknowledgements

I would like to thank all those who have contributed ideas, insights, and enthusiasm to this book. In particular, thanks to Malcolm Dando and Nick Lewer, and other former colleagues at the Department of Peace Studies, University of Bradford; Jamie Revill, Paul Rogers, Simon Whitby, and Jim Whitman. Many thanks to Jürgen Altmann for reviewing earlier drafts of Chapters 6 and 7. Thanks also to Robin Coupland, Toby Feakin, David Hambling, Alastair Hay, David Koplow, Dominique Loye, Richard Moyes, Alan Pearson, Brian Rappert, Julian Perry Robinson, Jonathan Rosenhead, Mark Wheelis, and Steve Wright.

Special thanks to Hannah Jones for proofreading some chapters, but particularly for the endless support and patience. Thanks to all my family and friends for their support.

Thanks to Ross Clarke (ross@makeaccessible.com) for the excellent cover illustration.

Finally, thanks to Alexandra Webster, Gemma D'Arcy Hughes at Palgrave Macmillan and the Staff of Macmillan Publishing Solutions, India.

Abbreviations

A3D	Aversive Audible Acoustic Device
ABL	Airborne Laser
ACCM	Aircraft Countermeasures system
ACPO	Association of Chief Police Officers (UK)
ADS	Active Denial System
AEP	Attenuating Energy Projectile
AFOSR	Air Force Office of Scientific Research (US)
AFRL	Air Force Research Laboratory (US)
AGARD	Advisory Group for Aerospace Research and Development
AHD	Acoustic Hailing Device
ANLM	Airburst Non-Lethal Munition
APL	Advanced Polymer Laboratory, University of New Hampshire
ARCAD	Advanced Riot Control Agent Device
ARDEC	Armament Research, Development, and Engineering Center (US Army)
ARL	Army Research Laboratory (US)
ARPA	Advanced Research Projects Agency (also DARPA)
ASRAP	Advanced Segmented Ring Airfoil Projectile
ATC	American Technology Corporation
ATL	Advanced Tactical Laser
BNLM	Bounding Non-Lethal Munition
BOSS	Battlefield Optical Surveillance System
BWC	Biological Weapons Convention
CCD	Conference of the Committee on Disarmament
CCK	cholecystokinin
CCW	Convention on Certain Conventional Weapons
CHP	Compact High Power (Laser Dazzler)
CIA	Central Intelligence Agency
CLADS	Canister Launched Area Denial System
CN	chloroacetophenone
COIL	chemical oxygen iodine laser
CR	dibenz(b,f)-1:4-oxazepine
CRDEC	Chemical Research, Development, and Engineering Center (US Army)
CRF	corticotrophin-releasing factor
CS	2-chlorobenzalmalononitrile
CSIS	Center for Strategic and International Studies
CWC	Chemical Weapons Convention
CWS	Chemical Warfare Service (US Army)

DARPA	Defense Advanced Research Projects Agency (US)
dB	decibels
DBBL	Dismounted Battlefield Battle Laboratory
DE	Directed Energy
DEPSCoR	Department of Defense Experimental Program to Stimulate Competitive Research
DHS	Department of Homeland Security
DIP	Discriminating Irritant Projectile
DOD	Department of Defense (US)
DOE	Department of Energy (US)
DOJ	Department of Justice (US)
DOMILL	DSAC Sub-Committee on the Medical Implications of Less-lethal Weapons
DRG	Defence Research Group
DSAC	Defence Scientific Advisory Council (UK)
DSB	Defense Science Board (US)
Dstl	Defence Science and Technology Laboratory (UK)
ECBC	Edgewood Chemical and Biological Center (US Army)
ELF	extremely low frequency
EPIC	Electromagnetic Personnel Interdiction Control
ERDEC	Edgewood Research, Development, and Engineering Center (US Army)
ERGM	Extended Range Guided Munition
FAS	Federation of American Scientists
FBI	Federal Bureau of Investigation
GHz	gigahertz
HALT	Hinder Adversaries with Less-than-Lethal Technology
HEAP	Human Effects Advisory Panel
HECOE	Human Effects Center of Excellence
HED	Human Effectiveness Directorate (AFRL)
HEDJ	Joint Non-Lethal Weaponry Branch (AFRL HED)
HEDO	Optical Radiation Branch (AFRL HED)
HEDR	Radiofrequency Radiation Branch (AFRL HED)
HIDA	High Intensity Directed Acoustics
HOSDB	Home Office Scientific Development Branch (UK)
HPM	high power microwave
HSARPA	Homeland Security Advanced Research Projects Agency (US)
Hz	hertz
IACP	International Association of Chiefs of Police
ICRC	International Committee of the Red Cross
IEEE	Institute of Electrical and Electronics Engineers
IFBG	Improved Flash Bang Grenade
ILEF	International Law Enforcement Forum
ISNLS	Individual Serviceman Non-Lethal System

ITS	Infrasound Test Device
JAG	Judge Advocate General (US)
JNLWD	Joint Non-Lethal Weapons Directorate
JNLWM	Joint Non-Lethal Warning Munition
JNLWP	Joint Non-Lethal Weapons Program
LANL	Los Alamos National Laboratory
LAPD	Los Angeles Police Department
LCDM	Low Collateral Damage Munitions
LCMS	Laser Countermeasure System
LDS	Laser Dazzle Sight
LEAA	Law Enforcement Assistance Administration (US)
LECTAC	Law Enforcement and Corrections Technology Advisory Council (US)
LF	low frequency
LLNL	Lawrence Livermore National Laboratory
LLW	'Less-Lethal' Weapon
LRAD	Long Range Acoustic Device
LVOSS	Light Vehicle Obscuration Smoke System
MCCM	Modular Crowd Control Munition
MCRU	Marine Corps Research University
MCWL	Marine Corps Warfighting Laboratory
MDS	Mobility Denial System
MEDUSA	Mob Excess Deterrent Using Silent Audio
MOD	Ministry of Defence (UK)
MPA	Metropolitan Police Authority (UK)
MPS	Metropolitan Police Service (UK)
MTR	Military Technical Revolution
mW	milliwatt
NATO	North Atlantic Treaty Organisation
NDIA	National Defense Industrial Association
NIHRC	Northern Ireland Human Rights Commission
NIJ	National Institute of Justice (US)
NILECJ	National Institute of Law Enforcement and Criminal Justice (US)
NIO	Northern Ireland Office (UK)
NLAW	Non-Lethal Acoustic Weapons
NLCS	Non-Lethal Capability Sets
NLECTC	National Law Enforcement and Corrections Technology Center (US)
NLW	'Non-Lethal' Weapon
NLWCC	Non-Lethal Weapons Steering Committee
NRC	National Research Council (US)
NSF	National Science Foundation (US)
NSWC	Naval Surface Warfare Center (US)
NTAR	Non-Lethal Technology and Academic Research Symposium

NTIC	Non-Lethal Technology Innovation Center
OC	oleoresin capsicum
OCADS	Overhead Chemical Agent Dispersion System
OFT	Office of Force Transformation (US)
OICW	Objective Individual Combat Weapon
OLDS	Overhead Liquid Dispersal System
OLETC	Office of Law Enforcement Technology Commercialization (US)
ONR	Office of Naval Research (US)
OSHA	Occupational Safety and Health Administration (US)
PADDS	Plasma Acoustic Dazzler Denial Systems
PADS	Portable Active Denial System
PAVA	pelargonic acid vanillylamide
PBR	plastic baton round
PCP	phencyclidine
PELT	Portable Efficient Laser Testbed
PEP	Pulsed Energy Projectile
PHaSR	Personnel Halting and Stimulation Response
PIKL	Pulsed Impulsive Kill Laser
PSDB	Police Scientific Development Branch (UK)
RAG	Ring Airfoil Grenade
RAP	Ring Airfoil Projectile
RCA	riot control agent
RCMP	Royal Canadian Mounted Police
RF	radio frequency
RPEWS	Rheostatic Pulsed Energy Weapon System
RTO	Research Technology Organisation
SADAG	Sequential Arc Discharge Generator
SARA	Scientific Applications & Research Associates Inc.
SDI	Strategic Defense Initiative
SEB	staphylococcal enterotoxin B
SIPRI	Stockholm International Peace Research Institute
SMBI	Stress and Motivated Behavior Institute
SNL	Sandia National Laboratories
SSRI	selective serotonin reuptake inhibitor
SwRI	Southwest Research Institute
TADICAMS	tactical air-delivered incapacitating munition system
TAPM	Taser anti-personnel munition
TBRL	Target Behavioral Response Laboratory
THC	tetrahydrocannabinol
THEL	Tactical High Energy Laser
TMS	transcranial magnetic stimulation
TRAD	Taser remote area denial
TUGV	tactical unmanned ground vehicle
UAV	unmanned aerial vehicle

UV	ultraviolet
VEE	Venezuelan equine encephalitis
VF	voice frequency
VLF	very low frequency
VMADS	Vehicle Mounted Active Denial System
WHO	World Health Organization
XADS	Xtreme Alternative Defense Systems
XREP	eXtended Range Electronic Projectile

1
Introduction

1.1 So-called 'non-lethal' weapons

'Non-lethal', 'less-lethal', 'less-than-lethal', 'soft-kill', 'pre-lethal', 'sub-lethal', and even 'worse-than-lethal'. Reflecting differing assessments, these are all terms used to describe weapons that are intended to incapacitate people without causing death or permanent injury, or to disable equipment with minimal damage to the surrounding environment. There are long-standing disagreements over the merits and definitions of the term 'non-lethal' or other terms related to lethality when applied to any weapon or group of weapons.[1] During the 1990s increasing military attention led to divisive and enduring debate between advocates of 'non-lethal' weapons and sceptics, as described by Fidler.[2] Advocates[3] emphasised what they viewed as the revolutionary promise of new weapons technologies and their potential to promote the humane use of force. The sceptics,[4] on the other hand, building on concerns first expressed in the 1970s,[5] cautioned against affording any weapons technologies special status and highlighted the need for critical technological, legal, and ethical assessment.

From the outset it has been acknowledged that no weapon can be entirely 'non-lethal'. As a 1972 report commissioned by the US National Science Foundation argued:

> 'Nonlethal' is a relative term. All weapons, and a wide variety of objects that are not intended to serve as weapons, create some primary or secondary risk of death or permanent injury. The probable seriousness of their effects (their lethality) depends on a number of factors, not all of which are determined by their design. Weapons not intended to kill or create permanent injury, if used with any degree of regularity, would undoubtedly cause some deaths because of physiological differences among those against whom they are employed, physical malfunctioning, improper utilization, and other circumstances.[6]

One of these additional circumstances is the frequency of use. As the report of a 1986 Department of Justice (DOJ) conference on 'non-lethal' weapons pointed out:

> The excessive use of non-lethal weapons may result in no net improvement in rates of fatal injury when compared to lethal weapons practice. If, for example, a less than lethal weapon is one-tenth as lethal as a handgun but is used ten times more frequently, an identical number of subjects will be fatally injured.[7]

From these observations came a preference, among police and law enforcement organisations,[8] for the term 'less-lethal' as a way of describing a weapon that was not entirely safe or 'non-lethal' but, if used according to certain parameters, was less likely to cause death or permanent injury than a device intended to have the capability of killing or permanently injuring.[9] The International Law Enforcement Forum (ILEF) on Minimal Force Options, a collaborative group of police forces in the US, Canada, Australia, New Zealand, the UK, and a number of other European countries established in 2001, has articulated its own definition of 'less-lethal' weapons: 'The application of tactics and technologies that are less likely to result in death or serious injury than conventional firearms and/or munitions'.[10]

Military organisations have favoured the 'non-lethal' terminology, which was formalised by the US Department of Defense (DOD) in Directive 3000.3 of July 1996:

> 3.1. Non-Lethal Weapons. Weapons that are explicitly designed and primarily employed so as to incapacitate personnel or materiel, while minimizing fatalities, permanent injury to personnel, and undesired damage to property and the environment.
>
> 3.1.1. Unlike conventional lethal weapons that destroy their targets principally through blast, penetration and fragmentation, non-lethal weapons employ means other than gross physical destruction to prevent the target from functioning.
>
> 3.1.2. Non-lethal weapons are intended to have one, or both, of the following characteristics:
>
> 3.1.2.1. They have relatively reversible effects on personnel or materiel.
>
> 3.1.2.2. They affect objects differently within their area of influence.[11]

The North Atlantic Treaty Organization (NATO) used the US example for its own definition:

> Non-Lethal Weapons are weapons which are explicitly designed and developed to incapacitate or repel personnel, with a low probability of

fatality or permanent injury, or to disable equipment, with minimal undesired damage or impact on the environment.[12]

Although different organisations use 'non-lethal', 'less-lethal', or 'less-than-lethal',[13] the terms are interchangeable in the sense that they are generally used to refer to the same group of varied weapons.

1.1.1 Questioning benign intent

Common to all definitions of 'non-lethal' weapons is the apparent *intent* to minimise permanent injury or death. This is the major factor offered by advocates in distinguishing between 'non-lethal' weapons and other weapons. It is also one of the main assertions subject to criticism.[14] This seemingly benign intent in the development and use of 'non-lethal' weapons is often assumed by advocates, but there are clear inconsistencies in both the policy governing these weapons and the realities of their use. The policies of the US DOD and NATO contain perhaps the most striking contradiction:

> Non-lethal weapons may be used in conjunction with lethal weapon systems to enhance the latter's effectiveness and efficiency in military operations. This shall apply across the range of military operations to include those situations where overwhelming force is employed.[15]

Using 'non-lethal' weapons to enhance the killing power of 'lethal' weapons would seem entirely inconsistent with the intent to minimise permanent injury and death. However, this contradictory policy is central to military considerations of 'non-lethal' weapons. The report of a seminar that brought together UK and US government officials in 2000 is indicative:

> NLWs ['non-lethal' weapons] may be used in a variety of different missions. In some cases they may be employed to save innocent lives and property, while in others they may be used to enhance the effectiveness of lethal weapons.[16]

The report contended that 'there must be a concerted effort to counter the perception of purely "non-lethal operations."'[17]

Contradictions are further evident in practice. During the Vietnam War the irritant chemical agent CS, also known as 'tear gas', was used on a massive scale to enhance the killing power of lethal fire rather than to reduce casualties.[18] A report published by the European Parliament in 2000 collected numerous examples of 'non-lethal' weapons use in conjunction with lethal firearms all over the world.[19] In 2002 Russian Special Forces used anaesthetic drugs to 'knock-out' hostage takers in a Moscow theatre, who were then shot and killed while unconscious.[20] This tactic of using 'non-lethal' weapons in a 'pre-lethal' manner has been specifically articulated in US Army doctrine:

> Nonlethal capabilities are required to cause enemy hiding in defilade, cover, and concealment; or hiding amid the nonbelligerent populace, to have to move from hiding, and thereby be exposed to lethal effects.[21]

Clearly reference to reduced lethality does not make sense in these contexts.[22] It is important to recognise that the examples given represent only a proportion of 'non-lethal' weapons usage and are far more relevant to military rather than police operations. Nevertheless the significant number of practical examples coupled with explicit supporting policies are sufficient to cast doubt on the veracity of the claims made about the intent behind the development and use of 'non-lethal' weapons, which underpins most definitions.

1.1.2   Alternatives to lethal force? Or compliance tools?

Another common characterisation of 'non-lethal' weapons is that they represent an *alternative* to lethal weapons. The research and development agency of the US DOJ states on its website that 'Less-lethal weapons have been developed to provide law enforcement, corrections, and military personnel with an alternative to lethal force'.[23] The rationale commonly given is that these weapons can be used in place of conventional firearms to reduce casualties and save lives. This message is asserted by military and police developers and subsequently portrayed in media reports of 'non-lethal' weapons deployment.[24] Again examples of policy and practice cast doubt on these claims. Authorities overseeing police use of 'non-lethal' weapons often caution specifically against using them as a replacement for lethal weapons. For example, a 2003 UK Metropolitan Police Authority (MPA) report noted:

> The Home Office, ACPO [Association of Chief Police Officers] and the MPS [Metropolitan Police Service] agree that less lethal options should not be a replacement to the police use of firearms. It remains the case that where a person is armed with a firearm, or is otherwise so dangerous as to put life in imminent danger, firearms will continue to be deployed, albeit now supported by less lethal options.[25]

As is expected, the military are even more reluctant to consider restrictions on the use of lethal force. As NATO and US DOD 'non-lethal' weapons policy states:

> Neither the existence, the presence nor the potential effect of Non-Lethal Weapons shall constitute an obligation to use Non-Lethal Weapons, or

impose a higher standard for, or additional restrictions on, the use of lethal force.[26]

In practice, while there are examples of 'non-lethal' weapons being used instead of firearms, often their introduction acts as a supplementary means of violence or an additional tier of force that can be more easily justified. This was recognised early on by Ackroyd et al. in their book *The Technology of Political Control*, first published in 1977:

> A further justification for the new riot-control technology is: 'If we weren't using gas (or rubber bullets, or whatever) we would have to use guns'. But we have seen from the case of Northern Ireland that it is not gas *or* guns but gas *and* guns. The new technology supplements the old: it does not replace it. As another Ministry of Defence official has admitted: 'CS gas is rarely of use against gunmen; its applications comes ... at a lower level of violence, in circumstances in which the use of firearms by the troops would be inappropriate if not unlawful'[27] [emphasis in original].

The widespread use of the Taser electrical weapon provides a more contemporary example of this supplementary use of force in practice. A 2004 Amnesty International report found:

> There is also evidence to suggest that, far from being used to avoid lethal force, many US police agencies are deploying tasers as a routine force option to subdue non-compliant or disturbed individuals who do not pose a serious danger to themselves or others.[28]

Widespread Taser deployment combined with relaxed policy on its use and a reluctance to employ it as an alternative to lethal force means that it is often used by the police and military to gain compliance, bypassing non-violent conflict resolution techniques such as simple negotiation.[29] The statistics on how the Taser is being used speak for themselves. A 2004 review of Taser use by police in one county in Colorado found that a third of the 112 victims had been handcuffed at the time.[30] A similar review of over 500 Taser uses[31] in the Seattle area found that victims were unarmed in 78 per cent of incidents where it was used by Seattle Police Department and 88 per cent of uses by King County Sheriff's Office.[32] A review of over 550 uses of the Taser by the Royal Canadian Mounted Police (RCMP) between 2002 and 2005 found that the victims were unarmed in 79 per cent of cases.[33]

1.1.3 Lethality by design

Critics question the notion implicit in definitions of 'non-lethal' weapons that lethality can be a function of design. The International Committee of the Red Cross (ICRC) has long drawn attention to the fact that 'lethality' is dependent on the context, contending that commonly used definitions are misleading in that they imply that conventional weapons are 100 per cent lethal, which is very often not the case.[34] Coupland has pointed out that the term 'non-lethal' is applied to a range of old and new weapons and that it cannot be an inherent property of a weapon because the outcome will be determined by a combination of risk factors in a given context.[35] He concludes that describing a weapon as 'non-lethal' or 'less-lethal' is misleading and moreover intentionally so: 'The notion has politically correct or even humanitarian connotations and is, therefore, an effective marketing strategy'.[36]

Indeed some weapons described as 'non-lethal' have been shown to have comparable fatality rates to those expected from 'lethal' weapons, in theory and in practice. A Federation of American Scientists (FAS) Working Group developed a mathematical model to show that incapacitating biochemical weapons, such as potent anaesthetic drugs, are likely to cause at least 10 per cent fatalities.[37] In practice this figure may be higher, as illustrated by the 2002 Moscow siege where the fatality rate was over 15 per cent.[38] The FAS authors make the comparison with weapons assumed to be 100 per cent lethal:

> For instance, in military combat, firearms typically cause about 35% deaths among total casualties, shells about 20%, and grenades about 10%. 'Lethal' chemical weapons are comparable; in World War I the lethality of gas was about 7%.[39]

1.1.4 Disingenuous advocacy

The feeling that the term 'non-lethal' is being used as a marketing strategy for new weapons technology is given added credence by two recent trends in policy and technology development. Firstly, there has been a conscious move by the military, police, and other advocates of 'non-lethal' weapons to soften the associated language and terminology with a view to facilitating increased policy, public, and legal acceptance, even in the face of existing legal constraints. Thus there is a strategy to describe 'non-lethal' weapons not as 'weapons', but as 'capabilities' or 'technologies'.[40] This extends to individual weapons types: chemical weapons become 'calmatives' or 'advanced riot control agents', low energy laser weapons become 'optical distractors', and acoustic weapons become 'acoustic hailing devices'. This has been articulated explicitly during discussions in 2000 between UK and US government officials:

> [T]here was considerable enthusiasm, principally from the UK, for dispensing with the term (and notion) of 'weapon' and instead focussing on non-lethal 'capabilities' that produce non-lethal 'effects'. This would

provide greater operational as well as policy/legal flexibility. The consensus of the group, then, favoured the term 'Non-Lethal Capabilities'.[41]

In order to promote this semantic shift the UK and the US agreed to promote a 'family of non-lethal "capabilities"' rather than weapons in policy and media circles.[42]

The second trend is well illustrated in a 2004 report by the Council on Foreign Relations, an influential US foreign policy think tank, which advocated a greater role for 'non-lethal' weapons in the US military. Stretching the definition of 'non-lethal' weapons seemingly beyond reason, the report described the ideal 'non-lethal' weapon as one with *intentionally* 'lethal' effects:

> In a sense, 'nonlethal weapons' is a misnomer ... And there is no requirement that NLW be incapable of killing or of causing permanent damage. Moreover, the ideal NLW would be a system with continuously variable intensity and influence, ranging from a warning tap to a stunning blow to a lethal effect.[43]

The desire for weapons or systems of weapons with variable or 'scalable' effects is not new.[44] From the outset of their formal 'non-lethal' weapons programme, the US DOD stressed the requirement for a 'rheostatic capability' to deliver 'varying levels of effects' as one of the guiding principles for research and development.[45] However, the first decade of the twenty-first century has seen increasing emphasis on the integration of 'non-lethal' and 'lethal' systems as well as continuing research and development towards individual weapons systems with variable effects from 'non-lethal' to 'lethal', particularly in the area of directed energy weapons.[46] Clearly the 'non-lethal' or 'less-lethal' terminology is becoming incompatible with the nature of many new weapons being developed under the 'non-lethal' banner. Describing some of these planned weapons systems as 'non-lethal' is disingenuous. It is akin to describing a shotgun as 'non-lethal' by virtue of the fact that it can fire sponge projectiles as well as lead shots.

1.1.5 The end of 'non-lethal' weapons?

In one of the earliest assessments of 'non-lethal' weapons, published in 1970, Coates cautioned:

> A major risk in the use of nonlethal weaponry is failure to keep the nonlethal aspect clean, that is, free of associations with lethal tactics. ... If nonlethal weapons are used to augment lethal tactics or strategy, the principal value of the nonlethal weapons may be lost.[47]

Policy guidelines, use in practice, and technology development in the intervening period have not heeded this warning. This may accelerate the demise, not only of the principal value of 'non-lethal' weapons but the entire concept of using less injurious weapons to minimise casualties, particularly in the military arena. In this context Dando's observation in his 1996 book seems apposite:

> It is suggested that, rather than arguments for a more benign mode of peacekeeping being the driving force, the main reason for the rise of non-lethal weaponry may be the possibility of using it as an adjunct to regular military operations, as part of an effort to maintain military advantage through technological superiority.[48]

For the most part 'non-lethal' weapons are new weapons, new means of violence, enabled by advances in technology.

And yet there still may be something in the idea of reducing the level of force used by the military and police by employing less injurious weapons. Recognising that no weapon can be 100 per cent 'non-lethal', especially given the variable susceptibilities among populations, Nick Lewer and I have argued for setting much tighter parameters on the concept:

> 'Non-lethal weapons' are explicitly intended, designed and employed to incapacitate people with *effects that are temporary and reversible*. So, a 'non-lethal' weapon should cause no permanent deleterious change to the person, whether physical, physiological or psychological. It should be discriminate and not cause unnecessary suffering. It should *provide an alternative to, and raise the threshold for the use of lethal force*.[49]

The key elements here are the temporary and reversible[50] nature of the effects and the unambiguous role for these weapons in reducing, and raising the threshold for, the use of lethal force rather than complementing or enhancing it. Policy and doctrine pronouncements by the military and police may seem unequivocal in their insistence that 'non-lethal' weapons can never replace 'lethal' weapons, but if technological development did provide some viable alternatives, then this position would likely become untenable given the political, legal, and ethical pressure that would result. One might cautiously suggest that, in the future, the use of certain 'non-lethal' weapons may indeed raise the threshold for the use of 'lethal' force.[51] However, developing a weapon technology that fits these tighter constraints may just as likely prove to be an unattainable goal.[52]

A crucial factor is that the underpinning policy for use of a given weapon and adherence to this policy fits within these tight constraints.[53] Some existing weapons described as 'non-lethal', such as irritant chemicals and electrical weapons, can for the most part deliver temporary and reversible effects, although deaths do occur and significant health concerns remain. But in many situations these weapons are not being used as an alternative to lethal force or to raise the threshold for lethal force.[54] Taking the example of electrical weapons such as the Taser, much stricter policy on deployment and use, both in terms of operation (e.g. prohibiting multiple shocks) and rules of engagement (i.e. restricting use solely to situations where lethal force would previously have been necessary), would bring them closer to the concept their developers espouse.

Overall, however, the issues discussed here urge caution and scepticism over existing and emerging 'non-lethal' weapons. The central concept of minimising injuries and casualties has been sullied by contradictory policy and practice. The banner of 'non-lethal' weapons development has been co-opted both for advanced 'lethal' weapons development[55] and for attempts to reintroduce prohibited weapons.[56] Existing weapons are becoming technologies of compliance, and emerging weapons may embody long-standing concerns over an expanding technology of political control.

In this context Lewer and Schofield's observation, concluding their 1997 critique of 'non-lethal' weapons, is all the more relevant over ten years later and should be kept in mind while reading subsequent chapters of this book:

> We have to resist the fatal attraction that NLWs ['non-lethal' weapons] transcend concerns surrounding conventional weapons, and the dilemmas surrounding the use of force. They are simply weapons, and it would be dangerous not to treat them in the same way as any other weapon.[57]

1.2   The technological imperative

Efforts to apply unconventional or exotic technologies to the development of new 'non-lethal' weapons have played a large part in attracting and sustaining interest in the topic since the 1970s. Discussions, analyses, and debates about 'non-lethal' weapons have tended to place emphasis on emerging or future technologies.[58] Paradoxically, despite increased research and development during the past 15 years, few 'non-lethal' weapons incorporating new technologies have actually been deployed on a large scale. However, the recent and imminent deployment of some new biochemical, directed energy, and acoustic weapons raises questions over the causal factors. Are these new weapons the result of particular scientific and technological advances? And if so, will military weapons programmes develop and expand to exploit these, as happened with biological weapons during the twentieth century?[59] It has been observed that all major technologies have been exploited for both peaceful and hostile purposes.[60] Is 'non-lethal' weapons development contributing to the hostile exploitation of various scientific fields, including biotechnology, pharmacology, neuroscience, bio-electromagnetics, and electromagnetic and acoustic engineering?

Equally important is the question of whether these weapons are what their developers and users purport them to be. Secrecy and a lack of inde-pendent scientific analysis have perpetuated unsubstantiated claims over the technological capability and maturity of 'non-lethal' weapons, as Altmann argued in 2001:

> Whenever decisions are taken on the basis of wrong or incomplete infor-mation, dangers arise. The history of the NLW ['non-lethal' weapons] debate illustrated some of these. Claims were made by proponents with-out giving valid references. Journalists reported what they had heard (or understood) of military projects. Instead of demanding evidence, later authors took the assertions for granted. As a consequence, studies from military academies as well as articles and books from peace researchers repeated this information, mutually increasing apparent credibility.[61]

The dangers of exaggerating the potential of 'non-lethal' weapons technolo-gies may be profound in terms of changes in military and police priorities and challenges to ethical and legal norms.

1.3   Chapter overview

In Chapters 2, 3, and 4 this book provides a history of the development of 'non-lethal' weapons by the military and police, from early interest in the 1960s to the present day. Although pieces of this story have been com-piled elsewhere, this is the first integrated history to be published. It aims to form a basis for accurate analysis of the surrounding issues and to help prevent the promotion of speculation over fact. The book also provides a detailed assessment of the role of advances in science and technology in the development of 'non-lethal' weapons, with particular attention to emerging biochemical, directed energy, and acoustic weapons in Chapters 5, 6, and 7. It places these developments in the broader context of institutional devel-opment, socio-political circumstances, strategic environment, legal con-straints, and military and police operational requirements. The conclusions, implications, and recommendations for policy are presented in Chapter 8.

'Non-lethal' weapons can be categorised, broadly speaking, by technology type used to exert the effect: kinetic energy, electrical, chemical, biochemical, optical, acoustic, and directed energy. In addition there are weapons that combine more than one effect, and delivery systems, which are another facet of these weapons. This book encompasses weapons systems that have been *described* as 'non-lethal' weapons. Their inclusion does not constitute a judgement about their relative lethality, only an acknowledgement of the way in which developers, users, policymakers, and observers have chosen to categorise them. Weapons that have been described in this way comprise a variety of unrelated systems, technologies, and techniques, including those directed at people and objects. This analysis considers only those that target people, that is, anti-personnel weapons. So-called 'anti-materiel' weapons, proposed for use against vehicles, electronic equipment, or other objects and materials, may have secondary effects on people. However, they are beyond the scope of this book.

Necessarily this book focuses on developments in the US,[62] where most interest in 'non-lethal' weapons has arisen and in particular the research and development activities sponsored by the DOD and the DOJ. This is also because sources of information on US weapons programmes are more readily available. Nevertheless there is a pervading veil of secrecy surrounding many military and police 'non-lethal' weapons research and development programmes, particularly those related to unconventional or exotic technologies, as many elements of these are classified. Therefore this analysis is limited by the availability of open literature, and has benefited from the requests made by other interested parties under the US Freedom of Information Act (FOIA).[63]

2
The Early History of 'Non-Lethal' Weapons

This chapter explores the early history of 'non-lethal' weapons development covering the period from the 1960s until 1989, just before the hugely increased interest in the field that developed during the 1990s. It describes the origins and emergence of new weapons, examining this process with reference to technological advances, wider socio-political context, legal developments, and the evolution of associated institutional structures.

2.1 The 1960s and 1970s: The new riot control

It was not until the 1960s that a group of varied weapons technologies began to be described collectively as 'non-lethal' weapons by policymakers and law enforcement end-users.[1] Irritant chemical weapons, also known as riot control agents (RCAs) or 'tear gas', were the most mature technology included in this category at that time, having been an integral part of military chemical weapons programmes since World War I and adopted by police forces around the world soon after. These were the primary 'non-lethal' weapons used by police forces in the US during the 1960s and 1970s as alternatives or additions to batons and firearms. They were used during riots and other civil disturbances arising from the civil rights and anti-war movements, which had given rise to the consideration of new techniques and weapons for riot control. In the standard police text on riot control of that era, *Riot Control – Materiel and Techniques* by Rex Applegate, a large section of the book is devoted to uses of 'riot chemicals'.[2]

The US law enforcement establishment, lacking any research budget of its own, took advantage of military investment, as Coates observed in 1972:

> Many of the easy gains that have been made in the development of non-lethal weapons have been based on the topical effects of tear agents. The basic agents and the innovations in their mode of delivery have come about, and found extensive use in the last few years, chiefly

as a result of the large and expensive research and development programs of the military services: they are a civilian by-product of military research.[3]

This military technology pull was combined with a policy push in the form of recommendations from two Presidential Commissions in the late 1960s. The 1967 report of the 'President's Crime Commission on Law Enforcement and the Administration of Justice' recommended that the use of lethal force by the police be restricted. It also recommended the wider application of the 'scientific and technological revolution' to the problems of law enforcement.[4] A second Presidential Commission was set up to investigate the summer 1967 riots in Newark and Detroit resulting from the gross racial inequality in the US at the time. The 1969 'Report of the National Advisory Commission on Civil Disorders' recommended that local officials 'Develop guidelines governing the use of control equipment and provide alternatives to the use of lethal weapons'.[5]

In June 1968, following the first Presidential Commission, the US Congress passed the Omnibus Crime Control and Safe Streets Act, which created the Law Enforcement Assistance Administration (LEAA) within the DOJ to provide grants to state and local police forces.[6] This soon had an impact on the deployment of irritant chemical weapons by police in the US, as Coates noted several years later:

> A major stimulus to the widespread use of tear gas was the Omnibus Crime Control and Safe Street [*sic*] Act of 1968, which made millions of dollars in federal money available to the states for general improvement of their criminal justice systems; ... The first order of business for the police was to increase their immediate capabilities for dealing with violence. This meant the procurement of a wider range of lethal and non-lethal weapons.[7]

The Act also established the National Institute of Law Enforcement and Criminal Justice (NILECJ) within the LEAA to make grants for research and to develop new methods for law enforcement.[8] Encouraged by the legislation, proponents of 'non-lethal' weapons were optimistic about the prospects for technological development. Writing in 1969, Applegate argued:

> More Buck Rogers developments in nonlethal equipment and allied fields, relating to the control of mob and individual violence, are already on the drawing boards or yet to come.[9]

Such science fiction analogies have continued to inform proponents' highest hopes for 'non-lethal' weapons.[10]

By 1971 Applegate's optimism was undiminished:

[N]o resource, idea, or known but unproved existing device will be neglected in the search for 'softer' weapons. Many development items that have died in the recent past for lack of funding or governmental backing yet may be given a new lease of life.[11]

This period saw an expansion of proposed 'non-lethal' weapons and exploration of new technologies. However, much of this innovation was characterised by small-scale commercial undertakings with significant limitations, as Coates pointed out:

Weapons research, conducted on very slim budgets, has largely taken the form of speculative endeavors by commercial organization[s] serving an uncertain market. As a result, new materials are frequently introduced on a shockingly slim basis of evidence as to their effectiveness, reliability or safety.[12]

Two growth areas were the development of blunt impact weapons, including wooden, rubber, and 'bean-bag' projectiles, and electrical weapons.

In the 1960s and the 1970s the majority of literature on 'non-lethal' weapons was focused on new equipment for policing tasks such as riot control with little reference to potential military application, although there had been discussions in both the military and peace research communities over the possibility of 'war without death'.[13] A significant exception was a 1970 paper by Coates, published by the Institute for Defense Analyses and entitled 'Nonlethal and Nondestructive Combat in Cities Overseas', which proposed a wider role for such weapons in 'limited and low-intensity warfare'. In a prescient assessment of future conflict, he put forward an argument for development of 'non-lethal' weapons that has since become commonplace:[14]

There will be both more intermingling of aggressors and civilians and a greater blurring of the distinction between the two in many anticipated types of conflict. This may be especially the case in urban combat.[15]

Having considered a whole range of potential mechanisms and techniques for 'non-lethal' weapons, he concluded:

By far the most tactically versatile and useful antipersonnel mechanisms for urban combat are chemical. Other techniques relying on impact, light, sound, and heat, while affording some operational effectiveness and substantial decrements in deadliness, are generally more restricted in their application. They are less versatile and most particularly applicable to riot control.[16]

He noted that research and development had concentrated on irritant chemicals, which had been used widely in the Vietnam War, but recommended that a research programme be undertaken to 'uncover, design, select, and evaluate nonlethal chemical agents with new or improved effects for urban combat'.[17] Among the other recommendations were for systematic studies 'to define limits of safety for both existing and potential electrical and impact weapons'.[18]

In 1971 the US National Science Foundation (NSF) sponsored a study on 'non-lethal' weapons under their broader programme to 'identify areas in which scientific research can help solve social problems'.[19] Central to the study was a two-day conference co-sponsored by the NSF and the LEAA of the DOJ. The 1972 report, 'Nonlethal Weapons for Law Enforcement: Research Needs and Priorities', included an assessment of the current state of various weapons technologies but found that there had been 'few advances in police weaponry':

> With the exception of chemical stream dispensers available to individual officers in some police departments, officers on the beat for the most part rely on the same weapons they did a century ago – their personal prowess, the nightstick, and the handgun.[20]

The report argued that most of the new weapons systems developed had not gained acceptance due to exaggerated claims on their effectiveness by the manufacturers and lack of sufficient testing and evaluation processes. However, it presented an optimistic view about the prospects for emerging technological solutions:

> In short, many of the objections to nonlethal weapons involve technical problems with specific weapons now in use or proposed. In theory, at least, most of these objections could be answered by improvement of the weapons. They should be the subject of research.[21]

Noting the already widespread use of irritant chemical weapons for controlling groups of people in riots or civil disturbances, the report stressed that priority should be given to the development of 'non-lethal' weapons for use by individual police officers in situations involving one or a few people.[22] The recommendations for research and development were similar to Coates's 1970 study for the military:

> Chemical and electrical weapons offer the greatest promise in the short term and should be given highest priority in development efforts. Secondary priority should be focused on overcoming the problems related to risks of serious injuries from less-than-lethal kinetic energy impact weapons.[23]

The scarcity of data about the effectiveness and safety of existing weapons informed a major recommendation for a government-funded programme for 'Testing and evaluation of existing and newly developed nonlethal weapons'.[24] The US Army Human Engineering Laboratory was contracted by the LEAA to carry out this work over a period of several years in the early and mid-1970s.[25] The purpose of the Army research effort was 'the development of a standardized methodology for the determination of less-lethal weapon effectiveness and safety characteristics'.[26] It addressed the three categories of 'non-lethal' weapons prevalent at the time: kinetic energy (blunt impact), chemical, and electrical.

A 1975 book on *Riot Control*, published in the UK, drew majority of its information on 'non-lethal' weapons from the US studies, acknowledging that the further development was occurring primarily in the US.[27] However, the UK and the US also had an information-sharing agreement covering 'non-lethal' weapons research.[28] The focus of research and development work in the UK had been the design of new blunt impact projectiles.

2.1.1   Irritant chemical weapons: From CN to CS

Irritant chemical agents, or RCAs, are characterised by the intense sensory irritation and pain they cause to the eyes and respiratory tract, and the temporary nature of these effects,[29] and were first used by the French police in 1912.[30] Irritant agents were the first chemical weapons to be then used during World War I before the rapid escalation to lethal agents.[31] A large variety of irritant agents, including bromoacetone (and vomiting agents such as adamsite), were used by both sides during World War I.[32] Towards the end of the War, the US Army began investigating chloroacetophenone (CN) as a new irritant agent, and in the post-war years this work was expanded with a renewed interest in the use of these chemicals for policing. The landmark 1971 study of chemical and biological warfare published by the Stockholm International Peace Research Institute (SIPRI) noted:

> In the 1920s the US Army Chemical Warfare Service (CWS) conducted more research on CN than on any other agent: in 1921 the CWS offered a CN device for experimental trial to the Philadelphia police, and built a manufacturing plant for the agent at Edgewood Arsenal the following year.[33]

A marketing effort orchestrated by the Chemical Warfare Service (CWS) in the early 1920s to promote civilian use of irritant agents led to CN becoming a common US police weapon as early as the mid-1920s.[34]

For the military, irritant agents were seen to have a specific function in chemical warfare doctrine, as volume II of the SIPRI study pointed out:

> [T]heir function is not to cause casualties (although their use alongside other weapons may well increase overall casualties) but to lower enemy combat efficiency, thus extending their users' ability to manoeuvre.[35]

Following the US initiative, militaries in other countries developed CN and by World War II it was the main irritant agent in the various countries' stockpiles,[36] although chemical weapons were not used during the War.[37]

Irritant chemical agents found widespread use among police around the world during the post-World War II period. Writing in 1971, the SIPRI authors note:

> For peacetime purposes irritant chemical agents were, and are, used by police forces to control riots and lesser civil disturbances, and to cope with situations such as those where an armed criminal barricades himself to resist capture. In some countries, for example the United States and South Africa, the agents are freely available commercially in 'personal protectors' and similar devices.[38]

In the mid-1950s CN had been found lacking by the British military when using it during civil disorders in Cyprus, and they screened numerous compounds to find a more effective irritant agent.[39] They selected 2-chlorobenzalmalononitrile (CS), which had first been investigated as a new irritant chemical weapon during the 1930s and 1940s.[40]

As Furmanski has noted, CS had a number of advantages over CN, in particular it was more potent:

> CS was more rapid in action, more severe in effect, and less toxic. While CN was a true 'tear gas' affecting the eyes almost exclusively, CS was a general mucosal irritant, and affected the upper and lower airways as well as the eyes, and was capable of causing skin blistering and nausea in heavy exposures. While tight fitting goggles (or even tightly closing the eyes) could protect against CN effects, a full gas mask was necessary to protect against CS.[41]

CS was first used by the British in Cyprus in 1958-9 and irritant agents were used 124 times in the British colonies between 1960 and 1965.[42]

2.1.1.1　CS in Vietnam

The Vietnam War saw massive use of CS by the US Army.[43] Promoted as a humane weapon to limit civilian deaths and injuries for use solely in riot control situations, it was soon being employed in combat operations and with ever increasing regularity during 1968 and 1969.[44] The initial decision in 1965 to use CS on the battlefield prompted a period of rapid research and development, as described by a US Army historian in 1970:

> When the decision was made, half way through the decade, to employ CS weaponry in Vietnam, neither standardised munitions nor developed concepts for such employment existed. Yet in succeeding months and years weapons were designed, produced, and shipped, concepts were

evolved, and effective employment was attained ... [I]t represented the first effort by an American force in half a century to develop and utilize a group of chemical weapons in actual combat.[45]

The extensive nature of CS integration into US military operations was described in the 1971 SIPRI study:

Almost every type of weapons delivery system in Viet-Nam had a CS capability, so that CS could swiftly be spread over almost any size of target area, at any range and, if necessary, in close coordination with other forms of firepower.[46]

As Meselson and Robinson have pointed out more recently:

25 different types of weapon disseminating the irritant agent CS, including heavy munitions ranging up to 155-mm artillery shell and 750-pound aircraft bombs, were used in Viet Nam. Ultimately more than 15 million pounds of CS were dispensed in these munitions.[47]

CS was used without restriction and in a manner entirely incompatible with any concept of reduced or 'non-lethal' application of force. A post-war US Army report found no evidence of its use to prevent enemy or civilian casualties, quite the opposite:

[T]he reduction in casualties has not been in enemy or noncombatant personnel but, rather, friendly troops, as a result of using CS to make other fires more effective.[48]

2.1.1.2   Police embrace CS

Irritant agents were also being used by police forces worldwide,[49] but CN remained the standard agent in the mid-1960s.[50] This began to change following the US experience in Vietnam, as police forces gradually switched to CS in the late 1960s, taking advantage of military research and development.[51]

Following the July 1967 riots in Newark and Detroit, the use of irritant chemical weapons in riot control gained increasing support in the US.[52] The 1968 'Report of the National Advisory Commission on Civil Disorders' commented that the Army's experience with the 'more effective and safer' agent CS meant that there should no longer be any concern about using 'massive amounts of gas in densely populated areas'.[53] Among the report's specific recommendations, which overlooked the military use of CS in concert with conventional weapons, was the following:

The commission recommends that in suppressing disorder, the police, whenever possible, follow the example of the U.S. Army in requiring the use of chemical agents before the use of deadly weapons.[54]

High-profile use of CS by the US National Guard that followed included spraying it from helicopters during student protests in Berkeley, California, in May 1969[55] and using it during anti-war demonstrations at Kent State University prior to the firing of live ammunition into the crowd, which killed four students.[56]

Although the British had long used CS abroad, it was first used on UK territory in 1969 during riots in Londonderry, Northern Ireland. There was a public outcry and an inquiry was commissioned to investigate the health effects of CS.[57] The 1971 'Himsworth Report', after the Chairman, recommended that irritant agents should be subject to the level of testing required for pharmaceutical drugs.[58]

A newer RCA, dibenz(b,f)-1:4-oxazepine (CR), synthesised by British scientists in 1962, was found to be more potent but less toxic than CS.[59] It was manufactured by the UK Ministry of Defence at a plant in Cornwall between 1968 and 1977,[60] authorised by the Ministry of Defence for use in Northern Ireland from 1973,[61] and approved by the US Army as a RCA in 1974.[62] CR has since found limited application in comparison with other agents, in part due to the relative lack of studies of its toxic effects.[63]

Capsaicin, an extract from the capsicum plant that is a derivative of vanillylamide, was also proposed for use as an irritant chemical weapon as early as World War I, and in the 1950s vanillylamides were considered alongside CS as a replacement for CN. By the early 1970s another extract, oleoresin capsicum (OC), was already being used as an irritant agent in several commercially available self-defence spray devices in the US.[64] Other research being conducted at the US Army's Edgewood Arsenal was a search for an irritant agent that would induce persistent effects lasting for 1–10 hours after exposure.[65]

A wide variety of devices were available to the military for dispersing CS and CN, including various grenades, shells, bombs, and bulk dispensers.[66] Three main methods were used for disseminating irritant chemicals: burning a solid agent to produce a smoke; micropulversing the agent for release as a fine powder or dust; and suspending in liquid for spraying, or vaporising.[67] Two types of powdered CS were developed: CS1, a micronised powder mixed with silica to aid dispersion; and CS2 with added water repellent agent that meant it remained active in the environment for up to 45 days.[68]

In the policing arena, the development of hand-held liquid irritant sprays that fired a stream of irritant agent in solution was one of the most significant innovations. Previous weapons had relied on explosive dissemination of powdered agent, producing a cloud that could not be directed at any one person.[69] Introduced in the US in 1965 under the name 'Chemical Mace', these devices were soon being used widely and described by some advocates at the time as the most important development in police weaponry since the advent of the handgun.[70] The projectors generally employed CN as it was easier to deliver in solution,[71] but a CS version was also developed at the suggestion of the US Army.[72]

2.1.2   Blunt impact projectiles: Inaccuracy and injury

During the 1960s existing 'non-lethal' weaponry was supplemented by the development of various blunt impact projectiles as alternatives to bullets.[73] They originated in Hong Kong where cylindrical inch-long wooden bullets made of teak were used by the police as early as 1958. These were 'skip fired' off the ground with the aim of striking people in the legs. Nevertheless they could cause serious injury or death, especially given the unpredictable ricochet off the ground.[74] Termed 'baton rounds' because they were deemed a substitute for wooden batons at longer ranges,[75] their limitations apparently precluded them from being considered by the British for use in Northern Ireland as the 'Troubles' there intensified in the late 1960s. Instead a much larger projectile, the L2A2, made of hard rubber, 15 cm long, 3.5 cm in diameter, and weighing 140 g,[76] was developed by the UK in a nine-month research effort and first introduced in July 1970. The rubber bullet was specifically developed by the Ministry of Defence for the British Army in Northern Ireland at the request of Army officers who wanted a weapon for use in civil disturbances with a range beyond stone-throwing distance.[77] Highly inaccurate, it caused numerous severe injuries and several deaths, which were compounded by misuse in the form of direct firing, firing at short range, as well as unpredictable ricochets from 'skip firing'.[78] From its initial deployment until the end of 1974 over 55,000 rubber bullets were fired in Northern Ireland. A shorter, lighter, more accurate projectile with a polyvinyl chloride (PVC) outer layer, the plastic bullet (LR L3A1), was developed in 1972 and first used in 1973. Initially presented as a complement to the rubber bullet for use at longer ranges, it replaced the rubber bullet in the mid-1970s. Unlike its predecessor, it was designed to be fired directly at a person and it proved even more dangerous at short range.[79]

Other projectiles to emerge in the late 1960s and early 1970s in the US included 37-mm wooden bullets, used against protestors in Berkley, California, in 1969, 'bean bags' consisting of a canvas pouch filled with lead shot, and 12-gauge shotgun cartridges filled with plastic pellets.[80] Golf ball-like projectiles and rubber projectiles filled with liquid were also developed.[81] The US Army developed a ring-shaped rubber projectile called the Ring Airfoil Grenade (RAG). Two versions were developed, the XM742 Soft RAG, which contained a CS payload released on impact, and the XM743 Sting RAG, made of solid rubber, both launched from an adapter on the M16 rifle. Over 500,000 Sting RAGs were produced and they were added to the Army inventory in 1978 but were never used and were eventually declared obsolete in 1995. The Soft RAG never entered production.[82]

Particular concerns were expressed on both sides of the Atlantic over the apparent lack of testing of all these new projectiles before their introduction and the dearth of data on their effects on the human body.[83] In the early 1970s US Army researchers observed that 'very little quantitative data on blunt trauma to the body were available'.[84] They tested various projectiles, including a 'bean-bag' type projectile called the Stun-bag, which they found highly likely to cause 'unsatisfactory' levels of injury at all ranges considered. Research on the UK's rubber bullet reached similar conclusions.[85] A 1978 SIPRI study of anti-personnel weapons noted an enduring problem with designing projectiles intended to be 'non-lethal':

> Obviously, the basic laws of physics apply as much to non-penetrating as to penetrating kinetic energy projectiles: additional energy applied to propel the missile further results in unnecessarily severe injuries at close range.[86]

2.1.3 Electrical weapons: From torture to Taser

Electrical weapons have their roots not in policing or riot control but in farming and torture. In 1930s Argentina the barbed cattle prod was replaced with an electrical version, the picana electrica. As Rejali has observed, 'the picana electrica combines portability, flexibility and low amperage. It is also cheap. In this sense, it qualifies as the first electric stun technology.'[87] It was soon adopted by the Argentinean police as a torture device for use during interrogation. Rejali's examination of the US patent record illustrates the close connection between the development of electrical weapons for use against animals, which had been patented from the early 1900s onwards, and those for use against humans:

> [A] new kind of cattleprod was used as the basis for a new kind of stun gun, a new kind of stun gun handle was then reused for a better stockprod. The same patent string included prods, grips, canes, flashlights, forks, guns and batons.[88]

He argues that the calls in the US during the 1960s and 1970s for the development of 'non-lethal' weapons simply led to a rebranding of existing electrical weaponry with the same devices patented as cattle prods now characterised as 'non-lethal' weapons. As in Argentina, the police in the US had already adopted the electric cattle prod, which was used against civil rights protestors in the Southern states as early as the 1950s[89] causing widespread public outrage.[90]

Applegate's 1969 book on riot control defended the police use of the cattle prod, characterising it, perplexingly, as a 'non-violent' technique. He advocated the 'shock baton', essentially a repackaged and redesigned cattle prod, as an important and 'humane tool' for police[91] and proposed that it be used as a compliance tool by police:

> Non violent individuals in its path will quickly 'melt away'. With it [shock baton], the passive laydown resister can be easily discouraged without having to carry him away.

Police on the beat can use it to handle and move, with a minimum of force, drunks of both sexes, teenagers, alcoholics, derelicts, etc. Prison guards, attendants at mental facilities, and plant security forces are also potential users.[92]

Worryingly some of these approaches are echoed in police use of electrical weapons in the US today.[93]

The two major studies of 'non lethal' weapons in the early 1970s saw electrical weapons as one of the most promising technologies for further development.[94] US Army researchers argued that electrical weapons offered many advantages over existing chemical and kinetic energy weapons, including 'Broad spectrum of incapacitation, predictable physiological effect, controllability of dose, rapid incapacitation etc.'.[95] Nevertheless public aversion to electrical weapons in the US was pervasive and it limited research and development, as the Army researchers noted:

It is rather strange that this particular area of less-lethal weapons has been curtailed because as shown above, electrical devices have, in concept, many of the desirable features of less-lethal devices except, of course, the most critical feature of public acceptance.[96]

But this should not, perhaps, have come as such a surprise. Applegate's rationale for their use characterised people's unease about electrical weapons: 'Almost all people have an instinctive dislike and fear of electricity and the shock effect which it produces, and will retreat when in this danger'.[97] This feeling is compounded by the history of torture with electric shock devices. However, Rejali has argued more recently that a misunderstanding about the origins of electrical torture, particularly the role of technological development, 'allows ordinary people, on the one hand, to condemn the diffusion of electric torture instruments and on the other hand, to tolerate its everyday use in their communities'.[98]

2.1.3.1 'Thomas A. Swift's Electrical Rifle'

SIPRI's 1978 study of anti-personnel weapons noted: 'Patents for electric guns, spears, arrows and harpoons have been awarded over the past 100 years but few have come into operation'.[99] The most significant exception was the Taser, invented by John Cover and named after 'Thomas A. Swift's Electrical Rifle' from a series of children's science fiction books. Cover developed the first prototype Taser in 1970, seemingly in response to the recommendations of the Presidential Commissions of the late 1960s.[100]

Overcoming the range limitations of an electric baton or 'touch stun' device, the Taser design, which incorporated a high-voltage low-amperage pulsed electric current, was summarised in the original 1974 patent:

A weapon for subduing and restraining includes a harmless projectile that is connected by means of a relatively fine, conductive wire to a launcher which contains an electrical power supply. The projectile is intended to contact a living target without serious trauma and to deliver an electric charge thereto sufficient to immobilize.[101]

Cover envisioned a capability to control the magnitude of the electrical current so that it would 'range in effect from immobilizing to potentially "lethal" levels'.[102]

The initial model, the TF-1 with an electrical power output of 5–7 watts, was marketed by Cover's company Taser Systems.[103] It was demonstrated to a number of law enforcement agencies in the US, the majority of which were unimpressed,[104] in part due to the unfavourable public opinion about electrical weapons. However, civilian markets, including the US airline industry, showed greater interest and over 2000 Tasers were sold in 1975 to members of the public, security guards, and some policemen.[105] Later in 1975 sales were halted by the Consumer Product Safety Commission pending an investigation. It concluded that the Taser was 'non-lethal' to healthy individuals and lifted its ban.[106] But in 1976 the Bureau of Alcohol, Tobacco and Firearms classified the Taser as a firearm, requiring registration and severely restricting sales. The State Department also limited its sale overseas due to concerns that it may be used for torture. Taser's profile was further raised as it was used in crimes such as robberies across the US. As a result two states, Michigan and New York, passed laws prohibiting possession by members of the public. Buying, selling, or possessing a Taser was made illegal in Canada.[107]

2.1.4   The technological imagination

Interest in 'non-lethal' weapons during the 1960s and 1970s generated numerous other ideas. In their 1977 book, *The Technology of Political Control*, Ackroyd et al. observed:

> Most of the new riot-control weapons produce their effect by impact or chemical harassment. But the technological/political imagination has not been idle. Other devices have been proposed, developed or marketed in these boom years of law-enforcement technology.[108]

In fact, all the major concepts and technologies that are considered for use in 'non-lethal' weapons today were either proposed, in development, or in use in some form by the late 1970s, as illustrated in Table 2.1.

Aside from irritant agents, a number of other types of chemicals were either being employed or suggested for use as 'non-lethal' weapons, including incapacitating agents, smokes, lubricants, foams, and malodorants. The major military weapons development effort in the 1960s focused on incapacitating biochemical agents. Like irritant agents, these emerged from long-established chemical weapons programmes of the US, the UK, and other countries.[110] Whereas irritant agents (or RCAs) act peripherally

Table 2.1 Status of 'non-lethal' weapons technologies in the late 1970s[109]

Technology	Type	Status (late 1970s)
Kinetic Energy	Baton	In use
	Water cannon	In use
	Blunt impact projectiles	In use
	Nets	Available, not in use
Electrical	'Stun baton'/'stun gun'	In use
	Taser	In use
	Wireless electrical weapon	Proposed
Chemical	Irritant/RCAs (CS/CN/CR/OC)	In use
	Smokes	In use
	Lubricants	Available, not in use
	Aqueous foams	Available, not in use
	Sticky foams	R&D
	Malodorants	R&D
Biochemical	Incapacitating agents	Military stockpile, not in use
Biological	Incapacitating bacteria, viruses, toxins	Prohibited, 1972 Biological Weapons Convention (BWC)
Optical and Optical/ Acoustic	Light-flash/flash-bang grenades	In use
	High-intensity lights	Limited use
	Stroboscopic lights	R&D
Acoustic	Audible sound generator	Limited use
	Infrasound/ultrasound generator	R&D
	Vortex generator	Proposed
Directed Energy	Lasers (low power)	R&D
	Lasers (high power)	R&D
	Radio frequency/microwave	R&D
Delivery Systems	Cartridges, grenades, mortars	In use
	Encapsulated projectiles	R&D
	Dart/injector gun	R&D
	Unmanned platforms	Proposed

on the body, causing intense sensory irritation primarily of the eyes, skin, and respiratory tract for a short time, proposed incapacitating agents would act centrally, producing profound effects on physiological processes for a longer period.[111] SIPRI's 1973 study of chemical and biological weapons observed:

> The objective of research on incapacitants is to find substances capable of reducing military effectiveness for lengthy periods without endangering life or causing permanent injury, and to do so at dosages comparable with the effective dosages of existing CW [chemical weapon] agents.[112]

A chapter in the 1997 US Army *Textbook of Military Medicine* summarised the history of US research on incapacitating agents during the 1950s, 1960s and early 1970s:

> Virtually every imaginable chemical technique for producing military incapacitation has been tried at some time. Between 1953 and 1973, at the predecessor laboratories to what is now the U.S. Army Medical Research Institute of Chemical Defense, many of these were discussed and, when deemed feasible, systematically tested. Chemicals whose predominant effects were in the central nervous system were of primary interest and received the most intensive study. But other substances capable of disrupting military performance were also investigated, including some biological toxins.[113]

Interestingly this text acknowledged the link between the search for incapacitating agents and research on other means to achieve incapacitation:

> Nor were chemical agents and toxins the only possibilities considered; other candidates included noise, microwaves, light, and foul odors.[114]

The focus on chemicals acting on the central nervous system was due to relevant developments in the pharmaceutical industry.[115] In the US the intensive search for an incapacitating agent resulted in the production, stockpiling, and standardisation, in 1962, of munitions filled with a glycollate agent, 3-quinuclidinyl benzilate, given the codename BZ, which was capable of causing physical weakness, delirium, and hallucinations in very small doses. Development of new agents to replace BZ, which was considered an unsatisfactory weapon due to its unpredictable effects, continued under a programme that finished in 1975 when it was removed from the US chemical weapons arsenal.[116]

In the law enforcement field, the application of dart guns delivering incapacitating chemicals, long used to immobilise wild animals, was suggested for use against people.[117] The US Army had not overlooked the potential application of its research to the police search for new weaponry. A 1968 Army technical report, 'Nonlethal Agents in Crime and Riot Control', argued:

> The intensive search at Edgewood to find incapacitating agents for military application has led to the discovery of several types of nonlethal agents with properties suitable for use in crime and riot control.[118]

A number of different classes of compounds were under investigation, including anaesthetics, analgesics, tranquillising agents, anticholinergics (e.g. glycollates such as BZ), and vomiting agents.[119] The development of incapacitating biochemical agents, including drugs, as weapons is explored in detail in Chapter 5.

Biological agents, including certain bacteria, viruses, and toxins, were also developed for use as incapacitating agents as part of military biological weapons programmes in the post-World War II period. The US military, for example, standardised viral agents *Coxiella burnetii* (Q fever) and Venezuelan equine encephalitis (VEE), bacterial agent *Brucella suis* (brucellosis), and toxin agent Staphylococcal enterotoxin B (SEB) as incapacitating biological weapons[120] alongside 'lethal' agents such as *Bacillus anthracis* (anthrax) and botulinum toxin.

From a military point of view, the development of incapacitating agents, whether biological or chemical, was carried out to enable greater flexibility in the use of chemical and biological weapons. As SIPRI's 1973 study of chemical and biological warfare noted, the political advantages of these agents were that their foreseen limited 'lethality' (the aim was to develop agents with a one-to-two per cent lethality) would enable greater freedom in the use of force. From a tactical perspective, these agents might be used to cause large-scale incapacitation and thus overwhelm medical and logistical services. They may also be used in situations where there was a risk to civilian or friendly forces.[121] In the US biological weapons programme, other factors, namely the relative ease of weaponising and conducting human tests with incapacitating agents as opposed to 'lethal' agents, meant that they were actually standardised earlier and investigated more fully.[122]

In his May 1970 paper, Coates considered biological agents as potential 'non-lethal' weapons for the military:

> The biological agents, while having much of the versatility of chemicals, lack a rapid onset of effect. Their tactical incisiveness is severely limited so they are less applicable to the class of conflict discussed in this paper [limited and urban warfare]. They may, however, have a substantial application in capturing and neutralizing hostile cities at highly intense levels of limited warfare.[123]

It is strange that biological agents were even considered given the timing. President Nixon had unilaterally renounced biological warfare and announced the closure of the US programme in November 1969.[124]

The military had long used smoke on the battlefield to obscure visibility and HC smoke, consisting of zinc oxide, hexachloroethane, and aluminium, emerged from a World War I research effort in the US and France to find an alternative to white phosphorous as an obscurant.[125] Writing in 1969, Applegate advocated the use of HC by police, arguing that 'obscuring smoke, one of history's oldest forms of chemical warfare, has emerged as one of the best, nonlethal, mob control tools'.[126] However, the 1972 NSF study maintained that smoke was only useful to police in a few specialised situations because it impeded both the police and the crowd and could make crowd dispersal even more difficult.[127] Contrary to early assertions concerning its safety,[128] HC material was later found to be toxic if inhaled, potentially resulting in lung damage or death at high concentrations.[129]

Another proposal was to use polymers mixed with water as lubricants to spray on the ground with the aim of restricting movement of people (or vehicles). The concept was demonstrated in the mid-1960s and dubbed 'instant banana peel'. Two products, Riotrol and Separan AP-30, were marketed to the police and the military, but they did not enter use.[130]

Aqueous foams were also proposed for use as a temporary barrier or to disorient groups of people. At the time rapid foam-producing machines were being used for firefighting in the US.[131] Applegate was optimistic about the potential for adding other chemical agents:

> With foam, a suggestion of 'witchcraft' can be enlarged upon. Its effects can be increased by the addition of dyes, stenches, eye irritants, tear-gas, slippery-footing material and special lighting effects. Doubtless few rioters, once subjected to foam treatment, would desire a second immersion.[132]

There was also an interest in the development of foam materials that would rapidly become sticky or rigid. The US Army were exploring the use of foams to form barriers that would last for days, weeks, or months.[133]

The use of foul-smelling chemical compounds, or malodorants, was considered as a potential means of area denial for military operations in the 1960s.[134] The origins of this type of weapon reached back to World War II when the US Office of Strategic Services developed a chemical sprayed via an atomiser, known as 'Who me?', which was designed to be used by the French resistance against German officers.[135] The British developed a similar device, the 'S Liquid Projector' in the 1940s.[136] US military studies were conducted by the Battelle Memorial Institute in 1966 as part of the Advanced Research Projects Agency's (ARPA) Project Agile with a view to using malodorous substances in Vietnam.[137] One study sought to assess cultural differences in olfaction (sense of smell) with the aim of using malodorants in psychological warfare.[138] In the 1970s malodorants were suggested as a possible weapon for police to use in crowd control.[139]

Writing in 1978, the authors of SIPRI's study of anti-personnel weapons observed: 'New developments in anti-personnel weapons derive from three main areas of physics: electricity, acoustics, and electromagnetic radiation'.[140] Considering electrical, acoustic, optical, and directed energy weapons they concluded:

> Apart from nuclear, biological and chemical weapons, they appear to offer the only possibilities for utilizing new scientific principles in the production of anti-personnel weapons.[141]

They pointed out that none of the existing weapons had 'any significant battlefield application' but that many of them had been used for 'paramilitary and police purposes, ranging from dispersing crowds of demonstrators to interrogating prisoners'.[142]

Optical devices designed to temporarily blind by producing flashes of bright light were under development and in limited use. However, conventional military illuminating munitions, such as the MK1 Illuminating Grenade, were already in widespread use.[143] These were designed to briefly light up areas at night and had the secondary effect of causing temporary flash blindness.[144] In the late 1960s Applegate had proposed that the use of military training grenades that produced a bright flash of light and a loud bang would be useful for police riot control operations.[145] A similar device was used in 1977 by German forces to overcome plane hijackers in Somalia.[146] Police in the US had also experimented with high-intensity light systems mounted on vehicles and flashed on and off to impair night vision.[147]

Stroboscopic lights were also investigated as a means of crowd control. In 1973 the *New Scientist* reported that a UK company had developed a device called the Photic Driver, which reportedly combined a strobe light and low-frequency sound, and that the US military had funded research on similar devices in 1964.[148] It had long been known that strobes at a certain frequency could cause physical symptoms, such as disorientation and vomiting, and also trigger photosensitive epileptic fits in a very small percentage of people. In the 1950s investigations of US military helicopter crashes found that pilots had become disorientated by the stroboscopic effect produced by the sun shining through rotating rotor blades.[149] Interest in the early 1970s coincided with concerns over the frequencies of strobes in London discotheques.[150]

The use of audible sound, high frequency (ultrasound), and low frequency (infrasound) were explored for potential weapons application. A powerful sound system, the HPS-1, was developed for the US military and used for psychological warfare in Vietnam, particularly to transmit messages or sounds over long distances from the air. An associated 'Curdler' unit could be fitted to enable the projection of unpleasant sounds at high volumes. It was acquired for use in riot control by some US police forces and the British Army in Northern Ireland.[151] During the 1970s there was research into the potential for ultrasound and infrasound to cause adverse physiological effects. In 1973 *New Scientist* reported that a device called the Squawk Box employing ultrasonic and infrasonic frequencies was being developed for the British Army but it is unclear whether or not it was actually produced.[152] Coates had also proposed the use of vortex rings and wind generation machines as possible 'non-lethal' weapons.[153] The development of acoustic weapons is explored in Chapter 7.

Directed energy weapons were in the very early stages of development during this period. Research and development was ongoing in the late

1960s and 1970s on laser weapons but primarily as 'lethal' weapons. By the late 1970s there was considerable investment by the US military and programmes in the UK, Germany, and the USSR. Potential anti-personnel effects could not be described as 'non-lethal' and included heat-induced damage to skin and soft tissue and eye damage.[154] In the US, work began on the development of tactical laser weapons for use against optical equipment or the human eye.[155] Consideration was also given to the use of microwave devices as weapons and initial research was carried out on the potential biological effects in the 1970s.[156] The development of directed energy weapons is explored in detail in Chapter 6.

The design of delivery systems was an important part of 'non-lethal' weapons development during this period. The new blunt impact projectiles were fired either with adaptations of existing pistols, rifles, shotguns, grenade launchers, or specially designed weapons such as the US Federal Riot Gun.[157] A wide variety of munitions and dispensers were developed for military use of irritant chemical agents during the 1960s and some of these systems were taken up for law enforcement use. Initial designs of frangible projectiles containing water, designed to rupture on impact, were also under development.[158]

2.1.5   Legal issues: Chemical and biological arms control

There were a number of relevant legal developments during the 1960s and 1970s, particularly in relation to proposed 'non-lethal' chemical and biological weapons. The use of chemical and bacteriological weapons had long been prohibited under international law by the 1925 *Protocol for the Prohibition of the Use in War of Asphyxiating, Poisonous or Other Gases, and of Bacteriological Methods of Warfare*, known as the Geneva Protocol.[159] However, the Protocol did not prohibit research, development, and possession of these weapons. Essentially it was seen as a 'no first use' agreement.[160] Nevertheless chemical weapons were used by Italy during the invasion of Abyssinia (now Ethiopia) in 1935–6 and Japan used chemical, and later biological, weapons against China during the Sino-Japanese War (1933–45).[161] Irritant chemical weapons were used extensively by the Japanese.[162] Large stockpiles of chemical weapons were built up during World War II but remained unused due to fears of retaliation in kind and doubts over their military utility.[163]

However, it was the large-scale use of irritant agents (i.e. RCAs) and herbicides by the US in Vietnam that brought international criticism and increased attention to the issue of chemical weapons arms control during the 1960s.[164] As Furmanski has described:

> The US faced increasing condemnation of its RCA [riot control agent] policy at home and abroad, and in 1966 faced a UN resolution calling for all states to abide by the 1925 Geneva Protocol banning chemical and biological warfare. ... [T]he US supported the resolution and voted in

favour, but contended, contrary to the general international consensus, that use of RCAs in war, because they were non-lethal agents, was not prohibited by the 1925 Geneva Protocol.[165]

Indeed, during the 1960s, the US military had intensified research, development, and testing of irritant agents as well as incapacitating agents, both chemical and biological.[166]

A 1969 report by the UN Secretary General called for States to affirm that the Geneva Protocol applied to all chemical weapons, including irritants. States at the Conference of the Committee on Disarmament (CCD), and the World Health Organization (WHO) warned of the dangers of escalation from the use of 'non-lethal' agents to the use of 'lethal' agents.[167] Use of 'lethal' chemical weapons during World War I had of course begun with the use of irritant agents.

In July 1969 the UK tabled a draft treaty banning biological weapons[168] and several months later President Nixon announced the closure of the US biological weapons programme, renouncing the use of all biological agents, including incapacitating agents, and in 1970 he extended this decision to toxins, whether of natural or synthetic origin. He also affirmed the non-first use of both lethal and incapacitating chemical weapons[169] and announced the resubmission of the Geneva Protocol to the US Senate for ratification. Although the US still maintained that it would reserve the right to use irritant chemical weapons (RCAs) in combat. This issue held up ratification until the Ford administration reached an agreement with the US military that would restrict, but not prohibit, the use of RCAs in combat.[170] In April 1975 President Ford signed Executive Order 11850 concerning use of RCAs and herbicides in warfare. It renounced first use of RCAs except under certain circumstances under Presidential approval but still permitted their use in combat situations such as: 'Use of riot control agents in situations in which civilians are used to mask or screen attacks and civilian casualties can be reduced or avoided'.[171] Furthermore the US reiterated its isolated view that the Geneva Protocol did not apply to riot control agents.[172]

The *Convention on the Prohibition of the Development, Production and Stockpiling of Bacteriological (Biological) and Toxin Weapons and on Their Destruction*, known as the Biological Weapons Convention (BWC), was signed in 1972 and came into force in 1975. It was the first treaty to ban an entire class of weapons and, critically, it prohibited the development, production, acquisition, and stockpiling of all biological weapons (including incapacitating agents), whereas the Geneva Protocol had only prohibited their use in warfare.[173]

Other relevant arms control discussions during the 1970s centred on weapons that may cause unnecessary suffering or have indiscriminate effects. The International Committee of the Red Cross (ICRC) convened meetings of government experts in 1974 and 1976 to discuss these issues.

The meetings focused on certain conventional weapons such as incendiary weapons and cluster bombs; however, brief reference was also made to new weapons that did not fit categories such as 'conventional' or 'chemical'. Many of these were technologies that would become relevant to proposed 'non-lethal' weapons, including directed energy (specifically laser and microwave devices), acoustic (specifically infrasound devices), and optical (specifically light-flash or stroboscopic devices).[174]

An important development in 1977 was the agreement of Additional Protocol I to the 1949 Geneva Conventions, which reaffirmed the three main principles of the law of war: the prohibition of weapons that cause superfluous injury or unnecessary suffering, the prohibition of weapons that strike military targets and civilians without distinction, and the prohibition of weapons that are abhorrent to the public conscience.[175] Furthermore it required that countries conduct a legal review of all new weapons to ensure compliance with these principles and those set out in specific international treaties.

2.2 The 1980s: Relative quiet

2.2.1 A police research programme

In the US new impetus was given to 'non-lethal' weapons development due to a Supreme Court decision, *Tennessee v. Garner* (1985), which limited the use of lethal force against fleeing suspects.[176] The case concerned an unarmed 15-year-old boy who was shot and killed by police in 1974 as he fled the scene of a burglary having stolen $10. The court ruled the existing law unconstitutional, concluding:

> [T]hat such [deadly] force may not be used unless it is necessary to pre-
> vent the escape and the officer has probable cause to believe that the
> suspect poses a significant threat of death or serious physical injury to
> the officer or others.[177]

In part as a response to this ruling, then Attorney General Edwin Meese convened a second conference on 'non-lethal' weapons in 1986.[178] It was held by the NIJ, the research arm of the DOJ, formerly the NILECJ.[179] The aim was to assess the progress in 'non-lethal' weapons development since the 1971 conference, to develop ideas for new weapons, and to plan future research and development.[180] The Foreword to the final report illustrated the dual humanitarian and economic drivers behind the search for alternatives to use of 'lethal' force for police:

> First, the use of deadly force frequently offends some of our highest
> national ideals – the preservation of life, and the right of a suspect to due

process. Second, a growing number of communities are suffering financial hardship as a result of civil liability suits alleging the use of excessive force by law enforcement officers.[181]

The conference focused on the three main types of 'non-lethal' weapons technologies available at the time: chemical, blunt impact, and electrical weapons, but the report observed a lack of progress in weapons development:

Notably, most of the current weapons reviewed here were also available in 1972. The apparent lack of significant innovation in the years between 1972 and 1986 indicated to participants the crucial need for central coordination and support of future development efforts.[182]

The 1987 report described five different types of situation for the use of 'non-lethal' weapons: 'close proximity encounters; fleeing persons; hostage/terrorist situations; barricade situations; and crowd/riot control'.[183] Developing new weapons for close proximity encounters was considered the most urgent need and, in keeping with assessments in the 1970s, the focus was on improvements to existing electrical weapons and the development of weapons to deliver incapacitating biochemical agents via a dart gun. The second priority area was hostage situations and here incapacitating agents, delivered as a gas or aerosol, were also considered to be the most promising option.[184] The focus for proposed research and development was clearly on centrally acting incapacitating chemicals rather than on peripherally acting irritant agents. The report concluded: 'Given the rapid pace of development in the drug industry, participants were optimistic that a targeted effort could produce effective, acceptable chemical agents'.[185] Indeed this research was the first major activity to be taken forward in a newly established Less-Than-Lethal (LTL) Technology Program. Writing in 2002, then Director of the NIJ recalled:

After the 1986 conference, NIJ established a less-than-lethal technologies program. The first research award under this program was made in 1987 to the U.S. Army Chemical Research, Development, and Engineering Center at Aberdeen Proving Ground for a single project – an assessment of the feasibility of a dart that could deliver a safe but incapacitating chemical to a fleeing suspect. The project evolved to the identification of a candidate chemical and the production of a prototype delivery system.[186]

2.2.1.1 UK tactics

In the UK, during the 1980s, the focus was not on developing new 'non-lethal' weapons but rather on introducing existing weapons to the police forces of the UK mainland that were already in use in Northern Ireland. Northam's 1988 book, *Shooting in the Dark*, chronicled the dramatic changes in police tactics and equipment. A number of riots, notably in the Brixton area of London in April 1981 and in the Toxeth area of Liverpool in July 1981, where the irritant agent CS was first used by police on the UK mainland, led ACPO to instigate a change in policy for dealing with public order situations with paramilitary style tactics and techniques imported from the Hong Kong police. By 1983 ACPO had drawn up a new Public Order Manual incorporating sections on the use of plastic bullets and CS. ACPO and the Home Office oversaw training of police forces all over the country and, with riots in 1985 giving further impetus to the changes, the Home Office made plastic bullets and CS available to all major police forces by the summer of 1986.[187]

2.2.2 Emerging military concepts

Although many of the 'non-lethal' weapons available to the police at this time were products of military research and development, the military were yet to take a significant interest in the concept. During the 1980s this situation did not change greatly since the technological arms race was driven by the Cold War stand-off between NATO and the Warsaw Pact countries focusing primarily on nuclear weapons development.[188] As Lewer and Schofield have pointed out:

> [M]any of the technologies that might form the basis of a non-lethal armoury had already been identified in the 1960s and 1970s but they were given no real priority in context of Cold War military planning.[189]

Nevertheless military research on unconventional weapons technologies during this period would provide a basis from which new 'non-lethal' weapons would later be put forward. As the report of the 1986 NIJ conference remarked:

> The military has undoubtedly conducted research and testing pertinent to the development of less than lethal weapons, but much of such work is classified.[190]

This secrecy concealed research and development of unconventional or 'exotic' weapons systems, such as directed energy weapons, which were given particular attention under the 1983 Strategic Defense Initiative (SDI).[191] The directed energy part of the SDI focused on high energy lasers for strategic defence against ballistic missiles, but the development of tactical laser weapons targeted at optical equipment and the human eye also intensified in the 1980s.[192]

In the late 1980s John Alexander, a Programme Manager in the Special Technologies Group at Los Alamos National Laboratory, who would soon emerge as one of the major advocates of 'non-lethal' weapons, was proposing the development of new technologies to disable military equipment such as tanks.[193] In a 1989 article, Alexander argued for the use of a variety of technologies such as chemicals, lasers, high-power microwaves, and high-intensity light to disable equipment and to a lesser extent people, describing these techniques collectively as 'antimateriel technology'.[194] However, in contrast to the emphasis on less-injurious weapons seen in law enforcement discussions,[195] Alexander's proposal was that these weapons would be force multipliers to enhance the lethality of existing weapons against the perceived Soviet threat, to increase the 'kill ratio'.[196] As he would recall in a 1999 book:

> The recent development of military non-lethal concepts arose from very lethal roots. While law enforcement has always been charged with using the minimum force necessary to restrain assailants, the post-Vietnam military embraced the concepts of overmatching enemy weapons and the use of overwhelming force.[197]

2.2.3   Electrical weapons: 'Stun guns' hit the streets

By the mid-1980s the Taser had been adopted by some police departments but it was not used widely.[198] In 1980 the Los Angeles Police Department (LAPD) had purchased 700 of the TF-76 Taser for patrol use.[199] The electrical power output of the TF-76 was larger than previous models at 11 watts.[200] In 1982 the LAPD approved the use of Tasers although they were only used around two times per month in the following three to four years.[201] By 1991 they had been used 'several thousand times' by the LAPD.[202] The Taser was considered to have limitations in reliability and effectiveness, particularly against those under the influence of drugs and those wearing heavy clothing, and improvements were considered a high priority.[203] By the time of the 1986 NIJ conference, the Taser Systems Company had filed for bankruptcy, in large part due to restrictions on sales to members of the public and to foreign countries resulting from the classification of Taser as a firearm.[204] Taser Systems was sold to investors who, from 1986 onwards, operated the company under the name Tasertron.[205] The first new model introduced was the TE-86, a two-shot weapon with a power output of 5-7 watts.[206] Tasertron electrical weapons were only sold to authorised police, security, and military agencies and were not made available to the civilian market.[207]

A variety of other hand-held 'stun guns', used at arms length with no projectiles, were available at the time. With fewer restrictions on their sale, since they were not classified as firearms, they were marketed widely to the public as well as the police.[208] Indeed the police had begun to raise concerns over the availability of electrical weapons to the general public.[209]

One new weapon was the Nova XR-5000 Stun Gun, which is still sold today. The report of the 1986 NIJ conference estimated that the number of Tasers purchased was in the thousands but that the number of Nova electrical weapons in circulation was 'in the order of a few hundred thousand'.[210]

Another available weapon was a glove fitted with an electrical generator that was in use in prisons.[211]

With increasing adoption of Tasers and other 'stun guns' by a few US police departments, medical attention was drawn to the adverse health effects. The use of Tasers had been followed by a number of deaths during the 1980s and, echoing contemporary debates, opinion was divided on the role of Taser.[212] Pathologists, Kornblum and Reddy, considered 16 deaths in the Los Angeles area following Taser use by police and concluded that drug overdose was the primary cause of death in the majority of cases.[213] Allen contested this conclusion arguing:

> As pathologists, we should warn law-enforcement agencies that tasers can cause death. It seems only logical that a device capable of depolarizing skeletal muscle can also depolarize heart muscle and cause fibrillation under certain circumstances. Furthermore, while the use of tasers may be generally safe in healthy adults, preexisitng heart disease, psychosis, and the use of drugs including cocaine, PCP, amphetamine and alcohol may substantially increase the risk of fatality.[214]

Amnesty International drew attention to the widespread use of electrical weapons for torture and in the 1980s they campaigned against the proliferation of these weapons to South Korea, Taiwan, and China. A 1997 Amnesty report observed that subsequently Taiwan and China became leading manufacturers and 'during the 1980s and 1990s production of stun weapons began in several other countries such as Brazil, France, Germany, Israel, Mexico and South Africa'.[215]

2.2.4 Other technical developments

There had been no significant development of blunt impact projectiles and little use of these in the US during the 1980s, although rubber and plastic bullets were still being used widely by the British in Northern Ireland.[216] The 1987 NIJ conference report noted:

> Few new concepts for impact weapons were presented to the conference. A host of unused impact weapons already exist, and most are generally considered ineffective or excessively dangerous.[217]

CS and CN remained the irritant chemical agents of choice and were widely deployed. In the US, the report observed:

> Tear gas has been standard in police inventories since the late 1960s. Officers frequently carry personal-issue hand dispensers, and most departments have tear gas shells for shooting dispensers past barricades. Large-volume dispensers can be used for crowd control.[218]

However, medical concerns over their safety were raised, as in a 1989 paper in the *Journal of the American Medical Association*:

> Proponents of their use claim that, if used correctly, the noxious effects of exposure are transient and of no long-term consequences. The use of tear gas in recent situations of civil unrest, however, demonstrates that exposure to the weapon is difficult to control and indiscriminate, and the weapon is often not used correctly. Severe traumatic injury from exploding tear gas bombs as well as lethal toxic injury have been documented. ... There is an ongoing need for investigation into the full toxicological potential of tear gas chemicals and renewed debate on whether their use can be condoned under any circumstances. [219]

With regard to incapacitating biochemical agents, which were the subject of NIJ's first research grant under the new LTL Technology Program, conference participants had noted past military research on these types of weapons: 'Military researchers have investigated a large number of tranquilizers; some of those not suitable for battle may well prove useful for law enforcement'.[220] In fact military attention to the development of these weapons, which had been conducted intensively from the 1950s through to the mid-1970s, had waned during the 1980s.[221] BZ weapons, having been declared obsolete in 1976, were not replaced with another incapacitating agent[222] and stockpiles of BZ weapons entered a destruction programme in the 1980s with incineration taking place between 1988 and 1990.[223] Exploratory research and development on incapacitating agents had continued at the Army's Edgewood Arsenal during the 1980s but it was not until the late 1980s that interest in military applications re-emerged,[224] perhaps as a result of the contracts awarded to the Army by the NIJ to study incapacitating agents for law enforcement purposes. The initial feasibility study, completed in 1989, favoured synthetic opioid analgesic drugs, in particular the fentanyl derivatives. However, the enduring problem remained that these potent compounds had low safety margins and potentially fatal side effects, such as respiratory depression, that would require close control of the dose received.[225]

Several other technologies were discussed at the 1986 NIJ conference. The report noted research on stroboscopic light devices by a number of groups, including testing on 100 people that produced discomfort and disorientation. Apparently military tests had produced similar effects. Consideration had also been given to the optimal frequencies and waveforms for inducing these effects.[226] The report argued: 'The fact that the brain can be severely affected by optic stimulation of a specific type offers clear possibilities for the development of less than lethal weapons'.[227]

In terms of directed energy weapons, the report described research on the use of long exposures to extremely low-frequency (ELF) radiation to cause nausea and disorientation. The potential for use of microwave frequencies was also discussed, although no mention was made of ongoing military research on directed energy weapons such as tactical lasers.[228] The British Navy, for example, deployed a shipboard laser system used to 'dazzle' aircraft pilots as early as 1982, during the Falklands war.[229] The US military funded work on aircraft-and vehicle-mounted laser weapons, and soon the development of portable laser weapons was initiated.[230] These battlefield lasers were being designed to target optical equipment, including night vision devices, but also to cause permanent damage to the human eye.[231] One proposed 'non-lethal' use of these lasers was to 'dazzle', causing temporary obscuration of vision or flash blindness.[232] The central problem, which remains an issue today, is that lasers designed to temporarily blind at a certain range can cause permanent damage and blindness at shorter ranges.[233] There was no mention of acoustic weapons in the report of the 1986 NIJ conference. However, research was continuing during the 1980s on the effects of infrasound on humans.[234]

2.2.5 Legal issues: Controlling inhumane weapons

Arms control discussions in the 1970s had led to a UN Conference on the issue of inhumane weapons. The result was the adoption of the *Convention on Prohibitions or Restrictions on the Use of Certain Conventional Weapons Which May Be Deemed to Be Excessively Injurious or to Have Indiscriminate Effects*,[235] known as the Convention on Certain Conventional Weapons (CCW) or the Inhumane Weapons Convention, which came into force in 1983 and would soon become relevant to proposed 'non-lethal' weapons. 'Future weapons', including lasers, microwaves, infrasound, light-flash, environmental warfare, and electronic warfare, had been discussed in the preceding experts meetings in 1974 and 1976 where it was considered too early to discuss restrictions on weapons still at the early stages of development. However, continued development of laser weapons during the 1980s led to particular concerns over those designed to blind.[236] The ICRC took an active interest in the issue and convened a meeting of experts in June 1989. The purpose of this meeting, which brought together technical, military, medical, and international legal experts, was later described by Doswald-Beck:

> [T]o establish whether such weapons were likely to be manufactured on any scale, whether they would indeed blind in most cases of anti-personnel use, whether such use would already be a violation of international humanitarian law and whether a legal regulation was possible or desirable.[237]

This turned out to be the first of a series of four meetings since the participants had recommended further investigation of the subject.[238]

2.3 Conclusion

It is clear that police and military interest in 'non-lethal' weapons did not share a common origin. In the 1960s and 1970s law enforcement organisations were responding to public, political, and legal pressure in their pursuit of weapons and tactics that would reduce the incidence of death and serious injury resulting from police use of force. Generally speaking, 'non-lethal' weapons were sought as *alternatives* to 'lethal' weapons, although they were not necessarily always used in this way. The military, on the other hand, did not have a particular interest in the concept of 'non-lethal' weaponry, although they had long incorporated 'non-lethal' irritant agents (or RCAs) into their chemical weapons stockpiles and were actively pursuing the development of incapacitating biochemical weapons. In contrast to the police, the military viewed these chemical weapons as *adjuncts* to 'lethal' weapons, developed and deployed to enable flexibility in achieving a military task rather than with the aim of limiting death and serious injury. Although the potential for reducing the number of civilian casualties through the use of 'non-lethal' weapons in certain conflict situations had been put forward, such as to justify the use of CS in the Vietnam War, this had not been borne out by their use in practice.

Despite the absence of an overall military programme, the majority of relevant technological advances were generated through military research and development. Many of these, including new irritant chemical agents, emerged from existing unconventional weapons programmes. The law enforcement community relied largely on this research base with little of its own capacity and only small-scale efforts in the private sector. It was this military expertise that the DOJ sought to exploit in its renewed search for 'non-lethal' weapons during the late 1980s. For the military the Cold War stand-off left little room for consideration of 'non-lethal' weapons and those ideas that were put forward stressed the potential of new incapacitating weapons as force multipliers.

In the law enforcement arena, the development of hand-held sprays for delivery of irritant agents was considered the most influential development. Despite the advent of electrical weapons in the private sector, doubts over their effectiveness and public acceptance precluded their widespread use. Both these types of weapons were marketed to the general public as well as the police. Various blunt impact projectiles, developed as alternatives to bullets, were not readily adopted by US police forces due to safety concerns, although the rubber and plastic bullet were used on a large scale by the British Army in Northern Ireland.

Numerous other technologies were considered for use by police, including smoke, lubricants, foams, malodorants, high intensity and stroboscopic lights, as well as acoustic and electromagnetic generators. Indeed this historical overview shows that the majority of weapons technologies under consideration as part of 'non-lethal' weapons programmes today were either in operation in some form, under research and development, or at least had been proposed by the late 1970s. However, these various devices and technologies were found wanting and by the late 1980s available 'non-lethal' weaponry had changed little from its 1960s roots. Moreover, these blunt impact, chemical and electrical, weapons suffered from significant deficiencies in terms of safety and effectiveness.

3
'Non-Lethal' Weapons in the 1990s

This chapter continues the history of 'non-lethal' weapons, addressing developments during the 1990s, and exploring the expansion of police and military interest. It focuses on the research and development activities conducted by the US DOJ and DOD.

3.1 Policing developments

3.1.1 Cooperation and collaboration

In the early 1990s the NIJ began to expand the LTL Technology Program to cover a wide variety of potential weapons.[1] As Pilant observed at the time: 'In 1992 and 1993, the NIJ initiated cooperative agreements, interagency agreements and a series of grants that focused on finding out what police needed'.[2] However, it continued to fund work at the Army Edgewood Research Development and Engineering Center (ERDEC) on the development of incapacitating biochemical weapons.[3]

In 1992 the NIJ enlisted technical support from the Department of Energy's (DOE) Office of Intelligence for further development of 'non-lethal' weapons through the Special Technologies Program.[4] This DOE programme was primarily concerned with development of technologies to protect and secure nuclear facilities but it encompassed the development of related counterterrorism technologies funded by other government departments.[5] Liaison with the DOE led to NIJ-funded projects at four of the DOE's national laboratories: Lawrence Livermore, Sandia, Oak Ridge, and Idaho.[6]

At Lawrence Livermore National Laboratory (LLNL) in California, the NIJ funded follow-on work on incapacitating biochemical weapons at the Forensic Science Center, which continued until at least 1997.[7] At Sandia National Laboratories in New Mexico, projects assessed whether sticky and aqueous foams could be used as 'non-lethal' weapons by police.[8] Sandia was the lead laboratory for research and development of physical security systems at the DOE, and a number of techniques were considered for impeding access to nuclear facilities,[9] as described in a 1992 Office of Technology Assessment report:

> Dispensable barriers and deterrents are designed to add physical encumbrances and to interfere with an adversary's personal sensory and motor processes. Such barriers include rapidly dispensable rigid foams, sticky foams, aqueous foams, sticky sprays, slippery sprays, sand columns, noise, lights, smoke, and rubble piles.[10]

At Oak Ridge National Laboratory in Tennessee a research project was initiated in September 1993 to address 'Physiological Responses to Energetic Stimuli'.[11] A 1998 history of police technology development described the research:

> This project entails ongoing research ... into various technologies to produce temporary physiological responses, such as nausea, dizziness, and disorientation. Under study is the body's susceptibility to sound, light, and ionizing and non-ionizing electromagnetic waves. The goal of the project is to learn what the body reacts to and develop a device, tool, or weapon that produces that reaction.[12]

At Idaho National Laboratory the NIJ funded research into airbag restraint systems for police vehicles.[13]

Other NIJ research projects initiated in 1992 and 1993 were studies by the American Correctional Association and the National Sheriffs' Association to assess the potential for use of 'non-lethal' weapons in prisons as well as in riot control and individual confrontations with police. The Police Foundation was contracted to analyse past scenarios where 'non-lethal' weapons may have been useful, and the Institute for Law and Justice began research on public attitudes to 'non-lethal' weapons.[14]

In addition to technological cooperation with the DOE, the NIJ also sought to review potentially applicable military technologies. An early recommendation of a panel of policy experts, funded by NIJ in early 1993, was that the DOJ should request an agreement with the defence and intelligence communities on technology development.[15] In June 1993 Attorney General Janet Reno wrote to the DOD and the Central Intelligence Agency (CIA) to suggest collaborative efforts to develop dual-use technologies for law enforcement and the military.[16] This led to a Memorandum of Understanding in April 1994 between the DOD and DOJ for sharing of technology and systems to enhance 'operations other than war' and law enforcement.[17] The programme was overseen by a Joint Program Steering Group at the DOD's Defense Advanced Research Projects Agency (DARPA)[18] with members from DARPA, NIJ, Federal Bureau of Investigation (FBI), Bureau of Prisons, and the

Army. It began in March 1995 with \$26 million to fund projects in seven technology areas, one of which was 'non-lethal' weapons.[19]

3.1.2   Influential events

A number of events had added urgency to the DOJ's 'non-lethal' weapons development efforts in the early 1990s.[20] In March 1991 Rodney King was apprehended and brutally beaten by Los Angeles police officers with batons. Two cartridges from a Taser electrical weapon were also fired during the incident.[21] For police, the ineffectiveness of the Taser in subduing him had indicated the requirement for further 'non-lethal' weapons development.[22] However, others have since highlighted the incident as an example of how 'non-lethal' weapons may be used by police to supplement more dangerous weapons rather than to replace them.[23] The acquittal of the four police officers involved in April 1992 led to the Los Angeles riots, which left over 50 people dead and over 2000 injured.[24] National Guard troops who were drafted in to control the situation did not have access to 'non-lethal' weapons[25] and these events bolstered research and development efforts.[26] In addition, the siege of a family at Ruby Ridge, Idaho, in August 1992, where snipers operated a 'shoot-on-sight' policy, led to a review of the FBI's rules for the use of lethal force.[27]

Perhaps the most significant incident, however, was the siege of the Branch Davidian compound at Waco by the Bureau of Alcohol, Tobacco, and Firearms and the FBI from 28 February to 19 April 1993, which left 76 people dead, including more than 20 children.[28] Attorney General Janet Reno had approved an FBI plan to use the irritant chemical agent CS to end the siege.[29] Armoured vehicles made holes in the walls through which CS was pumped into the building and additional barricade-penetrating CS cartridges were fired through the doors and windows.[30] The FBI also fired several military CS grenades.[31] Six hours into the operation, fires started in the building and there were just nine survivors.[32] Before the operation the FBI had sought other techniques to try get those inside to leave the compound, including shinning bright lights during the night and playing recordings of unpleasant sounds and music.[33] There were reports that they had flown in a Russian scientist who had been developing techniques to alter behaviour using subliminal messages with the aim of delivering these during phone conversations with negotiators.[34]

It was in the immediate aftermath of the Waco disaster that Janet Reno had set in motion the collaboration on law enforcement technologies with the DOD. These events were cited at the time as a reason for accelerating the NIJ's efforts on 'non-lethal' weapons technology[35] and even now the incident is used as an exemplar scenario to encourage further technological development.[36] Rappert later observed that failures in such interventions, even when they involve the use of existing 'non-lethal' weapons, are often used to bolster the case for developing new weapons technology rather than to question its use in the first place. He has argued that such a technological focus may be to the detriment of other priorities such as training or conflict management techniques.[37]

Another factor that contributed to the perceived need to develop new 'non-lethal' weapons in the early 1990s was the public concern over the safety of the irritant agent[38] OC, known as 'pepper spray' which threatened to restrict the widespread police use of these weapons.[39]

3.1.3   New technologies for policing

The NIJ collaboration with the DOE was part of a broader approach in the 1990s to exploit the expertise of existing government and private sector research and development infrastructure.[40] In 1994 the NIJ carried out a reorganisation specifically to assist in developing or adapting new technologies for law enforcement. This included the establishment of the Law Enforcement and Corrections Technology Advisory Council (LECTAC) to provide advice to a new system of National Law Enforcement and Corrections Technology Centers (NLECTC) tasked with testing and evaluating new technologies.[41] Furthermore, in 1995 the NIJ established an Office of Law Enforcement Technology Commercialization (OLETC). The LECTAC panel was to set the research agenda for NIJ's Office of Science and Technology and among its top priorities in the 1990s was the development of 'non-lethal' weapons.[42]

Specific recommendations on the direction of research and development were made by the LTL Technology and Policy Assessment Executive Panel and the LTL Liability Task Group. The former was described in a 1998 NIJ history of police technology:

> The LTL panel is made up of state and local law enforcement, elected officials, and current as well as former high-ranking federal government officials. It reviews technology needs, developments, and innovations from a national perspective and makes regular recommendations to NIJ.[43]

The formation of the related Liability Task Group reflected the potential impact of lawsuits on technology development:

> The Liability Task Group assesses civil liability issues associated with technologies in various stages of research, development, and use. The task group has examined the liability aspects of such technologies as pepper spray, chemical darts, sticky foam, aqueous foam, smart guns, projectable nets, disabling strobe lights, projectable bean bags, microwave devices to disable automobiles, weapons detection devices, thermal imaging and forward-looking infrared devices (FLIR), and rear seat airbag restraints.[44]

The topics and associated contractors of NIJ grants awarded from 1994 to 1999 for work related to anti-personnel 'non-lethal' weapons provide an overview of priorities during the 1990s and are shown in Table 3.1. The funding

Table 3.1   National Institute of Justice contracts relating to anti-personnel 'non-lethal' weapons for fiscal years 1994–9[46]

Initial funding*	Additional funding*	Description	Contractor
(1992)	1994	Application/Evaluation of LTL weapons in jails and patrol situations	National Sheriffs' Association
(1992)	1994	Field evaluation of LTL weapons in a prison setting, Phase Two	American Correctional Association
(1992)	1994	LTL weapons program – technical support	Office of Intelligence, DOE
(1993)	1994	LTL weapons technology and policy assessment	Burkhalter Associates, Inc.
(1993)	1998, 1999	Public acceptance of police technologies	Institute for Law and Justice, Inc.
1994	—	Airbag restraint system for patrol vehicles	Idaho National Engineering Laboratory
1994	—	Aqueous foam system	Sandia National Laboratories
1994	—	Evaluation of OC and stun device effectiveness	National Sheriffs' Association
1994	—	LTL weapons technology and policy liability – technical assistance	Burkhalter Associates, Inc.
1995	—	LTL technology assessment and transfer	Booz Allen Hamilton, Inc.
1995	—	Net deployment module for a snare net projectile	Foster-Miller, Inc.
1995	1996	Law enforcement technology, technology transfer, LTL technology, and policy assessment	Seaskate, Inc.
1995	1996	Law enforcement technology, technology transfer, LTL weapons technology, and policy liability assessment	Seaskate, Inc.
1996	1997, 1998, 1999, (2000)	LTL technology policy assessment panel	Seaskate, Inc.
1996	1998, 1999, (2000)	Law enforcement technology, technology transfer, LTL weapons technology, and policy liability assessment	Seaskate, Inc.
1997	—	Armstrong laboratory acoustic study	Armstrong Laboratory, US Air Force
1997	—	Development of a baton with a projectable restraining net	LRF, Inc.

(continued)

Table 3.1 Continued

Initial funding*	Additional funding*	Description	Contractor
1997	—	Evaluation of OC	University of North Carolina–Chapel Hill
1997	1998, 1999, (2000, 2001)	Ring Airfoil Projectile (RAP) system	Guilford Engineering Associates, Inc.
1997	—	Pepper Spray Projectile Disperser	Delta Defense, Inc.
1997	—	Health hazard assessment for kinetic energy impact weapons	US Army
1998	1999, (2000)	Biomechanical assessment of nonlethal weapons	Wayne State University
1998	—	Development of a database of the effects of LTL weapons	Pro Tac International
1998	—	Evaluation of the human effects of a prototype electric stun projectile	Pennsylvania State University
1998	—	Laser dazzler assessment	US Air Force Research Laboratory
1998	—	Impact of OC spray on respiratory function in the sitting and prone maximal restraint positions	University of California, San Diego
1999	—	Applicability of nonlethal weapons technology in schools	DynMeridian Corporation
1999	—	Preliminary characterisation and safety evaluation of defence technology's OC powder	Chemical Delivery Systems, Inc.

* Years in which funding was given for these projects outside the 1994–9 range are indicated in parentheses.

was modest during this period averaging at around $1.5 million per year.[45] However, this figure does not include cooperative projects funded from other sources such as the DOJ-DOD Joint Program Steering Group.

The focus of much research was on assessing existing weapons such as OC spray, electrical weapons, and blunt impact projectiles. However, NIJ also funded two projects to develop restraining nets, a project to modify the Army's Ring Airfoil Projectile (RAP), as well as Air Force studies of a 'dazzling' laser weapon and the potential use of low-frequency sound as an acoustic weapon. There were several projects assessing the human effects of various weapons, including a prototype electrical projectile, the 'Sticky Shocker'.[47]

One project funded by NIJ surveyed the use of various 'non-lethal' weapons and public attitudes towards them. As regards perceived effectiveness the study found:

> Compared to *all other* LTL alternatives included in the survey, OC received the most favorable ratings in all four categories of effectiveness. ... [P]rojectile weapons and stunning devices receive high scores for subduing suspects, fewer citizen complaints, and officer safety, but lower scores than most other weapons for public safety concerns[48] [their emphasis].

The report criticised police policies on the use of force observing that they 'fail to provide adequate guidelines on avoiding excessive force'.[49] The authors identified public opinion as a key issue for the acceptance, and therefore successful introduction, of any new 'non-lethal' weapon.[50]

Research on 'non-lethal' weapons received significant attention in the NIJ's annual reports to the US Congress during the late 1990s. The 1998 annual report set out the major aspects of the LTL Technology Program:

- Funding the development and improvement of existing LTL technologies.
- Testing and evaluating the safety and effectiveness of LTL technologies.
- Addressing the legal liabilities and social acceptability issues raised by LTL technologies.
- Coordinating with other Federal and international agencies to leverage LTL research, testing, and technology development.
- Providing information to law enforcement and corrections agencies about LTL technologies.[51]

3.1.4 International connections

The NIJ also initiated cooperative agreements on science and technology with other countries in the late 1990s that included the subject of 'non-lethal' weapons. A formal Memorandum of Understanding was signed with the UK Home Office Police Scientific Development Branch (PSDB)[52] in February 1997 as 'a framework for cooperation and collaboration in research, development, evaluation and operational use of law enforcement technologies'.[53] PSDB would soon draw heavily on NIJ research in its search for an alternative to the plastic bullet.[54] The NIJ signed a similar agreement with the Israeli Ministry of Public Security and also conducted collaborative research with the Canadian Police Research Centre (CPRC). These UK, Canadian, and Israeli organisations were all represented on the NIJ's LECTAC.[55]

In the UK there was little research and development ongoing during the 1990s apart from further development of the plastic baton round (PBR), known as the plastic bullet. A new, more accurate, launcher was introduced in 1994 and a research project to develop a new projectile was initiated in 1997. In 1996, during widespread rioting in Northern Ireland, over 8000 rounds were fired. A government commission reviewed their use and more restrictive guidelines were introduced in 1999.[56] The 1999 'Report of the Independent Commission on Policing in Northern Ireland' noted a lack of UK research and development:

> In view of the fatalities and serious injuries resulting from PBRs, and the controversy caused by their extensive use, we are surprised and concerned that the government, the Police Authority and the RUC [Royal Ulster Constabulary] have collectively failed to invest more time and money in a search for an acceptable alternative. We were able to discover very little research work being done in the United Kingdom (except in the development of more accurate PBRs).[57]

Among the Commission's recommendations were two that would guide future research and development in the UK:

> 69 We recommend that an immediate and substantial investment be made in a research programme to find an acceptable, effective and less potentially lethal alternative to the PBR.

> 70 We also recommend that the police be equipped with a broader range of public order equipment than the RUC currently possess, so that a commander has a number of options at his or her disposal which might reduce reliance on, or defer resort to, the PBR.[58]

In the UK the significant development in terms of deployment was the introduction of CS sprays to all police forces in England and Wales in August 1996 following a six-month operational trial among 16 police forces.[59]

3.2   Military developments

3.2.1   Advocates and emerging concepts

It was not until the early 1990s that military interest in 'non-lethal' weapons began to develop in earnest. This was made possible, as Lewer and Schofield have pointed out, by the changing international security environment:

> Only with the end of the Cold War and the re-evaluation of security issues was the potential of non-lethal weapons considered seriously. Compared to the 1970s, general technological advances had enhanced the prospects of developing fieldable equipment in terms of size, accuracy, speed of deployment etcetera. But, in themselves, technological advances would have been insufficient to secure funding without some

strategic rationale that could attract support from influential organiza-
tions and individuals including government policy makers and the
armed forces.[60]

This rationale was that 'non-lethal' weapons were needed in response to the
predicted rise in low-intensity conflict and interventions by 'Western' countries in regional conflicts, particularly in relation to 'operations other than
war' such as peacekeeping and peace enforcement, where conventional military weapons and tactics, it was argued, would not be effective. In the US,
interest was aroused through lobbying by the US Global Strategy Council in
Washington, DC, a conservative think tank then headed by a former Deputy
Director of the CIA.[61] Researchers at the Global Strategy Council, Janet and
Chris Morris, authored a series of papers in the early 1990s setting out their
vision of 'nonlethality' as a 'revolutionary strategic doctrine':

> Nonlethality will allow the U.S. to lead the world toward a new global
> order, away from war-fighting and toward peacekeeping, while enhanc-
> ing our diplomatic efforts and our ability to project American power,
> when necessary worldwide.

> Nonlethality augments our powerful high-technology deterrence
> capability by adding a new level of narrowly constrained use of force.
> Nonlethality means responding to conflict with the minimum force
> effective. Regional and low intensity conflict (adventurism, insurgency,
> ethnic violence, terrorism, narco-trafficking, domestic crime) can only
> be countered decisively with low lethality operations, tactics, and
> weapons.[62]

Initial lobbying had resulted in the formation of a Nonlethal Strategy Group
at the Department of Defense, established by then Secretary of Defense
Dick Cheney in March 1991 at the recommendation of then Undersecretary
of Defense for Policy, Paul Wolfowitz, who would head the group. A
Memorandum detailing this recommendation made the case for accelerated
research:

> A US lead in nonlethal technologies will increase our options and
> reinforce our position in the post-cold war world. Our R&D efforts
> must be increased in part to develop countermeasures for our own
> protection.[63]

The group subscribed to the Morris's view that 'non-lethal' weapons offered
revolutionary potential and that a 'Non-Lethal Defense Initiative' similar to
the SDI should be established.[64] This fitted into broader discussions in the
aftermath of the 1991 Gulf War about rapid advances in military technology,
described as a Military Technical Revolution (MTR), itself characterised as

part of a shift in military doctrine and operations portrayed as a Revolution in Military Affairs (RMA).[65] An early 1990s study on the MTR speculated on the revolutionary potential of 'non-lethal' weapons:

> If U.S. forces were able, through electronic, electromagnetic, directed energy, or other means to incapacitate or render ineffective enemy forces without destroying or killing them, the U.S. conduct of war would be revolutionized. The whole calculus of costs, benefits, and risks would change for both the United States and its potential adversaries.[66]

Ultimately the DOD working group met internal resistance to their proposed initiative and it was not until the Clinton administration came to power in 1992 that there were renewed efforts to put 'non-lethal' weapons back on the agenda as the new Secretary of Defense conducted a review of defence priorities.[67] John Alexander, Program Manager for Non-Lethal Defense within the Special Technologies Group at Los Alamos National Laboratory (LANL), presented a paper to Clinton's transition team advocating the establishment of a 'cohesive plan to study these capabilities and develop the supporting doctrine'.[68] Like Janet and Chris Morris, he presented his ideas in terms of revolutionary solutions to new security priorities. Consistent with his 1989 paper,[69] the focus of attention was anti-materiel rather than anti-personnel weapons:

> Non-Lethal Defence concepts propose employment of weapons other than smart hard bombs but that can achieve the same basic results in systems degradation: strategic paralysis of the adversary.[70]

3.2.2   Disparate research efforts

In the early 1990s it was the national laboratories that were setting the tone of 'non-lethal' weapons development. As a 1995 Council on Foreign Relations report observed:

> In the absence of any national policy on non-lethal weapons, development of non-lethal technologies has been largely driven by various scientific laboratories offering proposals as their nuclear warfare budgets were reduced.[71]

In addition to cuts in defence budgets, the Clinton administration had emphasised the need for the laboratories to focus on research with dual civil-military applications. Since the national laboratories already had expertise in relevant areas such as lasers and acoustics, 'non-lethal' weapons fitted into this framework and programmes were expanded.[72]

The major research and development efforts comprised collaborative projects between the Army's Armament Research, Development and

Engineering Center (ARDEC) and Los Alamos and Lawrence Livermore National Laboratories.[73] From 1991 to 1995 ARDEC operated a Low Collateral Damage Munitions (LCDM) programme at Picatinny Arsenal in New Jersey.[74] This programme sought to develop weapons that could 'effectively disable, dazzle or incapacitate aircraft, missiles, armoured vehicles, personnel and other equipment whilst minimizing collateral damage'.[75] Reflecting the approach at Los Alamos, the initial focus was on 'anti-materiel' concepts based on unconventional technologies. ARDEC proposed that these weapons would reduce 'collateral damage' and offer performance benefits over conventional weaponry. The stated purpose was to develop weapons with variable effects, from 'non-lethal' to lethal.[76] The Army also began to develop operational doctrine, circulating a draft 'Operations Concept for Disabling Measures' in 1992,[77] which led to the publication of the *Concept for Nonlethal Capabilities in Army Operations* in 1996.[78]

Projects in the ARDEC LCDM programme intended as anti-personnel weapons included research with Los Alamos on pulsed chemical lasers that would create a high-pressure plasma and resultant blast wave; contracted research by Scientific Applications & Research Associates (SARA) Inc. on two acoustic weapon concepts, one employing a low-frequency acoustic beam and the other termed an 'acoustic bullet'; and a joint research effort with the Army ERDEC on incapacitating chemicals as part of the Advanced Riot Control Agent Device (ARCAD) programme. In addition, researchers in the Armstrong Laboratory at the Brooks Air Force base had been tasked with assessing the bioeffects of laser weapons.[79] In their 1997 book, Lewer and Schofield summarised the roles of the different organisations involved:

> In simple terms, ARDEC is concentrating on the development of delivery systems and munitions while the laboratories provide important support through their expertise in the basic sciences and applied physics.[80]

The ARDEC programme itself had grown out of earlier work done by DARPA,[81] which in 1994 had been tasked with coordinating the joint DOJ-DOD effort on dual-use technologies. Within this joint initiative calls for proposals on 'non-lethal' weapons in May 1995 sought technologies for stopping a fleeing individual, controlling hostile crowds, and stopping moving vehicles.[82] Among those areas funded were projects on: high-intensity, low frequency acoustics at the Air Force Armstrong Laboratory; man-portable, and vehicle mounted 'dazzling' laser weapons at the Air Force Phillips Laboratory; a launched wireless electric shock projectile, the 'Sticky Shocker', with Jaycor Company; and smoke grenades at the Army's ERDEC.[83] By the time of a January 1997 review of the initiative, progress amounted to the demonstration of a vehicle-mounted 'dazzling' laser system and the prototype 'Sticky Shocker'.[84]

3.2.3   Operational cement

Military technology requirements and the overlap with law enforcement priorities had been noted by a working group convened by DARPA in 1993 to help formulate a research programme to 'enhance the effectiveness' of US forces involved in 'operations other than war'.[85] The number of UN peace-keeping operations had increased dramatically in the early 1990s including operations in the Former Yugoslavia, Somalia, and Haiti.[86] In 1993 the US Marines were sent to Somalia to assist the UN peacekeeping mission in a humanitarian operation to distribute food. The Marines had batons and OC sprays, which had little effect in controlling crowds. With escalating violence they relied on lethal force and many civilians were killed.[87]

In late 1994 the Marines were tasked with assisting the withdrawal of UN peacekeepers from Somalia in what would be Operation United Shield. They investigated the availability of weapons for use in crowd control and, with assistance from the Army,[88] acquired: five types of 40 mm grenade-launched blunt impact projectiles, three types of 12 gauge shotgun projectiles, various OC spray devices, stinger grenades, flash-bang grenades, sticky foam, and aqueous foam.[89] Two different laser systems were also supplied by the Air Force Phillips Laboratory: the Saber 203 Laser Illuminator, a red diode laser weapon intended to temporarily blind or 'dazzle'; and a prototype solid-state green laser weapon.[90] There was very little use of these weapons during the March 1995 operation. Sticky foam was used to augment barriers, and both laser systems were used on a limited basis to warn people off by illuminating them. They were not used to affect vision due to concerns over eye damage.[91] Nevertheless the deployment of these 'non-lethal' weapons, and associated media coverage, was considered to have played an important role in deterring violence and in the successful withdrawal. The Marine's interest in 'non-lethal' weapons was galvanised and the commander of the operation, Anthony Zinni, subsequently became an outspoken advocate. Some 'non-lethal' weapons were also deployed with US troops during Operation Uphold Democracy in Haiti in 1994–5, namely OC pepper spray, plastic baton rounds, and beanbag rounds for shotguns. This deployment was also viewed favourably with John Sheehan, the former Commander in Chief of US Atlantic Command, also becoming a strong supporter.[92]

3.2.4   Secrecy

The early 1990s saw the first major military conferences on 'non-lethal' weapons. 'Non Lethal Defense', in November 1993, was co-sponsored by Los Alamos National Laboratory and hosted by the Applied Physics Laboratory at Johns Hopkins University. It was followed by 'Non Lethal Defense II' in March 1996 and 'Non Lethal Defense III' in February 1998. The secrecy of ongoing weapons programmes was reflected in the requirement that participants for the first conference had to have Secret-level security clearances.[93] There was disagreement over the issue of secrecy from the outset, as Lewer and Schofield noted:

> Some of the leading advocates such as the Morrises argue that non-lethal weapons will achieve their greatest impact by means of an open assessment of capabilities and operational roles. Others, mainly from the traditional military establishments, argue that secrecy is of paramount importance to ensure maximum effectiveness.[94]

The latter approach won out, with the argument that secrecy was necessary to avoid the development of countermeasures, and much weapons development work was being conducted within classified projects.[95]

3.2.5 Policy and prioritisation

The first attempt to organise the disparate US military efforts were made in February 1994 when a Non-Lethal Weapons Steering Committee (NLWSC) was established at the DOD chaired by the Office of the Undersecretary for Defense for Acquisition and Technology and the Office of the Assistant Secretary of Defense for Special Operations and Low Intensity Conflict.[96] In July 1994 the NLWSC circulated a *Draft Policy for Non-Lethal Weapons*.[97]

A January 1995 report by influential think tank the Council on Foreign Relations is viewed as having a significant impact on the subsequent institutionalisation of 'non-lethal' weapons in the DOD.[98] The report considered their potential use in conflicts such as that in Somalia and the ongoing conflict in Bosnia, concluding that 'vigorous exploration of non-lethal technologies is politically, militarily, and morally appropriate, and affordable as well'.[99]

In July 1996 US policy was formalised by Department of Defense Directive 3000.3, *Policy for Non-Lethal Weapons*, which established the Joint Non-Lethal Weapons Program (JNLWP). The policy defined 'non-lethal' weapons as:

> Weapons that are explicitly designed and primarily employed so as to incapacitate personnel or materiel, while minimizing fatalities, permanent injury to personnel, and undesired damage to property and the environment.[100]

The Directive assigned responsibility for the development of 'non-lethal' weapons to the Marine Corps, who would be 'responsible for program recommendations and for stimulating and coordinating non-lethal weapons requirements'.[101] There was to be no doubt as to the military's view on the role for 'non-lethal' weapons. They were not foreseen as ushering in a new era of humane warfare replacing conventional weaponry to some degree, as some analysts and commentators had speculated, but would be used to achieve better specified military objectives:

> Discourage, delay, or prevent hostile actions;
> Limit escalation;
> Take military action in situations where use of lethal force is not the preferred option;
> Better protect our forces;
> Temporarily disable equipment facilities, and personnel.[102]

Moreover their use in combination with conventional 'lethal' weapons, in a pre-lethal manner, to enhance the killing power of conventional weapons was officially endorsed.[103] Coates's advice to the military in 1970 that 'non-lethal' and 'lethal' tactics should be kept separate was long forgotten.[104]

In January 1997 the JNLWP became operational with the establishment of an organisational structure. The Joint Non-Lethal Weapons Directorate (JNLWD), run by the Marines, would be the focal point for coordination of all 'non-lethal' weapons development activities, guided by a Joint Non-Lethal Weapons Integrated Product Team (JIPT) and a Joint Coordination and Integration Group (JCIG).[105] Shortly after the JNLWD was established it conducted a review of existing 'non-lethal' weapons programmes.[106] Anti-personnel non-lethal weapons selected for further development are shown in Table 3.2 in the order they were prioritised.

The majority of existing programmes were part of the Army's Low Collateral Damage Munitions (LCDM) programme.[108] Many involved the development of new delivery systems for low-tech payloads such as rubber balls, and RCAs. Initially considerable priority was also given to acoustic weapons research.[109] However, the Non-Lethal Acoustic Weapons (NLAW) programme was closed down in 1999.[110] Another programme that had attracted considerable interest was the Air Force Research Laboratory's (AFRL) classified development of so-called 'Active Denial Technology', employing millimetre wave electromagnetic radiation to heat the skin and cause pain. The prototype system was fitted to a 'Humvee' armoured vehicle and called the Vehicle Mounted Active Denial System (VMADS).[111] The JNLWD review did not consider ongoing Air Force and DARPA research on 'dazzling' laser weapons, although there was certainly significant interest in these devices. Several war gaming exercises were conducted in the late 1990s that focused on existing and conceptual directed energy weapons including the Emerald Express exercise in May 1999, which addressed the use of 'dazzling' lasers and surrounding policy issues.[112]

Army research and development of incapacitating biochemical agents and associated delivery systems, as part of the ARCAD programme, apparently

Table 3.2   Review and prioritisation of anti-personnel 'non-lethal' weapons programmes by the Joint Non-Lethal Weapons Directorate[107]

Weapon	Details	Developer*
40-mm non-lethal crowd dispersal cartridge	M203 grenade launched munition with range of 10–50 metres and payload of rubber 'sting' balls.	ARDEC
Acoustic bioeffects and acoustic generators	Use of extremely low frequency sound (infrasound) as an acoustic weapon. *(Programme closed in 1999.)*	ARDEC and SARA Inc.
Modular Crowd Control Munition (MCCM)	Variant of the Claymore mine delivering a payload of rubber balls.	ARDEC
Vehicle-Mounted Active Denial System (VMADS)	Prototype directed energy millimetre wave weapon mounted on a 'Humvee' armoured vehicle. *(Programme classified at the time.)*	AFRL
66-mm vehicle-launched grenade	Grenade launched munition from Light Vehicle Obscuration Smoke System (LVOSS) with a range of 50–100 metres and payload of either rubber balls or flash-bang.	ARDEC
Unmanned Aerial Vehicle (UAV) non-lethal payload programme	Dispenser developed for UAV's such as the Dragon Drone to deliver various payloads: riot control agents, malodorants, electronic noise/siren, rubber balls, and marker dye.	NSWCDD and MCWL
Bounding Non-Lethal Munition (BNLM)	Variant of the M16A2 anti-personnel mine with various payloads proposed: rubber 'sting' balls, electric shock net, malodorants, riot control agents, and marker dye. *(Programme closed post 2002.)*	ARDEC
Canister Launched Area Denial System (CLADS)	Adaptation of Volcano Mine Dispenser System, mounted on HMMWV armoured vehicle to rapidly deliver 20 mines containing rubber balls. *(Programme closed post 2002.)*	ARDEC
Foam systems	Non-lethal slippery foam to deny access to people and vehicles. (Also rigid foam but for anti-materiel applications.)	ERDEC/ ECBC and SwRI
Vortex ring gun	Adaptation of the Mk19-3 grenade launcher to deliver payloads such as riot control agents, malodorants, or smokes via gas vortices. *(Programme closed in 1998.)*	ARL and ARDEC
Under-barrel tactical payload delivery system	Devices for delivery of various payloads, mounted under M16A2 and M4 rifles. *(Programme closed post 2002.)*	ARDEC

* Abbreviations as follows: Armament Research, Development and Engineering Center (ARDEC); Air Force Research Laboratory (AFRL); Army Research Laboratory (ARL); Edgewood Chemical Biological Center (ECBC); Edgewood Research, Development, and Engineering Center (ERDEC); Marine Corps Warfighting Laboratory (MCWL); Naval Surface Warfare Center, Dahlgren Division (NSWCDD); Scientific Applications & Research Associates (SARA Inc.); and Southwest Research Institute (SwRI).

was not included in the JNLWD's review. Ostensibly the programme had been halted due to the negotiation of the Chemical Weapons Convention (CWC), which was opened for signature in January 1993.[113] However, although full development of the ARCAD weapon was curtailed, research and development persisted.[114] In any case, the DOJ continued to sponsor related research at LLNL, building on previous ERDEC work. And soon the JNLWD would revisit the Army research programme.

3.2.6 Technology investment

The JNLWD soon sought new ideas and in 1997 instigated a Technology Investment Program to fund 1–2 year research initiatives in 'state-of-the-art' technologies within government laboratories, industry, and academia. Having received 63 initial proposals, three projects were selected for funding in fiscal year 1998 of which two were anti-personnel related. The first was a study of malodorant chemicals at the Army's ERDEC.[115] The second was on the development of spider fibre as an entangling material,[116] which was carried out by the Naval Surface Warfare Center, Dahlgren Division (NSWCDD) until the programme was closed in late 1998.[117]

The selection of the spider fibre project reflected the JNLWD's rather ambitious approach to technology development, as set out in the 1998 *Joint Concept for Non-Lethal Weapons*. It provided guiding principles for the JNLWP, emphasising efforts to 'leverage high technology':

> The exploitation of advanced technologies with potential non-lethal weapons applicability calls for innovative, creative thinking. The Department of Defense non-lethal weapons approach must encourage the pursuit of nontraditional concepts. Our experimental and developmental approaches must be bound only by the limits of physical possibility. Otherwise, we impose artificial and unnecessary limits on our thinking and thus on the potential utility of non-lethal systems. Electronic, acoustic, and nanotechnological approaches, among others, may offer high-payoff avenues of investigation and application.[118]

In fiscal year 1998 the budget for the 'non-lethal' weapons programme was just over $16 million.[119] The majority of this was spent on further development of the programmes prioritised by the JNLWD in their initial review and just under $730,000 was spent on the three projects selected through the Technology Investment Program.[120] However, from the outset additional funding for certain projects was provided by other armed services. Significant funding for directed energy weapons research came from the Air Force for the joint 'Active Denial Technology' programme as well as independent Air Force programmes such as the Saber 203 Laser Illuminator.[121]

In May 1998 the JNLWD sought new ideas as part of its ongoing Technology Investment Program for: (1) A rheostatic weapon system ('A single weapon whose effects are tunable across the entire force spectrum (from no effect up to lethal effect) is desired'); (2) Technology to employ non-lethal weapons at greater range (beyond 100 metres); (3) Various operational capabilities – (a) incapacitate personnel, (b) seize personnel, (c) denial of area to vehicles, (d) clear facilities of personnel, (e) denial of area to personnel, (f) disable/ neutralize vehicles, aircraft, vessels, and facilities; and (4) Non-lethal alternatives to anti-personnel landmines.[122] From 83 proposals submitted eight were selected for funding in fiscal year 1999, as shown in Table 3.3.

Table 3.3 Proposals selected for funding through the Joint Non-Lethal Weapons Directorate's Technology Investment Program in fiscal year 1999[123]

Weapon	Details	Developer*
Pulsed Energy Projectile (PEP)	Development of a pulsed high energy chemical laser to produce a high temperature plasma at the target surface with variable effects from 'non-lethal' to lethal.	Mission Research Corp.
81 mm mortar	Development of an 81mm mortar round to deliver 'non-lethal' payloads ranges of up to 1.5 km.	United Defense Inc., ARL, and ECBC
Overhead Chemical Agent Dispersion System (OCADS)	Development of a dispersal system to deliver chemical agents over a wide area. Later called the Overhead Liquid Dispersal System (OLDS).	Primex Aerospace Co.
Frangible mortar	Investigation of material for a proposed frangible (later combustible) 120 mm mortar round.	ARDEC
Extended Range Guided Munition (ERGM)	Feasibility study of using an existing munition to deliver 'non-lethal' payloads over long ranges.	Raytheon Corp.
Advanced Tactical Laser (ATL)	Feasibility study of an airborne high energy chemical laser for 'non-lethal' and lethal applications. It was presented as 'non-lethal' by virtue of its intended targets being objects but would be lethal if used against people.	Boeing Co.
Microencapsulation of chemical agents	Investigation of the use of microcapsules for delivering chemical agents.	APL, University of New Hampshire
Taser anti-personnel mine	Development of a Taser-based electrical anti-personnel mine.	Primex Aerospace Co. and Tasertron Co.

* Abbreviations as follows: Advanced Polymer Laboratory (APL), University of New Hampshire. (Other abbreviations as for Table 3.2).

3.2.7 Institutionalising 'non-lethal' weapons

The JNLWD also initiated partnerships with academic departments in the late 1990s in order to institutionalise 'non-lethal' weapons research and development.[124] In November 1997 the Applied Research Laboratory at Pennsylvania State University established the Institute for Non-Lethal Defense Technologies (INLDT) to conduct interdisciplinary research in support of DOD and DOJ 'non-lethal' weapons programmes by carrying out technical, human effects, and policy research. From the outset the INLDT was supported both politically and financially by the Marine Corps. Initial work funded by the JNLWD was the establishment of a Human Effects Advisory Panel (HEAP) to assess data on 'non-lethal' weapons effects.[125] In June 1999 the Marines signed an agreement with Pennsylvania State University, establishing it as the Marine Corps Research University (MCRU) to fulfil military research contracts covering a variety of topics including 'non-lethal' weapons, thus further strengthening the links between the organisations.[126]

Also in 1999 the JNLWD extended efforts to investigate new technologies by providing a grant to the University of New Hampshire to establish the Non-Lethal Technology Innovation Center (NTIC) with a mission 'to effect the next generation of nonlethal capabilities by identifying and promoting the development of innovative concepts, materials, and technologies'.[127] NTIC was set up to award JNLWD funding for research on new technologies and hold an annual Non-Lethal Technology and Academic Research (NTAR) Symposium, the first of which was held in May 1999.[128] Both the INLDT and the NTIC are essentially extensions of the JNLWD.[129]

By the end of the decade the JNLWP budget had increased substantially from $9.3 million in fiscal year 1997 and $16.1 million in fiscal year 1998 to $33.9 million in fiscal year 1999.[130] However, despite this increase, the JNLWP still only commanded a very small portion of the overall defence budget.

There appeared to be a growing momentum on 'non-lethal' weapons issues in 1999 with the publication of two studies by influential think tanks. The first was a policy study commissioned by the Office of the Secretary of Defense at the request of the National Security Council, funded by the JNLWD and authored by the Center for Strategic and International Studies (CSIS). It considered the strategic use of 'non-lethal' weapons for large-scale, long-range attacks in a variety of conflict scenarios, concluding that they had significant potential and that an expanded three-year research effort be undertaken by the JNLWD with funding of $100 million per year.[131] In October 1999 the second Council on Foreign Relations report on 'non-lethal' weapons concluded that progress in both development and deployment had been limited due to lack of support from senior policymakers and insufficient funding.[132] The report also recommended a substantial increase in funding arguing 'there is a high probability of major benefit from a large, urgent investment in nonlethal weapons and technologies'.[133]

3.2.8 Following the US lead

International interest during the 1990s centred on NATO, which in turn was guided by the US.[134] In 1994 NATO's Defence Research Group (DRG) was tasked with assessing the potential of 'non-lethal' weapons for peacekeeping and peace support operations.[135] Meanwhile the Advisory Group for Aerospace Research and Development (AGARD), a forum for information exchange on science and technology, began a study on 'Non-Lethal Means for Diverting or Forcing Non-Cooperative Aircraft to Land'. The report identified a concept of 'non-lethal air defence' for protecting airspace and enforcing no-fly zones.[136] In May 1997 AGARD published a second study addressing lethal and 'non-lethal' weapons for peace support operations.[137] As Lewer observed at the time:

> The study was commissioned to explore innovative means to attack (both lethal and non-lethal), with minimal risk of collateral damage, discrete ground targets from airborne platforms supporting NATO Peace Support Operations. A basic set of 50 lethal, 11 non-lethal, and 4 UAV concepts were identified and analysed in relevant target situations.[138]

'Non-lethal' concepts put forward included: the use of crop dusters to deliver irritant chemical weapons or aqueous foams; helicopters as platforms for a variety of weapons such as nets, acoustic systems, kinetic impact rounds, and 'dazzling' lasers; and the use of UAV's as delivery systems.[139] By September 1997, the work of NATO's DRG had led to the establishment of an NLW Policy Team[140] and two years later, in September 1999, NATO issued its Policy on NLW, which was closely aligned with US policy.[141]

Other collaboration occurred directly between the US JNLWD and interested countries in the late 1990s, as their 1999 Annual Report noted:

> Over the past year, the JNLWD had numerous foreign enquiries on DoD Non-Lethal Weapons (NLW) efforts. In response, the Directorate has provided overview briefs to France, Italy, Germany, Republic of Korea, Japan and the United Kingdom (UK), and replied to correspondence from many others such as Australia, Columbia, Sweden, Canada and Norway.[142]

Furthermore the JNLWD signed information exchange agreements with the UK Ministry of Defense in February 1998 and Israel in September 1999.[143] Meetings with the UK in 1998 and 1999[144] focused on training and doctrine as well as specific technologies such as anti-personnel landmine alternatives and 'dazzling' laser weapons. The UK and the US had starting planning for a series of joint war gaming exercises.[145]

3.3   Irritant chemical weapons: 'Pepper spray' preferred

Despite their availability as early as the 1970s there was a greatly increased uptake of OC sprays (also known as 'pepper spray') by US police departments during the early 1990s with OC preferred to CS.[146] A 1989 FBI study was the catalyst for this change because it claimed to find no adverse effects in over 800 subjects exposed to OC. As it was an unregulated product there was a proliferation of manufacturers and large numbers of sprays were marketed to both police and the general public.[147] A 1996 paper described the impact of the FBI study:

> Following release of this study, the use of OC sprays became so popular that a 1992 Washington Post article reported over 2000 law enforcement agencies were using pepper sprays. The popularity of OC sprays has now increased so much that current industry estimates indicate at least 15 million defense spray canisters (a majority containing OC) were manufactured in the three year period from 1992 through 1994.[148]

However, OC had been widely introduced with little assessment of the potential for adverse health effects.[149] There were a number of in-custody deaths following OC exposure, which threatened to limit the use of these weapons by police. In response the NIJ undertook a study that concluded OC was not the cause of these deaths.[150] The NIJ funded several other studies during the 1990s, which reached favourable conclusions about effectiveness and associated health risks of OC sprays.[151] However, Rappert's subsequent analysis of these studies indicated that there was a lack of balanced and objective assessment. Research with significant limitations was cited to reinforce favourable assessments of OC while research reaching unfavourable conclusions was disregarded.[152] A 1994 technical report by the Army's ERDEC expressed concerns over adverse health effects and the lack of data available for effects on varied population.[153] In a worrying twist to the debate in 1996, the agent overseeing the original FBI study was found guilty of receiving a bribe from the manufacturers of the CAP-STUN brand sprays used in the tests.[154]

Some research on alternatives to OC and CS irritant agents was funded by the NIJ in 1998 and 1999. Researchers assessed the potential of a potent irritant compound called tropilidene, which was studied by the US Army in the early 1970s. It was initially designated EA 4923 before being given the code CHT.[155]

3.4 Electrical weapons: Raising the voltage

One of the most significant developments in 'non-lethal' weaponry during the 1990s was the modification of a long established electrical weapon technology, the Taser. The changes originated not from government sponsored research endeavours but rather from the private sector. In 1993 a new company, Air Taser, later Taser International, entered the US market for Tasers. At the time Tasertron had a legal agreement that made it the only company allowed to sell Tasers to law enforcement agencies and it did not sell its products to the civilian market. Air Taser launched their first model in January 1995, the Air Taser 34000, which had the same power output (5–7 watts) as the Tasertron TE85, TE95, and TE93 Patrol Taser. The Air Taser 34000, like the Tasertron TE93, was a single-shot device and had the capability to be used in 'touch stun' mode. It was smaller and lighter than the TE93 but the most significant difference was that the Air Taser cartridges employed compressed nitrogen to launch the barbed projectiles whereas Tasertron cartridges used gunpowder. This meant that Air Tasers were not classified as firearms by the Bureau of Alcohol, Tobacco, and Firearms and could be widely sold to the general public as 'self defence' weapons.[156] This was the market targeted at the outset by the founder of Air Taser who described the company strategy in a 1996 conference presentation:

> Since the vast majority of firearm related fatalities [in the US] are committed by armed citizens (vis-a-vis police officers), the greatest societal gains will be realized by implementing policies that effect migration towards non-lethals by the general public.[157]

Unsurprisingly perhaps, his analysis of available 'non-lethal' weapons technology considered electrical weapons to be most suitable for implementing this ostensibly altruistic shift in the armoury of the US citizen. Nevertheless while powerful lobby groups such as the National Rifle Association have assisted many US citizens in maintaining their eighteenth century 'right to bear arms', there proved to be a substantial civilian market for electrical weapons to supplement them. By late 1996 'tens of thousands' of Air Taser units had been sold to the general public.[158] In 1997 Air Taser launched the Auto Taser, an anti-theft device similar to a steering wheel lock, but it was not a commercial success.[159] In early 1998, with the expiry of Tasertron's exclusive patent agreement for sales to law enforcement agencies, Air Taser (renamed Taser International) entered the law enforcement market.

By 1999, according to Tasertron, over 400 law enforcement agencies were using its electrical weapons and there had been over 50,000 deployments.[160] The Victoria Police Department in Canada introduced Tasertron Tasers in 1999 following a six-month trial. Until that point Tasers and similar weapons had been prohibited in Canada.[161]

Meanwhile Taser International had begun to develop a new weapon with a much higher power output of 26 watts, four times more powerful than the existing devices, which was redesigned to look like a handgun. Company tests showed that the prototype device, which would later be called the M26 Advanced Taser, was more effective at incapacitating victims, including those who had been able to fight through the effects of lower powered devices.[162] The first 30 M26 Advanced Tasers were sold to the New York City police department for field testing in November 1999.[163] This modification to the Taser design would prove to be very significant in terms of increased deployment of electrical weapons in the US and elsewhere. However, one concern noted just prior to its introduction was that all existing research on the human effects of electrical weapons was based around the lower power 5–7 watt weapons.[164]

In addition to hand-held electrical weapons, Tasertron had been conducting research and development of an electrical landmine, in collaboration with Primex Aerospace Company and the Army's ARDEC, as part of the JNLWD's initiative on 'non-lethal' alternatives to anti-personnel landmines. They developed a prototype Taser Area Denial Device that fired seven sets of Taser cartridges in a 120-degree arc and a prototype multi-shot system called the Taser Sentinel, which incorporated a modified Taser Area Denial Device and a camera to fire cartridges by remote control at varied angles.[165]

Other research funded by the DOJ-DOD collaborative effort on 'non-lethal' weapons sought to overcome the range limitations of hand-held Tasers with trailing wires by developing a wireless electrical projectile. The research was carried out by Jaycor Company who, by 1996, had developed the 'Sticky Shocker'. The prototype, fired from a compressed gas launcher, contained a battery pack to transmit an electric discharge on contact with the target person. Tests on the blunt impact force carried out by the company showed that it delivered similar impact to rubber bullets and 'bean bag' rounds.[166] It therefore shared the limitations of these projectiles in terms of potential for severe injury. A 1999 NIJ-sponsored assessment of the 'Sticky Shocker' conducted by the Human Effects Advisory Panel at Pennsylvania State University warned that the impact had the potential to kill or cause serious injury and expressed concerns over the electrical discharge:

> The Shocker's electrical insult could cause acidosis [increase in acidity of the blood], which can lead to death. It also has a high probability of skin burns. The Sticky Shocker's electrical insult also may cause other serious injuries. The problem is, little data exists regarding how electrical current passes through the human body.[167]

This knowledge gap concerning the interaction of electrical currents with the human body applied to all electrical weapons.

During the 1990s Amnesty International continued to raise concerns over the use of electrical weapons for torture. In a 1997 report, 'Arming the Torturers: Electro-shock Torture and the Spread of Stun Technology' the organisation described reports of torture with hand-held electrical weapons in numerous countries, noting:

> The portability and ease with which electro-shock weapons can be concealed, means that the incapacitating, painful and other effects of such weapons may be attractive to unscrupulous security, police and prison officers, especially since traces of their use on victims can afterwards be difficult to detect. Aware of the growing international marketing of electro-shock weapons, Amnesty International is publishing this report to warn the international community of this danger.[168]

3.5 Other technologies

There were no major developments in blunt impact projectiles during the 1990s. In 1997 the NIJ began funding a project to assess the potential of the rubber Ring Airfoil Projectile (RAP), which had been developed by the US Army in the 1970s under the name Ring Airfoil Grenade (RAG). The renewed research effort sought to develop the version that would release a three-foot diameter cloud of OC powder on impact. The project was ongoing at the end of the 1990s.[169] In the UK, research was ongoing on a replacement for the L5A6/7 plastic bullets.[170]

Substantial work on chemical-based 'non-lethal' weapons had been conducted during this period including further development of lubricants, foams, malodorants, and incapacitating agents. The NIJ funded a project in 1992 to assess the application of sticky foam to subdue prisoners and by 1994 scientists had conducted toxicology tests and developed a prototype delivery system.[171] These systems were considered too dangerous for use against people due to the risk of suffocation.[172] The sticky foam also presented problems in terms of clean-up.[173] In late 1994 the NIJ also funded the development of a prototype cell extraction system employing aqueous foam laced with OC irritant agent. They conducted a feasibility study to assess the use of this irritant foam to fill the entire stairwell of a prison building in the event of a large-scale disturbance.[174]

Research on slippery substances was another development effort inherited by the JNLWD. New research at the Army Edgewood Chemical Biological Center (ECBC) had begun in 1996 with the screening of a variety of water-activated polyacrylamide and polyacrylic acid-based substances and resulted in the selection of several commercial compounds for further consideration, including Agefloc WT 603 and various Percol powders. Testing highlighted logistical difficulties, which led to collaboration with the Southwest Research Institute (SwRI) in early 1999 to consider a wider range of chemical compounds.[175]

Research on malodorant chemicals at ECBC was ongoing to deliver: an 'odour index' relating to the effects of odours on specific population; techniques for microencapsulating these chemicals; and a prototype hand-held delivery system.[176] Malodorants were being considered as potential payloads for a variety of delivery systems. Initial research, conducted in collaboration with the Monell Chemical Senses Center in Philadelphia, involved assessing the most aversive chemical mixtures and ascertaining the human response. Two chemical mixtures, 'US Government Bathroom Malodor', the smell of human faeces, and 'Who me?', the smell of body odour, were found to be the most unpleasant. Some of the symptoms reported by human volunteers included nausea and gagging.[177]

The Army programme to develop the ARCAD employing an incapacitating chemical agent was ongoing in the early 1990s. This programme had close connections with the NIJ programme. Further NIJ-funded research on agents and delivery systems was carried out by LLNL during the mid-1990s. Synthetic opioid drugs, namely fentanyl analogues, were the major agents under consideration by both the Army and the NIJ, with the military also clearly interested in alpha-2 adrenergic drugs to induce sedation. Both groups were investigating the use of agent and antidote combinations in an attempt to control life threatening side effects such as respiratory depression. The ARCAD programme was developing a grenade-like delivery system[178] while the Livermore research was investigating transdermal (through skin) delivery systems for use against individuals.[179] The development of incapacitating biochemical agents as weapons is explored in detail in Chapter 5.

Other unusual uses of chemicals were put forward during the 1990s. A 1994 research proposal by the Air Force Wright Laboratory, 'Harassing, Annoying and 'Bad Guy' Identifying Chemicals', proposed three categories of chemical-based weapons including: 'Chemicals that attract annoying creatures to the enemy position'; 'Chemicals that make lasting but non-lethal markings on the personnel'; and 'Chemicals that effect human behaviour so that discipline and morale in enemy units is adversely effected'. The latter category included a bizarre suggestion: 'One distasteful but completely non-lethal example would be strong aphrodisiacs, especially if the chemical also caused homosexual behaviour'.[180]

Research programmes on acoustic weapons were conducted throughout the 1990s, investigating various acoustic weapons concepts including a high power infrasound generator, and a vortex ring generator. However, in 1998 and 1999 both projects ended with the closure of the programme after almost ten years of research and development work that had yielded little more than a prototype infrasound generator that failed to produce predictable, repeatable effects at the minimum required range.[181] Nevertheless Army research and development of other acoustic weapons persisted,[182] as did interest in the commercial sector.[183] The development of acoustic weapons is explored in Chapter 7.

Development of anti-personnel directed energy weapons expanded greatly during the 1990s. In the early 1990s tactical laser weapons designed to blind and to degrade sensors and optics had emerged. Despite their destructive and irreversible effects on the human eye some of these were even presented as 'non-lethal' weapons.[184] International pressure led to a ban on laser weapons intentionally designed to blind in 1995. Subsequently attention turned to those designed to temporarily blind or 'dazzle' a person. A number of prototype devices were produced including the Saber 203 Illuminator, a red diode laser developed by the Air Force Phillips Laboratory prior to the ban on blinding lasers. This weapon was eventually discarded in 1999, in part due to concerns over eye safety.[185] A comparable device called the Laser Dissuader was developed by Science and Engineering Associates. In the late 1990s the Air Force tested a number of these weapons and by 1999 had begun to develop a weapon incorporating similar optics called the Hinder Adversaries with Less-than-Lethal Technology (HALT) as a replacement for the Saber 203 Illuminator.[186] Other weapons included the Laser Dazzler, a green solid-state laser weapon developed by LE Systems with funding from the joint DOJ-DOD initiative on 'non-lethal' weapons.

Air Force research on using millimetre wave electromagnetic energy to heat up human skin and cause a painful burning sensation, which they termed 'Active Denial Technology', had been ongoing throughout the 1990s and this research and development was given high priority by the JNLWD in their initial review of 'non-lethal' weapons programmes. There was also investigative research being conducted on the use of high energy chemical lasers for 'non-lethal' weapons applications such as the development of pulsed lasers to create plasma induced shock waves. Nevertheless proposed 'non-lethal' directed energy weapons formed a very small part of the larger US programme (and indeed programmes in other countries) to develop technological alternatives or complements to conventional weapons. The vast majority of funding, which had decreased considerably in the 1990s in comparison to efforts under the SDI in the 1980s, was going towards development of high energy laser weapons, such as the Airborne Laser (ABL) intended to shoot down ballistic missiles, and High-Power Microwave (HPM) weapons designed to destroy electronic equipment.[187] The development of directed energy weapons is explored in detail in Chapter 6.

Many of the 'non-lethal' weapons programmes inherited from the Army and prioritised by the JNLWD in the late 1990s involved the development delivery systems, compatible with existing conventional weapons, for firing a variety of payloads at extended ranges. These included the development of grenades, mortars, and other munitions, in addition to a dispersal device to deliver chemical agents over large areas. Unmanned aerial vehicles (UAVs), which were being developed primarily for carrying sensors or conventional weapons, were also under consideration for delivering 'non-lethal' weapons,[188] including for law enforcement purposes.[189] In the commercial sector a significant development was the PepperBall System, essentially a paintball-type frangible projectile for delivering various payloads including OC powder. It had been developed by Jaycor Tactical Systems and used for the first time by the Seattle Police Department during protests at the World Trade Organisation meeting in 1999.[190]

3.6 Legal issues: Consensus on chemicals and lasers

Three further meetings of experts to assess the dangers from the development of anti-personnel lasers designed to blind were held by the ICRC in 1990 and 1991. They first studied the technical aspects of laser weapons and the effects on the eye, the second assessed the effects of different types of battlefield injuries and the problems associated with blindness, and the final meeting examined whether, on the basis of findings from the previous meetings, laser weapons designed to blind were already illegal. The majority view was that legal regulation to ban these weapons would be desirable through the negotiation of an additional Protocol to the 1980 Convention on Certain Conventional Weapons (CCW). In the face of opposition from some States who were actively developing these weapons and indifference from others, in 1993 the ICRC published the findings of its four meetings in order to gain international support for a ban. Meetings of government experts preceding the 1995 Review Conference of the CCW provided an opportunity for the Swedish Government and the ICRC to raise the issue. By this stage the only country that declared opposition to a ban was the US.[191] Significantly, Human Rights Watch published research in May 1995 detailing a number of US laser weapons systems under development with the capability to blind.[192] Meanwhile a small group of US politicians sought to raise the issue with the Clinton administration. This led to a reversal of US policy several weeks before the opening of the CCW Review Conference in late September 1995.[193] An Additional Protocol, *Protocol IV on Blinding Laser Weapons*, was negotiated and agreed upon in 1995 and came into force in 1998. Article I stated:

> It is prohibited to employ laser weapons specifically designed, as their sole combat function or as one of their combat functions, to cause permanent blindness to unenhanced vision, that is to the naked eye or to the eye with corrective eyesight devices.[194]

Furthermore, Article II required that in using other laser systems, such as rangefinders and target designators, countries 'shall take all feasible precautions to avoid the incidence of permanent blindness to unenhanced vision'.[195]

Another particularly significant legal development was the negotiation of the *Convention on the Prohibition of the Development, Production, Stockpiling and Use of Chemical Weapons and on their Destruction,* known as the Chemical Weapons Convention (CWC), which was finally agreed in late 1992.[196] It was opened for signature in January 1993 and came into force in April 1997. Building on the 1925 Geneva Protocol, the CWC bound States 'never under any circumstances' to use chemical weapons or to 'develop, produce, otherwise acquire, stockpile or retain chemical weapons, or transfer, directly or indirectly, chemical weapons to anyone'.[197] However, concerns were immediately raised about ambiguities in the Convention that could weaken its prohibitions, particularly in relation to RCAs and proposed incapacitating chemical weapons.[198] The subject of RCAs had been contentious during the negotiations and the text reflected a compromise between differing positions.[199] RCAs were defined as:

[A]ny chemical not listed in a Schedule, which can produce rapidly in humans sensory irritation or disabling physical effects which disappear within a short time following termination of exposure.[200]

Article I of the Convention specifically prohibited the use of RCAs, such as the irritant agents CS and OC, as a 'method of warfare'. This was to prevent military use of type that was seen during US operations in the Vietnam War and to avoid the danger of escalation to 'lethal' agents. However, what constituted a 'method of warfare' was not defined in the Convention. Other ambiguities lay in the 'purposes not prohibited', which included the use of toxic chemicals for 'law enforcement including domestic riot control purposes' in Article II 9(d).[201] This permitted the continued use of irritant chemical weapons by police on a domestic basis, as had long become commonplace. However, 'law enforcement' was not defined anywhere in the Convention and neither were law enforcement chemicals. This lack of definition left room for differing interpretations concerning not only the use of toxic chemical agents by the military or police in the grey area between warfare and domestic law enforcement, such as peacekeeping and peace enforcement, but also the types of chemicals that could be used.[202] As the March 1994 editorial of the *Chemical Weapons Convention Bulletin* noted:

Some, by no means a majority, of the negotiating states wished to protect possible applications of disabling chemicals that would either go beyond, or might be criticized as going beyond, applications hitherto customary in the hands of domestic police forces.[203]

One of the principal disputes was the long-standing US position, not shared by any other States, that they did not consider RCAs to be chemical weapons.[204] Furthermore, when the Senate ratified the CWC it made clear the US position and that the Convention would not detract from the 1975 US law, Executive Order 11850, which permitted the use of RCAs in certain situations, and maintained the right to use them against combatants in several types of military operation.[205] This was despite some of the Executive Order's provisions being incompatible with the CWC's prohibition on the use of RCAs as a method of warfare.[206] This isolated US position was defended in a preliminary legal review of proposed chemical 'non-lethal' weapons produced by the Navy Office of the Judge Advocate General in November 1997 that was requested by the JNLWD shortly after the CWC came into force.[207]

The legal review also considered incapacitating chemical agents, suggesting that they 'may also be RCAs'. This contradicted accepted wisdom distinguishing incapacitating agents, with their central mechanism of action and profound effects, from RCAs, which act peripherally as sensory irritants. It also contradicted prior recognition by the US of three main categories of chemical weapons: lethal, incapacitating, and RCAs. Nevertheless with the negotiation of the CWC, the US had begun to describe incapacitating agents as 'advanced riot control agents' or 'calmatives' in what was a seemingly disingenuous exercise to facilitate their continued development by the military in the face of the CWC's prohibition of chemical weapons. The legal review document acknowledged, rather naively, that these incapacitating agents 'may rely on their toxic properties to have a physiological effect on humans', arguing that they would then only be permitted for 'purposes not prohibited' by the Convention. Of course this brought the issue around full circle to the ambiguity in the Convention over what constituted 'law enforcement purposes' and whether chemicals used for these purposes were limited to RCAs. The preliminary legal review also argued that malodorant chemicals were not restricted by the CWC because they did not rely on their toxic properties to exert their effects.[208]

Another relevant legal development was the negotiation of the 1997 *Convention on the Prohibition of the Use, Stockpiling, Production and Transfer of Anti-Personnel Mines and on their Destruction*, known as the Ottawa Treaty or the Mine Ban Treaty.[209] The US was not a signatory but later said that it would sign if alternatives to land mines could be developed.[210] A Department of Defense initiative to develop alternatives to anti-personnel landmines had begun in 1996 and the JNLWD was tasked with developing 'non-lethal' alternatives.[211]

A development that shaped police consideration of 'non-lethal' weapons was the adoption of the United Nations *Basic Principles on the Use of Force and Firearms by Law Enforcement Officials* in 1990. Although not legally binding, these principles set out moral and practical guidance to police forces. General provisions 2, 3, and 4 addressed 'non-lethal' weapons, advising that governments and law enforcement agencies should develop these as alternatives to firearms 'with a view to increasingly restraining the application of means capable of causing death or injury to persons'.[212] However, the Principles cautioned that they should be 'carefully evaluated' and 'carefully controlled', and furthermore that law enforcement officials should 'as far as possible, apply non-violent means before resorting to the use of force and firearms'.[213]

3.7   Conclusion

It was not until the end of the Cold War with a shift in security priorities that 'non-lethal' weapons for the military began to be considered seriously by US policymakers, and the subject matter broadened beyond the search for new police weaponry. However, with no overall policy, many early research and development activities were characterised by secretive and opportunistic endeavours at the DOE's national laboratories and collaborative efforts linked to the Army's LCDM programme, which sought weapons with variable effects from 'lethal' to 'non-lethal'. Advocacy by a handful of proponents eventually led to the formalisation of policy in 1996 and the establishment of the JNLWP, bringing together disparate military research efforts under the control of the JNLWD. Inherited programmes were augmented with ambitious efforts to pursue new technologies. However, the perceived revolutionary potential of new 'non-lethal' weapons to restrict the use of 'lethal' force, on which they had been sold, was not reflected in the cautious policy that seemingly solidified their position as adjuncts rather than alternatives to 'lethal' force. Furthermore, the policy specifically endorsed their use as force multipliers, contradicting the central concept of minimising fatalities and permanent injury.

In the policing sphere high profile events, in particular the disaster at Waco, had given impetus to the expanded efforts of the DOJ LTL Technology Program. Close connections were maintained with military research as NIJ initially sought technical support from the DOE and then collaborated with the DOD. A significant amount of research necessarily focused on safety and effectiveness concerns over existing police weaponry but NIJ also supported the development of acoustic, directed energy, and incapacitating biochemical weapons.

With the growing military interest in 'non-lethal' weapons more research was conducted on these unconventional technologies with mixed results. Decade long research and development of acoustic weapons came to nothing but work on directed energy weapons led to new devices. Prototype 'dazzling' laser weapons emerged in the mid-1990s but concerns remained over their potential to cause permanent eye damage and their limited effectiveness. The classified 'Active Denial Technology' was given high priority. Other concepts based on high energy lasers were at the very early stages of development. In the early 1990s the Army intended to proceed with the full-scale development of a munition delivering incapacitating biochemical agents but the negotiation of the CWC halted the project. Nevertheless related research and development continued under the auspices of the DOJ and military interest persisted.

The most significant immediate developments were not novel military systems but variations of existing technologies marketed to both the police and the general public. Due to safety claims, OC became hugely popular, eclipsing CS as the irritant chemical weapon of choice for US police forces. A new design of the Taser electrical weapon opened up a significant civilian 'self defence' market due to a technicality and the commercial contest for the police market led to the development of a higher-powered Taser, which would soon be deployed very widely. Advocates had predicted revolutionary developments based around novel technologies but these pronouncements seemed premature with the organisation of the military programme only recently established and limited results from ambitious research and development efforts.

4
The Contemporary Development of 'Non-Lethal' Weapons

The Chapter completes the historical assessment of 'non-lethal' weapons, covering contemporary research and development efforts from 2000 to the present day, again with particular attention to the research and development programmes of the US DOJ and DOD.

4.1 Police developments

4.1.1 Safety and effectiveness

During 2000 the NIJ had 17 ongoing projects on 'non-lethal' weapons that had begun during the mid to late 1990s. The focus of research was on safety and effectiveness studies of blunt impact projectiles and OC ('pepper spray'). Development of the Laser Dazzler weapon was ongoing as was investigation of a so-called 'active light barrier'. The latter involved the use of a bright light source shone onto scattered particles to provide a visual obstacle to a crowd.[1] Further assessment and development of the Ring Airfoil Projectile (RAP) and the 'Sticky Shocker' electrical projectile was ongoing.[2]

In 2001, NIJ began an association with the Institute for Non-Lethal Defense Technologies (INLDT) at Pennsylvania State University, the group working closely with the JNLWD, funding a new three-phase project. Phase One contributed towards a joint study testing the accuracy and impact force of a range of blunt impact projectiles to augment the often scant and unverified information provided by manufacturers.[3] Phase Two research was 'an investigation of controlled exposure to calmative-based oleoresin capsicum' and Phase Three was the establishment of an online E-Forum 'to support an operational needs assessment for less-than-lethal technologies'.[4]

4.1.2 The influence of 9/11

After the attacks in New York and Washington on 11 September 2001, attention quickly turned to the potential for using 'non-lethal' weapons aboard aircraft.[5] The November 2001 Aviation and Transportation Security Act required NIJ to conduct an assessment of 'non-lethal' weapons for aircraft security,[6] which was completed in April 2002.[7] The report concluded that electrical weapons such as the Taser showed the most promise but that blunt impact projectiles may also be useful. It advised that more tests were needed on safety issues such as the effects of electrical weaponry discharged on aircraft equipment and the use of impact projectiles in confined spaces. It also noted that light and acoustic weapons needed more development before being considered, adding that light levels that are 'truly disabling' often require power levels that cause permanent eye damage. The NIJ study considered irritant chemical sprays to be insufficiently incapacitating against determined people but noted that a system for remote release of incapacitating biochemical agents into the cabin was under study or was in development.[8]

It later emerged that the use of 'non-lethal' weapons had in fact played a role in the 11 September 2001 attacks. The 9/11 Commission Report described reports of the use of 'pepper spray' to overcome passengers and flight attendants on both planes that eventually crashed into the World Trade Center.[9]

Airlines have not sought to deploy 'non-lethal' weapons on commercial aircraft in recent years. A May 2006 report by the US Government Accountability office noted:

> Due primarily to other enhancements in aviation security since 2001, there appears to be no demonstrated interest on the part of air carriers to introduce less-than-lethal weapons, including electric stun devices, on their aircraft.[10]

4.1.3 Programme drivers

A May 2002 statement by the Director of NIJ also gave a general overview of the direction and focus of the LTL Technology Program:

> Typically, NIJ-funded projects in this area have focused on:
>
> I. Improving the safety of blunt-trauma projectile weapons;
> II. Improving the delivery accuracy and dispersal efficiency of pepper spray for barricade scenarios;
> III. Evaluating the safety and effectiveness of pepper spray;
> IV. Developing and evaluating technology useful for disorienting suspects; and
> V. Evaluating the safety and effectiveness of electrical shock weapons.[11]

Further information on the focus of the programme at that time is provided in a late 2001 conference presentation by the NIJ, which gave an overview of the perceived differences between military and law enforcement requirements for 'non-lethal' weapons, as shown in Table 4.1.[12]

Table 4.1 National Institute of Justice assessment of the differences between law enforcement and military requirements for 'non-lethal' weapons[13]

End User	Military	Law Enforcement
Range	100 to 1000 ft.	0 to 100 ft.
Size/Weight	Vehicle mount or smaller	Person portable
Cost	Tolerate higher costs	$500 or less
Operation	Crowd control	one-on-one confrontation
	Area of Denial (AOD)	AOD – limited use
	Tolerate preparation time	Ready to use
Logistics	Personnel available for:	Limited personnel
	Planning, set-up, and maintenance	On belt or in trunk [car boot]
	Trained, practiced, and specialised	Trained Generalist
Use of chemicals	Extremely Restrictive	Restrictive (excluding RCAs)
Personnel encountered	Men, women, and children (non-military)	Men, women, and children
	'Good' physical condition	Alcohol and drugs a factor
Legal implications	Global media present	Local/National media
	Non-citizen peacekeeping	Citizen peacekeeping
	International law	Local/State diverse laws

An important difference is the lower acceptance of injury in the law enforcement arena, as Boyd has argued:

> These devices – at least when used by law enforcement – have to be effective, yet not sacrifice safety, where safety is defined as totally reversible effects with a duration no longer than is necessary. Unfortunately, the most effective technologies can push the bounds of safety, while very safe technologies are often not very effective at all.[14]

4.1.4 Funding research

In February 2002 the NIJ sought proposals for new or improved 'non-lethal' weapons technologies as well as evaluation of existing technologies.[15] Reflecting the focus on homeland security in the aftermath of the 11 September 2001 attacks they were looking for concepts for use in protecting public buildings or airports and weapons that could act at longer ranges than existing blunt impact projectiles.[16]

NIJ funded eight new projects for fiscal year 2002. Three of these involved testing and modelling to assess the injuries likely to be caused by blunt impact projectiles. Other research funded included: development of a multiple-shot launcher for the RAP, assessment of eight different flash-bang devices,[17] and a two-year assessment of how 'non-lethal' weapons could be integrated into airport security.[18]

As regards new weapons technologies NIJ also funded two projects being conducted in collaboration with the military: continued development work on a 'non-lethal' thermobaric or fuel-air explosive device[19] and an assessment of the utility of a Multi-Sensory Grenade for law enforcement applications. In 2003 one new project was funded, a study on injuries caused by various 'non-lethal' weapons. Table 4.2 details all projects on anti-personnel 'non-lethal' weapons funded by NIJ for fiscal years 2000 to 2008.

Table 4.2   National Institute of Justice contracts relating to anti-personnel 'non-lethal' weapons for fiscal years 2000–8[20]

Initial Funding*	Additional Funding*	Description	Contractor
(1996)	(1997), (1998), (1999), 2000	LTL technology policy assessment panel	Seaskate, Inc.
(1996)	(1998), (1999), 2000	Law enforcement technology, technology transfer, LTL weapons technology, and policy liability assessment	Seaskate, Inc.
(1997)	(1998), (1999), 2000, 2001	RAP system	Guilford Engineering Associates, Inc.
(1998)	(1999), 2000	Biomechanical assessment of NLW	Wayne State University
2000	—	LTL ballistic Weapon	Law Enforcement Technologies, Inc.
2001	—	LTL equipment review	National Security Research, Inc.
2001	—	LTL technology support	Pennsylvania State University
2002	—	Feasibility study of a finite element model to assess LTL munitions	Wayne State University
2002	—	Multi-sensory grenade and field evaluation	Scientific Applications and Research Associates, Inc.
2002	—	Multishot launcher with advanced LTL RAPs	Vanek Prototype Co.
2002	—	Penetration assessment of LTL munitions	Wayne State University
2002	—	Performance characterisation study of noise-flash diversionary device	E-LABS, Inc.
2002	—	Variable-range less-lethal ballistic, Phase Two	Law Enforcement Technologies, Inc.
2002	2005	Biomechanical assessment of blunt ballistic impacts to the abdomen	Wayne State University

(Continued)

Table 4.2   Continued

Initial Funding*	Additional Funding*	Description	Contractor
2002	—	Analysis of airport security measures and the role of LTL weapons	National Security Research, Inc
2003	—	Injuries produced by law enforcement use of LTL weapons	University of Florida – Gainesville
2004	2005	Collection and dissemination of less-lethal databases to law enforcement	Pennsylvania State University
2004	—	Compact and rugged pulsed laser technology for less-lethal weapons	Sterling Photonics, Inc.
2004	—	Independent assessment and evaluation of less-lethal devices	Pennsylvania State University
2004	2008	Injuries produced by law enforcement's use of less-lethal weapons: A multicentre trial	Wake Forest University Health Sciences
2004	2005	Less-lethal weapon technology review and operational needs assessment	Pennsylvania State University
2004	—	Modelling electric current through the human body from a less-lethal electromuscular device	University of Wisconsin
2004	—	Multishot launcher with advanced segmented RAPs	Chester F. Vanek
2004	—	RAP system: Operational testing guidance	Aerospace Corporation
2004	—	Multiwave dazzler	Scientific Applications and Research Associates, Inc.
2004	—	Solid-state Active Denial System (ADS) demonstration program	Raytheon Co.
2005	—	Analysis of human injuries and taser deployment: Effect of less-lethal weapons in the de-escalation of force	Florida Gulf Coast University
2005	—	Analysis of less-lethal technologies: Taser versus Stinger	Florida Gulf Coast University

(*Continued*)

Table 4.2 Continued

Initial Funding*	Additional Funding*	Description	Contractor
2005	—	Effect of Taser on cardiac, respiratory, and metabolic physiology in human subjects	University of California – San Diego
2005	2008	Human electromuscular incapacitation devices in trainees	New Jersey Medical School – Medicine and Dentistry
2005	—	Interdisciplinary working group for review of kinetic energy impact injuries	Wayne State University
2006	—	Evaluation of less-lethal technologies on police use-of-force outcomes	Police Executive Research Forum
2006	—	Injuries produced by law enforcement's use of less-lethal weapons	Wake Forest University Health Sciences
2006	—	Electronic control weapons and unexpected deaths-in-custody	International Association of Chiefs of Police
2007	—	Less-Lethal Weapons: Policies, Practices and Technologies	Pennsylvania State University
2007	—	Operationalizing Calmatives – Legal Issues, Concepts and Technologies	Pennsylvania State University
2007	2008	Physiological Model of Excited Delirium	Wayne State University
2007	2008	Resuscitation Therapy for Human Electromuscular Incapacitation (HEMI) Device-Induced Fatal Hyperthermia	Maroon Biotech, Inc.

* Years in which funding was given for these projects outside the 2000–8 range are indicated in parentheses.

By late 2003 NIJ's attention had turned to military directed energy weapons technologies and considerations of how they might be adapted for law enforcement applications. For fiscal year 2004 the NIJ sought proposals for new 'area denial' technologies:

> The goal of research in this area is to enable law enforcement agencies to safely and effectively deny individuals or groups of people access to specific areas. An example could be the use of directed energy to induce an epidermal heating sensation in targeted persons.[21]

The example given was a reference to the 'Active Denial Technology' developed by the Air Force in collaboration with Raytheon Company, which was subsequently awarded a $500,000 contract to work towards a prototype portable version of the technology for law enforcement use.[22]

Other directed energy weapons research funded in fiscal year 2004 included a contract to Sterling Photonics for development of a portable pulsed laser weapon that would act by producing a plasma shock wave.[23] This weapon development effort is similar to the US military's Pulsed Energy Projectile (PEP). The JNLWD also funded Sterling Photonics in 2004, which was likely to be directed towards the same project.[24] NIJ provided funding to the AFRL for development of a classified portable laser weapon system called the Portable Efficient Laser Testbed (PELT),[25] which was also co-funded by the JNLWD.[26] This Air Force research effort began in-house during 2001 and in 2004 the name was changed from PELT to Personnel Halting and Stimulation Response (PHaSR). The PHaSR is being designed to employ a two-wavelength laser system, one to heat the skin of the target person and the other as a 'dazzling' weapon against the eyes.[27] Another directed energy project funded in 2004 was a 'dazzling' laser weapon under development by SARA Inc. called the Multiwave Dazzler.[28]

Two other projects funded in 2004 reflected the NIJ's stated requirement for research on 'electromuscular device modelling' and 'less-lethal device-induced injury data'.[29] There was also funding for two projects continuing the development of the RAP.

Over $1 million in funding was provided to the INLDT at Pennsylvania State University in 2004 and 2005 for three contracts that included the development of a 'non-lethal' weapons database and statistical research on the outcomes of uses of electrical weapons such as the Taser.[30] It is unclear what other research was funded as part of these contracts. One possibility is further work on OC and incapacitating chemical mixtures that was ongoing in 2003. The Director of the INDLT certainly considered incapacitating chemicals among future 'non-lethal' weapons technologies for law enforcement in a 2005 conference presentation.[31]

For fiscal year 2005 the NIJ sought to fund research on 'Less-Lethal Pursuit Management Technologies' calling for proposals for:

Developing new technologies to incapacitate personnel.
Developing means to deliver effectively less-lethal force independent of range or environment.
Acquiring, recording, and analyzing less-lethal device-induced injury data.[32]

NIJ also sought to fund research on 'relative likelihood of injury to officers, suspected offenders, and bystanders in situations where the police do or do not have access to less-lethal weaponry'.[33]

Of the five new projects funded in 2005, four concerned electrical weapons, in particular the Taser, including studies of the human effects, impact on injuries resulting from police use of force, and comparison with the Stinger electrical weapon. The other was a two-year project to establish a working group to review injury data from blunt impact munitions.

In late 2005 the NIJ announced its specific intention to fund the development of new technologies during fiscal year 2006 rather than the evaluation of existing weapons:

NIJ seeks concept papers that describe the development of new, innovative devices that incapacitate individuals without risk of death or serious or permanent injury. NIJ is seeking devices that:

- Discretely incapacitate an individual (who may be in a crowd) at a distance.
- Compel near-instantaneous compliance at arms length.
- Compel one or more individuals to rapidly exit or not enter an area.

Possible Technical Approaches
Solutions to meet the needs described in this solicitation might include but are not limited to:

- Chemically based devices.
- Directed energy based devices.
- Conductive energy devices.[34]

Another announcement indicated that the NIJ was also seeking to develop or adapt 'non-lethal' weapons for use in schools.[35]

Despite these calls for development of new concepts in both 2005 and 2006, no projects on new weapons technologies were announced, although it is certainly conceivable that classified programmes were funded. It is known that NIJ awarded $250,000 to the AFRL for continued development of a rangefinder for the PHaSR portable laser weapon, which is being co-sponsored by the JNLWD.[36]

Three new projects funded in 2006 were for work on evaluating the safety and effectiveness of existing 'non-lethal' weapons. In addition to those shown in Table 4.2, a two-year study led by the NIJ began in 2006 to assess the increasingly controversial area of deaths following the use of electrical weapons such as the Taser. It will comprise mortality reviews by a panel of doctors to assess deaths that have occurred following the use of these weapons. An interim report of this work was published in 2008.[37]

NIJ calls for research proposals for fiscal years 2007 and 2008 highlighted particular interest in a variety of technologies including 'chemically based devices (e.g. anesthetics or calmatives)'; 'directed energy-based devices'; 'conductive energy devices'; and 'low-level force devices'.[38]

In April 2007 the NIJ convened a panel to discuss incapacitating biochemical weapons, so called calmatives, and subsequently funded Pennsylvania State University to carry out further research on potential drugs, delivery systems, and legal issues.[39]

Despite the range of 'non-lethal' weapons projects funded by the NIJ, including research on new technologies, the impact of the programme on emerging weaponry has been limited due to relatively low funding averaging $1.5 million per year for the fiscal year period 2000 to 2006.[40] As a 2003 National Research Council (NRC) report noted:

> The total research budget for non-lethal weapons development is modest, and the NIJ program has tended toward leveraging past R&D or modifying existing weapons to improve and extend effectiveness.[41]

The Department of Homeland Security (DHS) has also begun to fund research and development through the Homeland Security Advanced Research Projects Agency (HSARPA) with particular interest in radio frequency, 'dazzling' lasers or bright lights, and wireless electrical weapons.[42] Following initial funding in 2005 three companies were awarded $750,000 for two-year research efforts to produce prototype weapons and conduct animal and human tests.[43] Lynntech is developing two types of electrical projectile, one to be fired from a 12-gauge shotgun and the other a larger 40 mm projectile, and Mide Technology is also developing a shotgun-fired electrical projectile. Intelligent Optical Systems is developing an optical weapon that produces very bright flashing light to cause flash blindness and disorientation that will apparently 'operate at power levels close to the eye-damage threshold'.[44]

4.1.5   UK alternatives to the plastic bullet

In the UK 'non-lethal' weapons research has focused on the development of new blunt impact projectiles and assessments of existing 'off-the-shelf' weapons as alternatives to the plastic bullet. Following the recommendations of the Independent Commission on Policing for Northern Ireland in 1999, a UK Steering Group chaired by the Northern Ireland Office was set up in Summer 2000 with the following objective:

> To establish whether a less potentially lethal alternative to baton rounds is available; and to review the public order equipment which is presently available or could be developed in order to expand the range of tactical options available to operational commanders.[45]

The work of the Steering Group has been conducted in five phases thus far. The Phase One report, published in April 2001, set out criteria against which proposed alternatives could be judged and provided a literature review.

The Steering Group prioritised technologies for further research and tasked the Police Scientific Development Branch (PSDB) with carrying out initial testing and evaluation.[46] Meanwhile a new plastic bullet, the L21A1, was adopted by the Army and police in the UK and Northern Ireland in June 2001.[47]

The Phase Two report of the Steering Group's work was published in November 2001. It incorporated PSDB's testing and evaluation work and presented an initial medical assessment of 'non-lethal' weapons. The latter was carried out by a subcommittee of the Ministry of Defence's (MOD) Defence Scientific Advisory Council (DSAC), the DSAC subcommittee on the Medical Implications of Less-lethal weapons (DOMILL).[48]

By the time of the publication of the Phase Three report in December 2002, the Steering Group ruled out all commercially available impact projectiles as alternatives to the baton round and had commissioned the MOD's Defence Science and Technology Laboratory (Dstl) to develop two new projectiles: one with a crushable body to reduce the impact with the aim of reducing the risk of serious head injuries, the Attenuating Energy Projectile (AEP); and the other designed to deliver a CS irritant powder released from a frangible tip upon impact, the Discriminating Irritant Projectile (DIP).[49] The Phase Three report also presented testing and evaluation carried out by PSDB on the M26 Taser, which had been given a high priority for further testing, together with a medical assessment carried out by DOMILL.[50]

The Phase Four report[51] was published in January 2004 and by that time the ACPO proposal for an operational trial of the Taser M26 had been accepted with a one-year trial beginning in April 2003 with five police forces. In September 2004, use of the Taser was extended to firearms officers in all police forces in England and Wales.[52] In mid-2003 Taser International had introduced a new model, the Taser X26, which was also approved for use by UK police forces in March 2005.[53]

In November 2008 the Home Office announced that it would make 10,000 Tasers available to police forces across the UK and, following a one-year trial in 10 police forces, decided to extend their use beyond specialist firearms officers.[54]

However, London's Metropolitan Police Authority (MPA) rejected the offer of wider Taser availability, arguing:

> The MPA recognises the potential to cause fear and damage public confidence if the use of tasers is extended to non specialist trained police officers and is perceived by the public to be indiscriminate.
> The Authority scrutinises every incident during which a taser is discharged. While there is no doubt that in some circumstances tasers are a very effective alternative to firearms or asps [batons], their use must be tightly controlled and we have seen no case made out to extend their availability.[55]

The Phase Four Steering Group report discussed development of the AEP, which was eventually introduced as a replacement for the L21A1 plastic bullet in June 2005.[56] In 2006 the Northern Ireland Office published the Phase Five report, which described the introduction of the AEP and noted that technical issues with regard to the DIP needed to be resolved but that it may be introduced in 2009 or 2010.[57]

Unlike the programme at the US NIJ the UK Home Office has not become involved in developing new technologies. PSDB, renamed the Home Office Scientific Development Branch (HOSDB) in 2005, has conducted extensive evaluation of existing 'non-lethal' weapons but has not carried out research and development of new technologies. Development of new impact projectiles has been carried out by the MOD's Dstl who, together with the private company QinetiQ, are the primary centres for research on new 'non-lethal' weapons in the UK.

The UK Steering Group on 'non-lethal' weapons maintains close ties with police and military organisations in Europe, Canada, and particularly the US. The HOSDB has maintained an information sharing agreement with the NIJ since 1997. Early on in its work the Steering Group forged close links with the INLDT, which led to the establishment of a collaborative group called the International Law Enforcement Forum (ILEF) on Minimal Force Options, which has held a series of meetings of invited police, military, and academic organisations involved in the development and use of 'non-lethal' weapons for law enforcement in the US, UK, Canada, and Europe.[58]

4.2 Military developments

4.2.1 Defining research and development needs

In 2000 the US military conducted a year-long 'Joint Mission Area Analysis' to assess the status of the JNLWP to provide direction for subsequent weapons development. It identified the requirement of weapons in three areas: counter-personnel, counter-materiel, and counter-capability. With regard to the former, four types of tasks were emphasised: control crowds; incapacitate individuals; deny area to personnel; and clear facilities, structures, or areas.[59] The study evaluated 45 potential 'non-lethal' weapons technologies, assessing their potential for application to over 100 different types of military mission, and 12 were identified for further development:

1. millimeter wave
2. chemical oxygen iodine laser (COIL)
3. antitraction materials
4. non-lethal delivery and deployment
5. malodorants

6. calmatives
7. high-power microwave (HPM)
8. rigid foams
9. tagging and tracking
10. nanoparticles
11. laser scattering obscuration
12. deuterium-fluoride/hydrogen-fluoride (DF/HF) lasers.[60]

High priority was given to directed energy weapons concepts, the millimetre wave 'Active Denial Technology' and high energy biochemical lasers, and to new biochemical weapons, namely incapacitating chemicals (so-called calmatives) and malodorant chemicals.

The following year the JNLWD and the Office of Naval Research (ONR) requested that the Naval Studies Board of the NRC at the US National Academy of Sciences carry out an assessment of 'non-lethal' weapons science and technology. A Committee with members from the US national laboratories, academia, and the private sector began work in 2001 to review existing programmes and published its final report in early 2003.[61]

The committee identified several technology areas that it considered to be most important for further investigation ONR. In terms of anti-personnel weapons, they highlighted three in particular: development of incapacitating biochemical weapons for use in 'crowd control' and 'clearing facilities'; accelerated research on directed energy weapons, in particular solid-state lasers for 'operational non-lethal weapons applications'; and the use of unmanned vehicles as delivery systems.[62]

For chemical weapons development the report recommended a 'strong partnership' with the Army's ECBC, noting their prior work and suggesting that the ONR contribution could be on weaponisation, with attention to means and to effectively stabilise and encapsulate the agents as well as systems to deliver and disperse them. More specifically the committee recommended three steps. The first was to 'identify opportunities for potential applications of malodorants', arguing that more research was needed on the cultural variations in susceptibility, health effects, and behavioural responses. The second was to 'increase research in the field of human response to calmatives', emphasising the development of agents with wide safety-margins apparently with the aim of altering behaviour or incapacitating without causing unconsciousness. The third was to 'target efforts to develop chemical delivery systems', noting that more advanced delivery systems were required to enable control of the 'dose' of chemical agent delivered.[63]

As regards anti-personnel directed energy weapons the report recommended careful assessment of the Active Denial System (ADS) for naval applications cautioning that logistical, health effects, and effectiveness issues needed further investigation.[64] The committee was unimpressed with the two ongoing JNLWD chemical laser weapons programmes, the PEP and the Advanced Tactical Laser (ATL) arguing that JNLWD should 'reassess its investments in these programs'.[65] However, they suggested that more research should be conducted on the potential of solid-state lasers for 'non-lethal' weapons applications.[66]

The committee's major recommendation on delivery systems was for programmes to explore the use of unmanned vehicles to deliver chemical and other payloads:

> Considerable research in robotic and remote precision delivery of lethal weapons systems is well underway in many agencies. Small UAVs [unmanned aerial vehicles], UUVs [unmanned underwater vehicles] and remote controlled surface (water) vehicles offer attractive ways to deliver NLWs at large standoff distances with greater accuracy.[67]

More generally the committee recommended that the JNLWD should focus on two areas: encouraging and exploring new 'non-lethal' weapon concepts; and increasing efforts to characterise the effects and effectiveness of these weapons.[68]

The report observed that JNLWD had necessarily concentrated on relatively mature technologies and bringing commercial 'off-the-shelf' systems to the field but warned that it may soon run out of new ideas due to limited funding for research and development, lack of understanding of human effects, and lack of resources for establishing the military effectiveness of 'non-lethal' weapons.[69] The committee urged the organisation to 'aggressively stimulate and explore new ideas', recommending,

> JNLWD build a significantly more robust outreach and exploratory investment program, to include partnerships with DARPA [Defense Advanced Research Projects Agency], U.S. government laboratories and law enforcement communities, and allies, as well as frequent interactions with the industrial base in which the directorate reiterates its requirements for potential developers.[70]

The committee pointed out that the limited funding available for research and development was insufficient to attract major defence contractors and national laboratories, and recommended an increase of the $500,000 funding for the JNLWD's Technology Investment Program by 'an order of magnitude'.[71] By the time of the NRC report, several new projects had been funded under this Technology Investment Program:

- *Non-lethal loitering system.* An assessment of an autonomous delivery system for nonlethal applications.

- *Microencapsulation.* A demonstration of the ability to encapsulate non-lethal chemical payloads.
- *Front-end analysis.* A series of workshops and analyses culminating in a database of potential riot control agents and calmatives, with emphasis on technology advances in the past 10 years.
- *Thermobaric technology.* A feasibility study to determine the usefulness of thermobaric weapons to conduct non-lethal missions.
- *Veiling glare laser.* A study to demonstrate the ability of an ultraviolet laser to create a fluorescence-induced glare on excised human cadaver lenses.[72]

Recognising that the characterisation of human effects of various 'non-lethal' weapons may be central to acceptance by policymakers and military leaders, the committee argued for the creation of a 'centre of excellence' for each technology area (blunt impact, chemical, electrical etc.) and to create models for assessing human effects drawing on relevant scientific expertise.[73] This would build on the existing Human Effects Center of Excellence (HECOE) at the AFRL's Human Effectiveness Directorate. The HECOE, established under a memorandum of understanding between JNLWD and AFRL in 2001, is the central organisation for 'non-lethal' weapons human effects research.[74] The recommendation for human effects modelling is at the root of an emerging 'effects-based' approach to 'non-lethal' weapons research and development. In essence it is a form of reverse engineering, starting with the effect desired and then devising a mechanism to induce it.[75]

The report also drew attention to the major technical characteristics the committee considered desirable for a given weapon:

Technical Characteristics of Non-Lethal Weapons[76]

1. Effects on target (significant, repeatable effects)
2. Rheostatic capability
3. Selective targeting
4. Portable by a person or existing vehicle
5. Standoff/range
6. Ease of cleanup
7. Developmental maturity
8. Complementary or synergistic technology
9. Acquisition and operational costs (training, maintenance, reuse, and so on)
10. Robustness to countermeasures

Two of the issues the report raised that are commonly expressed in military circles include the perceived need for weapons with extended range up to hundreds of metres or even kilometres and the desire for weapons with scalable or rheostatic effects from 'non-lethal' to 'lethal'.[77]

The committee also highlighted a broader issue with profound implications for the speed of development of new 'non-lethal' weapons. That is a lack of genuine institutional support in the DOD:

> The committee finds a wide gap between the rhetoric on the importance of non-lethal weapons as expounded by senior leadership in the unified commands and the U.S. Marine Corps, and the limited attention in planning, assessment, R&D, and acquisition given to NLWs throughout DOD, in general, and the Department of the Navy in particular.[78]

4.2.2 Secrecy and 9/11

One issue raised again with the publication of the report was that of the secrecy surrounding 'non-lethal' weapons development. Although the study was unclassified, the JNLWD instructed the National Academy of Sciences to withhold public access to all of the documents collected during the study that would ordinarily become US public records.[79] The history of 'non-lethal' weapons development illustrates endemic secrecy surrounding many different aspects of these programmes. However, it seems likely that one area, that of continuing military interest in the development of new chemical weapons and its incompatibility with international law, is a major cause of this sensitivity. The preface to the NRC report noted that the differing interpretations of the prohibitions of the CWC within the US government, between the DOD and the Department of State, led to the removal of the section on legal issues from the final version of the report.[80]

Of course the reason given for *de facto* classification of the documents collected for the report was that security concerns following the attacks of 11 September 2001 precluded their release.[81] The report had already been drafted when those events unfolded but the prologue to the report indicated that the field of 'non-lethal' weapons, like every aspect of US defence and national security policy, would be reshaped and refocused in the light of the perceived new threat:

> In rooting out terrorism's infrastructure, there will be times when controlled application of force will be essential and unconstrained violence counterproductive to our strategic goals. ... [T]he need to isolate a few individuals, both in the United States and abroad, most likely in and amongst civilian populations, will remain critically important. In that context, non-lethal weapons may play an even greater role in matters of national security.[82]

Another event that had raised the Navy's interest in 'non-lethal' weapons was the attack on the USS Cole warship in October 2000.

4.2.3 Lack of institutional support and funding

In late 2002 a senior DOD advisory group, the Joint Requirements Oversight Council, approved a 'Mission Needs Statement' describing the development and acquisition of 'non-lethal' weapons as a high priority, arguing that the US military lacked the capability to 'engage targets' in situations where the use of lethal force would be counterproductive. One of the major requirements they articulated was the development of weapons with increased range suggesting various technologies that could be used such as frangible munitions, microencapsulation, and proximity fuses.[83]

In early 2003 the Council on Foreign Relations embarked on a third study of 'non-lethal' weapons, which was published in February 2004. Written during the development of the insurgency in the aftermath of the US-led invasion of Iraq, the report proposed that wider integration of existing 'non-lethal' weapons could have helped reduce the looting and sabotage and help re-establish law and order, arguing,

> [i]ncorporating these and additional forms of nonlethal capabilities more broadly into the equipment, training, and doctrine of the armed services could substantially improve U.S. effectiveness in achieving the goals of modern war.[84]

Like the NRC study, the Council on Foreign Relations group found a lack of institutional support at the top levels of the Pentagon and noted that 'NLW have not entered the mainstream of defense thinking and procurement'.[85]

The report recommended that the JNLWP refocus on four areas. Firstly, noting that the primary users were currently the military police, it advocated the wider deployment of existing short-range 'non-lethal' weapons (i.e. kinetic impact, Taser, flash-bang, etc.) in the Marine Corps and the Army, and encouraged uptake of 'non-lethal' weapons by the Navy and Air Force. Secondly, it recommended that the range of current 'non-lethal' weapons should be extended beyond 100 metres, through development of precision delivery systems. Thirdly, it urged that testing and human effects assessment of the millimetre wave ADS should be completed so that it could be fielded. And finally it called for increased funding and technical support for development of weapons such as the ATL and laser guided 'non-lethal' payloads.[86] The support for the ATL was in contrast to the unfavourable assessment by the NRC.

The Council on Foreign Relations report also recommended that the JNLWD should be greatly expanded with a sevenfold increase in funding levels and greater support from the Joint Forces Command. For fiscal years 2000 to 2003 the JNLWD's core budget had averaged at $22 million per year. For fiscal year 2004 it had almost doubled to just under $44 million. The Council on Foreign Relations wanted to see an annual budget of $300 million,[87] however, the budget remained around $44 million for fiscal years 2005, 2006, and 2007.[88] When set in the context of total US defence spending, the JNLWP really is a very minor effort, representing 0.01 per cent of the $440 billion defence budget for fiscal year 2007. There have been some indications, however, that overall funding for the JNLWP may increase again, perhaps doubling existing investment by 2013.[89]

4.2.4 Current 'non-lethal' weapons capabilities

Table 4.3 illustrates the various 'non-lethal' weapons currently employed by the US military. The majority of these are furnished in the form of Non-Lethal Capability Sets (NLCS), which have been deployed since 1997, containing a particular number of each item. The Army sets, for example, are designed to equip a platoon of 30 soldiers.[90] The 'non-lethal' weapons included in the sets are primarily low-technology kinetic, chemical, optical, and flash-bang systems. However, a few new weapons, such as the M26 and X26 Tasers, have been added as they have become available. The sets also contain various 'riot control' equipment such as batons, shields, plastic handcuffs, and bullhorns. By early 2004 around 80 of these sets had been deployed to various locations, including Iraq and Kosovo, mainly with the Marines and the Army.[91] Several of the newer weapons are not included in the standard NLCS but have been fielded on a more limited basis such as the Long Range Acoustic Device (LRAD), the FN 303 launcher system, and various 'dazzling' laser weapons, all of which have been sent to Iraq. The FN 303 was designated as the Individual Serviceman Non-Lethal System (ISNLS).[92]

It is notable that new 'non-lethal' weapons that have been recently adopted by the military are primarily commercial 'off-the-shelf' technologies (Taser X26, LRAD, FN 303, green 'dazzling' laser weapons) rather than the product of military sponsored research and development. The only deployed anti-personnel weapons to have emerged from weapons programmes administered by the JNLWD itself are the Modular Crowd Control Munition and the 66 mm grenades.[93]

Operational use of available 'non-lethal' weapons by the military has been limited.[94] In Iraq, the type of urban operations often used to promote their development has been ongoing for several years, it seems the major area of employment has been as compliance tools for controlling prisoners. However, bright lights, 'dazzling' laser weapons, Tasers, and the LRAD have also been used in protecting convoys and stopping vehicles at checkpoints.[95]

4.2.5 Current weapons development programmes

The foci of ongoing weapons development programmes reflect the perceived need to increase the range of existing systems and to incorporate new technologies with less emphasis on blunt impact effects. The major US military weapons development programmes are shown in Table 4.4. In the area of electrical weapons efforts are directed at developing an electric shock projectile that overcomes the range limitations of the Taser as well as an electrical anti-personnel mine. The majority of programmes, however, focus on directed energy weapons and new delivery systems. The millimetre wave electromagnetic 'Active Denial Technology' has been under development at the Air Force Research Laboratory (AFRL) since the early 1990s and the main contractor, Raytheon, has been tasked with producing various different

Table 4.3 US military anti-personnel 'non-lethal' weapons and delivery systems[96]

Type	Weapon	Description/Manufacturer	Users
Kinetic	12-gauge shotgun rounds	Fin stabilised rubber, wooden, multiple rubber balls (Defense Technology Corp.), beanbag, dye containing (Technical Solutions Group).	Army, Marines, Navy, Air Force, Coast Guard
Kinetic	40 mm M203 grenade launcher rounds	Multiple rubber balls, foam rubber baton (Defense Technology Corp.), sponge tip grenade (AMTEC).	Army, Marines, Navy, Air Force
Kinetic	Rifle-launched rounds	Multiple rubber balls – 'point' and 'area' rounds – delivered at ranges of 30–80 metres (Alliant Techsystems).	Army
Kinetic	Rubber ball grenade	Hand grenade containing multiple rubber balls (Combined Tactical Systems).	Marines, Navy, Air Force
Kinetic	66 mm grenade Light Vehicle Obscurant Smoke System (LVOSS)	66 mm multiple rubber ball grenade delivered at ranges of 80–100 metres (PW Defence).	Army, Marines
Kinetic	Modular Crowd Control Munition (MCCM)	Variant of claymore anti-personnel mine delivering rubber balls (Lone Star).	Army
Kinetic/Chemical	FN 303 System (Individual Serviceman Non-Lethal System (ISNLS))	Compressed air launcher firing various projectiles with different payloads (solid kinetic impact, containing OC, and containing paint) (FN Herstal).	Army, Marines, Military Police
Chemical	OC spray	Various spray devices from small short-range to large with range of 25 feet or more (Defense Technology Corp.).	Army, Marines, Air Force
Chemical	CR spray	Various spray devices from small short-range to large with range of 25 feet or more (ACALA).	Army
Chemical	Grenade for 66 mm LVOSS	66 mm L96A1 CS grenade with range of 65–95 metres (PW Defence).	Army
Electrical	Taser M26/X26	Electrical weapon, also described as electro-muscular incapacitation weapon (Taser International).	Army, Marines, Military Police

(Continued)

Table 4.3　Continued

Type	Weapon	Description/Manufacturer	Users
Optical	High-intensity light	Fixed-mounted bright xenon or infrared flashlight to illuminate people at up to 1900 yards (Xenonics).	Army, Marines
Optical	High-intensity light	Hand-held bright xenon flashlight to illuminate or obscure vision (Sure Fire).	Army, Marines
Optical/ Acoustic	12-gauge shotgun round	Flash-bang round that produces a loud bang and bright flash to disorientate (Defense Technology Corp.).	Army, Air Force
Optical/ Acoustic	Flash-bang grenade	Hand-thrown grenade that produces a loud bang and bright flash to disorientate (Universal Propulsion).	Army
Optical/ Acoustic	66 mm grenade for LVOSS	66 mm flash-bang grenade that produces a loud bang and bright flash to disorientate at ranges of 80–100 metres (PW Defence).	Army, Marines
Acoustic	Long Range Acoustic Device (LRAD)	Directional high-intensity acoustic device that can be used as loudhailer and also to cause ear pain and discomfort. (American Technology Corp.).	Army, Marines, Navy, Military Police
Directed energy	Dissuader Laser Illuminator	Flashlight sized red laser diode 'dazzling' weapon that causes glare or flash blindness but can cause permanent eye damage at close range (SEA Technology).	Air Force
Directed Energy	Various 'dazzling' laser weapons	Hand-held or weapon-mounted green 'dazzling' laser weapons approved for use by the Army include: XADS PD/G-105 (Xtreme Alternative Defense Systems Ltd.), MiniGreen, GBD-IIIC (BE Myers & Co. Inc.), HELIOS, and GHOST.	Army
Delivery	12-gauge shotgun	Standard shotgun (Mossberg).	Army, Marines
Delivery	XM26 Lightweight shotgun system	Under-barrel shotgun attachment for standard rifle (C-More Systems).	Army
Delivery	40 mm M203 grenade launcher	Standard 40 mm grenade launcher attachment for rifles such as the M16.	Army, Marines, Navy, Air Force
Delivery	66 mm LVOSS	Vehicle mounted 66 mm grenade launcher (Centech).	Army, Marines

Table 4.4 Major unclassified US military anti-personnel 'non-lethal' weapons development programmes[97]

Type	Weapon	Description	Main Developers[98]	Status
Kinetic	Mk19 Non-Lethal Munition (NLM)	Blunt trauma munition containing one plastic RAP fired from Mk19 grenade machine gun at ranges up 100 metres. Long-range version under development.	ARDEC, JNLWD	Prototype: Human effects testing carried out.
Chemical	Mobility Denial System (MDS)	Lubricant chemicals to deny access to people (or vehicles) delivered from backpack or vehicle mounted spray device.	JNLWD, ECBC, Southwest Research Institute, DARPA	Prototype: Ongoing testing of material and delivery systems.
Electrical	Taser Anti-Personnel Munition (TAPM)	Taser anti-personnel mine with range of 21feet triggered by infrared sensors. Development as part of Army's Hand-Emplaced Non-Lethal Munition (HENLM) programme. Also known as Taser Remote Area Denial (TRAD) system.	ARDEC, Taser International, General Dynamics Corp.	Prototype
Electrical	Extended Range Electronic Projectile (XREP)	Electrical projectile fired from 12-gauge shotgun with 30m range.	Office of Naval Research, Taser International	Prototype: Demonstrated in 2006; pilot programme in 2008
Optical/ Acoustic	Joint Non-Lethal Warning Munition (JNLWM)	12-gauge and 40 mm flash-bang munitions designed to discharge at fixed 100, 200, and 300m ranges.	NSWC Crane, JNLWD, Combined Systems Inc.	12-gauge munitions fielded. 40 mm munitions in testing.
Acoustic	Acoustic Hailing Devices	Acoustic devices that deliver directional sound at long-range. Used for communication but can also cause ear pain and damage at high-power levels and closer ranges.	ARDEC, JNLWD	LRAD in use, other devices under consideration.
Directed Energy	Active Denial System (ADS)	Millimetre wave directed energy weapon that causes pain through skin heating – 100 kilowatt, >750 m range.	AFRL, JNLWD, Raytheon Co.	Prototype: Ongoing military assessment and evaluation.
Directed Energy	Silent Guardian	Fixed site or truck-mounted version of ADS for medium range applications – 30 kilowatt, >250 m range.	Raytheon Co.	Offered for sale by company.
Directed Energy	Portable Active Denial System (PADS)	Tripod-mounted version of ADS – 400 watt, short-range.	AFRL, DOE, OFT, Raytheon Co.	Prototype: Ongoing human effects and utility testing.

(Continued)

Table 4.4 Continued

Type	Weapon	Description	Main Developers	Status
Directed Energy	Hand-held Active Denial System	Research towards the development of a hand-held Active Denial weapon.	DOJ, JNLWD, Raytheon Co.	Prototype: Ongoing R&D
Directed Energy	Pulsed Energy Projectile (PEP)	Proposed weapon employing high-power pulsed chemical laser to create a plasma shock wave at the target surface. Research now focusing on solid-state lasers.	JNLWD, Mission Research Corp.	R&D: Ongoing development of laser hardware and human effects testing.
Directed Energy	Personnel Halting and Stimulation Response (PHaSR)	Laser weapon employing two wavelengths, one to 'dazzle' the other to 'repel' by heating the skin. Formerly known as PELT.	AFRL, JNLWD	Prototype: Ongoing development of 'eye safe' rangefinder.
Delivery	Airburst Non-Lethal Munition (ANLM)	Munition that bursts just before it reaches a target, releasing the payload at 250 m range. Low and high-velocity versions of 25 mm and 40 mm munitions under development. Payload may be chemical, kinetic impact, 'flash-bang', or electrical.	ARDEC, JNLWD, Pennsylvania State University, ECBC	Prototype: Ongoing development and evaluation of payloads.
Delivery	81 mm Non-Lethal Mortar	Development of a mortar round to deliver 'non-lethal' payloads at ranges up to 2.5km. Primary consideration of chemical payloads through integration of the Overhead Liquid Dispersal System (OLDS).	ARL, ECBC, United Defense LP	Prototype: Ongoing development and evaluation of payloads.
Delivery	XM1063	155 mm cargo round containing numerous submunitions for delivery of various payloads at ranges of 15–25km. Liquid chemical payloads under consideration.	ARDEC, ECBC, General Dynamics Corp.	Prototype: Ongoing testing and evaluation of payloads.
Delivery	Mission Payload Module – Non-Lethal Weapon System (MPM-NLWS)	Programme to integrate a delivery system to vehicle platforms that will deliver a range of munitions, both lethal and 'non-lethal' including smoke, flash-bang, and blunt impact. VENOM 40 mm and Metal Storm systems under consideration.	ARDEC, JNLWD	System evaluation and human effects testing.
Delivery	Tactical Unmanned Ground Vehicle (TUGV)	Robotic ground vehicle designed as platform for remote control delivery of both lethal and 'non-lethal' weapons. Various 'non-lethal' payloads under consideration for integration.	JNLWD, Office of Naval Research	In production.

sizes of weapon incorporating this technology, one of which, called Silent Guardian, the company is already offering for sale.[99] Another prototype to emerge from AFRL is a dual-wavelength laser weapon, the PHaSR. The third major development programme has been the PEP, which employs a pulsed laser to produce a high energy plasma shock wave.

Programmes to mount 'non-lethal' weapons delivery systems on military vehicles and unmanned ground vehicles are underway. Several different types of munition under development, each designed to burst near or above the target person or group and release a 'non-lethal' payload. Although these munitions may be configured to release blunt impact projectiles and flash-bang devices, there has been particular attention to the employment of chemicals such as irritant agents (OC, PAVA, CS), malodorants, and incapacitating agents. PAVA, a synthetic form of OC, is under assessment for wide-area dispersal.[100] Given the nature of these delivery systems and the types of chemical agents that have been proposed it would be strange if there were no ongoing programmes to characterise and test these agents. It is unclear whether such research is being carried out under classified projects or whether policy concerns, relating to the prohibitions of the CWC, have prevented this from continuing. Whereas the 2003 NRC report strongly advocated the further development of incapacitating biochemical weapons, the 2004 report from the Council on Foreign Relations cautioned against this.[101] Nevertheless, closely linked research on incapacitating biochemical weapons has continued to be funded by NIJ.

4.2.6 Key research players

Research and development activities under the JNLWP are spread across the military services, where research is conducted both in-house and contracted to the private sector. The Marine Corps funds research at Pennsylvania State University, including the Applied Research Laboratory, which operates the INLDT. Projects draw on expertise from other departments at the university including the College of Medicine.[102] The other major Marine Corps research centre is the Non-Lethal Technology Innovation Center (NTIC) at the University of New Hampshire, which is tasked with identifying new technologies in the academic community.[103]

Within the Army, the Armament Research, Development and Engineering Center (ARDEC) at Picatinny in New Jersey remains the major site of research and development. In a similar vein to the Low Collateral Damage Munitions (LCDM) programme of the early 1990s ARDEC's Scalable Effects programme seeks to develop weapons with variable effects from 'lethal' to 'non-lethal' and incorporates the development of new delivery systems as well as acoustic and directed energy technologies.[104] Within ARDEC the Target Behavioral Response Laboratory (TBRL) has been established as part of a homeland security initiative.[105]

In 2002 ARDEC established the Stress and Motivated Behaviour Institute (SMBI) at the New Jersey Medical School.[106] Research at SMBI concerns the neurobiological basis of stress and anxiety with the aim of developing new techniques of 'personnel suppression' for the military and police. Researchers are investigating the use of bright light and acoustic stimuli.[107]

The Army Research Laboratory (ARL) is involved in 'non-lethal' weapons research through joint efforts with ARDEC on delivery systems.[108] ARL also conducts research into directed energy weapons for lethal and 'non-lethal' applications.[109] The Army's Edgewood Chemical Biological Center (ECBC) is the major centre of expertise on chemical agents and is involved in development and evaluation of irritant chemical agents (RCAs), malodorants, and incapacitating biochemical agents.[110]

AFRL is the main site of 'non-lethal' weapons research within the Air Force. AFRL's Directed Energy Directorate at Kirtland Air Force Base in New Mexico is the US military's centre of expertise for directed energy weapons.[111] The Directed Energy Bioeffects Division of AFRL's Human Effectiveness Directorate (HED) at Brooks Air Force Base in Texas is the focal point for 'non-lethal' weapons human effects research. There are three branches within the Directed Energy Bioeffects Division that are carrying out relevant work: the Joint Non-Lethal Weaponry Branch (HEDJ), the Optical Radiation Branch (HEDO), and the Radiofrequency Radiation Branch (HEDR).[112]

The main organisations conducting 'non-lethal' weapons research within the Navy are the Office of Naval Research (ONR) and the Naval Surface Warfare Center (NSWC). In addition to coordinating the joint DOJ-DOD initiative, DARPA is also exploring some 'non-lethal' weapons concepts, including those for urban combat operations.[113] The national laboratories of the DOE, such as Sandia National Laboratories, also continue to carry out relevant research.

4.2.7 Emerging research and development focus

The direction and focus of ongoing research and development efforts can be gleaned from announcements soliciting proposals for research. In January 2006 the JNLWD was seeking proposals for applied research to develop next-generation 'non-lethal' weapons with the overall purpose of overcoming existing limitations with regard to: 'range, accuracy and precision'; 'effectiveness and the ability to quantify it'; 'providing universal, repeatable and robust NL [non-lethal] effect'; and 'target safety, particularly across a wide-spectrum of the population'.[114] As regards anti-personnel weapons the overall focus of research requirements was:

- Develop novel non-lethal directed energy weapons.
- Develop long-range acoustic and/or ocular devices.
- Research and develop capabilities to incapacitate humans for extended durations (more than three minutes).

- Characterise the non-lethal human effects associated with non-lethal directed energy exposures.
- Explore innovative non-lethal technologies and stimuli through the development of prototype systems and characterization of non-lethal human effects.[115]

For fiscal year 2006 specific areas of research identified included the design of long-range acoustic and optical weapons and the further development of 'Active Denial Technology'. For fiscal year 2007 the research objectives included development of anti-traction materials, extended range wireless electrical weapons, and acoustic array systems as well as investigation of the human effects of various acoustic frequencies, incoherent light sources, and overpressures.[116] Areas of focus for proposed research in fiscal year 2009 included analysing human effects of: optical and thermal lasers, high-power microwaves, and millimetre wave radiation.[117]

There is a clear focus on directed energy and acoustic weapons technologies as well as extending the range of existing technologies such as electrical weapons. Although calls for research proposals do not mention of the further development of chemical weapons,[118] these are foreseen by the JNLWD as part of future capabilities.[119]

The way in which new directed energy, acoustic, and chemical 'non-lethal' weapons are designed has begun to change with a focus on 'effects-based' weapons design underpinned by research on human effects. The HEDJ within the Directed Energy Bioeffects Division of AFRL's HED is at the centre of this reorientation. Essentially this group is carrying out and funding basic and applied research in order to characterize the physiological and psychological effects of various 'non-lethal' weapons technologies on individuals and groups. The long-term goal is to develop the theory and supporting predictive models to enable the design of new weapons based around a desired behavioural effect. This research effort is very broad, seeking to investigate incapacitating effects that can be induced through interfering with the human senses of hearing, vision, touch, and smell. It will also address the effects of electrical current on various physiological systems including the central nervous system, neuromuscular interface, and endocrine system. Perhaps most profoundly some research will seek to investigate suppressive effects on the central nervous system through, for example, influencing neurotransmitter function.[120]

4.2.8   Increasing institutional support?

Although the field of 'non-lethal' weapons remains a niche area within the DOD there have been signs of increasing institutional support. In 2004 a Defense Science Board (DSB) report on 'Future Strategic Strike Forces' advocated further development of 'non-lethal' weapons affecting physiological or psychological functions, advising that 'applications of biological, chemical, or electromagnetic radiation effects on humans should be pursued'.[121] In 2005 the DOD's 'Strategy for Homeland Defense and Civil Support' stated that 'non-lethal' weapons would be further investigated for use in 'homeland defense', noting that basic research into physiological effects would be expanded and opportunities to share military technology with law enforcement agencies identified.[122] The 2006 'Quadrennial Defense Review Report', authored by senior leaders in the DOD and setting the tone for the future direction of the military also articulated a role for 'non-lethal' weapons as one of the capabilities required to achieve the major objective of 'defeating terrorist networks'.[123]

4.2.9 NATO studies

In 1999 NATO had launched its Defence Capabilities Initiative to align military capabilities with 'new security challenges' such as the intervention in Kosovo.[124] NATO's Research Technology Organisation (RTO) was tasked with investigating 'non-lethal' weapons technologies.[125] The RTO has conducted several technical studies through its Studies, Analysis and Simulation (SAS) and Human Factors and Medicine (HFM) panels. A 2004 report, 'SAS-035 Non-Lethal Weapons Effectiveness Assessment', developed a mathematical model for assessing 'non-lethal' weapon effectiveness, which was developed in a follow-on study, 'SAS-060 Non-Lethal Weapons Effectiveness Assessment Development and Verification Study'.[126] In December 2004 the SAS panel published the report of its technical study, 'SAS-040 Non-Lethal Weapons and Future Peace Enforcement Operations', which assessed 'non-lethal' weapons technologies for use in NATO peace enforcement operations for the period up to 2020.[127] Five technologies were identified as best suited to accomplish various operational tasks: radio frequency devices, rapid barriers (acoustic, electromagnetic, mechanical), anti-traction materials, electrical weapons, and nets.[128] The report recommended that NATO should conduct focused research and development efforts in these five areas, noting that they 'could be made scalable from non-lethal to lethal'.[129]

A 2006 technical report, 'HFM-073 Human Effects of Non-Lethal Technologies', found a lack of information on human effects and recommended the formation of an international database for this information, arguing that these data were critical to public and military acceptance. It concluded that there was a particular need for human effects data concerning new concepts, such as directed energy weapons.[130] A follow on study, 'HFM-145 Human Effects of Non-Lethal Technologies', is underway.[131]

4.3   Irritant chemical weapons: The rise of PAVA

Irritant chemical agents such as CS and OC ('pepper spray') continue to be used widely by police forces across the world, delivered by various spray devices, frangible projectiles, shells, and grenades.[132] One of the most significant developments in recent years has been an increase in the usage of pelargonic acid vanillylamide (PAVA), a synthetic version of OC that is more potent than the natural product and less variable in its potency. It is used widely by law enforcement organisations in North America and some European countries, including police forces in the UK,[133] and the US military is also investigating its use.[134] There are enduring concerns over the safety and health effects of irritant chemical weapons and the variability of different products. For example, a 2004 study by scientists at Guy's and St. Thomas' Hospital in London found that the specific CS sprays used by UK police forces may cause more adverse and long-lasting effects than other sprays.[135] An issue that clouds assessments of the safety and effectiveness of irritant chemical sprays is the variation in concentrations of active ingredient, composition of carrier substances, and types of delivery system.[136]

4.4 Blunt impact projectiles: Continuing injury concerns

There are now a large variety of blunt impact projectiles commercially available to the police and military. Many of them are designed for use with a standard 12-guage shotgun, 37 mm launcher, or 40 mm launcher. Others are fired with specially designed weapons such as the FN 303 or the PepperBall system. Beanbag and plastic baton projectiles are the most commonly used types of impact projectiles by US law enforcement.[137] A 2001 US study tested 80 different projectiles and categorised them in seven broad classes: airfoil; baton (foam, plastic, rubber, styrofoam, wooden); drag-stabilised; encapsulated; fin-stabilised; pads; and pellets.[138] Despite the continuous use of impact munitions since the 1970s a major finding was the 'general inaccuracy' of these weapons. A similar UK study evaluated 36 different impact projectiles and only two of those were considered sufficiently accurate to be taken forward for further evaluation.[139] Accuracy is a major concern as these projectiles can cause serious injury or death if they hit a sensitive part of the body such as the head and neck. The 2003 NRC report on 'non-lethal' weapons acknowledged: 'control of trauma level from blunt projectiles remains a serious problem'[140] and a 2004 NIJ report noted that the range is a key factor in the severity of injury caused.[141]

In the UK the L5A7 plastic baton round, the 'plastic bullet', was replaced with the L21A1 round in 2001, which was designed to be more accurate and therefore reduce the likelihood of causing death or serious injury.[142] However, a 2003 report by the Northern Ireland Human Rights Commission (NIHRC) found that the new round hit harder, was 2.5 times more likely to penetrate the skin, and had a higher potential for ricochet. The report found that the L21A1 was more likely to cause injury, with 10.3 per cent having caused injury compared to 1.14 per cent of the old L5A7 projectiles.[143] Dstl has since developed the AEP, which was introduced in 2005 as a replacement for the L21A1. The AEP is a plastic projectile with an air pocket that causes it to crush on impact with the intent of reducing the likelihood of death or serious injury.[144] It was used extensively in Northern Ireland during riots in late 2005.[145] The first medical study of injuries caused by the AEP in 2007 concluded:

> The stated objective for the AEP development and introduction was to decrease the possible risk of serious or fatal head injury. Although no deaths were attributable to the use of the AEP, a combined total of 50% of the injuries sustained were to the thorax or above the clavicle. ... It is clear that the AEP requires ongoing evaluation, and it is too early to conclude that it provides a safer alternative to the L21A1.[146]

4.5 Electrical weapons: Taser expansion and diversification

Since the introduction of a higher-powered Advanced Taser M26 in late 1999 these electrical weapons have proliferated in law enforcement agencies in the US and worldwide. According to the company by October 2006 they had sold 184,000 Tasers to 9100 law enforcement and military agencies, including law enforcement organisations in 44 different countries.[147] They are widely used by police across the US and Canada, and have been adopted in the UK. In 2003 Taser International introduced the Taser X26, which apparently improves on the effectiveness of the M26 model. A variety of cartridges are sold by the company with ranges of 15, 21, 25, and 35 feet and longer barbs have been developed for use against people wearing thick clothing.[148]

The company sells a version of the X26, the X26c, to the general public for 'personal defence' and in 2007 they introduced the Taser C2, which is aimed at expanding their consumer market. It is smaller and therefore easily carried, cheaper, and does not look like a weapon. Marketed to women, it is available with metallic pink and leopard skin patterns and is even available with a holster incorporating an mp3 player.[149] Both police groups such as the International Association of Chiefs of Police (IACP) and human rights organisations including Amnesty International have expressed concern over this step towards the wider marketing and availability of electrical weapons to the general public.[150] Criminal use of these and other 'non-lethal' weapons for crimes such as robbery, assault, and rape is already widespread in the US and elsewhere.[151]

For the military Taser has developed the X-Rail System for attaching a Taser X26 to rifles. Earlier models were developed for use by the military in Iraq and Afghanistan.[152] In August 2006 the company announced the formation of an advisory board of former military officers indicating that it hopes to expand sales to the military.[153]

For several years Taser International was the only company in the US manufacturing this type of weapon, having acquired its main competitor,

Tasertron, in June 2003. However, more recently a company called Stinger Systems has started selling similar wire-tethered electrical weapons, having developed two-shot and four-shot models.[154] The same company also sells electrical riot shields, and stun-belts, so-called prisoner worn stun devices, to US law enforcement and military agencies. Stun-belts are banned in the European Community under legislation that classifies them as torture devices.[155]

Very little medical testing of the new Taser weapons was carried out prior to their wide introduction across North America but increasing concerns over deaths following the use of Tasers, as raised by various organisations including Amnesty International, have led to further research sponsored by the DOJ and DOD.[156] Concerns remain over the human effects, particularly in relation to the administering of multiple shocks, use on those under the influence of drugs, and use on children or other vulnerable groups. Moreover there is unease that the weapons are not being employed as an alternative to lethal force but often as a compliance tool for police.[157]

Ongoing research and development of electrical weapons in recent years has focussed on longer-range systems. The US Navy has funded development by Taser International of a projectile that delivers an electric shock. A prototype of the XREP (Extended Range Electronic Projectile), which is fired from a 12-gauge shotgun, was demonstrated to the military in February 2006 at ranges of 30 metres.[158]

Taser International has also been developing an electrical anti-personnel mine in collaboration with the US Army and General Dynamics Corporation.[159] The Taser Remote Area Denial (TRAD) system is being marketed to both the military and the police to protect buildings and facilities or deny access to an area. It fires multiple Taser cartridges triggered by motion sensors and an infrared camera, and multiple units can be networked to cover a wide area.[160] The first incarnation of this system is called the Taser Shockwave, which was announced in 2007.[161] Also revealed in 2007 was a strategic alliance formed between Taser International and iRobot Corp. to integrate Taser electrical weapons on to the PackBot Explorer unmanned ground vehicle.[162]

4.6   Other technologies

The NIJ has been funding the development of a new 'flash-bang' weapon to replace existing grenade-type devices, in use for over 30 years, which combine bright light and painful sound levels to disorientate. The concept is to release a cloud of powdered fuel that is ignited to form a bright fireball, loud noise, and pressure wave in the same manner as a fuel-air explosive or thermobaric weapon. The developers are working on a fusing system that would enable it to detonate next to the victim at ranges of 15 to 100 metres and there are plans to incorporate a chemical irritant agent. With sound levels of up to 170 db the weapon would present a serious danger of permanent hearing damage.[163] The JNLWP is taking a similar concept forward through a research and development programme called the Improved Flash Bang Grenade (IFBG).[164]

Several other weapons have been pursued that combine a number of different effects to target multiple human senses.[165] The JNLWP has aimed to produce a so-called clear-a-space device to clear buildings.[166] Under this programme SARA Inc. have been developing a Multi-Sensory Grenade that produces a bright flash, loud noise, and also releases a malodorant or other chemical agents.[167] The NIJ has also funded an evaluation of this weapon.[168]

There has been continued development of a system to deliver anti-traction materials, called the Mobility Denial System (MDS). The Southwest Research Institute (SwRI) has developed a prototype system that sprays a highly slippery gel, formed from a mixture of polymers and water, onto surfaces to restrict the movement of people and of vehicles. A backpack system has a capacity of five gallons and a range of 20 feet enabling coverage of 2000 square feet and a vehicle-mounted system dispenses 300 gallons of the gel with a range of 100 feet and covering 120,000 square feet.[169] The gel, which remains slippery for around 12 hours, is being developed for both military and law enforcement applications.[170] The DAPRA Polymer Ice programme 'aims to replicate the properties of "black ice" for use in a broad range of hot, arid environments as found in the Middle East'.[171]

Researchers at the Emulsion Polymers Institute at Lehigh University have been working on the microencapsulation of anti-traction materials, producing millimetre-sized beads that rupture under pressure of a person's foot or a vehicle tyre.[172] Particles with a sticky outer surface for adhesion to walls or other surfaces have also been developed. Research is being carried out into the development of beads that would release material when triggered by specific environmental factors such as temperature or moisture.[173] This technology is also being applied to the delivery of other chemical agents such as incapacitating agents and malodorants.

Malodorant chemicals continue to be considered as potential payloads for chemical delivery systems under development by the JNLWP and the NIJ. Building on research initiated in the late 1990s the Army's ECBC has continued to investigate these agents in partnership with the Monell Chemical Senses Center in Philadelphia. Research has been conducted on cultural differences in susceptibilities to different odours.[174] The 2003 NRC report on 'non-lethal' weapons argued that malodorants 'have a strong potential for controlling crowds, clearing facilities, and area denial' and recommended further research.[175] It appears that some malodorant systems are already commercially available. A report published by the NIHRC notes that 'cadaver stench systems were being promoted at the Milipol Police and Internal Security Exhibition in Paris in November 2001'.[176] Apparently police forces in the US have begun to use foul smelling materials to prevent occupation of vacant buildings.[177]

Research and development of incapacitating biochemical agents has continued in recent years with interest from the US military and the DOJ in using these agents as payloads for various delivery systems. Given the controversial nature of research in this area, especially with regard to military involvement, little information is available. In 2000 the JNLWD's Technology Investment Program funded a 'Front End Analysis' of anti-personnel chemicals at ECBC with the objective of identifying chemicals for 'immobilizing adversaries'.[178] The Applied Research Laboratory at Pennsylvania State University carried out a literature review to assess the potential of incapacitating agents.[179] The NRC report in 2003 strongly advocated further development of incapacitating agents noting that they were being studied at ECBC after a 'lull in R&D for 10 years'.[180] NIJ funded further research at Pennsylvania State University in 2007. Research and development work is progressing elsewhere including in Russia.[181] In Moscow in late 2002 Russian authorities ended the siege of a theatre using an aerosolised fentanyl derivative[182] with devastating results.[183] In the Czech Republic the military have teamed up with anaesthesiologists to carry out research and development of different mixtures of agents with a focus on opioids, alpha-2 agonists, and dissociative anaesthetics such as ketamine.[184] The development of incapacitating biochemical agents, including drugs, as weapons is explored in detail in Chapter 5.

Despite research attempting to harness acoustic energy for use as weapons, few devices have emerged. It has proved difficult to produce acoustic energy in a directional beam and there are no proven effects of non-audible frequencies, infrasound and ultrasound, or viable effects of audible frequencies at levels that do not risk hearing damage. The major development in this field has come from the commercial sector. American Technology Corp. has developed a device, comprising an array of acoustic emitters, for projecting loud audible sound over long distances (up to 1 km), called the LRAD, first introduced in 2003.[185] It transmits speech or recordings but also has a piercing warning tone. Referred to by the military as an 'acoustic hailing device' rather than a weapon, it can be used in this manner but at high-power levels and at close ranges it can cause ear discomfort and permanent hearing damage.[186] By September 2005, around 350 LRAD systems had been deployed primarily with US military and law enforcement agencies.[187] A number of other companies have developed similar systems[188] and the JNLWD has been evaluating some of these.[189] ARDEC has also continued research and development of its own Aversive Audible Acoustic Device (A3D) and is working with American Technology Corp. and the SMBI to investigate the 'aggressive' use of the LRAD as a weapon rather than a hailing device.[190] Meanwhile JNLWD is developing a device called the Distributed Sound and Light Array (DSLA), which combines an acoustic array with a 'dazzling' laser and bright white lights.[191] Research has continued in the US and other countries on the development of vortex ring generators for use as projectiles or as a delivery system for various chemical payloads.[192] The development of acoustic weapons is explored in Chapter 7.

Research and development of directed energy weapons that employ various types of electromagnetic energy, including equipment generating radio frequency, microwave and millimetre wave beams, low energy lasers, and high energy lasers, for proposed 'non-lethal' applications has intensified in recent years. In the case of high energy lasers, some work is barely distinguishable from research on 'lethal' systems. The major US military programme is the ADS, which employs millimetre wave energy to heat the skin, causing a painful burning sensation. A prototype ADS System 0 was developed by the AFRL and declassified in late 2000. In recent years a vehicle-mounted ADS System 1 has been undergoing human testing and military evaluation but despite reports of its imminent use in Iraq,[193] it will not be deployed until 2010 at the earliest.[194] Another major US military development programme is the PEP, which would theoretically employ a high energy pulsed laser to produce a plasma blast wave stimulating nerves in the skin to cause pain and incapacitation.[195]

Development of a variety of low energy 'dazzling' laser weapons by the US military, the DOJ, and private companies has continued. Many of these, while 'dazzling' at a certain range, can cause permanent eye damage at shorter ranges. Some green 'dazzling' laser weapons are in use by the US military in Iraq and a prototype system, the PHaSR, that fires two different laser wavelengths, one to 'dazzle' and one to heat the skin, is under development at AFRL.[196] Another research area promoted by several companies and funded by the US military is the use of lasers to produce an ionised plasma along which an electrical charge is conducted to incapacitate or kill.[197] The development of directed energy weapons is explored in detail in Chapter 6.

With the range of existing 'non-lethal' weapons seen as a major limitation, a significant number of US military research and development programmes focus on new munitions, including shells, grenades, and mortars, that may enable delivery of various payloads at greater distances while minimising injury from the munition casing. There has been particular attention to the delivery of various chemical agents including irritant chemicals, malodorants, and incapacitating biochemical agents. In the private sector frangible encapsulated projectiles containing irritant chemicals for use against individuals, such as those fired by the Pepperball and FN 303 systems, have been adopted by US law enforcement agencies and more recently by the US military.[198] In the UK Dstl is developing a similar chemical delivery system for irritant chemicals called the DIP.[199] Increasingly unmanned air vehicles are being deployed by the US military in their operations and other unmanned platforms that have been developed include surface watercraft, underwater vehicles, and ground vehicles. While they have been primarily developed for use in sensing, surveillance, or 'lethal' weapons delivery, they are under consideration for delivering 'non-lethal' payloads.[200]

4.7   Legal issues: Stresses on international law

No new international agreements that relate to 'non-lethal' weapons have emerged in recent years, however, debates surrounding the impact of these new weapons on existing arms control treaties and international humanitarian law have intensified.[201] Fidler has argued that there are three perspectives on the future of 'non-lethal' weapons and international law:

> The compliance perspective insists that NLWs ['non-lethal' weapons] comply with existing rules of international law. The selective change perspective seeks limited changes in international law to allow more robust use of NLWs. The radical change perspective sees in NLWs the potential to reform radically international law on the use of force and armed conflict.[202]

Fidler has also pointed out that technological development will continue to stress international law on the development and use of these weapons in ways that are 'politically charged, legally complicated, and ethically challenging'.[203]

Much of the debate in recent years has centred on the development and proposed usage of incapacitating biochemical weapons. This intensified following the siege of the Moscow theatre in 2002 where Russian Special Forces used incapacitating agents for the first time killing over 120 people. However, the subject was intentionally avoided at both the First Review Conference of the CWC in early 2003,[204] and the Second Review Conference in 2008.[205] The issue has also been raised in peripheral discussions in relation to the BWC since proposed biochemical weapons agents may be covered by both conventions.[206] As regards the CWC, events in Moscow refocused attention on the permitted uses of chemical weapons for 'law enforcement purposes' and differing interpretations over the types of chemicals that are permitted in different circumstances.[207] Continuing military interest in these weapons is seen as the greatest threat to the prohibitions of the CWC and the BWC and the established norms outlawing chemical and biological warfare.[208]

The age-old issue of military use of irritant chemical weapons, or RCAs, have come to the fore again in recent years. In 2003, in the run-up to the war in Iraq, the US Secretary of Defense testified to the Congress House Armed Services Committee, stating that the US was attempting to 'fashion rules of engagement' to enable their use in combat[209] despite the fact that the CWC prohibits the use of RCAs 'as a method of warfare'.[210] This notion is unsupported by all other countries, including the UK. The UK Defence Secretary made it clear that the UK military would not use RCAs in any military operations or on any battlefield.[211] There is even disagreement within the US government on this issue with the Department of State in opposition to calls by the DOD for wider military use of RCAs and indeed military development of new incapacitating agent weapons.[212] Nevertheless the DOD continues to press for changes in policy.[213] A related issue is the legal status of malodorants. Indications from the US military suggest a keenness not to classify them as RCAs, which would prohibit their use in warfare.[214] However, their proposed action as sensory irritants would seemingly class them as RCAs.[215]

For emerging acoustic and directed energy weapons, however, there are no international agreements restricting their development and proliferation beyond compliance with international humanitarian law, and the additional protocol to the CCW that prohibits laser weapons intentionally designed to blind. Military establishments are keen to resist additional constraints on the development and use of 'non-lethal' weapons technologies, as exemplified in a recent NATO report:

> In order to ensure that NATO forces retain the ability to accomplish missions, it will be important that nations participating in NATO operations remain vigilant against the development of specific legal regimes which unnecessarily limit the ability to use NLWs.[216]

Another consideration surrounds the everincreasing tendency of the military to refer to 'non-lethal' weapons not as weapons but as 'capabilities' or 'technologies'. This semantic strategy is largely for policy and public relations effect in gaining acceptance of new weapons. However, it seems there have been legal implications. The LRAD has avoided the military legal review that is required for all new weapons systems apparently because it is not classified by the US military as a weapon.[217]

In late 2006 the ICRC published a document to assist states in ensuring new weapons and means of warfare comply with the fundamental principles of the law of war and treaties prohibiting specific weapons.[218]

4.8   Conclusion

At the turn of the century, with the JNLWP less than four-years-old, the military set out to assess progress and set priorities for research and development. The Joint Mission Area Analysis in 2000 and the NRC review in 2001 concurred on the required focus of technological development: directed energy weapons, chemical weapons, and delivery systems. A Council on Foreign Relations report in 2003 broadly agreed with these assessments, although it argued that the costs of pursuing new chemical weapons outweighed the benefits. Both reports emphasised the broader perceived requirement for weapons with greater range, more precise delivery, and rheostatic effects from 'non-lethal' to 'lethal'.

Two overarching issues for 'non-lethal' weapons development are the lack of broad institutional support in the DOD, and the lack of funding for the

JNLWP, in particular for research and development. The NRC and Council on Foreign Relations reports argued that increased funding would need to be made available for the development of new technologies and assessment of human effects, and effectiveness if new 'non-lethal' weapons were to be successfully fielded. Notably, this increased support, both financial and institutional, has not been forthcoming.

Since the late 1990s the US military has fielded a range of 'non-lethal' weapons that are primarily low-technology. New weapons that have been fielded in recent years include the Taser M26 and X26, the FN 303, the LRAD, and various 'dazzling' laser weapons. For the most part these have emerged from the private sector rather than from military research and development programmes.

From an operational perspective, the rhetoric of the revolutionary potential of 'non-lethal' weapons has not been realised in practice. In Iraq, where the type of urban combat put forward as the ideal for 'non-lethal' weapons deployment has been prevalent, their use thus far has been very limited outside prison camps. Whether this is due to the pervading limitations of existing low-technology weapons or broader limitations on the practicality or military willingness to substitute 'non-lethal' for 'lethal' force remains to be seen.

The JNLWP is putting its hope firmly in directed energy weapons for the future. The millimetre wave ADS, may be fielded in the next few years and a number of other research and development efforts are focusing on high energy lasers and other electromagnetic radiation systems, in particular elucidating biological effects. This move towards 'effects-based' design applies to the programme as a whole. In recent years, perhaps because of the popularity of the LRAD among military services, acoustic weapons concepts have also been revisited.

Another focus is on new delivery systems, in part to extend the range of existing technologies such as electrical weapons, but also to develop mid and long-range airburst munitions. The key issue here is what they will contain. All signs point towards some form of chemical agent and the most attractive from a purely operational perspective may be incapacitating agents, which offer the potential for far more profound effects than irritant, malodorant, or slippery chemicals. Of course, the CWC prohibits the use of toxic chemicals in warfare and limits the use of RCAs to 'law enforcement including domestic riot control'. Even the most unrestrictive interpretations of the CWC would also limit the use of incapacitating agents to these circumstances. Nevertheless military interest persists and the political inertia, in terms of addressing the issue at the international level, has not been broken.

The NIJ programme is peripheral with regard to weapons development, with a smaller scope and lower funding. For the most part, research continues on assessing the safety limitations and extending the effectiveness of existing technologies. Although NIJ maintains close connections with the DOD and has co-sponsored research on directed energy weapons and incapacitating biochemical weapons. Moreover, it is in domestic policing rather than military operations that 'non-lethal' weapons continue to be used most widely. It may be that emerging military weapons technologies follow this pattern. The ongoing development of incapacitating biochemical weapons, directed energy weapons, and acoustic weapons are examined in more detail in the subsequent chapters.

5
Chemical and Biochemical Weapons

This chapter addresses military and law enforcement efforts to develop incapacitating biochemical agents as weapons, which have spanned almost 60 years. It focuses on events in the US, tracking the weapons programmes administered by the DOD and related research funded by the DOJ to develop these agents and associated delivery systems. Recent developments in several other countries are also discussed.

5.1   Definitions

The long-standing military definition of an incapacitating agent is 'a chemical agent which produces a temporary disabling condition that persists for hours to days after exposure to the agent (unlike that produced by riot control agents)'.[1] From a military perspective, specific characteristics have been seen as follows:

1. Highly potent (an extremely low dose is effective) and logistically feasible.
2. Able to produce their effects by altering the higher regulatory activity of the central nervous system.
3. Of a duration of action lasting hours or days, rather than of a momentary or fleeting action.
4. Not seriously dangerous to life except at doses many times the effective dose.
5. Not likely to produce permanent injury in concentrations which are militarily effective.[2]

However, contemporary definitions emphasise rapid onset of action and short duration of effects, characteristics which reflect the current preoccupation with counterterrorism and the associated convergence of military and policing requirements.[3] Generally for reasons of politics and public relations these weapons have also been referred to as 'calmatives' and 'advanced riot control agents'. Particularly in the light of this intentionally cloudy termi-nology it is important to note that incapacitating agents are distinct from irritant chemical agents, often called riot control agents (RCAs), both in terms of their mechanism of action and their effects. RCAs act peripherally on the eyes, mucous membranes, and skin to produce local sensory irritant effects, whereas incapacitating agents act on receptors in the nervous system to produce central effects on cognition, perception, and consciousness.

While incapacitating agents have commonly been viewed as chemical weapons, the term 'biochemical weapons' is also used to reflect the conflu-ence of chemistry and biology in this area.[4] Greater understanding of bio-chemical processes in the body at the molecular level means that it is now more appropriate to think of a biochemical weapons spectrum rather than distinct chemical and biological weapons,[5] as shown in Table 5.1.

Midspectrum agents are those that fall in between 'classical' chemical weapons and biological weapons and share the characteristics of both.[7] Such agents generally exert their effects through acting on particular cell receptors in the body and can have either a synthetic chemical origin (i.e. drugs or poisons) or a natural biological origin (i.e. bioregulators, peptides, toxins). These midspectrum biochemical agents can have a variety of effects ranging from incapacitation to death, determined by the dose. They can act on a wide variety of physiological processes including blood pressure, tem-perature regulation, nervous system function, and immune response.[8]

Sight should not be lost of the variety of biochemical pathways and systems that are potential targets for incapacitating agent development.[9] Nevertheless the focus of 'non-lethal' weapons development has long been on agents that depress or inhibit the function of the central nervous system.[10] Neurotransmitters mediate chemical transmission in the nervous

Table 5.1 The biochemical weapons spectrum[6]

Classical chemical weapons	Industrial pharmaceutical chemicals	Bioregulators and peptides	Toxins	Genetically modified biological weapons	Traditional biological weapons
cyanide blister agents nerve agents	fentanyl ketamine midazolam	neurotransmitters hormones cytokines	botulinum toxin ricin saxitoxin	modified bacteria and viruses	anthrax plague yellow fever

CWC
◄──────────────────────►

BWC
◄─────────────────────────────►

poison ◄────────────────────► | infect ◄──────────►

system through their interactions with specific receptors. In the central nervous system these neurotransmitter-receptor interactions have a major role in regulating consciousness, mood, anxiety, perception, and cognition. While neurotransmitters are the naturally occurring bioregulatory peptides that bind to cell receptors in the central nervous system, these receptors can also be bound by synthetic chemicals (i.e. drugs or poisons). Among these are a number of classes of agents under consideration as incapacitating biochemical weapons.[11]

5.2 Past programmes

5.2.1 'Off the rocker' and 'on the floor'

Military interest in centrally acting biochemical agents as weapons, like other types of chemical and biological weapons, has a long history. The concept of employing chemical agents to cause temporary incapacitation rather than death is also an old one that began to receive greater attention as acceptance of lethal chemical agents declined in the aftermath of World War I.[12] However, it was not until after World War II that the expansion of the pharmaceutical industry led to the discovery of chemicals that would be suitable for this purpose[13] and interest from the US Army and the CIA soon followed.[14] SIPRI's 1971 study of chemical and biological warfare noted:

> The US Army's interest in psychochemicals was probably stimulated by the rapid development of psychotropic drugs by a number of chemical manufacturers after World War II. With the increasing use and availability of tranquilizers, stimulants and even hard drugs for the general public, it was perhaps inevitable that the possible military uses of the new substances should be investigated.[15]

A 1949 report by the Army Chemical Corps ambitiously considered psychochemicals, affecting the state of mind or mood, such as LSD (lysergic acid diethylamide) as alternatives to weapons of mass destruction.[16] The profound effects of LSD on the brain had only recently been discovered by accident during a pharmaceutical company's drug development process.[17] Army research began in 1951 and included the solicitation of candidate chemicals from various pharmaceutical companies through its Industrial Liaison Program.[18] Efforts focused on mescaline, LSD, and tetrahydrocannabinol (THC) related chemicals, and by late 1955 45 different compounds had been studied.[19] During these early investigations a variety of mechanisms for incapacitation were considered in addition to psychotropic effects. These included agents that influenced blood pressure and thermoregulation, or induced anaesthesia, sedation, muscle paralysis, tremors, or emesis.[20] Broadly speaking agents were colloquially divided into 'off the rocker' agents having psychotropic effects and 'on the floor' agents causing incapacitation through effects on other physiological processes.[21] 'Off the rocker' agents prevailed since the safety margins for other agents, including anaesthetic agents, sedatives, and opiate analgesics, were not considered sufficiently wide for them to perform as safe military incapacitating agents.[22]

Human testing began in 1956 with research continuing to focus on the same three groups of agents. Tests on mescaline and derivatives found that too large a dose was required[23] and a candidate THC analogue was discounted due to limited effects.[24] LSD remained the primary agent under investigation.[25] It was sufficiently potent but it too was later discounted due to its high production costs and side effects.[26] A large part of the incapacitating agent programme consisted of scanning new chemicals emerging from industry with around 10,000 compounds screened by the Army's Edgewood Arsenal each year.[27] In 1959 the Army began to investigate a compound from the pharmaceutical industry called Sernyl, which was the chemical phencyclidine (PCP). Human tests were conducted and it was quickly approved for manufacturing as Agent SN despite its variable effects and the large doses required for incapacitation. However, munitions containing SN were never produced.[28]

Another chemical that came to the attention of the programme around this time was 3-quinuclidinyl benzilate, an anticholinergic glycollate agent that had been developed by Hoffman-La Roche Inc. in 1951. It acts by interfering with the transmission of acetylcholine, a major neurotransmitter in the central nervous system to cause physical weakness, delirium, and hallucinations in very small doses.[29] Designated Agent BZ, investigation and human testing began at Edgewood Arsenal and it was soon prioritised. A re-evaluation of the US chemical and biological weapons programmes in 1961 led to priority being given to the development of an incapacitating chemical weapon capability and a project began to produce BZ munitions resulting in the standardisation in March 1962 of the 750 lb M43 cluster bomb and the 175 lb M44 generator cluster, which released the solid BZ as a particulate smoke.[30] However, only 1500 of these munitions were stockpiled[31] and they were only ever considered interim weapons, never fully integrated into the operational chemical weapons arsenal.[32] This was due to a number of shortcomings with both the agent and the delivery system as Kirby has described:

> [T]he operational problems that BZ presented were numerous. Its visible white agent cloud warned of its presence. Improvised masks, such as several layers of folded cloth over the nose and mouth could defeat it. Its envelope-of-action was less than ideal. The rate-of-action was delayed ... , and the duration of action was variable from 36 to 96 hours. Additionally, 50% to 80% of the casualties required restraint to prevent self-injury, and

paranoia and mania were common personality traits during recovery. These uncertainties made BZ unattractive to military planners.[33]

Wide ranging research into new incapacitating agents continued after the standardisation of BZ. For example, Pfizer was carrying out contracted research for the military on various chemicals including those that might induce retrograde amnesia.[34] By the late 1960s a number of different classes of compounds were under active investigation including anaesthetics, analgesics, tranquilizing agents, anticholinergics (e.g. glycollates), and vomiting agents. Moreover, the Army's Edgewood Arsenal was also promoting the adoption of these agents for use in law enforcement.[35] Many of these chemicals had previously been discounted due to their low-safety margins.

Morphine-like opioid analgesics that were of interest to developers included a piperidinol compound given the code EA 3382 and a benzomorphan known as M-140. Research was ongoing to mix these compounds with antagonists[36] (antidotes) in order to improve their safety margins. Tranquillising agents under consideration included a phenothiazine compound called prolixin and a butyrophenone known as compound 302,089. However, glycollates were still viewed as the most important class of chemicals and one such compound, EA 3834, was under consideration as a replacement for BZ due to its faster onset time.[37] By 1969, with President Nixon's disavowal of biological weapons and reaffirmation of no first use of lethal and incapacitating chemical weapons, the US BZ weapons were officially recognised as an ineffective capability.[38]

Military research on incapacitating agents in the UK, including close liaison with the US, had been underway since the late 1950s but activities had intensified in 1963 when a specific directive for the development of an offensive capability was issued.[39] Researchers noted that the best way to develop an incapacitating agent would be to design an agent with a specific action but they observed that existing knowledge of the interactions between biochemicals and receptors was not advanced enough. Therefore the search, as in the US, took the form of a literature search and screening of compounds with promising effects. Efforts concentrated on those neurotransmitter-receptor systems that were better understood. Foremost among these was the interaction of the neurotransmitter acetylcholine with acetylcholine receptors, which were known as the site of action of the lethal nerve agents. Glycollates such as BZ also act on this neurotransmitter-receptor system. The programme investigated a variety of other compounds affecting known neurotransmitter systems including indoles, such as LSD; tryptamines; benzimidazoles; tremorine derivatives; and morphine-like opioids such as oripavine derivatives. By the mid to late 1960s research became more systematic, with increased efforts to gain a greater understanding of the target receptors.[40]

Research on incapacitating agents continued until at least the early 1970s, but no suitable agent was found, the British having not been convinced about the US Army's BZ weapon.[41] Doubts were expressed by UK officials over the feasibility of 'non-lethal' incapacitating agents:

> On general grounds I think it unlikely that ... a pure incapacitator agent will emerge. Any chemical agent, a small dose of which is capable of profound disturbance of bodily of mental function, is certain to be able to cause death in large dose ... and no attack with a chemical warfare agent is likely to be designed with the primary objective of avoiding overhitting.[42]

Nevertheless in the US in the early 1970s new incapacitating agent weapons were moving closer to deployment.[43] Dissemination tests of the new glycollate agent, EA 3834, were conducted and in 1973 it was accepted for weaponisation.[44] Due to similar dissemination properties, it was envisaged that the wide variety of existing CS munitions could be used for delivery of the new agent.[45] Also at this time the Army approved a requirement for a tactical air-delivered incapacitating munition system (TADICAMS) and carried out advanced development of a 155 mm projectile, the XM-723, and tests of an incapacitating agent dispensing submunition (SUU-30/B) with EA 3834. Other agents under investigation at this stage were analogues of thebaine and oripavine, morphine-related compounds, and phenothiazines. Dissemination tests with the latter were carried out during fiscal year 1974.[46]

By late 1975 increasing public interest had led to Senate hearings to examine the scope of human experimentation programmes conducted by the DOD and the CIA.[47] Dando and Furmanski have described the extent of testing in the Army's incapacitating agent programme:

> Over the 20-year period 1956–1975 at least 6,720 soldiers and approximately 1,000 civilian patients or prisoners participated in evaluation of 254 chemical agents in at least 2,000 trials of psychochemicals.[48]

The Army's own assessment concluded that from 1950 to 1975 $110 million had been invested in this exploratory research. In addition to intramural research, at least 25 external contracts had been awarded including to universities and hospitals, the majority of which involved human testing.[49]

Despite this increasing scrutiny, the Army continued with exploratory development in fiscal years 1975 and 1976, investigating a binary concept for agent dissemination, studying rocket, artillery, and mortar delivery systems, and exploring the potential of benzodiazepines such as Valium as incapacitating agents.[50] A result of the Senate hearings was the introduction of greater restrictions on human testing, and so in fiscal year 1977 the

Army conducted a literature review of agents previously tested with a view to selecting an agent effective through inhalation and contact with the skin. One avenue under investigation was combining a glycollate with an irritant agent. Also during this period the Army conducted some advanced development work on a pilot plant for production of the glycollate EA 3834A and a filling facility for a XM96 66 mm incapacitating agent rocket warhead.[51] This would be the last advanced development work until the early 1990s.[52]

In 1975, with the end of the Vietnam War, military interest in incapacitating agents had begun to fade. BZ was declared obsolete and soon decommissioned, and EA 3834 weapons were not standardised.[53] Some years later, between 1988 and 1990, the 90,000 lb stockpile of BZ in bulk chemical form and munitions was destroyed in an incinerator at Pine Bluff Arsenal.[54]

During the nine-year period from fiscal year 1978 to 1986 the programme at the Army's Edgewood Arsenal continued. However, efforts were limited to relatively low-level exploratory research into new compounds and improved delivery systems.[55] Nevertheless significant progress was made, particularly in terms of increased understanding of the mechanism of action of potential incapacitating agents and how they might be weaponised.[56] Several research efforts in the early to mid 1980s involved the study of structure-activity relationships of various chemicals. By 1984 and 1985 emphasis appears to have shifted from psychomimetic compounds, such as the glycollate agents, to potent analgesics such as the opioid drug fentanyl and its analogues including carfentanil.[57] Fentanyl itself, which had been discovered in the late 1950s and was introduced as a clinical anaesthetic in the 1960s, had been considered as a candidate incapacitating agent as early as 1963.[58] However, its analogues (or derivatives) such as carfentanil were first synthesised in the 1970s, following a search in the pharmaceutical industry for more potent anaesthetics with wider safety margins.[59]

Some of these fentanyl derivatives had soon been introduced to anaesthesia practice and others were under consideration as veterinary tranquilisers.[60] Not long after their discovery they too were under consideration in the Army incapacitating agent programme. The Chemical Research, Development, and Engineering Center (CRDEC)[61] published research into the binding properties of carfentanil at different opioid receptor subtypes, illustrating the mechanism behind its wider safety margin.[62] Tests on primates were carried out with aerosolised carfentanil during the 1980s.[63] Also, in fiscal year 1984 the 155 mm munition containing incapacitating agent submunitions was redesigned and successfully tested. By fiscal year 1986 the search for new incapacitating agents continued drawing on academia and industry for new compounds.[64]

5.2.2   Advanced Riot Control Agent Device (ARCAD)

By 1987 the NIJ had established its LTL Technology Program following a conference where participants had urged investigation of chemical incapacitating agents. The first research contract under this new programme in 1987 was with the Army's CRDEC at Aberdeen Proving Ground for a feasibility assessment of a dart to deliver an incapacitating agent to stop a fleeing suspect.[65] NIJ added an additional $1 million to the research and development effort in 1989 and 1990[66] to identify a suitable chemical and produce a prototype delivery system.[67] The requirement for rapid immobilisation led to consideration of fentanyl analogues, in particular alfentanil, selected because of its high potency and quick action. However, its low-safety margin was a major problem and the prototype delivery system, comprising a standard police baton modified to fire a drug-filled dart, was a failure.[68]

It is not clear whether these NIJ contracts for new police chemical weapons rekindled the military's own interest but in any case activity in the Army's incapacitating agent programme increased markedly in the late 1980s and early 1990s,[69] and the Army adopted the NIJ's 'less-than-lethal' terminology. By fiscal year 1989, under Army Project A554, candidate opioid chemicals had been selected. Unsurprisingly, given the findings of research carried out for the NIJ, the fentanyl analogues were prioritised. Tests with primates found respiratory depression to be a major side effect and, in an effort to militate against this, studies were initiated on combining such opioids with antidotes (opioid antagonist drugs) in order to increase the safety margin.[70]

During fiscal year 1990 the Army terminated their 'Incapacitating Chemical Program' and reinvented it as the 'Riot Control Program'. This was most likely due to the ongoing negotiation of the CWC, which would soon prohibit the development of chemical weapons. The military apparently sought to place incapacitating agents in the same category as irritant RCAs, which the US had long maintained were not chemical weapons, an isolated position not shared by any other country.[71] As Perry Robinson observed in 1994:

> The chemicals themselves seem to be the same. The variant terminology reflects the changing status in international law of the weapons that are based on these chemicals.[72]

This attempt to soften the terminology was not a new idea. A report from the US Defense Science Board some 30 years previously, recommending a major effort on incapacitating agent development during the 1960s, had put forward new terminology to avoid legal restrictions and public opposition:

> It was argued that the ideal incapacitating agent should not be classed with the toxic biological or chemical agents and that it should be characterized by some new term, such as *'reinforced tear gas'*, or *'super tear gas'*, to emphasize its relatively innocuous nature[73] [emphasis added].

In 1990, 30 years later, incapacitating agents were being described as 'advanced riot control agents'.

During fiscal year 1990 further development work included evaluating candidate compounds, carrying out inhalation tests, investigating dissemination techniques, and developing production methods.[74] An acquisition plan for obtaining a incapacitating chemical weapon, the ARCAD, was approved by mid-1991. The weapon was described in the Army's 1992 'NBC Modernization Plan':

> The ARCAD consists of a hand held grenade, or device, that can also be shoulder fired from a weapon currently being used or developed. This device will deliver a potent riot control compound, which will provide a rapid onset of effects where the safety of the individual(s) is the primary concern. The candidate compound will be effective primarily through the respiratory tract.[75]

By fiscal year 1993 the ARCAD had entered advanced development under Project DE78, with $10.2 million funding for the year. Further work was conducted on the delivery system with a plan for testing and evaluation updated and a preliminary plan for manufacture completed.[76] A contract for development of the prototype weapon was scheduled to be awarded by late 1993,[77] but it seems that a decision was taken that the ARCAD would not move forward into the DOD's major systems development process.[78] This was due to the provisions of the CWC, which opened for signature in January 1993, prohibiting chemical weapons and limiting the use of RCAs to 'law enforcement including domestic riot control purposes'.[79] The US military had of course already sought to characterise these incapacitating biochemical weapons as RCAs.

Even though advanced development of the ARCAD was curtailed, the search for new agents continued. Researchers at ERDEC had carried out considerable work on fentanyl analogues for the ARCAD.[80] However, the limitations of these compounds fuelled the search for new compounds. As a DOD solicitation for research proposals on 'Less-Than-Lethal Immobilizing Chemicals' in late 1992 concluded:

> Most recent less-than-lethal (LTL) programs at US ARMY ERDEC focused on the fentanyls as candidate compounds. ... Many of these compounds are well-characterized, rapid acting, very potent and reliable in their activity. However, for many LTL applications, they have safety ratios that are too low and durations of action that are too long. Ideally one needs a material that will act safely, virtually instantaneously and last for just a few minutes. Thus, candidate chemical immobilizers with improved safety ratios and shorter duration of action are needed.[81]

Within the ERDEC research laboratories attention had turned to a class of sedative compounds called the alpha$_2$ adrenergic agonists and a multidisciplinary study of these compounds had been initiated in 1989.[82] Further research was carried out at Edgewood in the early 1990s with particular attention to a drug called medetomidine, which had been introduced as a sedative and analgesic for veterinary practice in 1989.[83] Work focused on modifying medetomidine to produce more selective analogues with potent sedative properties but without the cardiovascular side effects, such as low blood pressure.[84] By 1994 Army researchers were putting their faith in alpha$_2$ adrenergic agents as future incapacitating biochemical weapons:

> More selective α_2-adrenergic compounds with potent sedative activity have been considered to be ideal next generation anesthetic agents which can be developed and used in the Less-Than-Lethal Technology Program. Unlike opioids, these compounds are devoid of the usual liabilities associated with respiratory depression, physical dependence and environmental concern after dissemination.[85]

In April 1994 Technical Directors at ERDEC argued that the ARCAD Program should be revived, putting forward proposals for research and development. A three-year, $1.25 million Advanced Concept Technology Demonstration (ACTD)[86] effort, 'Demonstration of Chemical Immobilizers', was proposed, defining these agents as:

> [C]hemical compounds that produce incapacitation through immobilization, disorientation or unconsciousness. Among the classes of neuropharmacologic agents with potential as immobilizers are anesthetics, analgesics, sedatives and hypnotics.[87]

The objective of the proposed research was to: 'select, acquire and demonstrate the effectiveness and safety of a chemical immobilizer(s) on test animals, such as rodents and primates', focusing on agent delivery through inhalation and also carrying out limited tests of a prototype delivery system. The proposed research would comprise Phase 1 of a longer four phase programme, the latter phases envisaged as: expanded toxicological testing (Phase 2), delivery system development (Phase 3), and clinical trials for effectiveness and safety (Phase 4). For Phase 1 the proposal advocated a generic approach called 'Front End Analysis' to select the most suitable chemical compounds based on prior ERDEC research. Furthermore it was suggested that concurrent studies be conducted on two classes of compound likely to be selected in the 'Front End Analysis', namely synthetic opioid anaesthetics and alpha$_2$ adrenergic sedatives.[88]

These two lines of research were expanded in the supporting research proposals, entitled 'Antipersonnel Chemical Immobilizers: Synthetic Opioids'[89] and 'Antipersonnel Chemical Immobilizers: Sedatives'.[90] With regard to opioids the proposal noted that the major side effect of respiratory depression could be countered, and the safety margin increased, by combining the agent with an antidote as had been studied under the ARCAD programme.[91] An ERDEC patent illustrating just this strategy was filed in December 1994 claiming a novel combination of fentanyl derivative agonist and antagonist to induce analgesia, sedation, and anaesthesia with minimal respiratory depression, and noting that the sufentanil derivative was preferable. The patent pointed out that the development of opioid drugs without the side effect of respiratory depression had been 'an elusive goal' despite the emergence of more selective agents.[92]

The proposal for development of opioid incapacitating agents also referred to new fentanyl analogues with shorter durations of action, patented by Glaxo Pharmaceuticals in the early 1990s. One of these was remifentanil, since approved for use in anaesthesia.[93] At this point fentanyl analogues remained the prime candidates for the Army's incapacitating agent programme, as the proposal noted: 'Extensive studies have been carried out in the past and the most advanced technology exists for the fentanyls than for any other chemical immobilizer candidates'.[94]

The proposal relating to sedative compounds envisioned initial studies to design and synthesise new rapid acting alpha$_2$ adrenergic compounds that would 'cause immobilization by profound sedation'.[95] Interestingly, it also acknowledged some of the practical limitations that apply to any incapacitating chemical agent:

> Operational limitations include the potential use in mixed populations of the very young, the elderly, those in poor health and those who may react adversely to a specific chemical.[96]

In addition to the proposed work on fentanyl derivatives and alpha$_2$ adrenergic agonists as 'chemical immobilizers', researchers at Edgewood proposed a modest feasibility study of other potential incapacitating agents, which they termed 'calmative agents' and defined separately:

> A calmative agent can be defined as an antipersonnel chemical that leaves the victim awake and mobile but without the will or ability to meet military objectives or carry out criminal activity.[97]

Clearly the author of this proposal viewed 'calmatives' as distinct from 'immobilizing agents' in view of their mechanism of action not involving anaesthesia or sedation, it being more akin to the focus of early cold war efforts on psychomimetic action.[98] The impetus for this research proposal on 'calmatives' apparently arose from a Professor of Anaesthesiology at the University of Utah School of Medicine, who had passed on his observations of the effects of an experimental serotonin (5-HT) antagonist or blocker, which he had found to have a 'profound calming effect' on wild elk.

The proposed feasibility study envisaged a literature search to determine the structure-activity relationships of serotonin antagonists to find the receptor subtypes responsible for different pharmacological effects. Researchers would also seek to collaborate with outside experts in further investigating these agents as weapons:

> Identify and interact with expert(s) in academe, other government agency (OGA) or pharmaceutical laboratories to help identify or design compound(s) for desired effect.[99]

Although there is insufficient information available to reach a concrete conclusion, the three proposed research efforts do not appear to have been accepted at the time. In late 1995 the author of the proposals presented a paper to an ERDEC conference summarising the 40-year history of incapacitating agent research, which gave an overview of the compounds under consideration and the types of scenario envisaged for their use:

> Potential military missions include peacekeeping operations; crowd control; embassy protection; and counterterrorism. Law enforcement applications include use by local, state and national law enforcement agencies in hostage and barricade situations; crowd control; close proximity encounters; prison riots; and to halt fleeing suspects. Depending on the specific scenario, several classes of chemical have potential use, to include: potent analgesics/anesthetics as rapid acting immobilizers; sedatives as immobilizers; and calmatives that leave the subject awake and mobile but without the will or ability to meet objectives.[100]

5.2.2.1 Police-funded research

The NIJ had also continued to fund research into incapacitating agents and delivery systems during the 1990s. Following on from the contracted research at the Army's ERDEC in 1989 and 1990, NIJ initiated a project with Lawrence Livermore National Laboratory (LLNL) in late 1992 that continued to assess the feasibility of using fentanyl derivatives, with consideration of combining them with antidotes to enhance the safety margin, and solvents to enable delivery through the skin.[101] Initial work focused on alfentanil but by late 1993 attention had shifted to lofentanil because of its higher safety margin.[102] Research at the Forensic Science Center at LLNL continued until at least January 1997.[103]

LLNL researchers reviewed the most potent pharmaceutical agents available and, similarly to prior military efforts, a major theme was to investigate the viability of potent anaesthetic compounds in combination with antidotes. The major difference to military research was its aim to develop a weapon for use against an individual as opposed to a munition for delivering

Table 5.2 Lawrence Livermore National Laboratory literature review of clinical anaesthetics[105]

Drug class	Example	Clinical dose (IV)	Onset time (IV)	Side effects
Barbiturates	Sodium thiopental	200–500 mg	10–20 secs	Respiratory depression, hypotension
Benzodiazepines	Diazepam (Valium)	25 mg	1–2 mins	Some cardio-pulmonary depression
Opioids	Morphine Meperidine Fentanyl	1–2 mg (analgesic) 10–25 mg (analgesic) 0.05–0.1 mg (analgesic)	Not given Not given Seconds	Respiratory depression
Neuroleptic-opioid combinations	Butyrophenone (Droperidol) and Fentanyl mixture (Innovar)	0.1 ml/kg Innovar (2.5 mg Droperidol and 0.05 mg Fentanyl)	Not given	Respiratory depression, nausea, and vomiting

incapacitating agents over a wide area.[104] Their initial literature review considered clinical anaesthetics to compare the doses required, onset time, and side effects. A summary of their findings is shown in Table 5.2.

All the agents were found to have significant side effects, in particular respiratory depression. The most notable difference between the drugs considered was the potency and therefore the dose required, which led to the selection of fentanyl and its analogues for further investigation:

[I]t became apparent that fentanyl (Janssen Pharmaceuticals) is an uncommon and very powerful drug. Whereas other compounds, such as sodium pentothal, benzodiazepines, and morphine elicit an anesthetic response at dosage levels of 3–200 mg, fentanyl is highly effective in humans at microgram levels.[106]

Moreover fentanyl and its analogues were observed to be extremely fast acting, crossing the blood-brain barrier very quickly due to their lipophilic properties. They concluded, unsurprisingly in the light of prior military and NIJ-sponsored research that 'all pharmacologic and pharmacokinetic parameters point to this class of drugs [fentanyl and analogues] as an ideal candidate for less-than-lethal technology'.[107]

The report also described work carried out by LLNL researchers on a delivery system. Inhalation delivery was discounted due to the lack of dose control that would be possible in field conditions, a view clearly not shared by military developers[108] and injecting darts were ruled out following previous failed development attempts.[109] Researchers turned to alternative methods of drug delivery and drew their inspiration from drug skin patches, for example, nicotine patches for nicotine withdrawal, and fentanyl patches for severe burns, where the drug is combined with a solvent for delivery through the skin. They tested a prototype system comprising a felt pad soaked with dimethyl sufoxide (DMSO) solvent and fired from an air rifle. They found that a drug and DMSO mixture could be delivered in this way and would penetrate thin clothing. They also found that the delivery system would have to be encapsulated to enable practical use and carried out tests using a 38-calibre cartridge to deliver the felt pad. However, they proposed that future developments should consider smaller fully encapsulated 'paintball' type projectiles containing the drug and solvent mixture.[110]

The researchers considered the issue of mixing antidotes with the fentanyl-type drugs in order to increase the safety margin, noting that the antidote of choice for opioid toxicity is naloxone, an opioid antagonist which acts quickly and for a long duration to reverse the respiratory depression, low blood pressure, and sedative side effects of opioids. Since simply mixing naloxone with the opioid anaesthetic would defeat its effects the researchers proposed developing a delayed release mechanism for naloxone so that it reached maximum effect only after the anaesthetic drug had sufficient time to act.[111]

Researchers argued that in vitro tests of the drug and solvent soaked felt projectiles on animal and human cadaver skin should be the next step in the development of the weapon, followed by extensive animal testing, and then tests with human volunteers in cooperation with a university medical centre. They concluded that a final weapon system could be produced in two to five years depending on the level of funding and number of institutions involved.[112] It is unclear whether follow-on work was conducted but the US Army would later return to this concept of a fentanyl-DMSO felt projectile.

5.3   Contemporary programmes

5.3.1   Potential payloads

With the founding of the JNLWP in July 1996, research and development of 'non-lethal' weapons gained renewed impetus. A 1997 preliminary legal review of proposed chemical 'non-lethal' weapons, carried out by Navy lawyers at the request of the JNLWD, seemingly provided the legal ambiguity necessary for military research on incapacitating biochemical agents and delivery systems to proceed, despite the entering into force of the CWC.[113]

The first indication of a new research program emerged in December 1999. Following discussions with the JNLWD the Army issued a request for research on 'Chemical Immobilizing Agents for Non-lethal Applications'. Phase 1 of the proposed research would seek to identify new agents and agent combinations including an analysis of 'recent breakthroughs in the pharmacological classes such as Anesthetics/analgesics, tranquilizers, hypnotics and neuromuscular blockers' and subsequently 'establish the mode of immobilization, the effective dose(age) for immobilization, onset time and duration of effects, and safety ratio in the most appropriate animal species'.[114]

This research, it was envisaged, would be followed by Phase 2 of the project where input from various military and law enforcement agencies would be gathered in order to establish the required characteristics of chemical agents for potential scenarios of use, and the implications of the CWC's prohibitions. Following the selection of the preferred scenarios, tests would be conducted on non-human primates followed by clinical tests on humans to assess safety and operational characteristics. Furthermore an appropriate delivery system would be designed and demonstrated. Phase 3 would consider the dual use applications of the technology. Potential military uses given in the solicitation were 'meeting US and NATO objectives in peace-keeping missions; crowd control; embassy protection; rescue missions; and counter-terrorism' whereas law enforcement applications cited were 'hostage and barricade situations; crowd control; close proximity encounters, such as, domestic disturbances, bar fights and stopped motorists; to halt fleeing felons; and prison riots'.[115]

By June 2000 ECBC, formerly ERDEC, had awarded the contract for Phase 1 of the research to OptiMetrics, Inc.[116] The principal researcher would be a past ECBC scientist who has authored the 1994 Edgewood proposals for research and development of 'immobilizing agents' and 'calmatives'. The funding announcement noted that Phase 1 research would consist of a 'Front End Analysis' to 'determine feasibility for one or more candidates as immobilizing agents'.[117]

Unsurprisingly the description of the research, including the 'Front End Analysis' methodology, paralleled the 1994 ERDEC proposals. According to an employee of OptiMetrics, speaking in 2004, the contract award was $75,000,[118] and the research concentrated on fentanyl analogue and antidote mixtures.[119] It is not clear when this Phase 1 research was completed but it was carried out by November 2002 at the very latest. Neither is it apparent when or if the Phase 2 and Phase 3 research was undertaken.[120]

A related part of US research into incapacitating biochemical weapons at this time was a literature search and analysis carried out jointly by the Applied Research Laboratory and the College of Medicine at Pennsylvania State University. The Applied Research Laboratory is where the JNLWD-sponsored INLDT is located, itself run by a former JNLWD Director. On 3 October 2000 the Applied Research Laboratory published their study, 'The Advantages and Limitations of Calmatives for Use as a Non-Lethal Technique',[121] which aimed to provide a survey and comprehensive database of the medical literature on drugs that might be used as incapacitating biochemical weapons.[122]

The report defined 'calmatives' as 'compounds known to depress or inhibit the function of the central nervous system termed (depressants)', including 'sedative-hypnotic agents, anesthetic agents, skeletal muscle relaxants, opioid analgesics, anxiolytics, antipsychotics, antidepressants and selected drugs of abuse'.[123] In contrast to ECBC researchers, who distinguished between so-called immobilizing agents and so-called calmatives, the study grouped all potential incapacitating agents including potent anaesthetic chemicals as 'calmatives'. This softening of language in describing these chemical weapons is a feature of the report and reflects wider efforts to present new weaponry as 'techniques' or 'capabilities'.[124] Nowhere in the report is the word 'weapon' used, the authors preferring to use the phrase 'non-lethal technique'.

The report argued that different chemical agents would be required for different scenarios with 'different mechanisms of action, duration of effects and different depths of "calm"'.[125] The latter strange phrase meant that they considered effects ranging from a reduction of anxiety to anaesthetically induced unconsciousness, as illustrated with envisaged scenarios:

> For example, an individual running towards you with a gun may pose an immediate threat or perhaps be trying to protect you; in contrast with this immediate threat are a group of hungry refugees that are excited over the distribution of food and unwilling to wait patiently. In these two cases the degree of 'calm' required is vastly different in magnitude and the target populations are also different.[126]

Although the report did not consider delivery systems *per se*, the authors envisaged a variety of delivery routes including 'application to drinking water, topical administration to the skin, an aerosol spray inhalation route, or a drug filled rubber bullet'.[127]

The report proposed several classes of drugs that the researchers considered to have 'high potential' as incapacitating biochemical weapons, as shown in Table 5.3.

Unsurprisingly, the Pennsylvania State study drew attention to a number of classes of drugs that have long been considered as potential incapacitating agents including opioids, benzodiazepines, alpha$_2$ adrenergic agonists, and neurolept anaesthetics. With regard to opioid drugs, the report focused on one fentanyl analogue in particular, carfentanil, noting that it has long been used to immobilise large animals but had not been used in clinical anaesthesia for humans.[129]

The report's discussion of receptor function pointed out that the powerful analgesic properties of opioids such as fentanyl analogues are produced by action on the μ_1 subtype of opioid receptors, while the major side effect of respiratory depression is associated with μ_2 receptors. It follows that an opioid drug with selectivity for μ_1 over μ_2 receptors would be attractive

Table 5.3 Selected drugs as weapons[128]

Drug class	Examples	Site of action
Benzodiazepines	Diazepam, Midazolam, Etizolam	Gamma-aminobutyric acid (GABA) receptors
Alpha$_2$ Adrenergic Receptor Agonists	Dexmedetomidine	Alpha$_2$-adrenergic receptors
Dopamine D3 Receptor Agonists	Pramipexole, Cl-1007	D3 receptors
Selective Serotonin Reuptake Inhibitors	Fluoxetine, WO-09500194	5-HT transporter
Serotonin 5-HT$_{1A}$ Receptor Agonists	Busprione, Lesopitron	5-HT$_{1A}$ receptor
Opioid Receptors and Mu Agonists	Carfentanil	Mu opioid receptors
Neurolept Anesthetics	Propofol	GABA receptors
Corticotrophin-Releasing Factor Receptor Antagonists	CP 154,526; NBI 27914	CRF receptor (corticotrophin-releasing factor)
Cholecystokinin B receptor antagonists	Cl-988, Cl-1015	CCK-B receptor (cholecystokinin)

as an incapacitating agent because of an increased safety margin. This is something that researchers at the ERDEC were pursuing during the 1980s, publishing research that found carfentanil had a greater selectivity for μ_1 receptors than μ_2 receptors, thus resulting in lower respiratory depression than some other compounds with less selectivity.[130]

The report also reviewed benzodiazepines favourably, arguing that they are 'prototypical calmative agents with varying profiles from rapid onset and short acting, through intermediate acting, to very long term effects'.[131] Benzodiazepines exert their effects through action at GABA$_A$ receptors, causing sedation but also the side effects of respiratory and cardiovascular depression. An antagonist drug, flumazenil, can be used as an antidote. The Pennsylvania State researchers highlighted the development of new short acting compounds that have a rapid onset of effect with a short duration such as midazolam, which is described as: 'useful for sedation and anesthetic induction, processes which may occur in as little as two to five minutes following intravenous injection'.[132] The report noted that newer short acting compounds are under investigation including etizolam and Ro 48-6791.

Alpha$_2$ adrenergic agonist drugs, which had been singled out as candidate incapacitating agents some years previously by Army researchers, were also considered. The report focused on dexmedetomidine (Precedex), the stereoisomer of medetomidine initially developed as a veterinary drug and first approved for use in humans as recently as 1999, which causes sedation through highly selective action on the alpha$_{2A}$ receptor subtype over the alpha$_1$ subtype, which causes low blood pressure.[133] The Pennsylvania State report highlighted its synergistic action with other drugs:

> Used in conjunction with most other sedative agents, this drug markedly (23–90%) reduces the dose requirements for the primary agent, often reducing side effects leading to increased safety of the mixture of pharmaceutical agents.[134]

Furthermore the report noted that dexmedetomidine accentuates the effects of electrical currents on the body and suggested that it could be used to enhance the effects of electrical weapons.[135]

In the reports discussion of neurolept anaesthetics, propofol was given as an example of an agent that causes rapid anaesthesia through inhibiting nerve transmission at GABA receptors and requires no antidote due to rapid metabolism. Again the authors noted the synergistic properties. Clinically propofol is used with other GABA acting agents, such as the benzodiazepine midazolam, to decrease the dose requirements and safety margin of both agents. The report argued that the use of synergistic drugs warranted further research for the development of incapacitating weapons[136] and that examples of new synergistic combinations were emerging from anaesthesia practice.[137]

Like the LLNL researchers several years earlier, the report also addressed neurolept anaesthetic combinations, including the combination of droperidol and fentanyl, which produces a neuroleptic state 'characterized by marked tranquilization and sedation with a state of mental detachment and indifference while reflexes remain essentially intact'.[138] The authors noted that droperidol itself has too long a duration of action to be considered as an incapacitating agent and has significant side effects but that further research should be carried out on drugs inducing this neuroleptic state.[139]

In addition to the drug classes described above, that had commonly been considered as potential incapacitating agents in the past, the Pennsylvania State report argued for consideration of several other drug classes based on technical developments in the pharmaceutical industry. The report argued that dopamine D3 receptor agonists, in use for treatment of Parkinson's disease and under investigation for treatment of schizophrenia, could be of interest as incapacitating agents due to their anti-psychotic properties and effects on motivation and locomotion.[140]

The report also drew attention to drugs affecting serotonin (5-HT) receptors. In a discussion of selective serotonin reuptake inhibitors (SSRIs), such as fluoxetine (Prozac) and sertraline (Zoloft), which are used to treat depression and anxiety, the report noted their effect of increased drowsiness and reduced aggression. Although such drugs commonly have a very slow onset time (one week or more) for effects on mood, the report argued that it is likely that an SSRI with a rapid rate of onset can be identified especially given the ongoing intensive development of these types of drugs in the pharmaceutical industry.[141] Drugs that bind selectively to activate a particular serotonin receptor subtype, the 5-HT_{1A} receptor, were also considered due to their effects in reducing anxiety and aggression. The authors argued that 'the use of a selective 5-HT_{1A} receptor agonist would reduce symptoms of anxiety in an individual and promote a calmer and more compliant behavioral state'.[142]

Furthermore the report addressed the bioregulatory peptide corticotrophin-releasing factor (CRF), whose action at CRF receptors in the central nervous system is linked to mood and stress. It observed that a novel approach may be the use of CRF receptor antagonist peptides (or synthetic analogues) to produce 'a calm behavioral state', noting that improved delivery mechanisms for peptides would be required.[143] Another peptide system considered is that of cholecystokinin (CCK). Various CCK peptides act on CCK-A and CCK-B receptors in the brain with the latter receptors involved in anxiety and panic attacks. The report noted that CCK-B agonists have been shown to induce panic attacks, whereas CCK-B antagonists appear to inhibit panic and produce a calmer state, suggesting the need for further exploration and investigation of delivery mechanisms.[144]

Noting ongoing research on drug delivery, the report recommended that further research be carried out to investigate these various classes of drug as incapacitating biochemical weapons in collaboration with the pharmaceutical industry and that a similar review be conducted on drugs of abuse (including selected club drugs) and convulsants.[145] In summarising their literature review the authors argued that numerous drugs in clinical practice were candidate incapacitating agents and that a wide range of compounds were under investigation in the pharmaceutical industry for their ability to induce the sedative and behavioural effects of interest to weapons developers.

The preface to the Pennsylvania State report stated that the study was carried out as 'an internally funded initiative and basis for discussion'.[146] Both the JNLWD and the NIJ deny funding the report.[147] However, this is something of a moot point given the well known connections between Pennsylvania State University, the JNLWD, and the NIJ. Nevertheless it seems clear from the timing of the publication that the research was closely tied to ongoing military developments.

The report was published on 3 October 2000 and it was during a JNLWD review meeting held from 3 to 4 October 2000 that three new proposals were selected for funding under the JNLWD's Technology Investment Program for fiscal year 2001, one of which concerned the further research on incapacitating agents by the Army's ECBC. The research effort, which would appear to build on the Pennsylvania State literature review, was announced in 2001 with the objective of identifying 'non-lethal chemical materials for further testing which have minimal side effects for immobilizing adversaries in military and law enforcement scenarios'.[148] The project comprised 'a series of workshops and analyses culminating in a database of potential riot control agents and calmatives, with emphasis on technology advances in the past

10 years'.[149] The project was scheduled for completion in the third quarter of fiscal year 2002[150] with the aim of putting forward potential incapacitating agents for preliminary legal review.[151]

Information on the findings of this or subsequent research is not available. The NRC's study of 'non-lethal' weapons science and technology, published in early 2003, confirmed that military research on incapacitating biochemical weapons was ongoing noting that they were 'under study by ECBC after lull in R&D for 10 years'.[152] Researchers at ECBC had apparently returned to the concept of a sponge projectile soaked with a fentanyl derivative and antidote that LLNL researchers had previously explored. The report highlighted these weapons as one of the major technologies for further development. Despite concerns over compliance with the CWC discussed in the report, major recommendations were to 'increase research in the field of human response to calmatives', and to 'target efforts to develop chemical delivery systems'.[153]

With the military embarking on new research, the NIJ also funded further weapons development in this area. Given the prior interconnections between military and law enforcement programmes it is likely that there is close cooperation. Furthermore the US military is willing to subcontract weapons development to other government agencies in order to circumvent international legal prohibitions, as described in the report of a joint UK-US meeting on 'non-lethal' weapons:

> If there are promising technologies that DOD [Department of Defense] is prohibited from pursuing, set up MOA [Memorandum of Understanding] with DOJ [Department of Justice] or DOE [Department of Energy].[154]

In fiscal year 2001 NIJ funded research at the INLDT at Pennsylvania State University to 'conduct an investigation of controlled exposure to calmative-based oleoresin capsicum'.[155] There is very little information available about this project, combining incapacitating agents and irritant agents, although a February 2003 presentation by the Senior Program Manager for the NIJ LTL Technology Program indicated that the project had been reviewed by a liability panel and that work was progressing at Pennsylvania State University.[156] A potential application of incapacitating agents for law enforcement was suggested by the Director of the NIJ in 2002:

> Anesthetics or calmative chemicals could, in principle, be developed into a system whereby they could be remotely released into the cabin in order to incapacitate all passengers, and the hijackers, until the plane can be landed safely. Chemical systems of this type have not been employed in the field, however, and remain under study or in development.[157]

The same suggestion was made by the Director of the JNLWD in a presentation to the Airline Pilots Association in October 2001, arguing that suitable incapacitating chemicals could be available in '3 years +'.[158]

Since the 2003 NRC report recommending expanded research on incapacitating agents there has been no further openly available information on
the military programme due to likely classification of the ongoing work.[159]
However, some documentation has emerged relating to the continued development of associated delivery systems, as discussed later in this chapter. It
is unclear whether these types of biochemical weapons can now be accessed
for US military operations. Unconfirmed reports in 2003 quoted the Navy's
former Chief of Operational Testing and Evaluation as saying that Special
Forces had 'knock-out' gases available for use in Iraq.[160]

Recent announcements for research and development proposals in support of the JNLWP made no mention of incapacitating agents or any other
chemical agents. Although a major goal put forward was the development
of 'next generation', 'non-lethal' weapons and payloads for 'extended duration incapacitation of humans and material at ranges in access [*sic*] of small
arms range'.[161]

The most recent information to emerge on US interest in incapacitating
biochemical agents is from the law enforcement arena. Following requests
in 2006 for research proposals on so-called calmatives, NIJ convened a
'community acceptance panel' in late April 2007 to seek input on proposals
to fund further research. The panel based its discussions around the 2000
Pennsylvania State University report and recommended that NIJ fund further research, highlighting carfentanil for further investigation, and recommending collaboration with the pharmaceutical industry. Subsequently NIJ
awarded funding to Pennsylvania State University in 2007 to 'explore the
potential of operationalizing calmatives and to examine possible pharmaceuticals, technologies, and legal issues.'[162]

5.3.1.1 *Russia*

In late 2002, just as the NRC was preparing to publish its recommendations,
it emerged that at least one country had already developed and deployed
such weapons and was willing to use them within its own borders and on
its own citizens. On 23 October 2002 a group of around 50 armed men and
women claiming allegiance to the Chechen separatist movement took control of the Dubrovka theatre in Moscow, taking over 800 people hostage during a performance of the musical 'Nord Ost' and demanding the withdrawal
of Russian troops from Chechnya. In the morning of the third day of the
siege Russian authorities pumped an aerosolised biochemical incapacitating
agent into the auditorium through the ventilation system. Allowing at least
30 minutes for the agent to take affect, Special Forces stormed the building
shooting the majority of the hostage takers while unconscious.[163] At least
129 hostages were killed and many survivors needed hospital treatment[164]
All but one or two died due to exposure to the chemical agent.[165] It was not
until four days later that that the Russian Health minister finally released
the identity of the agent used, stating that it was 'based on derivatives of
fentanyl' and refusing to provide any further information.[166] The main side

effect of fentanyl derivatives is respiratory depression, which is thought to have been the major factor in the death of so many in Moscow. Although there is some debate as to whether the weapon used was a mixture of a fentanyl derivate and another inhalation anaesthetic, or perhaps even a novel agent, it seems certain that the aerosol contained an opioid agent since victims were treated with naloxone.[167] Indeed a 2003 paper by three US medical toxicologists commented:

> In the United States, naloxone, for a long time a critical antidote to treat heroin overdose and iatrogenic opioid toxicity, has now become a crucial component of our chemical warfare antidote repository.[168]

Various reports have suggested that the agent used was either sufentanil, remifentanil, or the most potent fentanyl analogue, carfentanil.[169] Experts in these anaesthetic compounds who have been involved in the US Army's programme to develop incapacitating agents have argued that it was most likely carfentanil.[170] Due to the size of the theatre the agent would need to have been extremely potent with a low concentration needed for the effect. According to one of these experts, only three classes of drugs are sufficiently potent: fentanyl derivatives such as carfentanil and sufentanil, the oripavines such as the wildlife tranquiliser etorphine (trade name M99/ Immobilon), and benzimidazoles such as etonitazene. All of these are opioid drugs, which have been considered in past US and UK military incapacitating agent programmes.[171] Some observers have claimed that the agent was called M99, an alternative name given to etorphine, which, like carfentanil, has long been used to immobilise large animals.[172]

As events in Moscow illustrated, Russia clearly has a significant programme to develop incapacitating biochemical weapons and, moreover, a deployable capability. It appears that these weapons may be stockpiled for rapid deployment when required. A Russian news source reported that the opioid antidote naloxone was made available to doctors during the 2004 school siege in Beslan in anticipation of Special Forces using incapacitating agents again.[173] And in October 2005 there were reports of the use of 'knockout gas' and antidotes by Special Forces during a hostage incident in the Russian town of Nalchik.[174]

As regards research and development a 2003 paper by Russian scientists addressed future avenues for research, arguing,

> [t]here is still no perfect tranquillizing agent, but the problem of safety can be solved by the succeeding or simultaneous application of calmative and antidote. This can minimize potential fatality.[175]

Of course this strategy of mixing agent and antidote has been a common characteristic of US incapacitating agent development efforts. Ongoing

Russian research in this area on computer modelling and simulation of pumping aerosolised chemical agents into buildings has concluded that in reality deaths cannot be avoided because dispersal and exposure levels cannot be sufficiently controlled.[176]

5.3.1.2 Czech Republic

The most openly available information about current research and development of incapacitating biochemical agents is that published by Czech researchers. In 2005 it emerged that the Czech military were funding the development of these weapons,[177] in a research effort that had begun in 2000,[178] to develop sedative and anaesthetic agent combinations for use as weapons under Czech Army Project No: MO 03021100007.[179] The researchers argued that: 'There is a possibility of pharmacological control of an individual behaving aggressively'.[180]

The types of drugs considered are similar to those highlighted in the Pennsylvania State University report from 2000,[181] as described in the introduction to a 2005 paper:

> They are highly receptor-specific agents with a well controllable effect. They are commonly used in anesthesiology practice and include benzodiazepines (midazolam), opioids (fentanyl and its derivatives), and alpha2 agonists (dexmedetomidine). There are specific antagonists to all these agents like flumazenil, naloxone or naltrexone and atipamezole. An important group of agents for these purposes are dissociative anesthetics (ketamine).[182]

In experiments conducted over several years researchers injected rhesus monkeys with different mixtures of agents to determine combinations and doses that would result in what they termed 'fully reversible immobilization'. In these experiments they administered the agents through intramuscular injection measuring the time to onset of the effect, the time to immobilisation, and the rate of recovery. Various combinations of medetomidine, ketamine, midazolam, dexmedetomidine, fentanyl, and hyaluronidase (an enzyme that speeds up absorption) were tested. The synergistic interactions of some of these drugs were incorporated into the experiments, such as the use of midazolam to decrease the effective dose of other drugs. One mixture, comprising midazolam, dexmedetomidine, and ketamine, was tested on ten nurses who were paid to participate in the experiments.[183] Following intramuscular injection the time taken for the subject to have to lie down was considered as the 'immobilization time', which in their experiments varied from two to four minutes. Another mixture of dexmedetomidine, midazolam, and fentanyl was tested on patients prior to surgery. Further experiments in rabbits employed opioids, including remifentanil, alfentanil combined with low doses of naloxone antidote, and etorphine (M99/Immobilon) combined with the antagonist butorphanole.

Animal tests explored various delivery routes, including nasal, transbuccal (across oral mucous membranes), and conjunctival (across the eye). Aerosol delivery was tested with rats and subsequently with 'volunteers', who were in fact children in hospital, using sprays with two different combinations of agents: ketamine and dexmedetomidine; and ketamine and midazolam. Transdermal delivery (across the skin) was tested in rabbits with etorphine and the solvent DMSO, which facilitates absorption through the skin. Researchers tested other mixtures combined with DMSO, proposing that incapacitating agents could be delivered in this way operationally:

> The transdermal technique of administration could possibly be used to induce long-term sedation with alpha$_2$ agonists, benzodiazepines, and a combination of them to pacify aggressive individuals. Using the paintball gun principle, anesthetic-containing balls could be used. Impact of the ball would be followed by their destruction and absorption of garment with the anesthetics which will be quickly absorbed via the skin.[184]

As discussed earlier in this chapter, the US LLNL had proposed the very same technique in the mid-1990s[185] and later experimented with a fentanyl-soaked sponge projectile[186] which was again under investigation by the US Army in 2001.

The Czech research appears to have taken inspiration from the US weapons research. Furthermore there has been broader international interest in this research through NATO links. The NATO Research and Technology Organisation panel on the human effects of 'non-lethal' weapons reviewed the Moscow incident favourably,[187] and the Chair of that panel expressed support for the Czech research.[188] The Czech representative to the NATO HFM-073 panel was, for some time, also one of the researchers, from the Army's Military Medical Academy, who has been involved in ongoing weapons research.[189]

5 3.1.3 Other countries

It seems likely that research and development of incapacitating agent weapons would be ongoing in other countries although there is no information available describing specific programmes. In 2004, report by The Sunshine Project included an assessment of French interest,[190] which illustrated military research on the behavioural and cognitive effects of various psychoactive and anaesthetic compounds, however, it noted that researchers did not find any indication of a weapons programme. Nevertheless a 2003 opinion piece by a leading French toxicologist and a military specialist in anaesthesiology, described the likely militarisation of drugs as weapons.[191] A subsequent paper by these authors warned of the dangers of using incapacitating biochemical weapons in hostage situations but supported further weapons development:

> [T]here is certainly a future for 'calmative' drugs in this scenario. Publication of these data demands caution as the terrorists themselves could use these new indications and methods. Other means of personnel control are under study, including use of microwaves and acoustic weapons. Secrecy in this research is essential for their future efficacy.[192]

The UK would at first appear to be less interested in these weapons. Having reviewed various 'non-lethal' weapons technologies, incapacitating bio-chemical weapons were downgraded as technologies not of immediate importance in a 2004 Northern Ireland Office report.[193] The report argued that 'use of calmatives in policing situations would not be a straightforward process'[194] and explained that the use of any drug would require knowledge of the subject's medical history. Nevertheless the Home Office is clearly not ruling out this type of weapon for the future with the caveat:

> PSDB [Police Scientific Development Branch] will continue to monitor this area, focussing on international research programmes and future developments in delivery methods and potential tranquilising agents.[195]

The UK MOD, despite long-lived collaboration with the US DOD on 'non-lethal' weapons,[196] has made clear its differing position in that the UK does not support the military development of incapacitating biochemical weapons.[197]

5.3.2   Weaponisation: Delivery systems

As discussed in earlier chapters, the US military has long desired to increase the range of various 'non-lethal' weapons by developing new delivery systems, many of which are being designed to deliver chemical agents.[198] Although the discussion of payloads is often non-specific, irritant chemi-cal agents (RCAs), malodorants, anti-traction chemicals, and incapacitating agents have all been discussed. This ambiguity allows delivery system devel-opment to proceed while minimising criticism of renewed military interest in biochemical weapons. Nevertheless the NRC report specifically recom-mended the development of delivery systems for incapacitating agents.[199] Even if these delivery systems were to be justified on the basis of use of RCAs for 'law enforcement including domestic riot control', serious concerns have been expressed that many of the munitions under development are not suit-able for this purpose, including a mortar round with a range of 2.5 km and an artillery projectile with a range of 28 km.[200]

In addition to the systems described in the following sections there are numerous delivery systems and associated technologies available for irritant chemical agents such as CS and OC that have a long history of development, as discussed in earlier chapters, including projectiles, grenades, smoke generators,[201] spray devices, and aerosol generators. Many of these may be adaptable or applicable to the delivery of incapacitating agents.

5.3.2.1   Drug bullets

Paintball-type encapsulated projectiles have been considered for delivery of incapacitating agents by researchers in the US and the Czech Republic. Such frangible projectiles and associated compressed air launchers, such as the PepperBall and FN303 weapons are used by US police for the delivery of powdered irritant agents such as CS, OC, or PAVA.[202] The FN303 has been designated as the US military's Individual Serviceman Non-Lethal System (ISNLS).[203] These are the types of projectiles that may be adapted for delivery of incapacitating agents against individuals.

During the late 1990s the NIJ began a project to reinvent the RAP, a rubber projectile developed by the US Army in the 1970s which would release a cloud of irritant agent upon impact from compartments inside the projectile. In 2002 the NIJ funded a research proposal to consider various payloads including incapacitating agents.[204] Further development of this projectile, now termed Advanced Segmented Ring Airfoil Projectile (ASRAP), was funded in 2004[205] and testing has been carried out at the at Pennsylvania State University.[206]

5.3.2.2   Chemical dispersal concepts

Relevant research and development conducted by the US military relates to delivery of chemical agents at long range and over wide areas to target groups of people. The JNLWD began funding the development of an Overhead Chemical Agent Dispersion System (OCADS), later called the Overhead Liquid Dispersion System (OLDS), in 1999 with the aim of providing the military with capability to quickly disperse chemical agents over large areas for crowd control or area denial.[207]

This work was carried out by Primex Aerospace Company (since acquired by General Dynamics) in collaboration with the Army's ARDEC. An April 2000 report described the successful design, testing, and demonstration of a system comprising a launcher and dispersal device. The latter consisting of a liquid-holding plastic canister with integrated gas generator to disperse the payload over an area 12 m in diameter at ranges of over 100 m. At the time OC was given as the payload under consideration although the report noted the system would be adaptable for delivering liquids with differing properties in varying droplet sizes and for delivering powders, encapsulated liquids, or projectiles, such as rubber pellets.[208]

5.3.2.3   81 mm mortar

In September 2001, General Dynamics Ordnance and Tactical Systems began further JNLWD-funded work building on the OLDS concept to develop liquid dispersal technology for an 81 mm mortar in collaboration with ARDEC.[209] By late 2003 this work was ongoing and ECBC had begun a study of potential malodorant payloads.[210] The programme to develop an 81 mm 'non-lethal' mortar had begun in 1999 under a joint project carried out by United Defense, the ARL, and ECBC.[211] The Applied Research Laboratory at Pennsylvania State University had also been involved in the assessment of this weapon.[212] The development aim is a mortar that can deliver a solid, liquid, aerosol, or powder payload from 200 m up to 2.5 km with a casing that does not cause any injury.[213] One prototype has a parachute system to slow the descent of the munition casing and another has a frangible casing. Tests were conducted in November 2002 and February 2003 on both prototypes including tests dispersing CS irritant simulants over an area of 25 square metres.[214]

5.3.2.4   Airburst munitions

Another type of munition, under development by the Army's ARDEC is the Airburst Non-Lethal Munition (ANLM), which is part of a wider programme to produce a new assault rifle for the Army called the Objective Individual Combat Weapon (OICW). The ANLM is designed to burst open just before it reaches its target, releasing a liquid, aerosol, or powder payload, for use at ranges of 5 to 1000 m.[215] Incapacitating agents have been presented as one potential payload.[216]

Initial testing by ARDEC and ECBC was conducted in January and April 2002 with CS irritant chemical payloads.[217] Shortly afterwards the Applied Research Laboratory at Pennsylvania State University carried out a technology assessment of the ANLM, which expressed doubts over the effectiveness of a CS payload and recommended that a 'Front End Analysis' be conducted to identify new, 'very concentrated agents'.[218] The authors, two of whom also authored the 2000 Pennsylvania State University review of incapacitating agents, were seemingly suggesting the use of incapacitating biochemical payloads. Work on the design of the ANLM munition has continued[219] but 2006 and 2008 JNLWD 'fact sheets' describe 'flash-bang' payloads and make no reference to consideration of chemical agents.[220]

5.3.2.5   155 mm artillery

The Army's ARDEC is also taking the lead in development of another munition in collaboration with General Dynamics Ordnance and Tactical Systems. This is a large 155 mm artillery projectile or 'cargo round' called the XM1063, which is adapted to carry a liquid payload.[221] To give some idea of the size and range, this munition is based on the 155 mm M864, which carries 72 conventional grenades at ranges of up to 28 km.[222] The XM1063, also referred to as the Non Lethal Personnel Suppression Projectile, will carry multiple submunitions at this range, which will be released above the target area and then fall to the ground via parachute and disperse their liquid payloads,[223] covering a minimum area of 5000 square metres.[224] General Dynamics is focussing on development of the submunitions, likely incorporating their overhead liquid dispersal technology.[225] Details of the proposed payload are scant but the available documentation describes it as a 'personnel suppression payload'.[226] There is no indication as to the exact nature of the liquid, although payload development and testing is being carried out by ECBC[227] and so it will certainly be some type of chemical agent.[228] When testing of the munition began in 2004 potential payloads had apparently already been selected.[229] Tests have continued[230] and by mid-2007 clinical trials had been conducted on the proposed payload.[231] With the weapon due to be ready for production in 2010 no further information has emerged on what it will contain.[232]

5.3.2.6 Patented concepts

ECBC has patented several other devices for dispersing chemical agents. A February 2003 patent for a 'Rifle-launched non-lethal cargo dispenser'[233] to deliver included among possible payloads both chemical and biological agents. Following pressure from The Sunshine Project, who noted that such a device would contravene the BWC,[234] a divisional patent was issued, replacing references to 'crowd control agents, biological agents, chemical agents' with the rather unspecific 'crowd control materials'.[235] Another ECBC patent is for a 'Particle aerosol belt', apparently designed to deliver payloads including 'pharmaceutical compositions'.[236]

5.3.2.7 Unmanned aerial vehicles (UAVs)

UAVs are under development primarily for military tasks such as lethal weapons delivery, sensing, and reconnaissance and it is a field of significant investment. The DOD invested over $3 billion in this area during the 1990s and planned to increase this to over $16 billion during the 2000s.[237] A very small but significant area of interest is the use of UAVs to deliver various 'non-lethal' payloads at long distances,[238] including chemical agents. In the mid-1990s a 'non-lethal' dispenser system was developed by the Naval Surface Warfare Center in collaboration with the Marine Corps Warfighting Laboratory (MCWL). Tests were carried out by the JNLWD with both Hunter and Exdrone UAVs during 1996 and 1997 using smoke munitions to simulate irritant chemicals.[239]

The JNLWD also funded the development of an unmanned platform to spray liquid payloads by remote control at the SwRI called the unmanned powered parafoil for use in crowd control operations.[240] Other projects carried out in the late 1990s included an assessment by Raytheon Corp. of the feasibility of using an Extended Range Guided Munition (ERGM)[241] to deliver 'non-lethal' payloads including chemical agents and the study of a 'Loitering Submunition' for autonomous delivery of 'non-lethal' payloads.[242] A major recommendation of the NRC panel in 2003 was for further development of unmanned vehicles to deliver 'non-lethal' weapons, including chemical agents, at long distance with greater accuracy.[243]

5.3.2.8 Microencapsulation

In 1999 the JNLWD funded a project at the University of New Hampshire to carry out research in to the use of microencapsulation for delivery of chemical agents and incapacitating agents such as anaesthetic drugs.[244] Reasons for encapsulating chemicals include enabling controlled release and compartmentalisation of binary systems. In addition microcapsules could conceivably be delivered from a variety of platforms such as shotguns, launchers, airburst munitions, mortars, and UAVs. Microcapsules may vary in size from centimetres to microns in diameter depending on the applications. Small microcapsules could even be inhaled for delivery of incapacitating agents. The researchers demonstrated a number of secondary release mechanisms that could be used to control the release of the materiel inside the capsule including mechanical rupture, thermal release, and hydrolytic release.[245] By 2003, researchers had already developed microencapsulated irritant agents, malodorants, and dyes.[246] The NRC panel argued that microencapsulation should be explored with a view to controlling the delivery of chemical agents as 'non-lethal' weapons.[247]

5.4   Major themes

5.4.1   Technical realities

This chapter illustrates that there have been a succession of failures to develop incapacitating biochemical weapons, beginning with the US and the UK efforts during the Cold War. In the US, despite great investment over twenty-five years including extensive human experimentation, the programme was a failure.[248] Although BZ was produced and weaponised in the early 1960s, it was never fully integrated into the US chemical weapons arsenal due to deficiencies in both the agent and delivery system.

The Army's concerted effort to produce the ARCAD in the early 1990s also faltered, as did the related NIJ research effort. On the basis of available information, the revived contemporary US military programme has yet to succeed in producing such a weapon. Although some proponents welcomed the Russian use of a fentanyl derivative in Moscow in 2002 and contended that it produced a better result than could have been expected with other types of force,[249] this event too exhibited the failure thus far to develop an incapacitating biochemical weapon that does not endanger life in operational conditions.

During the 1960s UK military researchers acknowledged the deficiency in their knowledge of the interaction between biochemical agents and receptors in the central nervous system. This meant that the search for new agents had to be carried out by trial and error rather than by design, reflecting the process of drug discovery at the time, and making it very difficult to elicit specific effects. For contemporary efforts these particular concerns have been ameliorated with an exponential increase in the understanding of receptor structure and function. The 1980s saw the identification of numerous peptide neurotransmitters that mediate chemical transmission in the nervous system alongside classical neurotransmitters such as acetylcholine. However, it is advances during the past 10–15 years that have revolutionised the field. This progress was particularly marked during the 1990s when there were more advances in neuroscience than all previous years combined.[250] The impact of genomics has led to a greater understanding of receptor systems and the elucidation of the structure and function of certain receptor subtypes that have now become potential targets for therapeutic drugs or indeed incapacitating agents. The key issue in relation to this change is specificity of effects through action on specific receptor subtypes, something that was lacking from early incapacitating agent development efforts.[251] By 2000, weapons developers boldly claimed that incapacitating agents could be tailored to have selective effects on consciousness, movement, and behaviour.[252]

Tailoring drugs for specific receptor targets has become easier through the emergence of combinatorial chemistry to create large libraries of potential compounds and high-throughput screening techniques to assess their activity. Moreover bioinformatics and computational biology permitting large-scale analysis of biological data have enabled development of computer modelling software that can be used to carry out virtual screening to identify new compounds.[253] As well as offering the opportunity to develop more effective new drugs to treat a variety of mental illnesses, this knowledge is dual use.[254] The US military and DOJ research has closely shadowed advances in the pharmaceutical industry and recently developers have advocated close collaboration with industry for ongoing weapons development.

An enduring barrier to development of incapacitating agents, interrelated with the issue of specificity, has been the problem of finding compounds with an adequate safety margin; that is a sufficiently wide difference between the dose of an agent which effectively incapacitates and the dose that kills. In pharmacological terms the safety margin is defined as the therapeutic index, which represents the ratio of the mean lethal dose (LD50) to the mean effective dose (ED50). The higher the therapeutic index (LD50/ED50) the higher the safety margin. The central requirements of an incapacitating agent are that it be sufficiently potent to be logistically feasible, thereby inducing the desired effect with a small dose, as well as having a wide enough safety margin to not risk serious injury or death in operational conditions. However, compounds that are very potent tend to have low safety margins and if a compound has a wide safety margin it will tend to have a long onset time or not be sufficiently potent.[255] In fact, researchers at the Federation of American Scientists developed a model illustrating that even with a safety margin higher than any known sedative or anaesthetic drug a chemical used as an incapacitating agent would be expected to cause at least 10 per cent fatalities.[256]

With the search for a potent yet safe incapacitating agent proving elusive, the strategy of mixing agents (agonists) with antidotes (antagonists) has been explored by weapons developers since the 1990s and more recently they have sought to explore the synergistic effects of different drugs that may reduce the dose of a certain drug required to elicit the desired effect, thereby reducing the dose-dependent side effects. Despite these attempted strategies, the problem of ensuring safety while retaining effectiveness does not appear to have been solved.[257]

Inducing the level of incapacitation desired while preventing adverse effects requires careful control of the dose received, especially with the types of powerful drug under consideration, which tend to have low-safety margins.[258] As Coupland has emphasised in relation to this issue, 'the only difference between a drug and a poison is the dose'.[259] In a clinical setting the dose of an anaesthetic or sedative drug to be administered is precisely calculated according to body weight, age, and health and, furthermore, vital signs are continuously monitored. Clearly in operational situations it is not possible to tailor the dose to each individual exposed. US military research-ers have concentrated on delivery of agents as an aerosol for inhalation and some have argued that this provides greater safety because children, for example, have smaller lungs and therefore inhale a smaller dose.[260] However, this crude measure does not take these individual characteristics into account nor the difficulties in predicting aerosol droplet dispersal inside a building let alone in the open air.[261] Moreover, there are the overarching problems of delivering an even concentration of the agent in a given area and cumulative intake of agent over time, which is even more pronounced in an enclosed space. As the researchers from the Federation of American Scientists have argued:

> The only practical way to maintain effectiveness in the face of uneven concentration is to use enough agent to guarantee that the minimal concentration in any area exceeds that needed to achieve effective inca-pacitation. However, this will mean that some areas will contain higher concentrations of the agent, enough to cause significant lethality.[262]

A 2007 report by the British Medical Association's Board of Science concluded that 'it seems almost impossible to create a delivery system which would ensure an evenly distributed dose and which would produce a response in a fast and effective way'.[263]

Whereas the military have sought to deliver incapacitating biochemical agents over a wide area to affect a group of people, police weapons developers have investigated projectiles targeted at an individual that deliver the agent by absorption through the skin. Even this approach, however, does not allow for tailoring the dose to each individual targeted. Dart guns for intramuscular delivery have been ruled out as impractical due to risks of causing serious injury through hitting an unintended area, and dangers of hitting a blood vessel, which could result in overdose.[264]

Based on these realities it seems inconceivable that the dose can be controlled beyond a certain extent through delivery system development alone. Therefore efforts are codependent on the aforementioned technical issues of developing agents, mixtures of agents, or combinations of agents and antidotes, which combine very high safety margins with sufficient potency. It is exactly this combination of technical advances that weapons developers appear to be relying on.[265] Writing in 2003, one proponent claimed that such developments may be within the reach of ongoing secretive research efforts.[266] However, the British Medical Association has cautioned that, independent of ethical issues, the use of drugs as 'non-lethal' weapons is not technically feasible, and an assessment by the Federation of American Scientists has concluded that 'genuinely non-lethal chemical weapons are beyond the reach of current science'.[267]

5.4.2   Pushing the legal boundaries

Clearly a major factor affecting the development of incapacitating biochemical weapons has been the emergence of international legal regimes prohibiting chemical and biological weapons. According to the NRC panel US military research and development of incapacitating agent weapons was initially halted in the early 1990s due to the negotiation of the CWC.[268] However, this respite was temporary and not all encompassing. Closely related research had continued to be sponsored by the NIJ and by the late 1990s the military programme itself had been revived. As discussed in earlier chapters, the CWC prohibits the development and use of any toxic chemical as a weapon. However, although it prohibits the use of RCAs (irritant chemical weapons) as a 'method of warfare', it permits their use for 'law enforcement including domestic riot control'.[269] Rather than limiting military interest in chemical weapons to irritant agents for use in specific circumstances such as civilian riot control, the US has pushed back against these restrictions in two interrelated ways. Firstly, the unique US position on RCAs, meaning that they do not view them as chemical weapons and that their national policy is not compatible with international law,[270] has been maintained with efforts by the DOD to advocate widening of RCA use to warfare.[271] Secondly, the US has attempted to present incapacitating agents as new RCAs despite their different mechanisms of action, and suggested that incapacitating agents could be designed that better fit the definition of RCAs.[272] The seeds for this strategy were sown during the negotiation of the CWC when ambiguities in the text were secured that left room for differing interpretations.[273]

The UK Northern Ireland Office has noted that the prohibition on the use of RCAs in warfare serves to provide legal obstacles to countries that want to develop inappropriate agents as RCAs and inappropriate delivery systems for RCAs, such as mortar and artillery rounds.[274] However, this has not prevented the US military from pursuing this exact strategy. In the 2000 report of a US/UK seminar the US has gone so far as to say:

> [A] research and development program with respect to ... chemically based calmatives as an RCA [riot control agent] ... [will] be continued as long as it is cost-productive to do so.[275]

This desire to circumnavigate legal strictures appears to be driven by a belief in the operational utility of incapacitating biochemical weapons for US military operations. The same 2000 report observed:

> During the war game scenarios, numerous participants expressed the desire to have a NLW [non-lethal weapon] that could quickly incapacitate individuals with little or no after-effects. The participants desired this NLW to be employed in a variety of scenarios ranging from crowd control to incapacitating enemy combatants. Generally, a chemically based calmative agent was viewed as the technology that could provide this capability.[276]

Of course, the use of chemical weapons for 'incapacitating enemy combatants' would clearly violate the CWC. Nevertheless it has been argued that the Convention does not prohibit their use by the military in situations such as crowd control, peacekeeping, and humanitarian relief operations.[277] And this leads back to the central issue of 'law enforcement' not being defined by the CWC from the outset.[278] This leaves open the possibility, as Dando has emphasised, of different interpretations on where law enforcement ends and a method of warfare begins.[279]

Furthermore there are differences of opinion on whether the CWC permits the use of any other chemical agents apart from RCAs (i.e. irritant chemical weapons) for 'law enforcement including domestic riot control'. Krutzsch and others have argued that it does not,[280] whereas Fidler has argued that chemical agents permitted for these purposes are not limited to RCAs.[281] Fidler notes that this point of view is reinforced by the muted reaction by other States to the Russian use of incapacitating agents in 2002. Indeed events in Moscow are likely to have increased interest in the development of incapacitating agents,[282] especially as the operation was considered a success among many observers including NATO's panel on 'non-lethal' weapons.[283]

Pearson has expressed concerns that observing ongoing developments in Russia and the US, more countries may become interested in these weapons, believing 'not only that effective and acceptably "non-lethal" incapacitating agents can be found, but that their use will be legitimized'.[284] This 'creeping legitimization' of new biochemical weapons, as described by Perry Robinson,[285] is seen as the greatest threat to the existing prohibitions on chemical and biological weapons by arms control researchers[286] and a contributing factor to what Wheelis and Dando have termed the imminent 'militarization of biology'.[287] However, the political response to the legal challenge presented by continued development of incapacitating biochemical weapons has been avoidance of the issue. The First Review Conference of the CWC in 2003 failed to address the topic, even with events of Moscow fresh in the memory.[288] At the Second Review Conference in 2008 there were some efforts to begin a discussion between countries on this issue although these were ultimately fruitless.[289] Discussions in the context of the BWC have remained peripheral.[290] However, with the confluence of chemistry and biology brought about by an increasingly molecular basis of understanding life processes, the relevance of the BWC to this issue has been emphasised.[291] There is no exemption in the BWC akin to the CWC's 'law enforcement' provision.[292] Naturally occurring bioregulators and toxins are covered by the BWC as well as their synthetic chemical analogues (i.e. drugs) that bind to the same receptor sites in the body.[293] Nevertheless even naturally occurring peptide bioregulators have been put forward as potential incapacitating agents.[294]

All the while others in related defence communities warn of the emergence of 'advanced biological warfare agents' that may be 'rationally engineered to target specific human biological systems at the molecular level' having a variety of effects 'including death, incapacitation, neurological impairment'.[295] Bioregulator agents are one potential class of advanced biological weapon, considered in the past as more potent replacements for classical chemical weapons.[296] A joint committee of the US Institute of Medicine and the NRC addressing 'Advances in Technology and the Prevention of Their Application to Next Generation Biowarfare Threats' also drew attention to the danger of bioregulator weapons.[297] The contradiction is glaring when biochemical weapons are promoted, on the one hand, as counterterrorist weapons while warnings are issued of the grave threat to international security from the development and proliferation of the very same class of weapons. The two are separated by the gulf in terminology: 'non-lethal' weapons versus weapons of mass destruction.

5.4.3 Advocacy

Advocacy has been another important factor affecting the development of incapacitating biochemical agents during past[298] and under contemporary weapons programmes. One of the most prominent US organisations addressing the issue of 'non-lethal' weapons has been the Washington, DC-based think tank the Council on Foreign Relations. In their 1995 report the panel acknowledged the CWC's prohibitions of chemical weapons but argued: 'It would, of course, be a tragic irony if nations used lethal means against non-combatants because non-lethal means were banned by an international convention'.[299] A follow-up report published in 1999 argued that: 'On occasion, U.S. security might be improved by a modification to a treaty such as the Chemical Weapons Convention or the Biological Weapons Convention'.[300] However, Fidler has reflected on a possible 'sea change' in opinion illustrated by their most recent report from 2004.[301] With a realisation of the wider dangers associated with pursuing new biochemical weapons the their report concluded:

> The Task Force believes that to press for an amendment to the CWC or even to assert a right to use RCAs as a method of warfare risks impairing the legitimacy of all NLW. This would also free others to openly and legitimately conduct focused governmental R&D that could more readily yield advanced lethal agents than improved nonlethal capabilities. ... Accordingly, the Task Force judges that on balance the best course for the United States is to reaffirm its commitment to the CWC and the BWC and to be a leader in ensuring that other nations comply with the treaties.[302]

Furthermore the report even expressed doubt about the operational viability of military incapacitating agent weapons:

> We note also that we have seen no full scenarios for the use of calmatives. What happens in a situation where, after everyone is confused or knocked out, they begin to revive, and the United States does not have an overwhelming presence?[303]

As was clear from the preface to the 2003 NRC report on 'non-lethal' weapons, the State Department seems to concur with the concerns expressed by the Council on Foreign Relations.[304] Nevertheless this message seems to receive scant recognition at the DOD, where advocates have continued to argue against this position. The DSB, which advises the DOD on science and technology matters, has urged the development of biochemical weapons regardless of the international legal prohibitions, as in a 1994 report on urban operations:

> [I]t seems reasonable to us that the U.S. should develop promising non-lethal chemical agents that can disperse crowds, calm rioters, or disable hostiles, and as a minimum, have select capabilities on hand *even though we may be prohibited from employing them*[305] [emphasis added].

Ten years later, in a 2004 report addressing 'Future Strategic Strike Forces', the DSB recommended that: 'Applications of biological, chemical or electromagnetic radiation effects on humans should be pursued'.[306] In the section on 'strategic payload concepts' the report argued that: 'Calmatives might be considered to deal with otherwise difficult situations in which neutralizing individuals could enable ultimate mission success'.[307]

A 2004 NATO report also listed incapacitating biochemical weapons among 'technologies of interest'.[308] Nevertheless military frustrations were evident at a 2005 JNLWD conference on 'non-lethal' weapons, where a military lawyer from the office of the US Navy's Judge Advocate General (JAG) doubted the legality of incapacitating biochemical weapons for the military.[309] More recently, a 2006 paper published by the US Air War College argued for the US to reject the CWC in order to enable the development and use of incapacitating biochemical weapons in the so-called 'war on terror'.[310]

An important element of advocacy, evident throughout the history of efforts to develop incapacitating biochemical weapons, has been that emanating from the institutions that are responsible for weapons research and development. In an editorial rueing the missed opportunity to address the issue at the First Review Conference of the CWC in 2003, Meselson and Perry Robinson made the point succinctly:

> There is another kind of escalation, which is the fostering of the growth and influence of institutions that are dependent upon the development and weaponization of chemical agents. Such institutions and their associated bureaucracies and dependent communities inevitably become a source of pressure for doing more in this area, and for promoting the assimilation of chemical weapons into the structures and doctrine of state forces.[311]

5.4.4   The role of scientists and public opinion

Another related factor has been the support and collaboration of scientists outside these dependent military institutions. Many of these have been medical doctors since weapons developers have sought to draw on expertise in anaesthesiology. Following the Moscow theatre siege, a prominent US anaesthesiologist advocated the further research and development of incapacitating biochemical weapons.[312] Writing in the *Annals of Emergency Medicine*, three medical toxicologists expressed the same view:

> The use of a 'sleeping gas' or calmative agent in this setting is a novel attempt at saving the most lives. ... Greater collaboration between clinicians and military planners is encouraged.[313]

Similarly, the broad-brush issue of counterterrorism is apparently a driver for the Czech anaesthetists currently collaborating on the development of these weapons, who have argued:

> [M]any agents used in everyday practice in anesthesiology can be employed as pharmacological non-lethal weapons. An anesthetist familiar with the pharmacokinetics and pharmacodynamics of these agents is thus familiar with this use. As a result, he or she can play a role in combating terrorism.[314]

Issues of medical ethics go unaddressed in these papers, the powerful combination of the 'non-lethal' weapons moniker and the rhetoric of the 'war on terror' apparently reducing the concerns that a doctor might have in collaborating with the development of drugs as weapons rather than as treatments. Others have raised concerns about these issues.[315] Coupland, for example, has pointed out that 'medical professionals could easily be caught in a spiral of weapon development and counter-measure'.[316] The British Medical Association has warned against the use of drugs as weapons, raising pharmacological, clinical, ethical, and legal concerns.[317]

Of course wider public opinion also influences the development of these weapons. As the international prohibitions of chemical and biological weapons have become normalised, so public opinion has tended to reflect these norms. This is reinforced by the overriding contemporary discourse of terrorism, which emphasises the threat of weapons of mass destruction, chemical and biological weapons included. For these reasons developers of incapacitating biochemical weapons have sought to reframe them as somehow separate while carrying out research and development in secret. In fact, the issue of secrecy may turn out to be counterproductive in terms of garnering support for these weapons. During the Cold War programme, as Furmanski has observed, secrecy contributed to the lack of public and political support for incapacitating agents while the more open consideration of sensory irritant chemicals aided their acceptance.[318] Nevertheless the softening and manipulation of language is a powerful tool. Under the overall 'non-lethal' banner, toxic biochemical agents are described as 'calmatives' and weapons are put forward as 'techniques' or 'capabilities'. Invoking the fear of terrorism, including chemical terrorism and bioterrorism, the development of these very weapons is then, paradoxically, presented as a practical counterterrorism solution. Perhaps the tacit support of the US President and the UK Prime Minister of the use of biochemical weapons by Russian forces during the Moscow theatre siege in 2002 is a measure of proponent's success in clouding the issue.[319]

5.5 Conclusion

Although significant advances in science and technology over the past 60 years of weapons development have certainly lowered the bar considerably to producing a 'non-lethal' incapacitating biochemical weapon, these efforts have failed due to technical realities that may prove insurmountable. Nevertheless the perceived potential for a scientific solution has seemingly been sufficient to maintain interest and sustain weapons research and development despite international legal constraints.[320] Meanwhile operational demand has increased due to the contemporary focus on counterterrorism and the perceived requirement for 'non-lethal' weapons. This process has perhaps gained new impetus since the first large-scale use of these weapons in Moscow in 2002, which apparently proved acceptable to the international community, even though the results could not conceivably be described as 'non-lethal'.[321] The continuing military and police interest in incapacitating biochemical weapons means that we now sit at the brink of wider proliferation, and erosion of the international prohibitions of chemical and biological weapons, unless greater political attention can be brought to bear in constraining weapons development.

6
Directed Energy Weapons

This chapter explores programmes to develop 'non-lethal' directed energy weapons. It focuses on events in the US, tracking the weapons programmes administered by the DOD and the DOJ. Although related research and development efforts were underway in the 1960s and 1970s, 'non-lethal' applications were not proposed seriously until the late 1980s.

6.1 Definitions

The DOD defines directed energy as 'an umbrella term covering technologies that relate to the production of a beam of concentrated electromagnetic energy or atomic or subatomic particles' and a directed energy weapon as 'a system using directed energy primarily as a direct means to damage or destroy enemy equipment, facilities, and personnel'.[1] Proposed directed energy weapons employ beams of energy in various regions of the electromagnetic spectrum, as illustrated in Table 6.1. Generally speaking the field of directed energy weapons encompasses two major areas: lasers[2] operating in the visible, ultraviolet, or infrared part of the spectrum; and equipment generating radio frequency, microwave, or millimetre wave beams.

First and foremost it is important to note, as the DOD definition would suggest, that the primary impetus for research on directed energy weapons is the development of revolutionary new 'lethal' weapons systems having the advantages of speed-of-light action, precision effects, and unlimited 'ammunition'.[4] As Rogers noted in 2002:

> The impact of directed energy weapons over the next quarter of a century could be huge, and some analysts argue that they are as potentially revolutionary as was the development of nuclear weapons sixty years ago.[5]

The main areas of research and development focus on high energy lasers, for strategic defence against ballistic missiles and tactical destruction of various military targets (e.g. aircraft, rockets, people) and high-power

Table 6.1　The electromagnetic spectrum[3]

Type	ELF, VF, VLF, LF	Radio-, Micro-, Millimetre-wave	Infrared	Visible – ROYGBIV	UV	X-ray, γ-ray
Frequency →	Less than 300 kHz	300 kHz –300 GHz	300 GHz –375 THz	375 THz –750 THz	375 THz –30 PHz	More than 30 PHz
Wavelength ←	More than 1 km	1 km–1 mm	1 mm– 800 nm	800 nm –400 nm	400 nm– 10 nm	Less than 10 nm
Effect	←――――――――― Non-ionizing ――――――――→				←―― Ionizing ――→	

microwaves (HPM) for tactical or strategic destruction of electronic infrastructure. Nevertheless certain 'non-lethal' directed energy applications have been proposed and presented as the foremost area of 'non-lethal' weapons development.[6]

Confusing matters even further is the concept of weapons with variable effects from 'lethal' to 'non-lethal', which was outlined by the Marine Corps in 1998 when the JNLWP was established.[7] In 2004 the Council on Foreign Relations went so far as to suggest that the ideal 'non-lethal' weapon '... would be a system with continuously variable intensity and influence, ranging from a warning tap to a stunning blow to a lethal effect'.[8]

Directed energy weapons are seen by the military as the most promising opportunity to develop such a capability.[9]

Those directed energy weapons presented as 'non-lethal' weapons can be divided into three main categories: low energy lasers; high energy lasers; and radio frequency, microwave, and millimetre wave devices.[10] The latter are often referred to by some authors as 'radiofrequency weapons' or 'microwave weapons' although concepts span a variety of frequencies.

6.1.1　Lasers

Prior to the ban on blinding laser weapons, agreed in 1995, the primary purpose of anti-personnel low energy laser weapons was to cause permanent eye damage. Subsequently, the aim of weapons developers has been to target the human eye to cause temporary visual disturbance (glare) or flashblindness, defined as follows:

> Glare can be defined as a relatively bright light in the visual field that degrades vision and may cause discomfort as long as the light is in the visual field. With flashblindness, the light is bright enough to cause a significant effect on the retinal adaptation level so that there is a period of a loss of visual sensitivity after the light source has been removed.[11]

These laser weapons commonly employ either laser diodes producing laser light in the red portion of the visible spectrum or solid-state lasers producing green light. Generally speaking these devices use Class 3b lasers, with powers from 5 milliwatts (mW) to a maximum of 500 mW. In contrast, laser pointers have power levels below 5 mW.[12] It is important to note that Class 3b lasers are capable of causing permanent eye damage depending on the power level entering the eye, itself dependent on the range, power output, and duration of exposure. Lasers with power levels above 500 mW are classified as Class 4 and can present a hazard to both the eyes and skin.[13] Even lasers with powers of up to several watts have been proposed as 'non-lethal' 'dazzling' lasers for use at long range.

There is no set definition of high energy laser weapons in terms of power levels although they are generally considered to be from tens of thousands of watts up to megawatt (a million watts) levels.[14] They may be defined in terms of effects, as Anderberg and Wolbarsht have noted:

> High-energy lasers may be used to melt holes through metal and plastic structures at reasonable distances, to set fire to objects, to burn a soldier's skin, and to destroy optics and electro-optical systems at long ranges.[15]

As such, high energy lasers are 'lethal' weapons technologies. Nevertheless, several conceptual mechanisms have been proposed for eliciting 'non-lethal' effects. One is the use of a pulsed laser to form a high energy plasma at the surface of the target person that explodes to produce a kinetic shock wave. Another is the use of a pulsed laser to form plasma 'channels' that might conduct electrical energy, with a view to developing wireless electrical weapons. A further concept is the use of a high energy laser to heat the skin to levels below the threshold for permanent damage.

Lasers are classified according to the type of material ('lasing medium') used to generate the laser beam. Solid-state lasers use a rod of crystal or glass containing ('doped with') an active material (e.g. alexandrite, neodymium). Semiconductor lasers or laser diodes, use a semiconductor material as the lasing medium doped with thin layers of active material. Fibre lasers use optical fibres as the medium doped with an active material. The laser beam is created by energising ('pumping') the lasing medium. Solid-state lasers can be pumped with a bright light source ('optical pumping') or a laser diode ('diode pumping'). Laser diodes are pumped with an electrical current. Fibre lasers tend to be pumped with a laser diode. Solid-state, laser diode, and fibre laser systems can all be powered electrically. Chemical lasers, on the other hand, use various chemicals as the lasing medium and require special chemical fuel to operate. Gas lasers use various gases as the lasing medium and are often pumped by an electrical discharge.[16]

6.1.2   Radio frequency, microwave, and millimetre wave beams

Electromagnetic generators employ a wide range of electromagnetic energy, from radio wave to microwave and up to millimetre wave frequencies, depending on the application. The primary area of known weapons development relates to HPM weapons to destroy or degrade electronic systems.[17] However, radio frequencies, microwaves, and millimetre waves can have a variety of biological effects on humans depending on numerous parameters including the power level, frequency, exposure duration, nature of the beam, and the part of the body affected.[18] As Geis has observed:

> [S]cientists have demonstrated a myriad of microwave effects among which are biological changes on the cellular level, changes in brain chemistry and function, changes in cardiovascular function, creation of lesions within the eye, temporary incapacitation, and even death.[19]

The complex human effects of radio frequencies, microwaves, and millimetre waves are not fully understood and research is ongoing. The main mechanism of action on biological tissue is heating and many effects are mediated by a rise in temperature in a given area of the body. Other effects are thought not to be related to heating, so-called non-thermal effects.[20] Clearly, damaging and lethal effects are possible through this heating mechanism at high power levels in the same way that a microwave oven cooks food. However, 'non-lethal' weapons applications have been proposed based on certain exposure types. Major areas of investigation include: the use of millimetre wave energy to heat skin and cause pain; and the use of microwaves to interfere with brain function, alter behaviour, and interfere with hearing, among other effects.[21] Like many areas of 'non-lethal' weapons development, research is rather secretive and so the exact scope and extent of weapons programmes, whether intended as 'non-lethal' or 'lethal', is difficult to ascertain. It is also obscured by the conspiracy theories that surround this field, which arise from the reality of military interest in using electromagnetic radiation to modify or control behaviour; so-called 'mind control'.[22]

6.2   Low energy laser weapons

6.2.1   Past programmes

Military investigation quickly followed the discovery of the laser in 1960, but concepts of revolutionary laser weaponry were unrealistic due to the low power of existing devices. Nevertheless low power lasers soon entered use as rangefinders and, during the Vietnam War, laser designators were developed to enable more accurate targeting of conventional bombs.[23] However, reports and rumours of the use of these devices against human eyes[24] combined with their widespread proliferation led to increased concerns over the risk of laser injuries in combat.[25]

By 1980 laser weapons intentionally targeting the human eye were already under development. The logistical limitations of high energy lasers had led to consideration of battlefield targets that would be particularly vulnerable to low energy lasers, such as electro-optical sensors and human eyes.[26] Furthermore, the relatively cheap nature of low energy lasers made them attractive weapons.[27] Their perceived tactical role was described in a 1987 *Military Review* article:

> BLWs [battlefield laser weapons] primarily seek to destroy vision systems – systems that have never before been specifically attacked. ... BLWs attack episcopes, periscopes, telescopes, night vision scopes, tracking devices or fire-and-forget missiles and 'remoted' [*sic*] close-circuit television. ... BLWs can directly attack the enemy's eyes.[28]

The author envisaged three levels of attack: to distract and cause the enemy to employ protective equipment, to temporarily 'dazzle' or flash-blind, or to permanently damage optical systems and human eyes. The concept of temporary 'dazzling', which would later become the focus of 'non-lethal' weapons concepts, was conceived as a means of temporary incapacitation without causing eye damage.[29]

The article noted that the use of this 'dazzling' tactic could prove far more dangerous if used against a person flying an aircraft, for example. In fact a ship-mounted system for that very purpose called the Laser Dazzle Sight (LDS) had already been deployed by the British Navy and used during the Falklands War in 1982. Despite its name the LDS was capable of causing eye damage at considerable distances.[30]

6.2.1.1 *Blinding lasers*

In any case, the development of weapons specifically designed to cause *permanent* eye damage, either directly or indirectly through targeted optical equipment, had been continuing apace during the 1980s.[31] Although these could not be described as 'non-lethal' weapons due to the irreversible damage caused to human eyes, it is necessary to detail the various programmes for two reasons. Firstly, they were presented as one of the major technologies in new concepts of 'antimateriel' or 'disabling' technologies emerging in the 1980s.[32] These same concepts, which initially emphasised incapacitation of military equipment (e.g. damage of sensors by lasers) to increase vulnerability to conventional attack, were essentially reframed as 'non-lethal' weapons technologies in the early 1990s, but the weapons remained the same and included lasers designed to blind.[33] Secondly, these laser weapons are the systems from which lasers designed to cause only temporary blinding or 'dazzling' would later emerge.

Early US laser weapons under development included the helicopter-mounted ALQ-169 Optical Warning Location/Detection device, which was developed in the late 1970s before the programme was cancelled in 1986.[34] Another was the Close Combat Laser Assault Weapon (C-CLAW) developed by the Army in the early 1980s, which was envisaged as a weapon for damaging glass optics and windscreens. Press reports that the prototype weapon, called Roadrunner, would be capable of blinding were not well received and this may have contributed to its demise in 1983. However, the Army's attention turned to another system under development by Martin Marietta Electronic Systems called the Stingray, also capable of blinding those viewing the optical sensors it was designed to target. A vehicle-mounted prototype was field tested in 1986 and two were deployed during the 1991 Gulf War but not used.[35] Alexander's 1989 article described the Stingray as 'classic antimateriel technology'.[36] By 1995 it had reached the advanced development stage.[37] A related prototype employing the same laser technology but in a more compact design was the Outrider weapon, also a vehicle-mounted laser that was being described by Martin Marietta in 1994 as a 'nonlethal technology option for low intensity conflicts and special operations'.[38] Another Stingray-related weapon called the Cameo Bluejay was developed by Lockheed Sanders for the Army in a programme that was cancelled in 1989.[39]

Meanwhile the Air Force had also been developing blinding laser weapons, including a prototype weapon called the Coronet Prince (AN/ALQ-179), which was built in 1985 and flight tested in 1989 before plans for full-scale development were curtailed in 1991 due to other priorities.[40] An associated Air Force development programme was called Compass Hammer.[41]

6.2.1.2 Laser rifles

Although these weapons were capable of damaging the eye either directly or as a side effect of their use against sensors, their primary targets were presented as the electro-optical sensors on military equipment such as tanks and aircraft. However, programmes to develop smaller hand-held anti-eye weapons were also underway in the 1980s, enabled by the emergence of more powerful solid-state lasers, which allowed the design of smaller systems.[42]

Information about secretive US weapons programmes began to emerge in the late 1980s and early 1990s. Three companies were competing to develop such a laser weapon for the Army. The first to be made public was the Dazer developed by Allied Corp., which consisted of a laser rifle with associated backpack containing the electronics and battery pack, and employed a Class 4 alexandrite solid-state laser. One of the reasons for using this type of laser was that the wavelength could be varied in order to make countermeasures more difficult. With a range of 1 km and capable of permanent blinding, it was designed for use by infantry against sensors and the human eye and tested as early as 1981.[43]

The Dazer was not chosen by the Army and the prototypes were transferred to Special Operations Command (SOCOM).[44] A similar weapon called the Cobra was developed by McDonnell-Douglas, which employed a solid-state laser operating at three different wavelengths to defeat countermeasures.[45] A third system called the AN/PLQ-5, developed by Lockheed Sanders, was eventually selected as the Army's Laser Countermeasure System (LCMS). Similar in size and operation to the other two weapons it was mounted on an M-16 rifle and was capable of causing permanent eye damage and blindness at ranges up to 1 km.[46] In May 1995 the company was awarded a $12 million contract to produce 20 of these weapons by July 1997.[47] However, the LCMS programme was cancelled in October 1995 due to the agreement of Protocol IV[48] to the CCW, which banned blinding lasers.[49] As discussed in Chapters 3 and 4, international pressure from the ICRC,[50] Human Rights Watch,[51] and some countries led to the ban, which came into force in 1998. However, the Protocol specifically did not prohibit anti-optics laser weapons and development of these continued.[52] Indeed a 1997 editorial in the *British Medical Journal* warned of continued dangers:

> Unfortunately, although antipersonnel systems should now not be manufactured or deployed by signatory countries, the efficiency of rangefinders, target illuminators, and antisensor systems is such that no countries will relinquish them, and these are still effectively antipersonnel laser weapons.[53]

6.2.1.3 'Dazzling' lasers

There was initial optimism that development of laser weapons purposefully designed to target the human eye would cease.[54] However, this was short-lived as it emerged that attention had simply shifted towards the development of so-called 'dazzling' laser weapons[55] that would, it was envisaged, cause temporary blindness (flash-blindness) or visual disturbance without permanent adverse effects on the eyes. These were being promoted as a major 'non-lethal' weapons technology for the police and the military by the mid-1990s.[56] However, concern over the potential for permanent eye damage remained since a weapon that could cause reversible visual disturbance at long ranges could be capable of causing permanent damage at shorter ranges.[57] Some argued that these 'dazzling' weapons would only be viable at night:

> It is practically impossible to flash blind a person in broad daylight without also causing some lasting damage to the eyes. Flash blinding without any damage is only possible when the eye is dark adapted and, thus, much more sensitive to the incoming laser light.[58]

One 'dazzling' laser weapon that had already been developed by the time of the 1995 Protocol was the Saber 203 Laser Illuminator. It was a product of a research and development partnership from 1990 to 1993 between the Air Force Research Laboratory (AFRL), the Defense Nuclear Agency, and Science and Engineering Associates Inc.[59] It comprised a 250 mW red semiconductor laser diode system, which could be fitted to the M203 40 mm grenade launcher attachment for M-16 rifles, and fired a continuous beam for ten seconds before flickering on and off.[60]

Prototypes of the Saber 203 were taken by Marines to Somalia in 1995 where they were used a few times to deter armed men approaching soldiers at night. Apparently due to concerns over eye-safety they were not used to 'dazzle' but they were used to illuminate a large red laser spot on the person to indicate that lethal fire would follow if they approached.[61] Another prototype Air Force laser system taken to Somalia was a 532 nm green laser, which was also used to illuminate targets.[62] A 1996 AFRL paper described these two main categories of low energy laser weapons:

> The visible lasers that most readily lend themselves to these types of applications are 650-670nm (red) laser diodes. Solid-state lasers, such as doubled Nd/YAG that produce 532nm (green) light, are also being packaged into small (hand-held) units with high efficiencies. Both diode and solid-state laser types are small, lightweight, efficient, and capable of delivering watts of power with relatively small battery sources.[63]

6.2.2   Contemporary programmes: 'Dazzling' lasers

The use of these prototypes in Somalia was viewed favourably by the military and led to further development of 'dazzling' laser weapons by the Air Force. Operational tests of the Saber 203 were conducted during fiscal year 1998, but by the following year the programme was closed and attention shifted to two related weapons, the Laser Dissuader and the HALT (Hinder Adversaries with Less-than-lethal Technology).[64] The cancellation of the Saber 203 programme was largely due to concerns over eye-safety and limited utility during daylight conditions.[65] Another limitation had been the small diameter of the laser cone which was difficult to keep in the eyes of the target person, especially if they were moving.[66]

The Laser Dissuader, developed independently by Science and Engineering Associates Inc. by 1997, and shaped like a large torch of the kind used by US police, is built on the same laser diode technology of the Saber 203, but with a higher power and a variable beam. It operates in a continuous beam for the first ten seconds and then flickers on and off and can be focused in a narrow or wide beam to enable use at long and short ranges. Shortly after its development it was being marketed for use by a variety of US law enforcement agencies.[67] The HALT system was an adaptation of the Laser Dissuader technology for the Air Force, which enabled it to be either rifle-mounted or used independently. One of the major difference between the Laser Dissuader/HALT design and the Saber 203 was that the former was designed to be eye-safe at the aperture (i.e. point-blank range) whereas the latter was not eye-safe at ranges less than six metres.[68] However, this is somewhat misleading in that the Laser Dissuader/HALT would only be safe for a quarter of a second, representing the time taken for the blink response. The operational guideline for safe minimum range with the focused beam is 25 m, whereas the wide-angle setting can apparently be used at closer ranges. To illustrate the effects of optics, if viewing the beam through binoculars the Laser Dissuader would only be safe for a quarter of a second at a distance of 116 m or more.

Air Force tests found that Laser Dissuader would only cause 'minimal annoying glare' in daylight conditions but that at night it could cause flash-blindness at up to 50 m. The weapons passed the military legal review in 1999 and were given to other DOD organisations for operational evaluation[69] with bioeffects research carried out by the AFRL.[70] The Laser Dissuader weapon was listed as a standard US Air Force weapon in reviews of military 'non-lethal' weapons published by the DOJ in 2002 and 2004.[71] It costs $5000 and is available to the military and law enforcement agencies although it is not clear how widely it is used. Science and Engineering Associates Inc. merged with another company in 2004 to form Apogen Technologies,[72] which now sells the Laser Dissuader. It also sells related devices including the LazerShield, which incorporates a red laser diode on a plastic riot shield.[73]

As regards the HALT weapon, a review of the design and assessment of potential military and law enforcement users was conducted by the military in 1998[74] and a contract was awarded for development of two variants in 1999.[75] Further development and operational testing was carried out through to 2002[76] when the NRC report noted: 'Future plans for HALT include the capability for dual, red and blue wavelengths that flicker off and on to mitigate filtering by single-wavelength goggles'.[77] However, it appears that the HALT weapon programme has since been cancelled.

6.2.2.1 Green lasers

In addition to interest in red laser diodes as 'dazzling' weapons the Air Force has also investigated the use of green lasers. Building on experience of the use of the Saber 203 and a solid-state green laser in Somalia, the Air Force Phillips Laboratory developed the Humvee-mounted Battlefield Optical Surveillance System (BOSS) in the mid to late 1990s, which incorporated three different lasers: an 810 nm infrared laser for use with night vision equipment to illuminate; a 3 watt 670 nm red laser; and a 3 watt 532 nm green laser. These were significantly more powerful than the lasers employed in the Saber 203 and Laser Dissuader, and were designed for use at long range. The minimum range for use of the BOSS was 100 metres because of the danger of eye damage. A green laser was selected because the human eye is significantly more sensitive to that wavelength than the red laser.[78]

The development of 'dazzling' laser weapons had also been funded through the joint DOJ-DOD initiative on dual-use technologies for law enforcement and 'operations other than war'.[79] In June 1996 LE Systems Inc. was contracted to develop a torch-shaped laser weapon based around a diode pumped, solid state, 532 nm green laser.[80] The company gained input from the Air Force Phillips Laboratory and the NIJ on the design of the weapon and had produced ten prototypes by late 1997, calling the weapon the Laser Dazzler.[81] AFRL carried out an evaluation of the safety and effectiveness of the Laser Dazzler from September 1999 to October 2000.[82] The report of these tests compared the weapon with the red 'dazzling' laser weapons the Air Force itself had been developing and discussed some of the major issues surrounding the development of 'dazzling' laser weapons. It noted that the 650 nm red laser diode technology was available to the Air Force initially but that there was interest in shorter wavelength red lasers (632 nm) and green lasers (532 nm) in particular because the eye is over eight times more sensitive to the latter. The Air Force evaluation found the Laser Dazzler lacking, mainly because the divergent beam necessary for it to have a shorter eye hazard zone made it less effective during daytime. However, the report noted that this was the major limitation of all such eye-safe 'dazzling' laser weapons, which were only operationally effective at night. The authors suggested that if a green laser weapon was developed with an adjustable beam then it might be more effective during daytime conditions and have more potential for causing glare and flash-blinding due to the increased sensitivity of the eye to green light.[83]

Since the publication of the Air Force report LE Systems Inc. have made modifications to the Laser Dazzler weapon, adding a variable focus feature. The resulting torch-shaped system is a 200 mW green laser that is apparently eye-safe at the aperture for a quarter of a second exposure. By mid-2005 the company had also developed a more powerful weapon called the Compact High Power (CHP) Laser Dazzler with a 500 mW power output,[84] which is the upper limit classification as a Class 3b laser.[85] The CHP Laser Dazzler can cause permanent eye damage at close range and the company states that it should only be used at ranges of 25 m and beyond.[86] Subsequently the CHP Laser Dazzler has been approved for use by the Army and Special Operations Command but not by the Marine Corps, who requested it for use in Iraq in December 2006. It seems that testing at the Naval Surface Warfare Center raised some concerns over eye-safety.[87]

6.2.2.2 Deployment in Iraq

Several other green 'dazzling' laser weapons have now been approved for use by the US military in Iraq. This is a result of the problems experienced at vehicle checkpoints where soldiers have killed a number of innocent people who did not understand instructions to stop. Following the shooting of an Italian security agent in 2005 who was escorting a journalist recently freed from her kidnappers,[88] an enquiry recommended that more 'non-lethal' options should be considered.[89] A number of 'dazzling' laser weapons were evaluated by the JNLWD as a potential solution.[90] In February 2006, 2000 green laser devices were shipped to Iraq by the Army Rapid Equipping Force for use at checkpoints.[91]

An Army legal review approved the use of five different green 'dazzling' laser weapons, all of which are capable of causing permanent eye damage at short ranges, as described in an August 2006 paper in *Army Lawyer*:

> The XADS PD/G-105, MiniGreen, GBD III, HELIOS, and GHOST are Class 3b lasers with sufficient power (100, 75, 250, 465, and 120 mW, respectively) to cause ocular injury at short ranges (17, 18, 10, 10, and 8.2 meters, respectively, based on a 0.25-second unaided exposure) and temporary visual disorientation or flash-blindness at longer ranges. ... All five weapons have a disorienting or flash-blinding effect on targeted personnel up to at least 200 meters in daylight and 370 meters at night. These effects are temporary and have more impact in low-light conditions since the effect is exacerbated by the greater difference between the laser light and ambient light.[92]

In May 2006 the commanding general of US troops in Iraq said that the military had found 'dazzling' laser weapons 'very effective', were keen to deploy more, and were testing ten different weapons.[93] According to Xtreme Alternative Defense Systems (XADS), who manufacture the PD/G-105, their laser weapons have been deployed in Iraq and Afghanistan and have been purchased by various agencies including the Army Rapid Equipping Force and Special Operations Command.[94] Around 60 HELIOS systems had been deployed to Iraq by April 2006,[95] and at the end of 2006 the Marines purchased 400 GBD-IIIC weapons.[96] The company that manufactures the latter weapon, BE Meyers Inc., markets this technology in two devices called Glare and Glare MOUT. These 'dazzling' laser weapons were adapted from the GBD-III green laser system used for long-range target designating.[97] While the paper in *Army Lawyer* above mentions the potential for eye injury at up to 10 metres for a very short exposure, the company advises that its weapons can cause permanent eye damage at ranges up to 70 metres.[98]

6.2.2.3   *Enduring safety concerns*

Despite the increased power of these weapons, the JNLWD has softened the terminology used to describe them, now referring to them as 'optical distractors' rather than weapons.[99] A concern raised by the ICRC is that the safety of these weapons will be dependent on a soldier's ability to make quick judgements of safe distances in difficult operational conditions.[100] At the Third Review Conference of the CCW in November 2006 Germany and Sweden put forward a joint proposal to assess developments in laser technology since 1995 and considered design improvements for military lasers to avoid incidence of permanent blindness.[101] Human Rights Watch expressed particular concern over 'dazzling' lasers that might function as blinding lasers.[102] The proposal was not taken forward and the US delegation dismissed the need for the reassessment of 'dazzling' lasers arguing that they were old technologies.[103] However, given the increasing power of 'dazzling' laser weapons that have been deployed since 1995, it seems that these concerns are warranted.

6.2.2.4 Emerging prototypes

While a variety of low energy laser weapons have now reached deployment, research and development has continued. AFRL began an in-house project in 2001 to develop what they called the Portable Efficient Laser Testbed (PELT). JNLWD and NIJ provided funding for the system in fiscal year 2004[104] and further details emerged in November 2005,[105] by which time the name had been changed to Personnel Halting and Stimulation Response (PHaSR) and two rifle-sized prototypes had been built, one handed to JNLWD and the other to NIJ.[106] Initially the PELT was being designed as a laser weapon to heat the skin of the target person and was described as the 'first man-portable heat compliance weapon of its kind',[107] and the PHaSR appears to combine this function with a 'dazzling' laser, as described in a 2006 Air Force 'fact sheet':

> PHaSR achieves the desired degree of protection through the synergistic application of two non-lethal laser wavelengths during the course of protection activities that will deter, prevent, or mitigate an adversary's effectiveness. The laser light from PHaSR temporarily impairs aggressors by 'dazzling' them with one wavelength. The second wavelength causes a repel effect that discourages advancing aggressors.[108]

There is little information on the technical characteristics of the prototype PHaSR weapon but it uses two low power diode-pumped lasers. One has a visible wavelength, for 'dazzling', and the other a mid-infrared wavelength, presumably for causing the heating or 'repel effect'.[109] This latter mechanism appears to be described in a 2004 NATO report as a 'pain generation laser' for use against skin: 'It is an eye-safe laser which generates pain when the beam interacts with the skin (burning sensation without injuries). It can work through light clothes'.[110] Further details of the weapon, including the range, are reportedly classified.[111]

The ScorpWorks research group at AFRL's Directed Energy Directorate has been funded by the JNLWD and NIJ to develop a range finder[112] so that according to the developers, 'the maximum safe laser energy can be placed on target, regardless of range (near or far)'.[113]

AFRL unveiled another laser weapon in December 2005 called the Aircraft Countermeasures (ACCM) system, a 'dazzling' laser weapon apparently designed to be used in conjunction with helicopter machine guns to prevent attacks from individuals on the ground. Again there is little information available about the prototype system, which has been tested by AFRL and Air Force Special Operations Command.[114]

6.2.2.5 Alternative approaches to 'dazzling'

A variety of other techniques have been pursued in the development of 'dazzling' laser weapons. One is the so-called veiling glare laser, as described in the 2003 NRC report on 'non-lethal' weapons:

> A different approach to laser dazzlers, the proposed veiling glare system, would use a laser designed to produce violet light at 360 to 440 nm. At sufficiently high intensities, light as these wavelengths induces fluorescence in the human eye, which, in turn, produces diffuse, defocused light in the retina, appearing to the subject as omnidirectional.[115]

This technique had been investigated by researchers at AFRL in the early 1990s as a means of inducing longer lasting visual disturbance.[116] JNLWD funded further Air Force research,[117] which was due to be completed in fiscal year 2002.[118] When these details emerged some scientists expressed scepticism of the viability of the technique and warned that power of the beam needed to induce such an effect would damage the eye.[119] The NRC report acknowledged this gap in knowledge noting 'potential for optical damage to the retina or other portions of the eye remains uncertain'.[120] However, research into this veiling glare technique in partnership between AFRL and Northrop Grumman Corp. has continued with human testing of red, blue, and ultraviolet lasers.[121]

Another 'dazzling' laser weapons programme is underway through a collaboration of SARA Inc.,[122] Northeast Photosciences Inc.,[123] the Stress and Motivated Behaviour Institute (SMBI)[124] at New Jersey Medical School, and the Target Behavioral Response Laboratory (TBRL)[125] at the Army's ARDEC. SMBI itself was set up with funding from ARDEC in 2002 to provide the army with expertise in the neurobiology of stress and anxiety, particularly with the aim of developing new 'suppressive' weapons to induce these effects.[126] The TBRL and SMBI have been collaborating on investigating the effects of light (laser and white) as well as acoustics. The prototype 'dazzling' laser weapon is called the Multi-wavelength dazzler or 'ColorDazl' and was funded by NIJ in fiscal year 2004.[127] The system comprises two elements: a laser module with three lasers of different wavelengths, and a rangefinding technology. The latter operates by firing a low power infrared laser at the target person's eye and detecting the glint that is reflected. Based on the signal the power level of the laser module is adjusted to flash-blind the person, including if they are wearing protective eyewear.[128] The laser module itself contains three different lasers: a red 650 nm laser diode, a diode-pumped green 532 nm solid-state laser, and a violet/blue 405 nm laser diode, as proposed for the veiling glare effects.[129]

The developers claim that alternating red and blue laser light can create particular stroboscopic induced effects that can cause photosensitive epilepsy in a small percentage of the population and may cause nausea or dizziness in the general population.[130] This technique was discussed in a 2004 NATO report, which observed that laser glare and flash-blindness could be combined with a strobe for added effect, claiming: 'A stroboscopic effect of frequency between 7 and 12 Hz can provoke severe discomfort and nausea in a group of persons'.[131] However, a subsequent 2006 NATO report in 2006 cast doubt on the evidential basis for these effects.[132]

The US Army has also funded research and development of 'dazzling' laser weapons incorporating a strobe effect. In 2002 it funded Intelligent Optical Systems to develop a green laser weapon incorporating a multidirectional strobe effect for use against crowds.[133] The Department of Homeland Security (DHS) has funded the same company to develop a prototype 'dazzling' weapon in 2005 with follow-on funding until 2008 to carry out human tests with the prototype.[134] However, the weapon incorporates powerful light emitting diodes rather than lasers.[135] The use of bright flashing lights, as opposed to lasers, appears to be under consideration for use against groups of people since the 'dazzling' laser weapons can only be used against individuals due to the narrow beam. The Army has requested Peak Beam Systems to adapt its standard powerful searchlight with a strobe function.[136]

6.3 High energy laser weapons

Ever since the discovery of the laser in 1960 the US military has sought high energy laser weapons that might complement conventional weapons. The overwhelming majority of investment in directed energy weapons has concerned the development of high energy laser weapons to heat targets with sufficient power to elicit destructive effects. Billions of dollars have been spent on chemical laser programmes such as the Air Force's Airborne Laser (ABL),[137] designed to destroy ballistic missiles in flight, and the Army's Tactical High-Energy Laser (THEL) for defending against artillery rocket attacks.[138] As such, high energy lasers would appear to have little relevance to concepts of 'non-lethal' weaponry. However, in recent years they have been presented as potential 'non-lethal' weapons, primarily in terms of hypothetical use against various objects, as described in the 2003 NRC report,

> 'high-energy laser' refers to a system with sufficient energy (and/or power) to ablate, melt, or burn material. Such systems can be lethal if directed against human beings. Their use as NLWs [non-lethal weapons] is intended for applications such as bursting automobile tires, rupturing fuel tanks, selectively cutting through electrical or communication lines, or setting fires. The advantage of such a system, if achievable, would be its capability for selective and precise targeting.[139]

The main example of this type of weapon currently under development is the Advanced Tactical Laser (ATL), a relative of the ABL that employs an aircraft mounted with 300 kilowatt chemical oxygen iodine laser (COIL).[140] So-called anti-materiel weapons are beyond the scope of this book, however this example illustrates an important issue that is relevant to the field as a whole. A destructive and lethal weapon is being marketed as 'non-lethal', entirely by virtue of perceived precision and intended targets.[141] Of course there is nothing to prevent it being used as a lethal weapon against human targets once it has been deployed. A conventional rifle could also be used to target vehicle tyres but it would not be described as a 'non-lethal' weapon.

Nevertheless other types of high energy lasers are also being proposed as 'non-lethal' weapons for use against people. The major thrust of contemporary research and development efforts relates to the use of pulsed lasers to form a high energy plasma (ionized gas), which in turn produces a kinetic shock wave.[142] Another concept being pursued is the use of this laser-induced plasma phenomenon as a delivery system for electrical energy with a view to developing long-range, wireless electrical weapons. Research is also underway with the aim of using high energy lasers to heat the skin and cause pain without causing permanent damage.

6.3.1   Laser-induced plasma: The Pulsed Energy Projectile

Details of a US military programme to develop a pulsed chemical laser for use against people and objects began to emerge in the early 1990s.[143] The development effort was part of the Army's Low Collateral Damage Munitions (LCDM) programme,[144] which was charged with developing unconventional weapons with variable effects.[145] The laser weapons programme was called the Pulsed Impulsive Kill Laser (PIKL), a joint effort with Los Alamos National Laboratory (LANL) and the Air Force's Armstrong Laboratory to develop a vehicle-mounted weapon with a range of 1–2 km.[146] As the name would suggest the developers did not envision 'non-lethal' reversible effects. In 2000 and 2002 the Air Force researchers outlined the concept of a high energy laser pulse producing a plasma at the target surface, which in turn produces powerful impulses that 'can literally chew through target material'.[147] For a human target this would mean tissue damage resulting in 'incapacitation or death'.[148]

The PIKL programme began in 1992 and comprised two concurrent research efforts: the development of a prototype pulsed deuterium-fluoride (DF) chemical laser at LANL and studies of the bioeffects of pulsed lasers at the AFRL's Armstrong Laboratory. A chemical laser was selected to enable sufficient power and portability and the DF laser was chosen in particular because of its good transmission through the atmosphere.[149] In their 1992 book on laser weapons Anderberg and Wolbarsht observed that 'the DF laser is still a realistic option for a battlefield laser weapon'.[150] Laboratory tests were conducted in 1992 at LANL followed by tests with a compact prototype in May 1993. Further refinements were made before another prototype was tested in December 1993. This system demonstrated the principle of producing high energy pulses and was used to conduct tests on various surfaces including chamois leather as a skin simulant, military uniform material, and kevlar bulletproof vest material. The researchers concluded that the effects produced with single pulses were 'two orders of magnitude below those needed to produce serious injuries' but that multiple pulses caused 'moderate to severe damage'.[151]

By 1998 LANL had teamed up with Mission Research Corp., with funding from the JNLWD with the aim of developing the PIKL technology into a weapon with variable effects from 'non-lethal' to 'lethal'.[152] The developmental weapon was renamed the Pulsed Energy Projectile (PEP) and described by the JNLWD as follows:

> PEP would utilise a pulsed deuterium-fluoride (DF) laser designed to produce an ionised plasma at the target surface. In turn, the plasma would produce an ultrasonic pressure wave that would pass into the body, stimulating the cutaneous nerves in the skin to produce pain and induce temporary paralysis. The proposed PEP system would accomplish this at extended ranges.[153]

Despite the softening of the language and envisioned 'non-lethal' effects, the NRC panel were unconvinced, raising concerns over some tests with skin simulant where 'penetration depth was greater than expected' and others where 'it was found that clothing could be burned away by PEP radiation or by the plasma it produced'.[154] Hambling has been more explicit about the potential dangers of high-pressure shockwaves:

> A hit in the mouth could result in lung rupture from the blast pressure, and an impact on the chest or abdomen could damage internal organs. A strike anywhere near the ear would be literally deafening. There is also the question of what the effects might be on eyes. An explosion on the surface of the eyeball would probably result in blinding, and might be lethal.[155]

In addition to safety concerns, the NRC panel questioned the practicality of pursuing any chemical laser weapons.[156] However, they proposed that the solid-state lasers may present an alternative for development of the PEP and a major recommendation was for increased research in this area.[157] This shift from chemical to solid-state laser technology had previously been put forward by the PEP developers, who argued that solid-state lasers offered advantages in terms of smaller size, lower weight, and ease of use.[158]

In the period from fiscal year 2002 to 2006 the JNLWD spent around $13 million on the PEP with the aim of exploring the laser hardware and attempting to characterise human effects that might be viable for use as a 'non-lethal' weapon.[159] Further investment averaging around $4 million per year was planned for fiscal years 2007 to 2009.[160] There is little publicly available information about this secretive programme but some details have emerged. In July 2004 the Office of Naval Research funded a research project on 'Sensory Consequences of Electromagnetic Pulses Emitted by Laser Induced Plasmas'[161] to be conducted by the Neuroscience Division at The University of Florida College of Dentistry[162] and the College of Optics and Photonics at the University of Central Florida.[163] Although heavily redacted in parts, the contract document gives some insight into the development of the conceptual PEP weapon and its perceived utility:

> Recent advances in directed energy weapons technology suggests that scalable, non-lethal to lethal force systems may be possible. Such a system would be useful in many environments. Two systems currently under development, active denial and pulsed energy (ADS and PEP) offer mainly complimentary capacities that could address multiple tasks ... [REDACTED]. The full capability of these directed energy systems (DE) are still being explored. At their current stage of development, each system has clear non-lethal (ADS) and lethal (PEP) capacities suitable to the above tasks. Our experiments will examine the feasibility of using the plasma derived EMP [electromagnetic pulse] to induce pain suitable to disarm and deter individuals or form barriers to the movement of large hostile groups.
>
> The efficiency and lethality of PEP weapons systems are straightforward. The non-ballistic, instantaneous properties of DE make precise targeting a straightforward matter of line of sight. Terrific amounts of energy can be delivered over great distances with pinpoint accuracy.[164]

Clearly the pulsed laser technology is seen as viable for delivering sufficient energy to cause serious injury or death. However, the purpose of the research was to assess the viability of 'non-lethal' effects by causing pain without permanent damage.

The contract document also emphasised that advances in solid-state laser technology were increasing interest in the development of lasers as 'non-lethal' weapons. The researchers planned to apply technical developments in ultra-short pulse lasers, such as femtosecond lasers, to assess the potential of using laser-induced plasmas to cause pain by activating nociceptors in the skin. Nociceptors are part of the peripheral nervous system that sense pain and transmit this information to the central nervous system.[165] The researchers planned to use in vitro sensory cell preparations to assess whether nociceptors could be activated to cause pain without damaging the cells, to find out the threshold at which the damage is caused, to determine which type of laser (micro-, nano-, or femtosecond pulsed) and 'pulse parameters' would be most effective, and to determine whether the degree of activation of the nociceptors, and therefore amount of pain caused, could be varied.

Both lead researchers on the contract made presentations on their work at a JNLWD-funded conference in late 2004.[166] A 2006 conference featured two further papers, apparently related to this ongoing research, which is funded in part by the JNLWD.[167]

This investigative research is the main openly available information on research related to the conceptual PEP weapon, and the concepts are clearly at an early stage of development. It is unclear what other research and development is being conducted in support of the project with the $4 million per year funding allocated to it. In 2008, however, the JNLWD did confirm that the chemical laser-based PEP research had been curtailed, indicating that ongoing research will focus on solid-state lasers.[168]

A related research and development effort on pulsed laser-induced plasma weapons has been carried out Sterling Photonics Inc., which received funding from both the JNLWD and the NIJ in fiscal year 2004.[169] The year-long contract for development of solid-state laser weapon technology was reported in *New Scientist* in May 2005 and was described by the NIJ as follows:

NIJ awarded Sterling Photonics Inc. a grant of $358,259 to develop a Compact Rugged Pulsed Laser Technology Platform for Counter-Personnel less lethal weapons. The focus of the project will be on less lethal weapons based on infrared laser-induced plasma shock-wave generation (plasma flash bang), aimed at disorienting the target person. This electrical laser technology has the potential of being compact, rugged, and battery operable, and as such should be highly portable, either for short duration operation in a personnel-carried backpack, or for extended durations with the use of generators.[170]

The Army has also funded research and development of pulsed laser weapons concepts, including $2.7 million for the Plasma Acoustic Dazzler Denial Systems Initiative (PADDS) at a company called Stellar Photonics.[171]

Femtosecond lasers are seen as a potential new area of investigation weapons developers in this area due to their unusual characteristics, as described by Beason:

The laser pulses occur so quickly that these short beams can penetrate materials faster then the material can react ... , and as a result the material doesn't heat up and is not damaged.

Myriad other phenomena occur because femtosecond laser pulses are so short that they, unlike normal, longer pulse or CW [continuous wave] lasers, don't react with the environment. For example, femtosecond lasers create filaments, or strands of plasma channels, when they propagate through the atmosphere. This channeling creates a 'self-focusing' effect, which in turn causes the femtosecond pulse not to spread out or diffract like a normal laser, and instead focuses into a much smaller spot than expected.[172]

6.3.2 Wireless electrical weapons

These laser-induced plasma channels are another area of current research in terms of 'non-lethal' weapons based around high energy lasers. The theory is that the plasma channels can be used to conduct an electrical discharge to a target person or object thus acting as a long-range electrical weapon. The concept of transmitting electrical energy through the air using conducting channels was investigated as early as the 1890s by Nikola Tesla and potential weapons applications were soon proposed.[173] This was long before the invention of the laser. However, since the 1960s, scientists have investigated using laser beams to conduct electrical discharges, primarily with a view to enabling laser-guided lightning discharges from clouds.[174] During the 1990s, attention turned to the use of ultra-short pulsed lasers for this purpose and it is these that are now being considered as laser-guided electrical weapons,[175] particularly as technological advances in solid-state lasers have decreased the size of these systems considerably.[176]

In January 2004 AFRL entered into a collaborative research partnership with Ionatron, Inc. to explore the viability of such laser weaponry.[177] The company's aim is to develop weapons that can be used to direct an electrical discharge against people, vehicles, electronic systems, or to disable mines or improvised explosive devices. As regards anti-personnel weapons the company envisages variable effects from 'non-lethal' to 'lethal'.[178] Ionatron signed similar research agreements with the Army's ARDEC and the Naval Surface Warfare Center (NSWC).[179] In early 2006 the NSWC granted $2.8 million in funding for continued research and development.[180]

Related research on using ultra-short pulsed lasers to transmit electrical discharges is also ongoing at the Naval Research Laboratory.[181] Budget documentation allocating $10 million for the project in fiscal year 2006, described the ongoing development of a vehicle-mounted prototype weapon.[182] Meanwhile the Army are also developing a vehicle-mounted prototype weapon based on laser-induced plasma channel technology, which was initially explored for neutralising mines[183] but has broadened in scope and is now described as the Rheostatic Pulsed Energy Weapon System (RPEWS).[184]

Nevertheless this technology remains in the early stages of development. Laser experts have expressed doubts over the viability of laser-guided electrical weapons and existing experimental systems have not been able to conduct an electrical discharge more than a few metres, far below the 10–30 metre range sought by the military.[185] This range limitation is perhaps the reason for the nature of the first prototype weapon promoted by Ionatron in 2005:

> The system is designed to be installed as a corridor or passageway denial system … The system creates a laser guided electric barrier … The system

is designed to stop intruders in a passageway or at a vehicle check point, with a lethal or non-lethal electrical discharge.[186]

One expert in this area of laser physics has said that it may be possible to develop vehicle-mounted weapon systems but that hand-held weapons are unlikely.[187] Two other US companies have been promoting related concepts. Xtreme Alternative Defense Systems (XADS)[188] and HSV Technologies, which was issued with a patent for a weapon concept in 1997 but has not produced a prototype.[189]

6.3.3 Thermal lasers

One further research area involves the investigation of fibre lasers for 'non-lethal' weapons applications. NP Photonics Inc. was awarded two contracts by the JNLWD in late 2005 for applied research and technology development. The first was a two-year contract for just under $1.5 million that started in September 2005 for 'Research and Development of Non-Lethal Fiber Laser in support of Joint Non-Lethal Weapons Directorate'.[190] The second was another two-year contract for $1.3 million that started in October 2005 for 'Research and Development of Portable GHz Sources in support of Joint Non-Lethal Weapons Directorate'.[191] The company presented a paper to a 2006 'non-lethal' weapons conference entitled 'Compact highly efficient 2-micron fiber laser'.[192] The two-micrometer infrared wavelength is not in the visible part of the spectrum and so, rather than use for 'dazzling' eye effects, the rationale is to heat the skin or eyes. In general fibre lasers are seen as an emerging technology area offering the potential for higher power levels than conventional solid-state lasers.[193] As regards 'non-lethal' weapons, this type of thermal laser is under investigation by AFRL to heat the skin, with the aim of causing pain without permanent damage.[194] This is likely to be the approach under development for the Air Force's PHaSR weapon to heat skin and induce the so-called 'repel effect'.

6.4 Radio frequency, microwave, and millimetre wave weapons

6.4.1 Past programmes: Death rays and mind control

The development of microwave generators was pursued to improve military radar and communication systems in the 1940s, offering advantages over existing radio wave systems in terms of resolution, information handling, range, and signal quality.[195] Akin to prior conceptual proposals in the 1920s and 1930s to use radio waves to create so-called death ray weapons to bring down aircraft,[196] microwave generating technology was soon the subject of similarly unsuccessful investigations by the Japanese during World War II and later by the US Air Force in the 1960s.[197] Scientists had quickly discovered that microwave beams could heat materials and this led to the development of the first microwave ovens.[198] Of course these thermal effects raised safety issues surrounding the effect of radars and other microwave technologies on humans. Research continued on the biological effects during the 1950s, 1960s, and 1970s and one of the major issues to arise was disagreement over the potential for additional non-thermal effects, that is, not dependent on the heating of tissue. Scientists in the Former Soviet Union and East Europe emphasised these, whereas those in the US dismissed them, which led to greatly differing safety standards. The debate lasted until the early 1980s after which the potential for non-thermal effects began to be acknowledged in the US.[199]

Of course the undisputed thermal effects had clear potential in terms of weapons applications. At the Conference of Government Experts on Weapons which may Cause Unnecessary Suffering or have Indiscriminate Effects in 1974 concerns were expressed over the potential for microwave anti-personnel weapons. The *SIPRI Yearbook 1975* noted: 'High intensity microwaves can be generated by radar devices and lasers. Devices of this kind can cause heating of the tissues leading to an "internal burn"'.[200]

In the mid-1970s there was significant public concern over the potential for adverse effects from microwave ovens and radar devices. Other fears related to long term exposures to low intensity microwaves. These were heightened when it emerged that the US Government had harboured similar concerns for some years, in particular relating to low level microwave irradiation of its embassy in Moscow.[201] In 1965 DARPA had initiated a secret research programme called Project PANDORA to assess the biological and behavioural effects of low power microwaves. Scientists from the Applied Physics Laboratory at Johns Hopkins University helped establish a microwave facility at the Walter Reed Army Institute of Research, where tests were conducted on animals and human subjects.[202] Apparently the project concluded that embassy staff had not suffered ill effects.[203] Reportedly, however, the research programme pursued weapons applications and demonstrated the potential of low power microwaves to interfere with brain function.[204]

Furthermore, in the mid-1970s details had begun to emerge about the CIA's extensive research into techniques to modify or control human behaviour for use in interrogation and covert operations. It had originated with Navy research in the late 1940s and expanded in the 1950s encompassing several different CIA programmes including the most wide-ranging of these, MKULTRA. This programme was followed from the early 1960s until the early 1970s by continued research into behaviour modification techniques at the CIA's Office of Research and Development. Although research concentrated on the use of chemical and biological agents to influence behaviour, including experiments with LSD on unwitting human subjects, a variety of other psychiatric techniques including hypnosis, sensory deprivation, and electroshock were explored. Researchers also experimented with electrical stimulation of the brain and the effects of microwaves.[205]

Hecht observed in his 1984 book: 'It sometimes seems that whatever scares the public attracts the Pentagon, and that may have happened with microwaves'.[206] In the late 1970s limited military research was ongoing into the effects of microwaves on animals and materials.[207] However, this primarily involved 'anti-materiel' weapons concepts that would use high power microwaves to damage electronic equipment and to jam communications. The investigative US programme was very small in comparison to work on high energy lasers, commanding only 1 per cent of the total budget for all directed energy weapons research in the early 1980s.[208] Military interest in HPM weapons to damage electronics grew in the 1980s due to new serendipitous discoveries in methods of generating microwaves with higher powers and higher frequencies.[209] At the high end of the spectrum were millimetre waves, which were also under consideration for military radar and communications applications.[210]

Despite this apparent 'anti-materiel' focus, there was some military interest in the possibility of anti-personnel radio frequency weapons, as indicated by a 1982 Air Force Office of Scientific Research (AFOSR)[211] study to identify future research requirements. Proposed research on biological effects would inform three main areas: the development of anti-personnel weapons, the assessment of the anti-personnel effects of anti-materiel weapons, and the development of defences and countermeasures against these weapons, including protection for operators. A new initiative was proposed to investigate 'RFR [radio frequency radiation] Forced Disruptive Phenomena'[212] with the aim of assessing the potential of radio frequency radiation to disrupt nervous system function and other physiological processes such as cardiac and respiratory function. The report noted that degradation of human performance through thermal effects should be addressed first and that subsequent research should address the 'possibilities of directing and interrogating mental functioning'[213] [their emphasis], suggesting:

> A rapidly scanning RFR system could provide an effective stun or kill capability over a large area. System effectiveness will be a function of waveform, field intensity, pulse widths, repetition frequency and carrier frequency. The system can be developed using tissue and whole animal experimental studies, coupled with mechanisms and waveforms effects research.[214]

It is unknown whether the proposed research programme was actually carried out.

Other discussions on this topic included a paper presented to a 1984 workshop at the Air Force's Air University, 'The Electromagnetic Spectrum in Low-Intensity Conflict', which discussed research on the biological effects of electromagnetic energy and theoretical military applications but did not describe any specific programmes.[215] The concept of using electromagnetic energy to affect brain function had also been suggested by Alexander in a 1980 paper in *Military Review*.[216] In this paper he also promoted the investigation of unrelated paranormal concepts such as remote viewing and psychokinesis, areas that the US Army had actually begun to experiment with in earnest in the early 1980s.[217] There are unconfirmed reports that the Navy funded research on the effects of low frequency radiation on brain function for weapons applications during the early 1980s.[218]

In his 1984 book Hecht observed that the effects of microwaves on humans remained uncertain:

> Thermal effects can occur at high microwave powers because body tissue is a fairly good absorber of microwaves. ... The effects of long-term exposure to low levels of microwaves are harder to quantify.[219]

However, he pointed to the lack of military utility for long-term effects and the possibility of metal shielding as a countermeasure against any anti-personnel microwave weapon.[220]

As regards technical barriers to the development of microwave weapons Hecht highlighted several issues. First, directing and focusing a beam of high power microwaves over long distances would require a very large and hence impractical antenna dish. Second, the microwave beam would spread out as it moved further from the antenna, limiting the possibility of precise targeting.[221] Another issue that had been recognised by military researchers was that many potential 'anti-materiel' military targets were metal and would reflect microwaves. Of course these limitations in terms of range, beam properties, and reflection would not present a barrier to short-range anti-personnel microwave weapons. Furthermore the technology for angling a beam was well developed due to the use of phased array microwave emitters that enabled electronic control of the movement of a beam.[222]

6.4.1.1 *Exploring 'non-lethal' weapons applications*

One of the earliest mentions of microwaves specifically in relation to 'non-lethal' weapons was in the report of the 1986 DOJ conference on the topic. Participants considered new weapons ideas and discussed the potential of using various frequencies of electromagnetic radiation, including microwaves and extremely low frequency radiation, to cause incapacitation.[223] In the early 1990s, the NIJ sponsored research at Oak Ridge National Laboratory including a project, 'Physiological Responses to Energetic Stimuli', which began in September 1993 and comprised a literature search on the biological effects of various types of electromagnetic energy with the intention of identifying new mechanisms of incapacitation. There is very little information about this research but it does not appear to have gone beyond the conceptual stage. Several ideas were suggested including the use of microwaves to raise body temperature, the use of extremely low frequency radiation to produce sensations of light (magnetophosphenes) akin to those experienced when you get a blow to the head, and the use of electromagnetic energy (presumably flashing light) to induce epileptic seizures.[224]

As military concepts of 'non-lethal' weapons emerged in the late 1980s and early 1990s high power microwaves were presented as a major technology for tactical or strategic destruction of electronic systems with little mention of anti-personnel applications.[225] One project underway in the early 1990s as part of the Army's LCDM programme was a project to develop high power microwave 'projectiles' for this purpose.[226] Nevertheless anti-personnel weapons were under consideration, including by the US Army,[227] and a 1998 Air University occasional paper noted:

> High powered microwaves are normally considered an anti-material weapon, but they may have significant antipersonnel capabilities as well. Some directed energy weapons, such as microwaves, are able to produce a variety of effects on humans to include increasing levels of pain, incapacitation, and disorientation. Research is on-going. If the range and power of a future capability is sufficient, a high-powered microwave weapon may be used for area denial or as a force protection capability.[228]

This ongoing research was primarily centred at AFRL's site at Brooks Air Force Base in Texas, where a research programme into the bioeffects of radio frequency, microwave, and millimetre wave radiation had begun in 1968 to investigate the safety of radar systems. The programme expanded over the years to become one of the world's centres of expertise. As a 2002 paper summarising the programme explained:

> At the Air Force Research Laboratory facilities at Brooks, a wide range of RFR [radiofrequency radiation] exposure parameters are studied, including exposure to microwaves, millimeter waves, high power microwaves (HPM), ultrawideband radiation (UWB), and includes both pulsed and continuous wave, acute, chronic, and repeated exposures. The research is conducted at biological levels of organisation from sub-cellular fractions, to cells, rodents, goats, monkeys, and humans. Biological effects studied include the biochemical, genetic, neural, physiological, behavioral, and cognitive.[229]

While this research was used to set standards for exposure for military systems such as radars, and to assess the effects of human exposure to high power microwave weapons directed at electronic systems, it also provided a dual-use depth of knowledge that could be applied to developing anti-personnel weapons with particular effects.

6.4.2 Contemporary programmes: Active Denial and 'controlled effects'

6.4.2.1 The Active Denial System (ADS)

This Air Force classified programme began in the early 1990s, but related research began in the late 1980s and the requirement for a specifically 'non-lethal' directed energy weapon had apparently been identified in 1989.[230] During the 1980s and early 1990s the Air Force was develop- ing new technologies for protecting military facilities under the Base and Installation Security System programme. This encompassed the use of acoustic, electro-optical, laser, radar, and other technologies to develop new sensors and detection devices and included the consideration of directed energy weapons to 'repel' people.[231] Whereas sensors and detection devices were being developed as 'passive defences', various technologies, both new and old, were under consideration to delay or deny access as 'active defences'. The primary focus was the protection of nuclear facilities, and the Department of Energy (DOE) was considering a variety of different methods including foams, sounds, bright lights, and smoke.[232] Beginning in 1993 the Air Force began a research effort called the 'Active Denial Program' to develop a new system for 'repelling' intruders at nuclear weapons stor- age sites using a beam of electromagnetic radiation.[233] A 1998 Air Force Scientific Advisory Board report gave the first indication of the technology under development:[234]

> The Active Denial program is a joint exploratory development effort between Armstrong Laboratory (AL) and Phillips Laboratory (PL) to develop nonlethal security and area denial applications. A fielded system would delay intrusion to allow threat assessment and validation, initia- tion of tactical response, and interdiction of the threat. An Active Denial system will give an AEF [Air Force Expeditionary Forces] commander a nonlethal option for force protection with the option of immediate tran- sition to lethal force if necessary. The current focus of the program is to provide proof-of-concept for ground-mobile, helicopter, and C-130-based systems. The research emphasis is on understanding the biological effects of millimeter-wave exposures.[235]

As it would emerge several years later, the concept was to use a millimetre wave beam with a frequency of 95 gigahertz (GHz) to heat the surface layers of the skin at a depth of 0.3–0.4 mm to 45–55 degrees centigrade, causing intolerable pain within seconds but limiting the exposure duration in order to prevent burns.[236] The frequency was chosen in part because the 'atmospheric window' at that frequency would enable better transmission through the air.[237]

By the time of the 1998 report, consideration of potential applications had expanded beyond facility security:

> Active denial is a technique for using electromagnetic beams to control enemy troop formations. These technologies could be employed from space as well as from air vehicles by employing large, light weight antennas in space to project the same power densities on the targets. The technologies are similar to those for HPM [high power microwave] weapons.[238]

The Active Denial programme was given high priority when a review of existing programmes was conducted by the newly established JNLWD in 1997. It was also given high priority within the Air Force itself following a 1998–9 Air Force study of 'Directed Energy Applications for Tactical Airborne Combat'.[239] The JNLWD funded the construction of a full power system, ADS System 0, which was built by Raytheon Co. and mounted on a stationary vehicle container.[240] The prototype (and subsequent versions) employs a flat (as opposed to parabolic) antenna to project the beam, which offers better efficiency than conventional antennae.[241] The system for generating the beam is called a gyrotron, a technology introduced in the late 1970s, although power-generating capabilities have improved significantly in the intervening years.[242]

Prior to the construction of the prototype testing had been conducted on animals and small patches of human skin but only at the laboratory level. Field testing using the ADS System 0 began in 2000 but not on people due to strict guidelines on the conduct of secret human testing.[243] In order to enable human testing with the full size ADS System 0, the programme was declassified in December 2000.[244] The first publicly available information on the weapon appeared in March 2001 in an article entitled 'The People Zapper'.[245] The Air Force then released a 'fact sheet' describing it as the Vehicle Mounted Active Denial System (VMADS), reflecting the plan to integrate the weapon onto a 'Humvee' vehicle.[246]

Following a 'Joint Mission Area Analysis' for 'non-lethal' weapons in 2000 the ADS was given highest priority for further development, and a Marine Corps Warfighting Laboratory war game reached favourable conclusions on the use of such a weapon in urban operations.[247] Subsequently the NRC panel reviewed the weapon in 2001 as part of their assessment of 'non-lethal' weapons science and technology and highlighted it as one of the major technologies for further development. The NRC's final report noted: 'The present VMADS system and those under development are based on knowledge initially gained decades ago', and emphasised that the major focus for development would be further assessing the human effects:

> The VMADS effect – near instantaneous heating of an individual by the RF [Radio Frequency] energy – is well understood empirically, but much remains to be learned about the biological implications of such heating.[248]

From the beginning of the programme until 2005 the US military spent $51 million on the ADS with $9 million used for assessing the effects of the beam on the human body.[249] Laboratory research relating to the biological effects of the 95 GHz of millimetre wave energy has been carried out by Air Force scientists and associated contractors from academia and industry and published in several journals from 1997 onwards. This addressed a variety of topics including the thresholds for causing pain, effects on the eye, and potential for carcinogenic effects.[250] Field testing with the full-power ADS System 0 on human volunteers began in 2001 at ranges of over 700 metres.[251] The programme was designated as an Advanced Concept Technology Demonstration (ACTD) in 2002 with the intention of accelerating its development.[252] Subsequently the second generation prototype, ADS System 1, which is integrated into a 'Humvee' vehicle, was built by Raytheon Co. and delivered for testing in late 2004.[253] Experimental protocol documents for some of the testing conducted from 2001–6 became public following Freedom of Information Act requests by The Sunshine Project.[254] These showed that a variety of experiments were carried out, ranging from assessing the heating effects and human responses, to assessments of the utility of the system in staged military scenarios.[255] The latter 'military utility assessments' involved over 200 volunteers and more than 3500 exposures.[256] The system for generating the millimetre wave energy is battery powered and the antenna to direct the beam is mounted on the roof of the vehicle.[257] Although exact details have not been released it is thought the ADS has a range of up to 1 km and that the beam is wider than an individual with the capability to affect three or four people standing together.[258]

As the Air Force developers of the weapon have noted, the critical factor in terms of effects on the human body is the duration of exposure:

High intensity MMW [millimetre waves] act on human skin and cornea in an orderly, dose-dependent manner, with detection occurring at very low power densities, followed by pain at higher exposures, followed by physical damage at even higher levels.[259]

The military contend that injury will be prevented because the victim will move out of the beam before their skin heats up to the threshold for permanent damage and that the eyes, which are even more sensitive to the heating effects of the beam, will be protected by the blink reflex.[260] Apparently the latest prototype system has been fitted with sensors so that the operator can see the beam, which is invisible to the naked eye, as well as controls the limit of the duration of the beam once triggered.[261] However, even with these measures concerns remain. An independent technical assessment by Altmann calculates the 'safe' exposure time to be a matter of seconds and dependent on the intensity of the beam used.[262] It also raises the issue of retargeting, arguing that even with controls limiting the amount of energy delivered with one firing, repeated exposure could result in the skin temperature rising above the threshold for permanent damage.[263] One danger would be if the operator chose to follow a person or group of people with the beam to punish them.[264] Altmann argues that this possibility 'puts avoidance of burns at the discretion of the weapon operator', noting that the system has the potential to cause second or third-degree burns, which could be life threatening due to the width of the beam and therefore the area of the body affected.[265] Another concern is that those targeted may not be able to move out of the beam if constrained by other people or barriers especially if they have had to close their eyes due to the painful effects.

During testing of the 'Active Denial Technology' there have been at least six cases of skin blistering following exposure and two cases of second-degree burns requiring medical attention. One occurred in 1999 during laboratory testing and was a small burn the size of a coin. A more recent incident occurred during military evaluation tests with the ADS System 1 prototype in April 2007. An Air Force volunteer received second-degree burns and was admitted to hospital for treatment.[266]

Other concerns that have been raised relate to the possibility of long-term effects and non-thermal effects that are not related to skin heating.[267] Different frequencies of millimetre wave radiation at low-levels have long been used to induce physiological changes for medical applications in some parts of the world.[268] A 2004 NATO report identified the gap in knowledge with regard to long-term effects:

> The long-term physiological effects of the microwaves received by an individual are still being studied (maximum acceptable dose, cumulative effect of successive exposures). The absence of definitive results is the main obstacle to the use of radio frequencies.[269]

However, a study in mice carried out by the developers found no evidence of cancer causing potential.[270]

A modular version of the ADS, ADS System 2, designed for hotter environments and to be operated at a fixed site or transported on a vehicle, was completed in 2007.[271] There are now several other weapon systems under development as shown in Table 6.2. DOJ is interested in employing the technology as a portable police weapon. In fiscal year 2004 the NIJ funded Raytheon Co. to develop the millimetre wave technology on a smaller scale.[272] The NIJ have stated their desire for a hand-held, shotgun sized, heat generating directed energy weapon with a range of around 15 metres and a beam of 8 cm in diameter.[273] The military are also interested in the possibility of a hand-held version.[274] Despite bold claims by the company about the potential for miniaturisation, such a small weapon maybe some years away.[275] According to a 2004 technical assessment of the 'Active Denial Technology', solid-state technology is not powerful enough or able to produce the required frequencies.[276] Nevertheless the NIJ now have a prototype hand-held ADS weapon.[277]

With regard to the larger Active Denial weapons, the military envisions their use in a wide variety of scenarios from crowd control to warfighting:

> The ADS will support a full gamut of peacetime and wartime missions - non-lethal methods of crowd and mob dispersal, checkpoint security,

Table 6.2 Developmental weapon systems employing the 95 GHz millimeter wave 'Active Denial Technology'[278]

Name	Program	Description	Developers	Status
Active Denial System (ADS)	Military	Original long-range system developed by the Air Force and the JNLWP. 100 kilowatt power with a maximum range of 750–1000 m and a 2 m (approx.) diameter antenna. ADS System 1 is a Humvee-mounted prototype. The ADS System 2 prototype is a modular version that can be used at a fixed site or truck-mounted.	AFRL, JNLWD, Raytheon Co.	Ongoing military evaluation. ADS System 2 was completed in late 2007.
Airborne Active Denial System	Military	Air Force adaptation of ADS system so that it can be mounted on an aircraft such as a C-130. Includes effort that began in 2004 to make the power generation system lighter. May be more powerful with a greater range than the vehicle-mounted system since these aircraft operate at ranges of >3 km*.	AFRL, Communications, and Power Industries[†]	Ongoing research and development.
Silent Guardian	Commercial	Mid-range system developed by Raytheon. 30 kilowatt power with a maximum range of >250 m and a 1.14 m diameter antenna. The weapon system can be used at a fixed site or mounted on a military tactical vehicle or large pick-up truck.	Raytheon Co.	Offered for sale by company from mid-2006.
Portable Active Denial System (PADS)	Homeland Security and Military	Short-range system co-sponsored by the DOE and the DOD. 400 watt power, tripod mounted prototype. Sandia National Laboratories (SNL) is evaluating the prototype for use in security at nuclear facilities. The Office of Force Transformation (OFT) is considering the system for integration into its Full Spectrum Effect Platform ('Project Sheriff')[‡].	AFRL, SNL (DOE), OFT (DOD), Raytheon Co.	Prototype systems delivered for evaluation in 2005. Human testing carried out in 2005 and 2006.
Hand-held Active Denial System	Military and Law enforcement	Research towards the development of a hand-held Active Denial weapon.	NIJ, JNLWD, Raytheon Co.	Prototype: Ongoing research and development.

* As suggested by:: Hambling, D. (2006) Say Hello to the Goodbye Weapon. *Wired.com*, 5 December 2006.

[†] Communications and Power Industries makes the gyrotron transmitter for the ADS systems.

[‡] Roque, A. (2005) DOD To Contract with Industry For Project Sheriff Integration. *Inside the Army*, 1 August 2005; Raytheon Company (2005) *Raytheon Delivers Breakthrough Non-Lethal Sheriff Active Denial System*. Press Release, 8 September 2005.

perimeter security, area denial, port protection, infrastructure protection, and clarification of intent (identifying combatants from non-combatants).[279]

From a non-military perspective various uses have been proposed in terms of homeland security and law enforcement, including the protection of sensitive buildings or facilities, such as nuclear weapons storage sites,[280] and even border control.[281]

There has been much speculation as well as mixed messages over when the military might deploy the 100 kilowatt, long-range ADS. During 2004 and 2005 there were reports about a public demonstration and imminent deployment to Iraq as well as reports of delays.[282] Following three 'military utility assessments' carried out in 2005 and 2006[283] the ADS System 1 was finally demonstrated to the media in January 2007.[284] At this point it emerged that it will not be deployed in the field until 2010 at the earliest.[285] In mid-2008 the JNLWD Director asserted that the weapon would be deployed in Iraq within six to ten months.[286]

As regards the 30 kilowatt, medium-range Silent Guardian system, described by Raytheon Co. as 'available now and ready for action', there have been no reports of its deployment.[287] Its high cost, 'less than $10 million' according to the company, would limit potential buyers.[288] It may be purchased by the military or perhaps for homeland security applications at sensitive facilities.

Field tests on the human effects of the 400 watt, short-range weapon were carried out in 2005 and 2006.[289] Sandia National Laboratory (SNL) is considering this smaller ADS system for nuclear facilities security. Reports in 2005 stated that a considerable amount of further testing was required.[290] The military wants to integrate the system on to an armoured Stryker vehicle along with other 'non-lethal' and 'lethal' weapons. This overall system is called the Full Spectrum Effects Platform or 'Project Sheriff'. In 2005 the Chief of Staff for Multi-National Corps-Iraq had asked for funding to be made available to produce 14 'Project Sheriff' vehicles, four each for the Army's 18th Military Police Brigade and 42nd Military Police Brigade, and six for the Marines.[291] The concept was developed by the Office of Force Transformation (OFT) and the Army oversaw the construction of the first three vehicles in 2006 and 2007.[292] However, the 'Active Denial Technology' was not included on those that were eventually fielded in Iraq in 2008.[293]

6.4.2.2   Controlled effects

Research and development of other electromagnetic weapons is certainly ongoing as part of a broader effort to develop directed energy weapons with varied and variable (lethal to 'non-lethal') effects. An Air Force science and technology panel considering future capabilities for the 2020 to 2050 time frame identified a concept of 'controlled effects' against equipment, communications, and people, as described in a 2004 paper:

> For the Controlled Personnel Effects capability, the S&T [science and technology] panel explored the potential for targeting individuals with nonlethal force, from a militarily useful range, to make selected adversaries think or act according to our needs. Through the application of nonlethal force, it is possible to physically influence or incapacitate personnel. Advanced technologies could enable the warfighter to remotely create physical sensations such as pressure or temperature changes. A current example of this technology is Active Denial ... By studying and modeling the human brain and nervous system, the ability to mentally influence or confuse personnel is also possible.[294]

One method of influencing various physiological processes, including brain function, is by using radio frequency radiation. The NRC panel on 'non-lethal' weapons pointed to the potential for the development of new weapons of this type by exposing the body to both low and high-frequency energy as well as high-power pulses:

> Recent developments in broadening the bandwidth of RF [radiofrequency] generators and the development of systems capable of producing very short pulses and very high peak power provide a glimpse into the vast unexplored region of biological effects or human susceptibilities and potential avenues for NLWs. Single pulses of RF energy have been associated with stun and seizure, decreased spontaneous animal activity, microwave-induced whole body movements, thermal sensations, and startle modification. Some of these effects may be associated with the activation of specialized nerve endings and/or may be only partially mediated by heating. Little evidence has been identified to suggest that a bioelectromagnetics program exists to explore the vast domain of RF energy for application to NLWs.[295]

Although the panel did not identify a bioelectromagnetic weapons programme in their review, details of several research and development efforts have since emerged.

Researchers at the University of Nevada, Reno, from the School of Medicine and the Department of Electrical Engineering, began a three-year investigative research project funded by AFOSR in mid-2002 to study the effects of radio frequency and microwave energy on the release of neurotransmitters in the nervous system with a view to developing 'non-lethal' weapons. Experiments were conducted on nerve cells in vitro from the adrenal medulla section of the adrenal gland. The adrenal medulla controls release of the catecholamine neurotransmitters adrenaline and noradrenaline into the bloodstream. The main observation given in the 2005 final report was that they found an increase in release of catecholamines from these cells as a result of exposure to pulsed and continuous wave radio frequency radiation in the 750–850 MHz range.[296] Subsequently, the researchers noted that the changes in neurotransmitter release were not due to an increase in temperature.[297]

The research programme expanded to investigate the effects of radio frequency radiation in the broader 1–6 GHz range to elicit non-thermal effects on brain function, as described in a January 2006 report:

> Although the United States Department of Defense is one of the world's largest developers and users of RF [radiofrequency]/MW [microwave] –emitting systems for radar, communication and anti-electronic weaponry purposes, the use of RF/MW radiation as a non-lethal weapon per se has not yet been realized. Most likely this is because the effects of exposure of biological systems to RF/MW fields at levels that do not produce thermal effects are largely unknown. The overall objective of the research funded by this grant was to begin laying the foundation upon which RF/MW technology can be developed that would have an application for non-lethal weaponry purposes, such as stunning/immobilizing the enemy.[298]

In addition to non-thermal effects the researchers have also been investigating the effects of rapid changes in temperature on neurotransmitter release.[299] Furthermore, a concurrent three-year research project, which began in mid-2003 and was part-funded by the Department of Defense Experimental Program to Stimulate Competitive Research (DEPSCoR),[300] expanded the scope of the research to investigate the effects of radio frequency and microwave radiation on skeletal muscle contraction to assess potential weapons applications.[301]

While the specific purpose of these programmes has been for weapons development the university has disingenuously sought to present the work in an entirely different light, as illustrated in a 2003 press release:

> The Air Force Office of Scientific Research, which is sponsoring the researchers, wants to find out what exposure to radiofrequency fields does to neurotransmitters and skeletal muscle tissue, and to use the information toward the development of beneficial, non-invasive medical treatments for injuries and diseases of the nervous system and skeletal muscle, said Craviso.
>
> The team's research will benefit human health, said Chatterjee.[302]

6.4.2.3 Microwave hearing

Another area of research and development relates to the microwave auditory effect, or microwave hearing, as described in a 2006 NATO report:

> A phenomenon in which microwave pulses of certain characteristics are heard as clicks or buzzes. The mechanism of this phenomenon is believed to be a thermoelastic transduction of the rapid temperature rise caused by the RF pulse into a mechanical wave in the head that is heard by the normal hearing apparatus. It is not believed to be harmful, but some consider that it might be annoying.[303]

This mechanism was recognised during World War II in relation to high power radar devices. The first scientific assessment was published in 1961 and the subject received significant research attention during the 1970s.[304] The most recent research and development for weapons applications has been carried out by both the US Air Force and the Navy. In 1994 researchers at the AFRL apparently developed a method for encoding intelligible speech into a radio frequency carrier beam. Prior to this it seems that it was only possible to transmit tones since speech became too distorted for the target person to decipher. The developers envisioned various applications including wireless communications, and as a communication method for deaf people, but also as a 'useful Psychological Warfare communications tool' and 'a distraction or delaying tactic for Active Denial Technology applications'.[305] A patent for the mechanism and associated device was filed by the Air Force in 1996 and granted in 2002,[306] and a related patent was filed in 2002 and granted in 2003.[307]

The Navy, specifically the Marine Corps has also been pursuing a weapon based upon this mechanism under the acronym MEDUSA (Mob Excess Deterrent Using Silent Audio). In late 2003 the Navy provided a small amount of funding to Wavelab Corp. to explore the potential of a 'Remote Personnel Incapacitation System'[308] and initial research showed evidence of the microwave hearing effect.[309] This particular project does not appear to have progressed further although the Marines have continued to pursue this weapon concept.[310] In 2008 the Sierra Nevada Corp. claimed that it would be able to build a MEDUSA device.[311]

However, biophysics experts have dismissed the potential of using the microwave hearing effect as a 'non-lethal' weapon, warning that the high power outputs required to transmit sufficiently loud sound levels would heat the brain, causing tissue damage and death fairly rapidly.[312]

Another radio frequency weapon concept that the Marine Corps are investigating is given the acronym EPIC (Electromagnetic Personnel Interdiction Control). Under the same program as MEDUSA, the Navy awarded a small grant to Invocon Inc. in late 2003 to explore the possibility of using a radio frequency beam to upset balance and hearing, and ultimately cause motion sickness, through action on the inner ear.[313] Subsequently the company was given funding of $600,000 for a two-year project starting in June 2005 to further develop the concept and demonstrate the feasibility of the mechanism of action on animal tissue[314] Reports surfaced in 2007 that Invocon Inc. had developed a prototype device.[315]

6.4.2.4 Behavioural effects?

Meanwhile basic research on the biological effects of various types of electromagnetic radiation continues at AFRL. In 2003 a review of radio frequency effects was published in collaboration with AFRL in the journal *Bioelectromagnetics*, which addressed behavioural and cognitive effects, and other effects on the nervous system.[316] The project was requested by the Institute of Electrical and Electronics Engineers (IEEE) with the aim of revising standards for human exposure. However, this knowledge is clearly dual-use in terms of the potential to elucidate new mechanisms for weapons applications. Specific goals of Air Force research in this area, as part of a new effects-based approach to 'non-lethal' weapons development, proposed exactly this. For example AFRL research priorities for 2005–9 included: 'Identify novel uses of directed energy as a weapon against biological targets or as a non-lethal weapon'; 'Conduct bioeffects research to provide optimal parameters to [weapon] system designers'; 'Determine the effects of electromagnetic and biomechanical insults on the human body'.[317] One of the major areas envisioned for ongoing research at AFRL in support of the JNLWP is directed energy weapons.[318]

There is also the potential that broader military-sponsored research in neuroscience may contribute to the development of new weapons targeting the brain in addition to the use of incapacitating biochemical agents as weapons, as described in Chapter 5. In his 2008 book, Moreno discusses the wide-ranging interest in the area shown by DARPA in particular.[319] In a 2006 article on the implications of advances in neuroscience Rose observed:

> [I]n the panicky environment of the so-called 'war on terror' there is increasing military interest in the development of techniques that can survey and possibly control and manipulate the mental processes of potential enemies.[320]

Expanding on one potential application he noted:

> [T]here is a long history of attempts by DARPA to develop techniques for focusing microwave beams to disorient or confuse opponents. Whether microwave technology is capable of achieving this goal is uncertain. More promising, however, is a much newer technique – transcranial magnetic stimulation (TMS). This focuses an intense magnetic field on specific brain regions, and has been shown specifically to affect thoughts, perceptions and behaviours that are dependent on those regions.[321]

In 2008 the NRC published a report on 'Emerging Cognitive Neuroscience and Related Technologies', which included an assessment of the potential military and intelligence applications of advances in this science and technology, including functional neuroimaging, and neuropsychopharmacology. The latter is of course highly relevant to the development of incapacitating biochemical weapons discussed in Chapter 5.[322]

6.5 Major themes

6.5.1 Low energy laser weapons

6.5.1.1 *Technical issues*

Advances in solid-state lasers during the 1980s and in laser diode technology during the early 1990s meant that by the mid-1990s, sufficiently portable, cost-effective, and powerful lasers were available to form the basis of so-called dazzling weapons proposed at that time. The major technical barrier remaining has been the issue of balancing effectiveness, that is, causing significant visual obscuration or flash-blinding, with safety, that is, avoiding permanent eye damage. After the ban on blinding lasers, weapons developers designed 'dazzling' laser weapons that were intended to be eye-safe, for a very short exposure, at the aperture. This led to better margins of safety but decreased effectiveness; in particular it meant that the weapons would be of little use in daylight conditions. In recent years, efforts to improve the effectiveness in affecting vision in all conditions have led to the use of higher power lasers. However, these weapons, a number of which have now been deployed, present a significant risk of permanent eye damage at shorter ranges and longer exposures. And so the issue of safety versus effectiveness has not been resolved but rather weapons development has favoured effectiveness, relying on operational guidelines to avoid eye damage.

The focus of current research and development is to find a technological solution to the safety-effectiveness issue through the design of rangefinders that would adjust the power level of the laser according to the range so that energy levels are kept below the threshold for eye damage. The theory is that the maximum 'safe' energy level can then be directed at the eye thus ensuring the greatest effectiveness. Research remains in the early stages but could lead to wider use of 'dazzling' laser weapons. However, it is unclear whether there is in fact a clear threshold dividing permanent and temporary effects. Furthermore, there are likely to be variations in susceptibilities across populations.

6.5.1.2 *Legal constraints*

Clearly an important factor in terms of low energy laser weapons has been legal regulation in the form of the international ban on blinding lasers, agreed in 1995. This resulted in the closure of certain laser weapons programmes and, moreover, it dismissed the misguided notion that somehow blinding could be presented as a 'non-lethal' effect. However, the timing of this development, occurring as it did during a time of greatly increased military interest in the field of 'non-lethal' weapons, somewhat paradoxically led to increased investigation of anti-eye lasers in the form of 'dazzling' weapons.

Crucial factors in the adoption of the legal prohibition of blinding lasers were the research and associated advocacy work conducted by the ICRC and later by Human Rights Watch. Such advocacy may play a role in determining whether new 'dazzling' laser weapons targeting the eye become accepted.

An interrelated factor is public opinion, which was strongly against blinding laser weapons, and may become relevant to the acceptance of emerging 'dazzling' laser weapons. Comments included in the report of a US-UK Government meeting on 'non-lethal' weapons illustrate this issue:

> Although a clear policy exists in the U.S. on the prohibition of the development and use of laser weapons that are intended to blind, it has become apparent that a continuous education process is needed to inform the public that this protocol does not preclude the development and use of laser weapons not intended to blind.
>
> The UK agrees that the public perception has sprung from a strong revulsion to blinding and yet has tended to affect all lasers whether they are intended to blind or not.[323]

Of course there is also advocacy from the military and weapons developers, who may present existing 'dazzling' laser weapons as not harmful to the eye, often putting them forward not as weapons but as 'tools' or 'techniques'. This may prove sufficient for acceptance however it is unlikely to be sustained if wider use results in incidents of eye damage or blindness.

6.5.1.3 Operational demand

The wider deployment of 'dazzling' laser weapons by the US military has only occurred from 2006 onwards. This change appears to have been a direct result of operational priorities during current operations in Iraq. The issue of checkpoint security in particular has been stated as a major problem for US forces and these weapons have been put forward as a potential solution. Moreover, requests and feedback by military commanders in the field indicate that they view them favourably and would like them to become more widely available.[324] In essence the spread of 'dazzling' laser weapons may have been awaiting a suitable application.

6.5.2 High energy laser weapons

6.5.2.1 Technical realities

As regards high energy laser weapons, efforts to date have failed to produce a viable 'non-lethal' weapon. It should also be noted that high energy laser weapons proposed as 'lethal' weapons have yet to be fielded despite 40 years of research and development efforts.[325]

A major barrier to the development of 'lethal' high energy laser weapons since the 1970s has been producing sufficient power levels. As Lumsden noted in SIPRI's 1978 book on anti-personnel weapons: 'The principle problem associated with turning lasers into usable weapons is that of the size of the power source'.[326] Previously only chemical lasers, which present logistical problems due to the requirement for hazardous and bulky chemical fuels, have been capable of producing sufficient power. However, recent advances in the power levels of solid-state lasers and decreases in the size of the associated electrical power sources mean that tactical solid-state laser weapons are becoming increasingly viable.[327] Although it appears that neither chemical nor solid-state lasers are yet efficient enough for use as destructive weapons.[328]

'Non-lethal' weapons applications, on the other hand, have only been put forward since the early 1990s and research programmes have yet to develop a viable weapon. Proposed 'non-lethal' bioeffects remain speculative, and tests during the 1990s with pulsed laser technology indicated the potential for causing serious injuries but not temporary and reversible effects. The potential for heating the skin without causing permanent damage is yet to be fully determined. Using such lasers to direct an electrical discharge towards a person may be a viable 'non-lethal' effect in theory. However, despite the bold claims from companies involved in this type of weapons development, thus far researchers have failed to transmit an electrical discharge more than several metres, which is less than the range of existing hand-held electrical weapons such as the Taser.

6.5.2.2 Misguided notions

A common theme in 'non-lethal' weapons discourse is the military desire, and associated advocacy, for development of a weapon with adjustable effects, which rests entirely on the perceived potential of directed energy weapons concepts. This perception has heightened since it was first articulated in the early 1990s and high energy laser weapons are seen as the most likely to offer this capability. As the 2003 NRC report on 'non-lethal' weapons noted: 'The promise of adjustable power levels (i.e. rheostatic capability) makes laser-based NLWs [non-lethal weapons] attractive'.[329] This 'promise' has become accepted wisdom among some 'non-lethal' weapons proponents, even in the absence of a demonstrated mechanism to produce 'non-lethal' effects, and it feeds into further advocacy for high energy lasers as the next generation of 'non-lethal' weapons.

More sinister, perhaps, is the use of this claim of 'non-lethal' potential alongside other factors, such as precision and speed of action, to promote what is essentially the development of 'lethal' high energy laser weapons. This advocacy becomes more disingenuous where the argument is extended to weapons that have 'lethal' effects, such as the ATL, but are put forward as 'non-lethal' either by virtue of their intended targets being objects not people, or their precision effects enabling the killing of an enemy soldier leaving a nearby civilian untouched.[330] Here use of the term 'non-lethal' clearly becomes a marketing tool.[331] However, exactly this approach is used by the military and some policy lobby groups in urging the overall development of directed energy weapons.[332] A former Director of the JNLWD put it thus:

> So now, imagine, a battlefield scenario where lasers streak down from the sky and across the distant battlefields of the earth. A suite of 'directed energy' weapons so accurate they can strike enemy materiel while avoiding non-combatants and innocent civilians standing only inches away; weapons so manageable that their energy level can be tailored to the target effects required and the mission. When the JNLWP vision reaches fruition, these weapons and capabilities will be more than just mere imagination; they will be a reality.[333]

6.5.3 Radio frequency, microwave, and millimetre wave weapons

In the case of radio frequency, microwave, and millimetre wave weapons, limited available information makes it difficult to assess the extent of past research efforts although they appear to have comprised mostly basic research into potential biological effects. Concerted efforts at 'non-lethal' weapons development did not begin in earnest until the early 1990s with the Active Denial programme, which has led to the construction of the millimetre wave ADS, now at the advanced prototype stage.

As regards millimetre wave weapons designed to heat the human body, some of the main technical issues that would limit the development of long range 'lethal' weapons have not presented as much as a problem of short range 'non-lethal' weapons. In a sense they have encouraged 'non-lethal' applications. The impractical size of an antenna for directing a beam at long range, and the spreading of the beam in the air as it moves further from the antenna favour shorter range, up to 1 km, applications. Moreover the intention to cause pain rather than kill limits the power requirements.

6.5.3.1 *Biological effects*

In general terms the central technology for producing a high intensity millimetre wave beam has been available since the 1980s and knowledge of the heating effects of microwaves for considerably longer. Aside from aspects of the militarisation of this technology, the major technical issue has been scientific assessment of the human effects of millimetre wave radiation to rule out adverse effects and determine exposure levels that are effective but do not cause permanent damage. After over ten years of animal and human testing the military developers are confident that the ADS weapon will have no permanent adverse effects[334] but given the complexity of interactions between electromagnetic radiation and the human body there may still be unidentified long-term effects. Perhaps more significant is that the safety of the weapon, that is ensuring non-damaging temporary effects, rests on the duration of exposure, which will be dependent on the operator. Moreover, with the overall military goal of developing rheostatic directed energy weapons, the temptation to vary the power level may be difficult to resist in the long-term. And as a 2004 NATO report noted: 'excessive power levels can have serious consequences for human targets'.[335]

6.5.3.2 Targeting the brain

The main barrier to using other types of electromagnetic radiation to induce various physiological or behavioural effects is also determining the biological effects of different frequencies, powers, and pulses. Research and development in this area is secretive and so it is difficult to assess the scope of past and current efforts. However, it is clear that much remains to be learned about the potential effects of radio frequencies such as non-thermal mechanisms, particularly with regard to the brain, which appears to be a major target for future weapons. As the NRC panel on 'non-lethal' weapons observed in their 2003 report:

> Leap-ahead non-lethal weapons technologies will require a much more thorough knowledge of RF interactions with the human body than is in existence or can be envisioned within the current programmatic plans of the JNLWD. Such progress will require a prolonged effort by a multidisciplinary team of researchers skilled in a wide range of disciplines.[336]

Nevertheless the AFRL and the JNLWP are aligning their research efforts to gain greater understanding in this area and then take advantage of this in order to develop new weapons. Again interest here will likely expand beyond solely 'non-lethal' effects.

6.5.3.3 The court of public opinion

For the development of the ADS one of the most important factors has been the lack of acceptance of the technology by politicians, the public, and within the military itself. High level political support within the DOD has generally been lacking throughout the research programme and apparently delayed its development.[337] In recent years this has been linked to unfavourable public reactions to the weapon, which was not well received when the prototype was first unveiled in 2001.[338] As a result public relations exercises have become an important aspect of the military programme. Part of this process has been exaggeration of the state of readiness by the military with press reports surfacing in 2004 and 2005 that deployment to Iraq was imminent, combined with bold claims over the ability of the weapon to save lives. As it turned out, it seemed that decision makers were not yet satisfied with the safety of the weapon and understandably concerned over the potential for criticism if it were deployed. In late 2006 the Secretary for the US Air Force suggested that it should be tested domestically as a police weapon before being approved for use by the military overseas, in order to limit such reactions.[339] Such a strategy would perhaps raise confidence in the safety claims but it is unlikely to be popular with the general public in the US.

6.5.3.4 Ethical concerns

Aside from the safety debates, enduring ethical and moral concerns remain over the use of weapons solely designed to cause pain at the push of a button. This issue applies to other proposed pain-causing directed energy weapons but also to existing low-tech weapons, many of which work wholly or partly by pain compliance. Scientific experts in pain have expressed serious concern over the use of research in their field to develop new weapons.[340] As a *New Scientist* editorial commenting on the PEP weapon concept observed: 'There is something chilling about turning research intended to ease suffering into a weapon that can be used to hurt people'.[341] Moreover the very nature of a pain-causing device makes it open to misuse, namely use for torture and punishment.[342] Altmann has suggested that acceptance of the ADS will depend on the situation in which it is used:

> Judgement on the morality of ADS use will depend on the scenarios. Fending off intrusion into nuclear-weapons storage sites or preventing small boats from coming too close to navy ships in port would probably be assessed differently from repelling demonstrators on a public road.[343]

Nevertheless, the argument often repeated by those promoting new 'non-lethal' weapons that they can 'save lives' is a powerful one, even if flawed in some respects. The Taser was widely deployed on exactly this premise but since its introduction it has been used just as widely as a compliance device for police as an alternative to lethal force.[344] Such mission creep is likely to occur with other weapons.

However, the public relations issue may remain pertinent after any deployment. Deaths following the use of the Taser and videos of abusive use have brought criticism and some restrictions on its use.[345] If the ADS is indeed deployed and it burns victims or is used for punishment then it may have to be withdrawn.[346]

6.5.3.5 Secrecy

The issue of secrecy may also play a role in the acceptance of the ADS weapon, particularly by the public and the wider international community. Information about the weapon has been slow to emerge and crucial information for independent assessment, such as the power level of the beam used on the target person,[347] the safety margin, and the range, are still secret. Initial declassification of the project in late 2000 was borne not out of concern for public information but practical issues related to human testing. This type of secrecy leads to scepticism of confident safety claims. The military argue that such assessments cannot be released due to the potential to develop countermeasures; however keeping them secret may be counterproductive in terms of gaining wider acceptance. Indeed the JNLWD has now published an assessment by its Human Effects Advisory Panel (HEAP), which argued that the ADS has a 'low probability of injury'.[348]

6.5.3.6 *Operational pull*

Another influence on the latter stages of development and subsequent deployment of the ADS may be the operational concerns relating to the prevailing situation in Iraq. It seems that some military commanders believe the weapon can help them in certain situations and there have been a number of requests for accelerated deployment. In December 2005, *Inside the Army* reported that the Head of the US Army's Rapid Equipping Force had requested that the weapon be deployed to Iraq, as had the Commander of the 18th Military Police Brigade who had apparently requested the ADS 'to help "suppress" insurgent attacks and quell prison uprisings'.[349] In December 2006 the Marine Corps officer commanding troops in the Al-Anbar province of Iraq put in an urgent request for the weapon for use at checkpoints and in protecting convoys.[350] A December 2007 Defense Science Board (DSB) report on directed energy weapons confirmed that the weapon was initially intended for use in prison camps but that the DOD assessed such deployment as 'not politically tenable'.[351]

6.5.3.7 *International humanitarian law*

The ADS has been assessed by the DOD for compliance with international humanitarian law and with existing international treaties, receiving internal approval in April 2004 and May 2004 respectively. There are no existing treaties that prohibit directed energy weapons aside from lasers that are intentionally designed to blind. However, one issue that arises in relation to international humanitarian law is the targeting of civilians. As the ICRC have emphasised 'the law of war prohibits the use of any weapon against civilians'.[352] The military states that 'U.S. Central Command JAG [Judge Advocate General] concurred that ADS System 1 is employable under current Rules of Engagement'.[353] It may be assumed that the proposed rules of engagement, which are not public knowledge, do not permit the targeting of civilians. However, one of the most common roles mentioned in association with the weapon is planned use for 'clarification of intent (identifying combatants from non-combatants)'.[354] This implies targeting of people before it is determined whether they are combatants or not.

6.5.3.8 From conspiracy to reality

As regards the ongoing research and development of 'non-lethal' radio frequency, microwave, and millimetre wave weapons based on other mechanisms of incapacitation, public acceptance and ethical issues are arguably even more important, especially with regard to weapons that would interfere with brain function. The focus of some current research and development efforts resemble post-World War II CIA endeavours to identify techniques to control behaviour. Since then considerable conspiracy theories have emerged, centred on the belief of a loud minority that an authority or government is controlling their behaviour using radio frequency or microwave weapons. Such theories have perpetuated on the Internet for example.[355] The issue now is that, as regards the direction of weapons development, conspiracy is becoming reality. Even based on the limited information available it is clear that the military is funding basic research efforts in this area and it is occurring under the banner of 'non-lethal' weapons development. It is safe to say that the development of these weapons, if they do prove viable, can be expected to receive significant opposition from the public and concerned parties in the international community. The pervasive secrecy and reluctance to discuss such research reflects the sensitivity, that is, probable unpopularity, of this weapons research. The associated ethical issues are profound, especially due to the potential for social control if such weapons were actually realised and used either in policing or warfare.

6.6 Conclusion

Although directed energy weapons have been under investigation since the 1960s, this chapter has described the research into 'non-lethal' applications that did not begin in earnest until the early 1990s. Taking advantage of technical advances and the absence of legal constraints, research and development programmes have expanded and some new weapons have emerged including low energy 'dazzling' laser weapons.

Deployment of the millimetre wave ADS has been delayed by the need to gain a scientific understanding of the biological effects through research that has taken a number of years. Similarly to 'dazzling' laser weapons the issue of balancing safety and effectiveness means that the risk of permanent injury is dependent on exposure duration, itself dependent on operational factors and the intent of the operator rather than the weapon design. As with 'dazzling' laser weapons, increasing operational demand may hasten the adoption of the ADS. However, political and public acceptance has become the key factor that will govern the timing of deployment and the subsequent circumstances of use.

Meanwhile, the development of high energy lasers as 'non-lethal' weapons remains speculative despite the insistence of some proponents that they will offer the potential for variable effects from 'non-lethal' to 'lethal'. It should be noted that 'non-lethal' programmes are a very small part of overall directed energy weapons development efforts. Nevertheless 'non-lethal' directed energy weapons are emerging prior to 'lethal' systems and this may even ease the path to the primary goal that is the emergence of a whole new class of 'lethal' weapons based around directed energy technologies.[356] And here, of course, concerns over safety will not be a consideration.

7
Acoustic Weapons

This chapter explores programmes to develop 'non-lethal' acoustic weapons since the 1970s. It focuses on events in the US, examining military and police weapons development efforts, including concerted research and development efforts during the 1990s.

7.1 Definitions

Concepts of acoustic 'non-lethal' weapons generally involve the aim of developing a directional beam of powerful acoustic energy to disorientate or temporarily incapacitate an individual or group. The effects of sound waves on humans are complex and dependent on the frequency, sound pressure level, and duration. They may also vary from one individual to another. Table 7.1 provides a generalised summary of the threshold sound pressure levels, measured in decibels (dB), for various effects at different acoustic frequencies.

The majority of proposed acoustic 'non-lethal' weapon concepts aim to employ high-levels of either low frequencies (infrasound/low audio) or high audio frequencies to exert a physiological effect without damaging hearing. As detailed by Altmann[2] and more recently summarised by Jauchem and Cook,[3] both concepts have fundamental limitations, in terms of human effects and practicality, that appear to preclude the development of effective 'non-lethal' weapons. As regards low frequencies, infrasound can be unpleasant at high-levels but it does not have the profound effects often associated with it. Low audio can have incapacitating effects but only at very high-levels that pose a risk of permanent hearing damage. Furthermore low frequencies cannot be formed in to a directed beam and high-levels cannot be created at a distance, making indoor applications the only possibility.

High frequencies can be directed in a beam but very high-levels can only be projected a few tens of metres with acoustic sources of a practical size. More importantly, at high-levels, where some significant extra-aural effects may

Table 7.1 Threshold sound levels for various effects on humans at different acoustic frequencies in air[1]

Frequency range (Hz)	Infrasound 1–20 Hz	Low audio 20–250 Hz	High audio 250 Hz–8 kHz	Very high audio/ Ultrasound >8 kHz / >20 kHz
Ear pain	140–60 dB	135–40 dB	140 dB 120 dB – discomfort	140 dB
Permanent hearing damage from short exposure	none up to 170 dB	none up to 150 dB	135 dB (7 min) 150 dB (0.4 sec) (1–4 Hz worst)	none up to 156 dB
Eardrum rupture	>170 dB	160 dB	160 dB	Unknown
Vestibular effects (effects on balance)	none up to 170 dB	150 dB – mild nausea	140 dB – slight disturbance of equilibrium	None up to 154 dB
Effects on respiratory organs	none up to 170 dB	150 dB – intolerable effects	140 dB – tickling in mouth 160 dB – heating	140 dB – tickling in mouth 160 dB – heating

be induced with audible frequencies, there is likely to be permanent hearing damage, which is not a reversible 'extra-lethal' effect. At moderate levels, with no risk of hearing damage except for long exposures, the effect is purely psychological based around the annoyance caused by unpleasant sounds, which may not be very effective as an incapacitating weapon. Moreover, the aural effects of acoustic energy can be mitigated with earplugs or protectors.[4] Ultrasonic concepts have also been explored to induce heating effects but achieving sufficiently high-levels at a distance is a major limitation.

One further concept that is sometimes classified as an acoustic weapon technology is the vortex ring generator, which is used for the propagation of vortex rings. Contrary to the mechanism of action for other acoustic weapons the idea behind this technology is to project a vortex of air at high speed towards a target person to create an impact or alternatively to deliver a substance, such as an irritant chemical.

The focus of acoustic 'non-lethal' weapons concepts that have been explored were described in the 2003 NRC report on 'non-lethal' weapons science and technology:

The concept of acoustic NLWs [non-lethal weapons] has focused on acoustic generators projecting sound downrange to affect crowds, to pro-vide area denial, or to clear facilities. Generators that have been explored for producing these high intensities include sirens, whistles, pulse jets, vortex generators, explosives, and fuel-air devices. For interior use, very high intensity acoustics (>170 dB) have been investigated as an access-delay technology for physical security systems.[5]

Impulsive acoustic sources, such as explosives and fuel-air devices, produce a short non-directional, high-intensity shock wave that can kill in the case of explosive weapons. So-called flash-bang or stun grenades are 'non-lethal' weapons that produce a bright flash and a loud noise from a small explosion. However, they are not commonly considered as acoustic weapons and will not be addressed here. Electrical discharge devices have also been investigated for the potential to direct impulsive acoustic energy. Furthermore, loudspeakers have been considered as potential acoustic 'non-lethal' weapons, although with a view to producing psychological effects with irritating sounds rather than attempts to induce more profound physiological effects.

7.2 Past interest: Psychological operations

One of the earliest references to the use of sound as a 'non-lethal' weapon is in Applegate's 1969 book on riot control equipment and techniques. In a chapter entitled 'New Ways With Sound' he described the HPS-1 sound system, a portable loudspeaker device developed for the US military and used to communicate over long distances.[6] The battery powered system, consisting of an amplifier and four high power horn loudspeakers, could project a voice over 4 km and it was mounted on helicopters and used for psychological operations during the Vietnam War. By the late 1960s and early 1970s police forces in the US and elsewhere had acquired the system for limited use in crowd control, including the British Army for use in Northern Ireland.[7] From a law enforcement point of view the HPS-1 was primarily a very loud public address system enabling communication regardless of crowd noise. However, the system could also be fitted with an auxiliary unit called the 'Curdler', which would project unpleasant sounds designed to irritate, as Applegate enthusiastically explained:

> The Curdler unit, utilizing the full 350-watts power, emits a shrieking, shrill, blatting, pulsating, penetrating sound.
> It will break up slogan shouting, chanting, singing, handclapping, rhythmic noise beats and agitator control. By breaking up such agitation tactics, police can cause mob leaders to lose control and proceed to restore order. At close ranges, the dissonant sound is so piercing that it forces advancing would-be rioters to turn away, discard their weapons, banners, signs, etc., in order to free their hands to cover and protect their ears.[8]

The 1972 report of the US National Science Foundation (NSF) funded study on 'non-lethal' weapons paid little attention to acoustic weapons but did note with regard to the sound 'Curdler' that 'At physical distress levels [there is] serious risk of permanent impairment of hearing'.[9]

Interest had also arisen during the mid-1960s concerning the effects of infrasound and low frequency audio on the human body. Early research was carried out in relation to the US space programme in order to assess the risks from low frequency noise generated during the launch phase. It was concluded that the effects of frequencies from 1 Hz to 100 Hz at volumes of up to 150 dB, although unpleasant, were tolerable for short exposures. However, it was research conducted by the French researcher Vladimir Gavreau during the same period and published in the late 1960s, claiming to have identified profound effects of infrasound that attracted considerable publicity.[10] As Leventhall has explained, 'Gavreau made some misleading statements, which led to confusion of harmful effects of very high levels at higher frequencies with the effects of infrasound'.[11] This led to much popular speculation throughout the 1970s about the malign effects of infrasound including the potential for infrasonic weapons.[12]

Reports in *New Scientist* during 1973 claimed that the British Army had developed a device called the 'Squawk box' for use in Northern Ireland that employed two ultrasonic beams interacting to form infrasound that could incapacitate people. However, the MOD denied the existence of the weapon and instead acknowledged that they had acquired the HPS-1 audible sound system.[13] A contemporary technical analysis by Altmann discounts the possibility of developing a feasible weapon as described in *New Scientist* since, although the mechanism employing two ultrasonic beams can be used to produce infrasound, it would be impossible to produce sufficiently high-levels to have any effect.[14] In 1978 Broner published a review of the data on the effects of low frequency sound on people concluding 'the possible danger due to infrasound has been much over-rated'.[15] Nevertheless the mythology surrounding the potential for infrasonic weapons even reached the United Nations Conference of the Committee on Disarmament in Geneva, where a paper was presented by Hungary in August 1978.[16]

Although there is very little information available, it seems that the US Army investigated the potential of sound and light devices for use in crowd control during the mid-1970s in a programme called DISPERSE, which was carried out at the Army Research Laboratory (ARL), then called the Harry Diamond Laboratories.[17] Several reports were produced in 1975, including a literature review that noted:

[O]f the 'mountains' of literature dealing with sound and light, there is virtually a pittance treating the subjects in a manner directly beneficial to the DISPERSE effort. There exists ... sufficient technical information to support at least an exploratory investigation of ... aversive audible acoustic stimuli, infrasonic and ultrasonic systems, and bright flashing and flickering light.[18]

According to a recent description of this programme there were proposals to test equipment producing infrasound and audible sound and to evaluate the effects of irritating or painful sounds, although it is unclear whether these experiments were carried out.[19]

As regards vortex rings, there is limited information concerning the consideration of weapons applications during this period. However, Coates's 1970 review of potential 'non-lethal' weapons technologies for the US military did observe: 'specific devices meriting modest efforts for crowd and mob control are vortex rings and wind-generation machines'.[20] In the early 1970s the Army looked at the potential for delivering irritant chemical agents with vortex rings and the Navy were also investigating weapons applications.[21]

It appears that acoustic devices were not considered again in the context of 'non-lethal' weapons development, at least in the openly available literature, until the early 1990s. The report of the 1986 conference on 'non-lethal' weapons held by the NIJ considered a wide variety of technologies but made no mention of acoustic weapons.[22]

7.3   Weapons programmes during the 1990s

The first concerted effort to develop a 'non-lethal' acoustic weapon appears to have been research carried out as part of the Low Collateral Damage Munitions (LCDM) programme, conducted by the US Army's Armament Research, Development and Engineering Center (ARDEC) from 1991 to 1995. A request for proposals for new weapon concepts in 1991 led to a contract being awarded to SARA Inc. in June 1992 to develop two acoustic weapon prototypes, as described in a 1992 ARDEC press release:

> SARA is developing a high power, very low frequency acoustic beam weapon and is also investigating methods of projecting non-diffracting, high frequency, acoustic bullets.
>
> The beam weapon will be a piston or detonation driven pulser which forces compressed air into an array of impedanced matched tubes to generate a low frequency wave front. Very low frequency waves have shown a coupling effect in small enclosed volumes which presents an interesting potential offensive capability against threat positioned bunkers or vehicles.
>
> The acoustic bullet concept is based on a non-diffracting wave form that would offer incremental penalties (e.g. capable of inflicting a discomfort, incapacitation or lethal effect). The non-diffracting wave form will be emitted from 1-to-2 meter antenna dishes.[23]

SARA Inc. received a series of contracts during the early and mid-1990s, primarily from the Army but also from DARPA and the DOE, to investigate acoustic weapons concepts and build several prototype devices.[24] An early device was called the Infrasonic Pulser, which apparently used fuel combustion to generate infrasonic frequencies between 1 and 17 Hz. Subsequently they developed compressed air and combustion-driven sirens, all of which produced acoustic energy in the audible range.[25] They also carried out Army-sponsored research on new acoustic effects. In a 1996 report the company claimed to have identified a novel mechanism that they called Pulsed Period Stimuli:

> Under certain frequency and modulation formats, pulse acoustic waveforms potentially have the ability to interfere with the nervous system, causing disorientation, or inducing a passive state within the targeted subject.[26]

In the same document, a research proposal for the NIJ, the company put forward three concepts including a hand-held 'incapacitating weapon' employing ultrasonic frequencies, a vehicle mounted high-intensity audible sound weapon, and a low frequency sound generator weapon. They also made claims of the potential of their prototype devices to cause 'bodily discomfort', disorientation, fatigue, and nausea.[27]

7.3.1 Perpetuating myths

In the absence of scientific assessments of the potential bioeffects, claims made by weapons developers and 'non-lethal' weapons advocates were perpetuated in both the popular and the defence media from the early 1990s onwards.[28] For example, a 1993 article in *Defense Electronics* quoted John Alexander, a 'non-lethal' weapons advocate saying, 'proof of principle has been established, we can make relatively compact acoustic weapons'[29] and a 1997 story in *US News & World Report* reported that SARA Inc. had 'built a device that will make internal organs resonate: The effects can run from discomfort to damage to death'.[30] Altmann reviewed some of the claims made by SARA Inc. and others about the human effects of acoustic energy noting,

> [i]t is interesting that firms tasked by the military to look into acoustic weapons or even to do research and development of them, repeated some of the myths described [in the popular media].[31]

7.3.2 The NLAW programme

Following the establishment of the JNLWP and a review of existing 'non-lethal' weapons programmes by the JNLWD in 1997 considerable priority was given to a Non-Lethal Acoustic Weapons (NLAW) programme, led by the Army in collaboration with AFRL. At this stage the main purpose was to develop acoustic generators that could be used to demonstrate extra-aural bioeffects in people that had apparently been observed in laboratory tests. The JNLWD's 1997 Annual Report reflected a certain amount of scepticism, observing 'Identification of a target effect is the critical step needed for future acoustic weapons development'.[32]

In addition to the prototypes developed by SARA Inc., the Army had sponsored in-house research at the ARL to develop acoustic sources with potential 'non-lethal' weapons applications. ARL constructed a prototype device that produced acoustic impulses from high voltage electrical discharges called the Sequential Arc Discharge Generator (SADAG) for investigation of the effects of audible acoustic pulses at the laboratory scale.[33] Another device producing audible sound was developed by a Major in the Marine Corps and called the Gayl Blaster after the inventor.[34] The prototype comprised a series of piezoelectric transducers arranged inside a metre-long tube with the aim of producing directional audible frequencies.[35] A further concept was presented to a 1998 conference: Primex Physics International proposed to develop a weapon based upon an array of four pulsed acoustic sources to produce shock waves at ranges of 100 to 200 metres.[36]

In a similar vein to the DISPERSE programme in the 1970s, Army researchers were also revisiting the idea of combining strong sound and light. A 1996 conference paper was optimistic about the possibilities based on new developments:

One of the solutions to the problem can be the use of either acoustic energy or the combination of acoustic energy and flashing white light. Over the last decade or so, considerable efforts have been extended in the area of both acoustics and white lights. The type(s) of physiological effects can range from disorientation to even lethality.[37]

7.3.3 Testing prototypes

Research on the biological effects of infrasonic and audible 'non-lethal' acoustic weapons prototypes was carried out between mid-1996 and early 1999 at ARFL's Brooks Air Force Base site with funding from ARDEC, DARPA, and NIJ.[38] A 1998 AFRL paper acknowledged the large gap between the many ambitious claims and actual research:

[D]espite its supposed historical roots and the attention it has received in recent articles in the popular media, there is very little scientific research on the usability of acoustics as an NLW.[39]

DARPA and NIJ funding was for research on the effects of infrasound and low frequency audio.[40] The purpose of NIJ funding in 1997 was for: 'demonstrating the utility of ultra-low frequency sound as an incapacitation technology suitable for hostage rescue scenarios'.[41] AFRL researchers constructed an acoustic chamber, termed the Infrasound Test Device (ITS), and used an infrasound generator called the Mobile Acoustic System, a large trailer-mounted device with a horn 17 m wide that is normally used to test atmospheric propagation of infrasound,[42] as well as subwoofer speakers, to test the effects of infrasound on monkeys.[43] The research found little evidence of significant effects:

> The only potentially useful effect was an apparent panic response shown by rhesus monkeys in the ITS at greater than 160 dB. … The panic response we saw in monkeys might be a useful [effect], but the required intensity of infrasound would probably be hard to sustain in the 'battlespace' at any distance.[44]

Furthermore the volume of the test chamber used was described by researchers as 'too small to be relevant as an indoor acoustic weapon'.[45] Additional experimentation in larger spaces suggested that even indoor infrasound weapons would not be viable:

> Subsequently, a unique reverberant resonant chamber was designed and constructed of reinforced concrete. A moveable wall allowed tuning to specific frequencies, and creation of standing waves of maximal intensity at different frequencies. There were no significant effects on subject behavior. Due to the difficulty of obtaining high sound pressure levels in a large volume, further extensive experimentation was not suggested.[46]

The Army's ARDEC funded research on the effects of high-intensity audible acoustic devices, which was also conducted by scientists at AFRL:

> The primary goal of the project was to determine if narrow-band, high-intensity acoustic energy in the audible frequency range could be used as a non-lethal weapon; that is, could it disrupt the goal-directed behavior of a highly-motivated non-human surrogate without causing a permanent threshold shift in hearing.[47]

Five different acoustic weapon prototypes were tested on animals: two compressed air driven sirens designed and built by SARA Inc. for laboratory testing (one with a frequency range of 750 to 2500 Hz and the other 1500 to 10,000 Hz), which produced average sound levels of 110 and 129 dB during the experiments; a prototype truck-mounted combustion driven siren also built by SARA Inc. and called the Dismounted Battlefield Battle Laboratory (DBBL) Siren, measured to have a maximum sound level of 93 dB; the

Army's SADAG, producing a maximum sound level of 165 dB; and the Gayl Blaster with a maximum sound level of 126 dB. However, the researchers found no significant effects, leading them to conclude that 'none of the four devices tested would have obvious utility as a non-lethal weapon'.[48] Furthermore they argued:

> On the basis of our experimental results, it appears to be unlikely that acoustic energy in the audible frequency range up to approximately 165 dB in intensity will provide useful 'extra-aural' effects. Thus it appears that narrow-band, high intensity acoustic energy in the audible frequency range would not have much utility as a non-lethal weapon.[49]

One of the devices, the SADAG, did affect the behaviour of pigs but had no effect on monkeys while also causing permanent hearing damage. The researchers pointed out that 'hearing damage alone is probably sufficient cause to exclude the use of a device as a non-lethal weapon'.[50] The SADAG device also produced infrasound but another test found no effects on behaviour with these low frequencies when tested on monkeys with hearing protectors.[51]

It is likely that the negative results of the AFRL testing[52] on the effects of high-intensity audible and infrasonic frequencies produced by these prototype systems were the major factor in the decision of the JNLWD to terminate the NLAW programme in September 1999.[53] Similarly negative conclusions about the viability of acoustic 'non-lethal' weapons were reached in a 1996 study by the UK MOD[54] and also in an independent technical assessment by Altmann in 1999.[55]

7.3.4 Vortex rings

Vortex ring weapons concepts were also explored in the mid and late 1990s. At ARL, researchers proposed the concept of modifying the Mk19-3 40 mm grenade launcher to fire gas vortices for delivering chemical agents. In May 1997 a programme to develop a prototype device was funded by the recently established JNLWD:[56]

> The Vortex Ring Gun (VRG) program will design, build, and successfully demonstrate the capability to produce a combustion-driven, ring vortices that will deter and disorient hostile individuals and crowds. This effort includes integration of concussion, flash, chemical and impulsive methods into a single delivery system capable of being focused onto a specific individual. The gas could be air, CO_2, or a knockout or crowd control compound.[57]

Despite this initial optimism, the programme was ended in 1998 due to 'unpredictable vortices and limits on effective range'.[58]

7.3.5   The end of the road?

In a 2000 paper Altmann summarised the outlook for acoustic weapons thus:

> Many of the allegations about the effects and properties of acoustic weapons, in particular using infrasound, contradict scientific evidence.
>
> At audio frequencies, if more that 'annoyance' is required, marked effects can be produced at short range but only at sound levels that pose clear dangers to unprotected hearing.[59]

The same conclusion was reached by the NRC panel having reviewed the range of acoustic weapons concepts explored during the 1990s:

> Traditional acoustic methods have not been successful in causing reliable non-lethal effects in any but highly restricted conditions (e.g., when flash bangs are used). This is true despite decades of anecdotal references describing debilitating effects of certain low frequencies. No program is currently exploring more basic mechanisms for traditional acoustic susceptibilities.[60]

7.4   Contemporary developments

7.4.1   The Long Range Acoustic Device (LRAD)

Despite dismissing most acoustic 'non-lethal' weapons concepts, the National Research panel did discuss two areas that they considered worthy of further investigation. The first, which they observed 'might be more appropriately considered in the realm of psychological tools or communication technologies' rather than acoustic weapons, was a technology using ultrasonic frequencies with their shorter wavelengths to give greater directivity for projecting audible sound.[61] Two companies, American Technology Corp. (ATC) and Holosonic Research Labs Inc., had both been working on these technologies for projecting sound during the 1990s.[62] In the late 1990s, ATC released its HyperSonic Sound directional loudspeaker systems based on this principle.[63] As described by Altmann, the system,

> emits modulated ultrasound that is then demodulated by non-linear effects in the air to produce audible sound, but with much higher directivity due to the short wavelengths of the ultrasound.[64]

While this technology presented clear opportunities for use in the entertainment and advertising industries, it does not appear to have been pursued further for 'non-lethal' weapons applications. However, ATC had also begun working on a related directed acoustic technology for military applications, which it called High Intensity Directed Acoustics (HIDA):

> HIDA devices incorporate highly-directional long-range hailing capability with acoustic non-lethal weapon potential to meet the increasing need to warn and protect ships, vehicles and facilities from would-be intruders. HIDA has been successfully tested in field conditions in hailing intruders at 500 yards or more without unduly distracting bystanders.[65]

Rather than employing ultrasonic signals, this technology consists of an array of acoustic sources, essentially loudspeakers, moving together (in phase) to direct a beam of audible sound.[66] In 2002 the company was awarded a contract by the US Navy to build a prototype device, which it called the LRAD, and by 2003 the first six devices were deployed on Navy ships. According to the company, a major impetus for the development of the LRAD was consideration of ship defences following the attack on the USS Cole Navy warship in October 2000. The LRAD, which costs around $30,000,[67] is described by the company as follows:

> The Long Range Acoustic Device (LRAD) is highly directive acoustic array designed for long-range communication and unmistakable warning. The LRAD device can issue a verbal warning and has the capability of following up with a deterrent tone to influence behavior or determine intent.[68]

The LRAD 1000 is a circular dish 0.8 m in diameter and 15 cm thick. It comprises of an amplifier and an acoustic emitter made up of an array of acoustic sources. The maximum intensity is maintained in a beam 30 degrees wide. Outside that area the sound levels decrease considerably but not entirely, for instance the sound level behind the dish is 40 dB lower than in front.[69]

The company produce two main versions of the system, the LRAD 1000 and a smaller version called the LRAD 500,[70] and released three new systems in 2008.[71] Both the LRAD 1000 and LRAD 500 have two modes: voice mode for transmitting voices or other sounds via the audio input, and tone mode for transmitting a high pitched warning sound. In tone, or warning, mode the LRAD 1000 can produce a maximum sound level of 151 dB for a short burst or continuous power of 146 dB at a distance of 1 metre. Altmann estimated that this would fall off to a maximum of 130 dB at 4 m and 120 dB at 60 m, which fits with the manufacturers assessment.[72] In voice mode it produces a maximum of 120 dB at 1 m, which falls off with increasing distance. The LRAD 1000 is designed for use at ranges of up to 500 m in voice mode and up to 1 km in tone mode. The smaller LRAD 500 has a maximum power of 145 dB at 1 metre in tone mode and is designed for use at up to 300 m in voice mode and 500 m in tone mode.[73]

By September 2005 around 350 LRAD systems had been deployed, many with US forces in Iraq. US military users include: the Navy, for ship protection and maritime interdiction; the Army for use at checkpoints and for psychological operations; the Military Police, for use at prison camps; and the Marine Corps.[74] According to a July 2005 report, the 3rd Infantry Division of the US Army had deployed 150 LRADs.[75] LRAD systems have also been used on two UK Navy ships in the Gulf and have been acquired by wide variety of law enforcement and commercial organisations including the US Coast Guard, Arizona Border Patrol, New York Police Department, Los Angeles Police Department, and cruise ship companies such as Princess and P&O, among others.[76] Another report indicated that the LRAD was being tested for use in US prisons.[77] Marines supporting the relief effort in New Orleans in the aftermath of Hurricane Katrina had several systems for addressing the crowds[78] and in November 2005 the LRAD was used to repel a pirate attack on the cruise ship *Luxury Spirit* as it was at sea off the Somali coast.[79] In 2007 it was used against Government opposition protesters in Tbilisi, Georgia.[80] In 2008 it emerged that LRAD systems had been exported to Australia, Singapore, Korea, and China, the latter raising some human rights concerns.[81] The LRAD is also available in the UK,[82] where the Metropolitan Police, for example, recommended it be reviewed for use in crowd control.[83]

7.4.2 An acoustic weapon?

Rather than classifying the LRAD as an acoustic 'non-lethal' weapon the US Department of Defense has characterised it as an 'acoustic hailing device', which the JNLWP defines as follows:

> Acoustic Hailing Devices (AHDs) are non-lethal, non-kinetic, long-range hailing and warning devices. They use advanced directed acoustic energy technology to provide a non-lethal warning capability with a range beyond that of any current non-lethal device available to U.S. forces. AHDs are capable of producing highly directional sound beams that allow users to project warning tones and intelligible voice commands beyond small arms engagement range.[84]

The DOD funded a safety study of the LRAD, which was conducted at Pennsylvania State University and concluded:

> LRAD can be safely employed as a 'hailing and warning' device based on applying the MIL-STD 1474D standards for operator safety and OSHA [Occupational Safety and Health Administration] standards for target population.[85]

Essentially this means that operators of the LRAD must wear hearing protection and that for those exposed to the beam the duration must be limited according to the US guidelines for occupational noise at different sound pressure levels. The US legal guidelines for permissible noise exposure set by OSHA advise that exposure to sound levels of 115 dB should be less than 15 minutes, although guidelines on higher levels are not given.[86] However, the US National Institute for Occupational Health and Safety has recommended that much tighter guidelines on safe exposures be set to avoid hearing damage from occupational noise over the course of a lifetime. In a 1998 report, 'Criteria for a Recommended Standard: Occupational Noise Exposure', they advise that exposure should be a maximum of 28 seconds at 115 dB, 9 seconds at 120 dB, 1 second at 127 dB, and less than 1 second at 130–40 dB.[87]

The measurements of the maximum output of the LRAD taken as a basis for setting guidelines on its use were taken by the Pennsylvania State University researchers who recorded a maximum sound level in tone mode of 121 dB at 25 metres and 107 dB at 100 m. They recommended that use of maximum power in tone mode be limited to ranges beyond 75 m and beyond 15 m in voice mode.[88] This means that there is a risk of hearing damage within these ranges, which increases with shorter distance and longer exposure duration.[89] Others, including Altmann have argued for greater precautions:

Avoiding permanent hearing damage to unprotected target subjects requires keeping appropriate limits for intensity and duration, depending on the distance. Thus, the rules for weapon operation are decisive. In order to prevent operator errors and overdoses, technical precautions – limiting the sound power and/or duration according to the target distance – are recommended.[90]

Since the LRAD is not classified as a weapon it has not been through the international legal review required for all new weapons. The military argue that this is because it is intended to be used for long-range communication rather than as a weapon.[91] However, they have sought to enhance the effects of the LRAD by developing specific unpleasant sounds, such as the sound of a baby crying played backwards, that can be transmitted via the audio input.[92] The likely use of these sounds played at high levels is to clear people out of an area or a building, drawing parallels with the unsuccessful attempts using loud music to force Panamanian General Noriega to surrender in 1989 and using various unpleasant sounds and music to break the 1993 siege at Waco.[93] Unconfirmed reports on the use of the LRAD in Iraq by the US Army's 361st Psychological Operations company observe:

The LRAD has proven useful for clearing streets and rooftops during cordon and search, for disseminating command information, and for drawing out enemy snipers who are subsequently destroyed by our own snipers.[94]

A number of companies now produce similar acoustic systems that are promoted for military use, which use arrays of loudspeakers to direct a beam
of audible acoustic energy.[95] One company makes the claim that its systems
can function as 'non-lethal' weapon: 'turning up the volume and shortening
the distance between our systems and the enemy can provide a debilitating
sound'.[96]

In 2006 the JNLWD began evaluating a number of commercially available systems as potential 'Acoustic Hailing Devices' with testing carried
out by researchers from the Army's ARDEC, Navy, and Pennsylvania State
University.[97] A February 2006 article claimed that the JNLWD had tested a
device that 'cracked windshields'.[98]

7.4.3   Persistent research and development

Despite the closure of the Army-led programmes on 'non-lethal' acoustic
weapons in the late 1990s, ARDEC has continued research on acoustic weapons concepts. ARDEC began working on research and development with
ATC in 2002[99] and in 2005 it awarded $4 million in funding to New Jersey
Medical School to investigate whether devices such as the LRAD could be
used in a more weapon-like manner as described in a 2005 DOD report on
collaborative research:

> To assist Army Research Development and Engineering Center (ARDEC)
> in determining whether long range directional acoustic devices in gen-
> eral, and the Long Range Acoustic Device (LRAD) in particular, can be
> used *more aggressively* in protecting assets and controlling areas as part of
> the overall non-lethal mission capabilities[100] [emphasis added].

In a similar vein to claims made by SARA Inc.[101] during the 1990s the developers of the LRAD have made bold claims about the potential effects of their
directed acoustic systems. In the *New York Times* the inventor was reported
as saying: 'HIDA [high intensity directed acoustics] can instantaneously
cause loss of equilibrium, vomiting, migraines – really we can pretty much
pick our ailment'.[102]

Meanwhile, ARDEC has also continued work on the hand-held acoustic
weapon prototype, the Gayl Blaster, which has now been renamed the
Aversive Audible Acoustic Device (A3D).[103] As described above, it employs
piezoelectric acoustic devices arranged in a line in a long tube. A similar
technical approach was taken by German researchers in developing a hand-
held acoustic weapon concept called the Directed Stick Radiator.[104] The
patent was purchased by ATC and they have been working on a prototype
device since at least 2001[105] in collaboration with ARDEC.[106] In a possible
reference to the Directed Stick Radiator the company claimed in late 2003
that a version of its HIDA technology, which was at the concept stage, had
'potential application as a scaleable nonlethal weapon with significantly

increased output for specialized military and government applications'.[107] The proposed device has also been referred to as the 'Acoustic Bazooka'.[108] The technical concept is described by Altmann as follows:

> [T]his is a linear array of piezoelectric sound emitters. The signals fed to the latter are delayed by the sound propagation time from one speaker to the next, so that constructive superposition takes place in the forward direction and the emission cone is correspondingly narrower.[109]

The stated aim of ongoing ARDEC research is to 'develop an acoustic device that can be used for crowd control, clearing facilities, or incapacitating individuals'.[110] ARDEC researchers have also carried out development work on integrating acoustic technology into a 'non-lethal' landmine combined with bright flashing light.[111]

Much of the ongoing research and development at ARDEC is underpinned by a collaboration between ARDEC's Target Behavioral Response Laboratory (TBRL), which was set up to investigate the development of so-called scaleable effects weapons, that is, from 'non-lethal' to 'lethal', based on acoustic and directed energy technologies, and the New Jersey Medical School, where ARDEC has established the Stress and Motivated Behavior Institute (SMBI) to garner neurobehavioural expertise.[112] In addition to studying the human effects of sound and light with a view to developing more effective 'flash-bang' devices,[113] SMBI researchers have been carrying out work to assess which types of audible sounds are most aversive.[114] More surprisingly perhaps, given the termination research sponsored by the JNLWP in the late 1990s the Army has even continued to carry out research on infrasound. In 2000 an ARL scientist reported that work was underway to construct a new infrasonic test chamber to enable testing at sound levels of up to 155 dB.[115] Furthermore, ARDEC has funded animal testing at the SMBI to assess effects of infrasound. Research, exposing rats to various infrasonic frequencies and sound levels began in 2003.[116] A 2006 conference paper by SMBI scientists explained that the research with audible and infrasonic frequencies was being carried out to evaluate 'their effectiveness in disrupting targeting, balance, and high-order cognitive processes in both humans and animals'.[117] They drew the following interim conclusion:

> While our data suggest that there are unconditional aversive properties of sound, truly aversive sound has been elusive. Integrative experimental methods are necessary – incorporating physiology, behavior, self report – to advance the science of acoustics as nonlethal weapons and techniques.[118]

Research on acoustic weapons concepts has also been funded by the JNLWD through NTIC at the University of New Hampshire. This has included basic research on the biological effects of ultrasound, which has been carried out at Wayne State University.[119]

With the cancellation of the vortex ring research in the late 1990s the US military does not appear to be working on 'non-lethal' weapons based around that concept although in 2003 SARA Inc. was still advertising a Vortex Launcher claiming, 'the vortex feels like having a bucket of ice water thrown into your chest'.[120] However, research and development of vortex ring generator weapons, either to produce an impact or for delivery of irritant chemicals, has continued in several other countries including the UK, Germany, and Russia.[121] A 2004 Canadian report on 'non-lethal' weapons research and development observed:

> Early R&D indicates that vortex ring generators may be able to deliver low frequency periodic shock waves, which combined with high noise levels, could be used as a crowd control device. Single burst vortex rings are able to knock targets off balance at short ranges, without doing any long-term harm. Vortex rings could also transport irritants (gas or particulates) to enhance crowd control.[122]

7.4.4 Underwater weapons

Aside from systems using ultrasonic frequencies to direct audible sound in the air, the only other area specifically recommended for further investigation by the NRC panel on 'non-lethal' weapons in 2003 was the use of acoustic sources as underwater 'non-lethal' weapons:

> Underwater applications present a potentially more promising scenario ... due to the increased coupling of acoustic energy. Past investigations have considered the use of ship SONAR against underwater threats. Also being investigated are underwater acoustic sources as warning or non-lethal options against such threats.[123]

The Applied Research Laboratories at the University of Texas at Austin were contracted by the US Navy to review the potential of developing a 'non-lethal' weapon targeted at divers and swimmers. The 2002 final report addressed a variety of techniques but focused on acoustic sources, reviewing studies of the biological effects of acoustic energy on humans and animals underwater, many of which had been conducted to set exposure limits for divers near military sonar systems. They recommended that systems producing very low frequency sound should be pursued including impulsive sound sources because of the potential for extra-aural effects underwater:[124]

> From the results of all the experiments and studies reviewed for this report, it is likely that the 20–100 Hz band is the one most likely to cause lung and/or vestibular discomfort. The most consistent factor in noise induced bioeffects is not frequency, but intensity, with exposure time of nearly equal importance.

A number of systems, both existing and proposed, are capable of producing high intensity sound in the 20–100 Hz band. Historically, this
frequency range has been the most difficult to produce using traditional
piezoelectric transducers. Other approaches such as air guns, spark
sources, and explosives are more commonly used. Spark sources and
explosives produce impulse noise, which is high intensity, short duration
sound with the majority of its energy below 500 Hz.[125]

The researchers concluded that future research should include further
tests on the bioeffects of low frequency sound on animals and humans
in water.[126] One technology they identified in particular was a spark gap
sound source, also called a plasma sound source, which produces an acoustic impulse from an electrical discharge. This is a similar technique to that
used in the Army's prototype SADAG. The report describes the technology
as 'an attractive candidate for swimmer deterrence' because it can produce
low frequency sound as well as producing a bright flash and it can be pulsed
repetitively.[127] The University of Texas researchers noted that a company
had proposed such a device for port security in 1992.[128] More recently, at
two conferences in 2006, another company proposed this technology as
a 'non-lethal' weapon for use underwater[129] and on land.[130] Several other
companies have also made proposals for underwater acoustic 'non-lethal'
weapons in recent years.[131]

In 2005 the US Coast Guard introduced a security system called the
Integrated Anti-Swimmer System, which combines acoustic sensors to detect
people in the water and an underwater loud-hailing system.[132] Research has
been ongoing a more powerful loudhailer with a range of 500 metres and
a prototype was developed in 2006.[133] The Navy have also been evaluating several concepts for an acoustic 'non-lethal' weapon to be added to
the overall security system. A prototype Diver Interdiction System is under
development with funding from the US Coast Guard and the JNLWD.[134]
Also, in 2008 the Navy was seeking proposals for a Non-Lethal Surface
Swimmer Deterrent System, which might incorporate acoustic and electrical
devices.[135]

7.4.5   A failed enterprise

In general acoustic 'non-lethal' weapons concepts have been found to have
major limitations, as a 2004 Defence Research and Development Canada
report observed:

> The opportunities for weaponization of acoustic devices (for defence
> applications) seem limited at present, and despite some claims in the
> literature the technology does not seem to have passed the level of
> annoying/repelling people through the use of mere sound intensity.

Many countries have reduced the amount of their R&D effort in this direction.[136]

As regards use of acoustic devices to annoy or irritate, as with systems such as the LRAD, the University of Texas review of potential acoustic 'non-lethal' weapons concluded: 'A determined mindset can enable a committed attacker to overcome a purely psychological deterrent, making irritating audible sound a poor choice [as a non-lethal weapon]'.[137]

Researchers at AFRL who conducted the experiments with acoustic devices in the late 1990s have explicitly cautioned against ongoing research for some years.[138] Their comprehensive review published in *Military Medicine* in 2007 warned that more resources could be wasted in pursuing acoustic weapons for use on land, for which there is no evidential basis:

The lack of practicality in using acoustic weapons has not prevented patents related to such technology being issued. Some research on potential acoustic nonlethal weapon prototypes has continued despite the lack of a repeatable useful bioeffect. ... without sufficient attention to bioeffects regarding nonlethal weapon concepts (including acoustic energy), military services could end up developing expensive hardware that would be operationally useless.

On the basis of results of numerous investigations, it seems unlikely that high-intensity acoustic energy in the audible, infrasonic, or low-frequency ranges will provide a device suitable to be used as a nonlethal weapon.[139]

Nevertheless acoustic 'non-lethal' weapons concepts were emphasised in a 2006 announcement seeking proposals for research and development in support of the JNLWP. One of the major research goals for fiscal years 2006 and 2007 included:

Develop long-range acoustic and/or ocular devices to support operational requirements while minimizing adverse health consequences. This includes the development of military effective 'sounds', acoustic propagation/targeting tools, NL [non-lethal] Acoustic Weapon decision employment tools, scalable distributed (phased) arrays, remote acoustic measurement sensing tools (to ensure proper acoustic energy on target), scaleable and adaptive beam-forming tools, and novel NL Acoustic sources including compact ultra-sonic heterodyning systems.[140]

JNLWD and Pennsylvania State University are developing a device called the Distributed Sound and Light Array (DSLA), which combines an acoustic array with a 'dazzling' laser and bright white lights.[141]

7.5   Major themes

7.5.1   Failed attempts

As this chapter has shown, despite longstanding interest in the concept of acoustic 'non-lethal' weapons concerted weapons research programmes conducted during the 1990s, which aimed to employ infrasound, low frequencies, and audible frequencies at high intensities, failed to find either significant effects or practicality of these concepts.

The major barrier to development of acoustic 'non-lethal' weapons has not been a technical one. Rather it has been the fact that there are no extra-aural physiological effects on humans caused by high-intensity acoustics that may act as a means of incapacitation without causing permanent ear damage. This discovery had been made during the 1960s and 1970s, and so it is unsurprising that research in the context of 'non-lethal' weapons development during the 1990s reached the same conclusion.

7.5.2   Limits of technical advances

One significant development in recent years has been the introduction of devices such as the LRAD that employ arrays of speakers to direct audible sound over long distances. Seemingly, this has led to a refocusing of interest on the potential for using directed audible frequencies to cause psychological effects. Nevertheless at high intensities the risk of permanent hearing damage remains while the potential for incapacitation is very limited.

Underwater applications may prove feasible, due to the differing properties of acoustic energy in that environment, although it remains to be seen whether incapacitating effects can be demonstrated that will not put the swimmer or diver in immediate danger of drowning or decompression sickness due to rapid ascent to the surface. On land vortex ring generators may yet be able to be used to produce a limited impact or, more likely, as a delivery system for chemical agents. However, they remain at the research and development stage.

7.5.3   Misinformation

One of the main factors maintaining ongoing interest in the development of acoustic 'non-lethal' weapons has been misinformation concerning potential effects. Animal testing by the Air Force to evaluate these claims based on existing prototypes led to the cancellation of several weapons programmes in the late 1990s. However, this has not led to a cessation of research and development into extra-aural effects despite reiteration by Air Force researchers that acoustic 'non-lethal' weapons are not viable for use on land beyond use of loud audible sound for psychological effect.

This leads to another factor affecting ongoing development; that is the role of research and development institutions. The Army's ARDEC was the first group in the US military to investigate the potential of acoustic weaponry for 'non-lethal' weapons applications in the mid-1970s and, with the resurgence of interest in the field in the early 1990s, it was ARDEC that led research and development efforts both prior to and after the establishment of the JNLWD. Even now, following dismissal of most acoustic weapons concepts by AFRL, ARDEC has continued research and development. This has included research on infrasound, which is widely assessed to be both ineffective and impractical for weapons applications. It seems that the long-standing interest of ARDEC researchers and promotion of acoustic weapons concepts has sustained ongoing research that runs contrary to available scientific evidence.

7.5.4   Legal evasion

Discussions of legal restrictions with regard to acoustic weapons have been limited since many proposed acoustic weapons that might have presented cause for concern have failed to materialise.[142] Although the general provisions of humanitarian law prohibiting weapons that cause unnecessary suffering or indiscriminate effects apply, there are no specific legal regimes governing potential acoustic weapons. Interestingly, the only major new system to be deployed by the US military, the LRAD, has not been classified as a weapon and therefore has not been subject to the legal review required of new weapons. It has also avoided export controls that might limit its distribution to countries with poor human rights records. This is the current status even though it could be used at close ranges to cause damaging effects and despite ongoing research to assess the potential for using such devices more aggressively. Ultimately, however, weapons presented as 'non-lethal' that cause permanent hearing loss are very unlikely to find political and public acceptance.[143]

7.6   Conclusion

Efforts to develop 'non-lethal' acoustic weapons that have incapacitating effects have not been successful. The systems that have been deployed in recent years have been described as 'hailing devices' rather than 'non-lethal' weapons. Given past assessments that rule out extra-aural effects below the threshold for permanent hearing damage, applications of these 'hailing devices' appear limited to irritating or psychological effects and ongoing efforts to develop acoustic 'non-lethal' weapons seem likely to fail.[144]

8
Conclusion

Ostensibly the major driver for the development of 'non-lethal' weapons has been to apply force without causing permanent injury or death, and thereby to reduce the requirement for lethal force. However, the historical record sheds light on a much more complex story, with varied drivers, premeditated and unanticipated results, and challenges to social, ethical, and legal norms.

8.1 The police–military divide

For police forces these weapons have been sought primarily as *alternatives* to 'lethal' weapons. Initial impetus came from public, political, and legal demands for weapons and tactics that would reduce the dangers from police use of force. However, as more new weapons have been taken up by police forces, for the most part they have found their utility not as replacements for firearms, but as additional tools of force to supplement them. By their very nature, as pain caus-ing devices not intended to permanently injure or kill, they lend themselves to use in gaining compliance. This led early observers to characterise them as part of the 'technology of political control', reflecting the view that these weapons provided the opportunity to use force to control people and situations where conventional force could not be justified. To a certain extent emphasis has also shifted from the need to reduce the injury to the victim, to a requirement to reduce the likelihood of injury to a police officer in situations where force may be required. As such, the wide deployment of 'non-lethal' weapons can actually lead to an increase in the use of force, and a decrease in the overall threshold for police use of force. Of course this does not reflect all use of 'non-lethal' weapons, since there are numerous examples of plastic bullets, Tasers, and other weapons being used against individuals posing a threat with a knife or other dangerous weapon.

Although the pain causing nature of 'non-lethal' weapons provides high potential for misuse, it is the policy underpinning their use that can either minimise or exacerbate this inherent danger. For example, if a police officer is permitted to use a Taser against someone who is unarmed, in handcuffs, or simply not compliant with their instructions then a very different outcome might be expected to a situation where use of the Taser is restricted to circumstances where the use of a firearm, or other dangerous weapon, can be justified due to the threat from an armed individual. In the latter situation the use of the 'non-lethal' weapon does indeed offer an alternative to the use of 'lethal' force and the opportunity for reducing the likelihood of permanent injury or death.

For the military, the potential role for 'non-lethal' weapons is altogether more confused. From the outset the military have seen these weapons as *adjuncts* to 'lethal' weapons, and moreover, as force multipliers in certain situations. The marketing potential of the term 'non-lethal' was quickly recognised. In perhaps the most large-scale use of 'non-lethal' weapons in history, the US employment of CS during the Vietnam War, they were sold as tools for the humane use of force while being used to enhance the killing power of conventional bombs and bullets. It might be tempting to dismiss this historical example as, at best, unintended or unforeseen. However, when US military planners came to agree on a policy underlying the development, deployment, and use of 'non-lethal' weapons in the mid-1990s, while selling a revolution, they aimed for the status quo and enshrined the use of 'non-lethal' weapons to *increase* casualties in official policy. Such premeditated policy precludes force multiplication as an unanticipated consequence and contradicts the entire concept of using these weapons to reduce permanent injury and death. A recent example was the 2002 Moscow siege when Russian Special Forces executed hostage takers while they were unconscious from the effects of an anaesthetic drug.

While military research and development of 'non-lethal' weapons has grown considerably, the main end-users of 'non-lethal' weapons have continued to be police organisations, who have taken advantage of military and private sector advances. Before any overall concepts of 'non-lethal' weapons were first articulated in the 1960s, technical developments in military chemical weapons programmes were promoted to the police, and adoption of CN and then CS followed. Where the technological push comes from the military there are concerns over the potential for militarisation of the police. This should include wide public engagement. This process can also have the side effect of normalising public opinion about a weapon to allow less scrutiny of subsequent military use. For example, suggestions have been made that the Active Denial System (ADS) should be used by US police forces to pave the way for use by the military in Iraq. Thus military and police concepts of 'non-lethal' weapons are distinct, while technology sharing is fluid. However, the role of the private sector, and in the US for example, the commercial market for self-defence weapons, in the uptake of new weapons by police should not be overlooked. The widespread use of OC ('pepper spray'), and Tasers was driven in part by these commercial endeavours.

Even in the US military itself, the use of 'non-lethal' weapons has largely been limited to policing type functions, such as at prison camps for controlling prisoners, at checkpoints for stopping drivers, for crowd control in protecting military convoys, and some peacekeeping operations. The question remains whether this is due to the inadequacy of existing 'non-lethal' weapons or an unwillingness to substitute 'non-lethal' for 'lethal' force. In truth, it is likely a combination of the two, and relevant to both military and police use. It could be argued that 'non-lethal' weapons are filling their potential as tools of compliance, or 'technologies of political control', and that they cannot be expected to be used particularly widely against those wielding 'lethal' weapons, at least without a significant change in policy.

8.2   Conflict as a catalyst

A central theme to emerge in this book has been the role of operational priorities, themselves determined by prevailing conflict, in catalysing 'non-lethal' weapons development at certain points in time. Although the irritant chemical agent CS had been standardised by the US Army by the early 1960s, it was not until the Vietnam War that research and development was accelerated to develop new weapons systems, and associated military doctrine put into place to enable their use. New impetus had also been given to efforts to develop incapacitating biochemical weapons in the early to mid-1970s, which faded with the end of the Vietnam conflict. During the strategic stand-off of the Cold War 'non-lethal' weapons concepts were of little military value but as it drew to a close, and US involvement in peacekeeping operations expanded in the early and mid-1990s, attention to 'non-lethal' weapons as potential technologies to assist in military 'operations other than war' and urban warfare increased greatly. Most recently the war in Iraq, and particularly the subsequent occupation, has raised operational demand and led to the limited deployment of some new 'non-lethal' weapons. Moreover the prevailing preoccupation with counterterrorism in the context of the so-called 'war on terror' and the perceived utility of 'non-lethal' weapons has also enhanced demand for technology development.

This process is mirrored in the policing arena with changing operational priorities. Riots in the US were the reason for initial police interest in developing new 'non-lethal' weapons in the 1960s and 1970s, restrictions on the use of 'lethal' force in police confrontations were the drivers in 1980s, high-profile policing disasters such as Waco provided impetus during the 1990s, and in recent years the focus of homeland security and counterterrorism has sustained and expanded the demand.

8.3   A failed revolution?

As shown in Chapters 2, 3, and 4, numerous technologies have been explored and tested since the 1970s, including smokes, lubricants, foams, malodorants, high-intensity lights, vortex rings, and various delivery systems. The development of drugs, and other incapacitating biochemical agents, as weapons has been pursued from the 1950s onward, directed energy weapons for 'non-lethal' applications since the 1980s, and acoustic weapons since the 1970s. Despite these efforts, the successful development, integration, and use of new 'non-lethal' weapons has been limited. Irritant chemical weapons (RCAs), blunt impact projectiles, and electrical weapons are still the mainstay of both military and police 'non-lethal' weapons capabilities, and most continue to suffer from deficiencies in terms of safety and effectiveness. The list of 'non-lethal' weapons that are currently available[1] does not differ greatly from similar compilations 30 years previously[2] although there have certainly been some significant changes and additions made to the 1970s versions of these technologies. Of these, the most significant in terms of recent technical advances has been the development of the higher-powered Taser electrical weapons, which has increased effectiveness while also heightening safety concerns. However, advocates' promise of revolutionary technologies remains unfulfilled, an aspiration rather than a reality.

Nevertheless some new weapons have been deployed in recent years and others are emerging, such as the millimetre wave ADS. Incapacitating biochemical weapons have been used by Russian Special Forces, including the first use in Moscow in 2002. 'Dazzling' laser weapons were the first directed energy 'non-lethal' weapons to be deployed on any significant scale, when sent to Iraq in 2006. And the Long Range Acoustic Device (LRAD) has been deployed by the US military and some police forces since 2003. Ongoing research and development emphasises expanding range and precision, and weapons with variable effects.

It should be noted that this research, based on the available open literature, has sought to contribute to knowledge and analysis of 'non-lethal' weapons programmes in the US and to a lesser extent the UK. A challenge for future research is to investigate activities in other countries where research and development activities are underway.

8.3.1 Drugs and the mind

Chapter 5 showed that, despite considerable attention and investment at several points during the past 60 years, weapons programmes have failed to produce a viable 'non-lethal' biochemical weapon that would not cause significant mortality in operational conditions. Developers have looked to advances in science and technology to resolve technical barriers. Although efforts to elicit specific effects have been aided by advances in the understanding of the brain and drug discovery, the narrow safety margins of these potent drugs and the inability to control the dose delivered have kept the concept from fruition.

Of course this is not the whole story. The inability of the technology to deliver a 'non-lethal' effect did not prevent their use on a large scale in

2002 causing the deaths of over 15 per cent of those exposed, nor did the legal constraints of the CWC and the BWC, which have delayed but not prevented the emergence of these new biochemical weapons. Operational demand for the types of effects that these weapons are perceived to offer has increased, and advocacy by military institutions and related proponents seeking to influence policy has seemingly had a significant impact in sustaining research and development in the hope that a scientific solution will emerge.

8.3.2   Directed-energy evolution

8.3.2.1   'Dazzling' lasers

As described in Chapter 6, the technology for the development of the most basic directed energy weapons, low energy 'dazzling' lasers, has long been available but the problem of balancing safety with effectiveness has delayed deployment. While efforts in the mid-1990s failed to produce an effective weapon that was eye safe at short-range, in recent years weapons development has favoured higher power devices, relying on operational, rather than technological, controls to avoid eye damage. It seems that the major factors leading to the eventual deployment of 'dazzling' laser weapons have been operational demand, as seen recently during the conflict in Iraq, and a change of approach meaning that new higher-powered weapons are more effective but present greater risk of eye injury.

Advocacy by concerned organisations played a crucial role in drawing public attention to the development of blinding lasers, dismissing the suggestion that they could be put forward as valid 'non-lethal' weapons, and successfully reversing policy on weapons that proved abhorrent to the public consciousness. This has set tighter parameters on the development and use of laser weapons targeting the human eye. If the use of emerging 'dazzling' laser weapons, which are not intended to cause permanent damage, does in fact lead to eye injuries then their use could prove hard to sustain.

8.3.2.2   High energy lasers

Although promoted as a key area for the future by the US military, the development of high energy lasers as 'non-lethal' weapons remains speculative. No viable mechanism of action has been identified and the potential for destructive effects is seemingly incompatible with 'non-lethal' weapons applications. A case could be made that the 'non-lethal' terminology is being used purposefully to promote new 'lethal' weapons systems. Given the demonstrated effects and the stated aim of designing rheostatic weapons, describing programmes such as the PEP as 'non-lethal' appears disingenuous. At the very least, the potential of high energy lasers as 'non-lethal' weapons has been greatly exaggerated.

8.3.2.3 Radio frequency, microwave, and millimetre wave beams

Research and development of radio frequency, microwave, and millimetre wave weapons has yet to produce a fielded weapon, although the ADS is now at the advanced prototype stage. With heating as a clear mechanism of action, the main issue has been the requirement to characterise the complex interactions of certain frequencies and power levels in the human body. While the developers of the ADS believe that this understanding is sufficiently advanced to rule out long-term adverse effects, it remains to be seen whether operational constraints will be sufficient to ensure that permanent injury does not result due to overexposure to the dose-dependent effects of millimetre wave radiation.

More important than technical discussions, perhaps, is the issue of public acceptance and related political viability. Since the unveiling of the prototype weapon in 2001, support for deployment from both military and political decision makers has remained lukewarm, largely due to concerns over unfavourable reactions from the public and the international community. Public acceptance has become the major factor affecting ongoing development and potential deployment of the ADS, which has resulted in a concerted public relations campaign by the JNLWD and an uncertain future.

8.3.3 Acoustic murmurings

Attempts to develop acoustic 'non-lethal' weapons, as described in Chapter 7, have failed because no type of acoustic energy can produce suitable incapacitating effects without risking permanent hearing damage. Irreversible hearing damage would not be a politically or publicly acceptable effect for a 'non-lethal' weapon. Although new systems have emerged for directing audible sound, the absence of scientific evidence for extra-aural effects limits the capability of these new 'hailing devices' to psychological annoyance. Moreover, the risk of permanent hearing damage remains a concern at high-sound levels and short-ranges.

The potential for development of acoustic weapons has been greatly exaggerated, largely by those companies and institutions involved in their development, whose claims have been perpetuated in articles and news stories. Even following the dismissal of acoustic weapons concepts by US Air Force scientists, the strength of institutional interest on the part of the US Army has seemingly sustained research and development programmes.

8.4 Organisation and funding

Clearly another important factor for 'non-lethal' weapons development has been the level of organisation and associated level of funding for these programmes. Although police interest began in the 1960s it was not until the mid-1980s that a specific 'non-lethal' weapons programme was set up by the US DOJ. And from its inception the main remit has been the evaluation and improvement of existing technologies rather than development of new technologies. The latter has been the reserve of military programmes but it is important to remember that the first organised military research and development effort seeking to exploit a variety of technologies was the Army's Low Collateral Damage Munitions (LCDM) programme, which began in the early 1990s. The overall organisational base and policy for development of 'non-lethal' weapons was not put in to place until the JNLWD was established and the JNLWP began in 1996. Thus organised efforts to develop new 'non-lethal' weapons technologies are relatively young. This is particularly relevant to directed energy and acoustic weapons. For incapacitating biochemical weapons the situation is somewhat different because concerted efforts to develop these had begun in the 1950s as part of existing chemical weapons programmes.

A related inhibitory factor has been the level of institutional support within the US DOD and the government as a whole. This has been lacking, even following the establishment of the JNLWP, with the low priority afforded to development of these weapons reflected in the low-level of funding for the overall programme, and for the research and development of new technologies in particular. Annual funding of up to $50 million for the JNLWP pales in comparison with the US defence budget of over $500 billion. Advocacy by the institutional base, the JNLWD and partners, has gained some more support but failed to raise the profile and funding it has sought. The US military as a whole appears to remain uncertain of the operational utility of available 'non-lethal' weapons and it seems that this is limiting rather than encouraging support for the development of new 'non-lethal' weapons, especially with the limited use during the current conflict in Iraq.

8.5   Fixing policy

8.5.1   Untangling the concept

An overarching issue, discussed in Chapter 1, is the confusion and contradiction evident in the policy that underpins the development, deployment, and use of 'non-lethal' weapons. Current military policy in the US and NATO explicitly allows for the development and use of these weapons as force multipliers, to enhance the killing power of conventional weapons, or as preludes to 'lethal' force. This is not only disingenuous; it is simply not compatible with claimed goals to develop weapons that will reduce permanent injury and death. To emphasise humanitarian applications while at the same time planning to use them in a 'pre-lethal' manner is not tenable. For the concept of 'non-lethal' weapons to have any longevity in the military arena, this contradiction must be removed with a change in policy.

Interconnected to this is the insistence, also articulated in current policy, that the availability or potential of 'non-lethal' weapons should not impose a higher standard or further restrictions on the use of lethal force. In fact the opposite is true; the pursuit of 'non-lethal' weapons must indeed seek to raise the threshold for the use of 'lethal' force by providing an alternative to it. If these policy changes are not made then, in the absence of a conceptual and policy framework to support the intent to reduce casualties and permanent injury, these weapons should be simply viewed as new weapons with no reference to lethality.

This argument also applies to the development and use of 'non-lethal' weapons by police forces. Underlying policies must have, as their basis, the aims set out in the *United Nations Basic Principles on the Use of Force and Firearms by Law Enforcement Officials*, which states:

> Governments and law enforcement agencies should develop a range of means as broad as possible and equip law enforcement officials with various types of weapons and ammunition that would allow for a differentiated use of force and firearms. These should include the development of 'non-lethal' incapacitating weapons for use in appropriate situations, *with a view to increasingly restraining the application of means capable of causing death or injury to persons*.[3] [emphasis added]

Again policy should aim to restrict the use of 'non-lethal' weapons to those situations where they can fulfil this role. That is where they can be substituted for the use of firearms or other means of force *more likely* to cause death or permanent injury. As such, new 'non-lethal' weapons should not be introduced as a new tier of force, or supplementary means of violence. And policy on the use of existing weapons should be tightened.

8.5.2 Semantics and reason

Requisite clarity on the concept of 'non-lethal' weapons needs to be accompanied by increased transparency on the part of those advocating, developing, and using them. Semantic strategies to soften the language, and thereby the associated image, of 'non-lethal' weapons by describing them as 'technologies' and 'capabilities', and not acknowledging the simple fact that they are weapons, should be curtailed. They are not only deceptive, but clearly so, and therefore counterproductive in gaining wider support for the development and deployment of 'non-lethal' weapons. Predictably, and unsurprisingly, they are likely to draw increased scepticism and criticism, not to mention unfavourable political and public reactions when these 'capabilities' behave more like weapons in practice.

Interrelated is the issue of what types of weapons, or weapons concepts, could be considered to fit the category of 'non-lethal' weapons, and which clearly cannot. Obviously weapons with envisaged, intended 'lethal' effects should not be described as 'non-lethal' weapons. But, as discussed in Chapter 6, some high energy laser prototype weapons with evidently destructive effects, such as the Advanced Tactical Laser (ATL), and others where the evidence for 'non-lethal' effects is purely speculative, such as the Pulsed Energy Projectile (PEP), are being described in exactly this way.

Underlying these discussions is the issue of definitions. Some advocates have suggested that a weapon can be called 'non-lethal' even if it is capable of a, as yet theoretical, spectrum of effects from 'non-lethal' to 'lethal'. This is very dangerous ground. Taking the example of the ADS; if it were announced that it could be used to cause variable effects, from temporary pain with no lasting damage to whole body third degree burns, would it still be acceptable to describe it as a 'non-lethal' weapon? Regardless of any protestations by developers that it was capable of 'non-lethal' effects, it seems safe to assume that political and public opinion would not support this. Thus, it would rightly be viewed as a new weapon with 'lethal' effects, rather than a new 'non-lethal' weapon.

8.5.3   Avoiding a chemical and biological weapons renaissance

Most analysts consider the development of incapacitating biochemical weapons, as the greatest threat to the existing international prohibitions and norms against chemical and biological weapons. The utmost concern is expressed about the intentions or unknown activities of countries or sub-state groups who may or may not possess or wish to develop chemical or biological weapons as weapons of mass destruction. However, the one area where research and development of toxic biochemical agents and their delivery systems as weapons is proceeding unchecked is in the context of 'non-lethal' weapons programmes. At the very least the issues of 'law enforcement purposes' and permitted 'law enforcement chemicals' urgently need to be clarified by countries that have signed the Chemical Weapons Convention (CWC). However, the international community should aim higher in recognising that the costs of pursuing new biochemical weapons, as regards a likely renaissance of these prohibited weapons, are far greater than any potential short-term operational benefits for policing. Particularly as the use of any biological agent or toxin (or synthetic analogue) as a weapon is unequivocally prohibited by the Biological Weapons Convention (BWC) and the use of any toxic chemical as a weapon beyond 'law enforcement purposes' is unequivocally prohibited by the CWC. In this sense, countries espousing strong approaches to preventing external threats posed by chemical and biological weapons proliferation need to look inwards at the proliferation threats posed by their investigations into developing new biochemical weapons. They should seek to limit the use of toxic chemicals for law enforcement to the existing sensory irritant agents, such as CS, and strongly resist pressures to widen their use.

As Chapter 5 illustrated, the technology is not able to deliver the capabilities that are desired, perceived, or promoted, in terms of temporary incapacitation without permanent injury or death, as illustrated in Moscow in 2002. It is time to draw a line under these weapons programmes and create broad international consensus. This should include wide public engagement. After all, in policing, it is the general public who will be in the firing line. International doctors and scientists from academia and industry, whose expertise is required in the development of these weapons should build on the work of the British Medical Association in recognising the dangers of subverting drugs as weapons rather than as treatments. In this context they should not be seduced by the seemingly benign outcomes implied by the 'non-lethal' terminology or the perceived operational necessity in the culture of fear that surrounds the so-called 'war on terror'. The most ardent advocates have even suggested transgressing international law to allow for the development and wide use of incapacitating biochemical weapons. However, the technical realities, broader proliferation concerns, and risks of eroding the norm against chemical and biological weapons, clearly illustrate the grave dangers of pursuing these weapons for policing, let alone military use.

8.5.4 Directed energy weapons: Opportunities for preventative arms control?

Directed energy weapons are still something of an unknown quantity. What is clear is that they are being given a high priority in the context of ongoing 'non-lethal' weapons development efforts. The review of the further development of 'dazzling' laser weapons in Chapter 6 indicates that it would be sensible to examine the recent deployment of these weapons in the context of international prohibitions on blinding lasers. Although Additional Protocol IV to the Convention on Certain Conventional Weapons (CCW) only prohibits laser weapons specifically designed to cause permanent eye damage, the re-emergence of laser weapons targeting the human eye, and the increased power levels in comparison to past 'dazzling' weapon prototypes, mean that there is a need to reassess the dangers of permanent eye damage or blindness through either accidental or intentional misuse.

With regard to emerging directed energy weapons it may be an opportune time to consider whether there are any constraints that the international community wishes to place on this field of weapons development, as there are no specific international legal restrictions aside from the prohibition of blinding lasers. Prior to development and deployment there may be a window for preventative arms control. This could perhaps restrict the mechanisms for directed energy weapon effects. Emerging weapons, such as the ADS, act by heating the skin in a dose-dependent manner. However, researchers are exploring all manner of biological effects that may be used to cause profound incapacitating effects, including interfering with brain function. Policymakers, scientists, academics, and non-governmental organisations should expand their consideration of these issue with regard to emerging prototype weapons and basic research that may yield new weapons in the future. This should incorporate informed public discussion and consultation, which is already proving to be a decisive factor. Advocates are sensitive to any efforts to limit 'non-lethal' weapons development and a NATO report has even called for vigilance to prevent the development of any specific legal regimes that might limit their ability to use 'non-lethal' weapons. However, these issues are ripe for exploration.

8.5.5 Acoustic weapons: Misguided efforts

Chapter 7 of this book showed that 'non-lethal' acoustic weapons are not viable and that their continued development is misguided. Nevertheless given ongoing military programmes, it is important to recognise that existing weapons, such as the LRAD, could be used to cause permanent hearing damage, or to deafen. This is relevant given their classification as 'hailing devices' and associated effects on their use and proliferation. Since they are not classed as weapons they do not appear to be subjected to international legal review. Moreover, their sale is not restricted by export controls preventing the transfer of weapons to countries where human rights violations are commonplace. This situation holds an important lesson, relating to the discussion of semantics above, which is that attempt to classify any weapon, 'non-lethal' or otherwise, as a 'capability' or a 'technology', should be resisted, particularly because history has illustrated a desire on the part of 'non-lethal' weapons advocates to bend the rules of international law.

8.5.6 Complying with international humanitarian law

This analysis of various 'non-lethal' weapons development efforts illustrates the need to ward off challenges to existing international treaties, in the context of biochemical weapons, and consider establishing new control on weapons development, in the case of directed energy weapons. However, another area that needs to be considered is the relationship between 'non-lethal' weapons and international humanitarian law. The efforts to promote misleading terminology in describing emerging 'non-lethal' weapons are geared towards policy and public relations acceptance but they also may have legal implications, as the example of the LRAD illustrates. International humanitarian law requires countries to evaluate all new weapons for compliance with existing treaties as well as the laws of war set out in the Geneva Conventions.

A central tenet of international humanitarian law is the prohibition in warfare of using any weapon against civilians. However, emerging military concepts concerning the use of 'non-lethal' weapons often refer to 'determining intent' or 'separating combatants from non-combatants'. This doctrine implies the use of weapons against individuals before it is ascertained whether or not they are combatants. Essentially it advocates the targeting of civilians. Clearly, with emerging weapons such as the ADS, the rules of engagement need to comply with international humanitarian law. Use of any weapon in warfare, 'non-lethal' or otherwise, is restricted to those using force against you, whose intentions you know, not those whose intentions you do not know. Otherwise the risk of weapons being used indiscriminately against civilians increases greatly.

8.5.7   New technologies, profound concerns

The mechanism of action for the majority of current 'non-lethal' weapons, such as irritant chemicals (RCAs), blunt impact projectiles, and even the ADS, are based around pain compliance or, in the case of some electrical weapons, pain and loss of muscle control. However, emerging weapons are designed to exert their effects through more sophisticated effects on the human body. Largely these seek to interfere with brain function. This is the case with incapacitating biochemical weapons. It is also the case with some conceptual and basic research underpinning directed energy weapons development, and broader efforts by the military to seek neurobehavioral expertise for 'non-lethal' weapons development. Interrelated is the move towards 'effects-based' weapons design, where a desired behavioural effect is identified and then research is undertaken to identify a physiological mechanism to induce it.

Taken together these approaches could lead to a dramatic shift in the nature of so-called 'non-lethal' weapons leading, potentially, to weapons with profoundly controlling effects becoming available to military and police users. The relevant technological, social, and ethical issues need to be explored in considerable detail in the context of arms control discussions and public awareness raising. Public opinion could be a powerful tool in affecting policy in this area, in advance of further weapons development.

8.5.8   Avoiding mission creep

An important issue, indicated by a number of examples described in this book, is the danger of mission creep. While policy needs fixing to be clearer on the rationale for the development of 'non-lethal' weapons and the appropriate circumstances for their use, data on the way in which currently deployed 'non-lethal' weapons are being used by police and military forces needs to be collected, analysed, and fed back into policy. This is happening in an ad hoc way in some instances already. For example, review of Taser use in the US by police organisations, non-governmental organisations, newspapers, and other interested parties, has shown the way in which a weapon, ostensibly introduced as an alternative to lethal force, is now being used with a much wider remit as a compliance tool. However, more data is needed, particularly on the relatively undocumented area of military use, to form a sound basis for recommending changes or restrictions to policy on a variety of these weapons. With the Taser, some US police forces have subsequently tightened their policies, for example, no longer permitting use of the Taser on children or those in handcuffs. However, these messages need to be clearly communicated. In the UK, the Home Office is gradually moving towards the wider introduction of the Taser, underpinned by less restrictive guidelines on circumstances for its use, which runs the risk of leading to similar cases of misuse.

When policymakers claim that 'non-lethal' weapons are 'saving lives', there needs to be information to examine the claim. Such an examination may find that indeed the given weapon combined with correct policy and training, is saving lives. Alternatively it might find that use of the weapon has saved lives in some circumstances but it is also being used as a tool of compliance. The next step would be to ask why? Is there an underlying problem with policy, training, oversight, or some other factor? Only through this type of process can mission creep be mitigated and controlled.

The potential use of new weapons in ongoing and future conflicts will need to be monitored carefully. Rationales for the development and deployment of new 'non-lethal' weapons are often supported by proposed scenarios for their use. However, history illustrates that there can often be a mismatch between the way these weapons are promoted and the way they are used in practice.

8.6   Continued scrutiny

This assessment of efforts to develop 'non-lethal' weapons demonstrates the important role advocacy has played, particularly in sustaining controversial and unproven weapons research. Misinformation, exaggeration, and accepted wisdom, whether intentional or accidental, and whether technical or policy related, has been commonplace. Advocates and supply side institutions have inflated perceptions of both the capability of, and the need for, 'non-lethal' weapons technologies.[4] As regards incapacitating biochemical weapons, the advocacy of developers has succeeded in sustaining weapons research and development in the face of the international prohibitions of chemical and biological weapons and seemingly insurmountable technical barriers. Strong advocacy of directed energy weapons as revolutionary weapons has seen destructive high energy lasers continue to be promoted as 'non-lethal'. And support for the viability of acoustic 'non-lethal' weapons has been maintained in the face of scientific evidence to the contrary. Moreover, a military policy that contradicts the central concept of minimising casualties and permanent injury remains in place over ten years since its introduction. Continued critical independent assessment, both scientific and policy orientated, is required to ensure that the same myths about technological capability are not being repeated ten or more years from now, and that emerging 'non-lethal' weapons are not used to make killing easier.

Those seeking the wider use and expanded development of 'non-lethal' weapons often protest that there seems to be less resistance to the introduction of a new 'lethal' weapon than a proposed 'non-lethal' one. There is a good reason for this apparent contradiction. 'Lethal' weapons are used with the clear intent to injure or kill, which restricts the contexts in which a rationale can be made for their use. In contrast, 'non-lethal' weapons are used with the stated intent of causing temporary incapacitation without injury or death. As such they lend themselves to making the use of *any* force more likely, both in policing and warfare, unless their use is carefully and strictly controlled. Moreover, they are often explicitly intended for use against civilian populations. Consequently, any claim that the use of a particular weapon will provide an alternative to lethal force, and ultimately save lives, deserves the utmost scrutiny to ensure that the technology and underlying policy is capable of fulfilling this worthwhile but beleaguered goal.

Notes

1 Introduction

1. Quotation marks are used throughout this book surrounding the phrase 'non-lethal' to reflect these disagreements.
2. Fidler, D. (2005) The meaning of Moscow: "Non-lethal" weapons and international law in the early 21st century. *International Review of the Red Cross*, Vol. 87, No. 859, September 2005, pp. 525–52.
3. Advocate literature during the 1990s included Morris, C. and Morris, J. (1991) *Nonlethality: A Global Strategy White Paper*. Washington, DC: US Global Strategy Council; Council on Foreign Relations (1995) *Non-Lethal Technologies: Military Options and Implications. Report of an Independent Task Force*. New York: Council on Foreign Relations; Morehouse, D. (1996) *Nonlethal Weapons: War without Death*. Westport: Praeger; Alexander, J. (1999) *Future War: Non-Lethal Weapons in Twenty-First-Century Warfare*. New York: St. Martin's Press; Copernoll, M. (1999) The Nonlethal Weapons Debate. *Naval War College Review*, Vol. LII, No. 2, Spring 1999, pp. 112–31; Garwin, R. (1999) *Nonlethal Technologies: Progress and Prospects. Report of an Independent Task Force*. New York: Council on Foreign Relations.
4. Sceptic literature during the 1990s included Aftergood, S. (1994) The soft-kill fallacy. *Bulletin of the Atomic Scientists*, Vol. 50, No. 5, September–October 1994; Dando, M. (1996) *A New Form of Warfare: The Rise of Non-Lethal Weapons*. London: Brasseys; Coupland, R. (1997) "Non-lethal" weapons: precipitating a new arms race. *British Medical Journal*, Vol. 315, p. 72, 12 July 1997; Lewer, N. and Schofield, S. (1997) *Non-Lethal Weapons: A Fatal Attraction?* London: Zed Books; Wright, S. (1998) *An Appraisal of Technologies of Political Control*. Working Document, PE 166 499. Luxembourg: European Parliament, Directorate General for Research, Scientific and Technological Options Assessment; Altmann, J. (1999) *Acoustic Weapons – A Prospective Assessment: Sources, Propagation, and Effects of Strong Sound*. Occasional Paper No. 22, May 1999. Ithaca, NY: Cornell University.
5. Ackroyd, C., Margolis, K., Rosenhead, J., and Shallice, T. (1980) *The Technology of Political Control*. Second edition, London: Pluto Press; Wright, S. (1978) New Police Technologies: An exploration of the social implications and unforeseen impacts of some recent developments. *Journal of Peace Research*, Vol. 15, No. 4, pp. 305–22.
6. Security Planning Corporation (1972) *Non-Lethal Weapons for Law Enforcement: Research Needs and Priorities. A Report to the National Science Foundation*. Washington, DC: Security Planning Corporation, p. 14.
7. Sweetman, S. (1987) *Report on the Attorney General's Conference on Less Than Lethal Weapons*. National Institute of Justice. Washington, DC: US Government Printing Office, p. 26.
8. For example, the National Institute of Justice (NIJ) and police forces in the US; and the Northern Ireland Office (NIO), Association of Chief Police Officers (ACPO), and police forces in the UK.
9. Security Planning Corporation (1972) op. cit., p. 14.

10. International Law Enforcement Forum (2005) *Less-Lethal Weapons Definitions and Operational Test Criteria*. International Law Enforcement Forum Report, p. 17.
11. US Department of Defense (1996) *Policy for Non-Lethal Weapons*, Directive 3000.3, 9 July 1996. Washington, DC: Office of the Assistant Secretary of Defense, Special Operations/Low Intensity Conflict.
12. NATO (1999) *NATO Policy on Non-Lethal Weapons*, 13 October 1999. Brussels: NATO.
13. The latter is used by the NIJ in the US.
14. Lewer, N. and Schofield, S. (1997) op. cit., pp. 5–7; Rappert, B. (2003) *Non-Lethal Weapons as Legitimizing Forces? Technology, Politics and the Management of Conflict*. London: Frank Cass, pp. 17–34.
15. US Department of Defense (1996) op. cit.; also see, NATO (1999) op. cit.
16. United States/United Kingdom (2001) *US/UK Non-Lethal Weapons (NLW)/Urban Operations Executive Seminar*, 30 November 2000, London. Assessment Report. ONR-NLW-038, p. 7.
17. Ibid., p. 11.
18. Howard, P. (1973) *Operational Aspects of Agent CS*. USATECOM Deseret Test Center technical report DTC-FR-S700M, April 1973. Cited in Meselson, M. and Perry Robinson, J. (2003) 'Non Lethal' Weapons and Implementation of the Chemical and Biological Weapons Conventions. *Paper given at the 20th Pugwash Workshop Study Group on the Implementation of the CBW Conventions: The BWC Intersessional Process towards the Sixth Review Conference and Beyond*, Geneva, Switzerland, 8–9 November 2003.
19. European Parliament (2000) *Crowd Control Technologies: An Assessment of Crowd Control Technology Options for the European Union. Section C: Technical Annex*, EP/1/1V/B/STOA/99/14/01. Brussels: European Parliament, Scientific Technology Options Assessment, Appendix 6.
20. BBC News (2002) How special forces ended siege. *BBC News Online*, 29 October 2002. Accessed December 2006 at: http://news.bbc.co.uk/.
21. US Army (2005) *Force Operating Capabilities, TRADOC Pamphlet 525–66*. Fort Monroe: US Army, Training and Doctrine Command.
22. The rather cynical counter-arguments that have been made by military policy-makers are twofold. Firstly, that 'non-lethal' weapons can be used to identify combatants who are then killed more easily, thereby reducing the risk of causing civilian casualties through the use of 'lethal' weapons alone. Secondly, that the concept of reducing casualties can apply solely to your own side (i.e. 'friendly casualties'), while actually using 'non-lethal' weapons to increase enemy casualties. However, these arguments do not fit with the way in which 'non-lethal' weapons are commonly presented and advocated.
23. National Institute of Justice (2006), Less-Than-Lethal Technologies (LTL) program website. Accessed December 2006 at: http://www.ojp.usdoj.gov/.
24. For a recent example see Lardner, R. (2007) Marines In Iraq Decry Lack Of Laser System. *Tampa Tribune*, 31 January 2007.
25. Metropolitan Police Authority (2003) *Introduction of the taser (electronic stun gun) as a less lethal option*. London: Metropolitan Police Authority, Co-ordination and Policing Committee, 4 April 2003; also see, Association of Chief Police Officers (2007) *Extended operational Deployment of Taser for Specially Trained Units (excluding firearms incidents)*, Policy, Version 2 – July 2007.
26. NATO (1999) op. cit.; also see, US Department of Defense (1996) op. cit.

27. Ackroyd, C., Margolis, K., Rosenhead, J., and Shallice, T. (1980) op. cit., p. 199.
28. Amnesty International (2004) *United States of America: Excessive and lethal force?* AMR 51/139/2004. London: Amnesty International.
29. Lewer, N. and Davison, N. (2006) *Electrical stun weapons: alternative to lethal force or a compliance tool?* Bradford: University of Bradford.
30. Migoya, D. (2004) Police Tasers set to stun. *Denver Post*, 4 May 2004.
31. This included incidents where the Taser was either displayed, fired, or used as a 'stun gun'.
32. *Seattle-Post Intelligencer* (not dated) Taser use in King County. Sample of law enforcement agencies using tasers and a breakdown of incidents by agency. Accessed September 2008 at: http://seattlepi.nwsource.com/.
33. *The Canadian Press* (2007) Most people hit with RCMP Tasers unarmed: reports. 18 November 2007. Accessed September 2008 at: http://www.ctv.ca/.
34. Coupland, R. and Loye, D. (2000) Legal and Health Issues: International Humanitarian Law and the Lethality or Non-Lethality of Weapons. In: M. Dando (ed.) *Non-Lethal Weapons: Technological and Operational Prospects.* Coulsdon: Jane's, pp. 60–6.
35. Coupland, R. (2005) Modelling armed violence: a tool for humanitarian dialogue in disarmament and arms control. In: J. Borrie and V. Martin Randin (eds) *Alternative Approaches in Multilateral Decision Making: Disarmament as Humanitarian Action.* Geneva: United Nations Institute for Disarmament Research (UNDIR), May 2005, pp. 39–49.
36. Ibid.
37. Klotz, L., Furmanski, M., and Wheelis, M. (2003) *Beware the Siren's Song: Why "Non-Lethal" Incapacitating Chemical Agents are Lethal.* Washington D.C.: Federation of American Scientists.
38. Walsh, P. (2003) Families claim death toll from gas in Moscow siege kept secret. *The Guardian*, 18 October 2003.
39. Klotz, L., Furmanski, M., and Wheelis, M. (2003) op. cit.
40. See, for example: Allison, G., Kelley, P., and Garwin, R. (2004) *Nonlethal Weapons and Capabilities. Report of an Independent Task Force.* New York: Council on Foreign Relations Press.
41. United States/United Kingdom (2001) op. cit., p. 3.
42. Ibid.
43. Allison, G., Kelley, P., and Garwin, R. (2004) op. cit., p. 12.
44. The US Army ran a Low Collateral Damage Munitions (LCDM) programme at the Army Research, Development and Engineering Center (ARDEC) during the early 1990s, which emphasised variable effects weapons, describing them as 'non-lethal'. This is now referred to as the 'Scalable Effects' programme. See National Research Council (2003) *An Assessment of Non-Lethal Weapons Science and Technology.* Washington, DC: National Academies Press, pp. 63–4; Galvan, J. and Kang, T. (2006) The Future of the Army Nonlethal Scalable Effects Center. *Military Police*, PB-19-06-1, April 2006.
45. US Marine Corps (1998) *Joint Concept for Non-Lethal Weapons*, 5 January 1998. Quantico: US Marine Corps.
46. See Davison, N. and Lewer, N. (2003–6) *Bradford Non-Lethal Weapons Research Project Research Reports No. 4–8.* Bradford: University of Bradford.
47. Coates, J. (1970) *Nonlethal and Nondestructive Combat in Cities Overseas.* Washington, DC: Institute for Defense Analyses, Science and Technology Division, pp. 102–3.

48. Dando, M. (1996) Preface.
49. Adapted from Lewer, N. and Davison, N. (2005) Non-lethal technologies – an overview. *Disarmament Forum, Science, technology and the CBW regimes*, No. 1, pp. 36–51; Zueger has noted that the requirements for discriminate effects and not causing unnecessary suffering are already obligations under international humanitarian law, (Zueger, B. (2006) *So-called "Non-Lethal" Weapons through the Lens of Humanitarian and Human Rights Law: The Example of Chemical 'Incapacitants'*. Master's Thesis, Centre Universitaire de Droit International Humanitaire (CUDH), p. 13). However, it does no harm to emphasise these requirements in the definition.
50. Meaning that the effects are short acting and recovery is both complete and occurs quickly after the weapon has been used. This is different from the slow healing process resulting from a wound for example.
51. Davison, N. and Lewer, N. (2005) *Bradford Non-Lethal Weapons Research Project Research Report No. 7*. Bradford: University of Bradford, p. 27.
52. Even if a weapon caused no apparent physical injuries, the potential psychological effects could not be eliminated, as noted in: Zueger, B. (2006) op. cit., p. 10.
53. Feakin has proposed the 'ICE Equation' to show the interrelation between intent, context, and effect: Feakin, T. (2005) *Non-lethal weapons: technology for lowering casualties?* Ph.D. Thesis. Bradford: University of Bradford, pp. 72–4.
54. Amnesty International (2004) op. cit.
55. For example, the Advanced Tactical Laser (ATL), a high energy laser that would be lethal if used against people, but is promoted as 'non-lethal' on account of its claimed accuracy at destroying vehicles or other objects without affecting people nearby. See Karcher, D. and Wertheim, E. (not dated) Safeguarding Peace, Safeguarding Life: How Non-Lethal Directed Energy Weapons Promise Both. *Homeland Defense Jounrnal*. Accessed December 2006 at: http://www.homelanddefensejournal.com/.
56. Meselson, M. and Perry Robinson, J. (2003) Editorial: 'Non-Lethal' Weapons, the CWC and the BWC. *The CBW Conventions Bulletin*, No. 61, pp. 1–2.
57. Lewer, N. and Schofield, S. (1997) op. cit., p. 134.
58. In addition to the literature in the 1990s referenced under notes 3 and 4; Applegate, R. (1969) *Riot Control – Materiel and Techniques*. First edition, Harrisburg, PA: Stackpole Books; Coates, J. (1970) *Nonlethal and Nondestructive Combat in Cities Overseas*. Washington, DC: Institute for Defense Analyses, Science and Technology Division; Security Planning Corporation (1972) op. cit.; Ackroyd, C., Margolis, K., Rosenhead, J., and Shallice, T. (1980); Sweetman, S. (1987) op. cit.; Alexander, J. (1989) Antimateriel Technology. *Military Review*, Vol. 69 No. 10, October, pp. 29–41; Omega Foundation (2000) *Crowd Control Technologies (An appraisal of technologies for political control). Final Study*. Luxemburg, Brussels: European Parliament, Directorate General for Research, The STOA Programme; Lewer, N. (ed.) (2002) *The Future of Non-Lethal Weapons: Technologies, Operations, Ethics and Law*. London: Frank Cass; Alexander, J. (2003) *Winning the War: Advanced Weapons, Strategies, and Concepts for the Post 9/11 World*. New York: St. Martin's Press; National Research Council (2003) op. cit.; Rappert, B. (2003) op. cit.; Allison, G., Kelley, P., and Garwin, R. (2004) op. cit.; NATO (2004) *Non-Lethal Weapons and Future Peace Enforcement Operations*, RTO-TR-SAS-040. Brussels: NATO; Koplow, D. (2006) *Non-Lethal Weapons: The Law and Policy of Revolutionary Technologies for the Military and Law Enforcement*. New York: Cambridge University Press.

59. Dando, M. (1999) The Impact of the Development of Modern Biology and Medicine on the Evolution of Offensive Biological Warfare Programs in the Twentieth Century. *Defense Analysis*, Vol. 15, No. 1, pp. 43–62; Davison, N. (2005) *The Role of Scientific Discovery in the Establishment of the First Biological Weapons Programmes*. Bradford Science and Technology Report No. 5. Bradford: University of Bradford.
60. Meselson, M. (2000) Averting the Hostile Exploitation of Biotechnology. *The CBW Conventions Bulletin*, No. 48, June 2000, pp. 16–19.
61. Altmann, J. (2001) Non-lethal Weapons Technologies – the Case for Independent Scientific Analysis. *Medicine, Conflict and Survival*, Vol. 17, No. 3, pp. 234–47.
62. And to a lesser extent the UK.
63. In particular those made by The Sunshine Project, a non-governmental organisation, which obtained numerous documents on the US incapacitating biochemical weapons programmes.

2 The Early History of 'Non-Lethal' Weapons

1. Applegate, R. (1969) *Riot Control – Materiel and Techniques*. First edition, Harrisburg, PA: Stackpole Books; Feakin, T. (2005) *Non-lethal weapons: technology for lowering casualties?* Ph.D. thesis, Department of Peace Studies, University of Bradford, pp. 13–18.
2. Applegate, R. (1969) op. cit., pp. 126–211.
3. Coates, J. (1972) Non-Lethal Police Weapons. *Technology Review*, June, pp. 49–56.
4. Seaskate, Inc. (1998) The *Evolution and Development of Police Technology*. Washington, DC: National Institute of Justice, Department of Justice, p. 27.
5. National Advisory Commission on Civil Disorders (1969) *Report of the National Advisory Commission on Civil Disorders*. New York: Bantam Books, pp. 1–29.
6. O'Bryant, J. (2003) *Issue Brief for Congress, Crime Control: The Federal Response*. Washington, DC: Congressional Research Service, Library of Congress, pp. 2–3.
7. Coates, J. (1972) op. cit.
8. O'Bryant, J. (2003) op. cit., pp. 2–3.
9. Applegate, R. (1969) op. cit.
10. For recent examples see: Davison, N. and Lewer, N. (2004) *Bradford Non-Lethal Weapons Research Project Research Report No. 5*. Bradford: University of Bradford, pp. 4 and 21.
11. Applegate, R. (1971) Nonlethal Police Weapons. *Ordnance*, July–August, pp. 62–6.
12. Coates, J. (1972) op. cit.
13. Dando, M. (1996) *A New Form of Warfare: The Rise of Non-Lethal Weapons*. London: Brassey's, p. 10.
14. See, for example: Alexander, J. (2001) An overview of the future of non-lethal weapons. *Medicine, Conflict and Survival*, July–September, Vol. 17, No. 3, pp. 180–93.
15. Coates, J. (1970) *Nonlethal and Nondestructive Combat in Cities Overseas*. Arlington, VA: Institute for Defense Analyses, Science and Technology Division, p. 1.
16. Ibid., p. 107.
17. Ibid., p. 108.
18. Ibid., p. 110.
19. Security Planning Corporation (1972) *Non-Lethal Weapons for Law Enforcement: Research Needs and Priorities. A Report to the National Science Foundation*. Washington, DC: Security Planning Corporation, p. 3.

20. Ibid., p. 11.
21. Ibid., p. 43.
22. Ibid., p. 7.
23. Ibid., pp. 7–8.
24. Ibid., p. 8.
25. Egner, D. (1977) *The Evaluation of Less-Lethal Weapons, Technical Memorandum 37–77*. Aberdeen Proving Ground, MD: US Army Human Engineering Laboratory, pp. 9–12.
26. Ibid., p. 9.
27. Deane-Drummond, A. (1975) *Riot Control*. London: Royal United Services Institute, pp. 121–9.
28. Ackroyd, C., Margolis, K., Rosenhead, J., and Shallice, T. (1980) *The Technology of Political Control*. Second edition, London: Pluto Press, p. 208.
29. Sidell, F. (1997) Riot Control Agents. In: F. Sidell, E. Takafuji, and D. Franz, (eds) *Textbook of Military Medicine: Medical Aspects of Chemical and Biological Warfare*. Washington DC: Borden Institute, Walter Reed Army Medical Center, pp. 307–24.
30. Stockholm International Peace Research Institute (1971) *The Problem of Chemical and Biological Warfare. Volume I: The Rise of CB Weapons*. Stockholm: Almqvist & Wiksell, p. 212.
31. Ibid., p. 131.
32. Ibid., pp. 39–43.
33. Ibid., pp. 59–60.
34. Furmanski, M. (2005) Military Interest in Low-lethality Biochemical Agents: The Historical Interaction of Advocates, Experts, Pragmatists and Politicians. *Background Paper prepared for the Symposium on Incapacitating Biochemical Weapons: Scientific, Military Legal and Policy Perspectives and Prospects, Geneva, Switzerland, 11 June 2005*. Washington, DC: *Center for Arms Control and Non-Proliferation*, pp. 7–10.
35. Stockholm International Peace Research Institute (1973) op. cit., p. 121.
36. Ibid., pp. 59–60.
37. Stockholm International Peace Research Institute (1971) op. cit., pp. 332–5.
38. Ibid., p. 212.
39. Furmanski, M. (2005) op. cit., p. 14.
40. Stockholm International Peace Research Institute (1971) op. cit., pp. 69–70.
41. Furmanski, M. (2005) op. cit., p. 14.
42. Stockholm International Peace Research Institute (1971) op. cit., pp. 212–13.
43. Ibid., pp. 85–203.
44. Ibid., pp. 187–90.
45. Davis, S. (1970) *Riot Control Weapons for the Vietnam War*. US Army Munitions Command Historical Monograph AMC 56M, Edgewood Arsenal, June 1970. Cited in: Perry Robinson, J. (2003) *Disabling Chemical Weapons: A Documented Chronology of Events, 1945–2003*. Harvard-Sussex Program, University of Sussex, unpublished version dated 8 October 2003, p. 64.
46. Stockholm International Peace Research Institute (1971) op. cit., p. 190.
47. Meselson, M. and Perry Robinson, J. (2003) 'Non Lethal' Weapons and Implementation of the Chemical and Biological Weapons Conventions. *Paper given at the 20th Pugwash Workshop Study Group on the Implementation of the CBW Conventions, Geneva, Switzerland, 8–9 November 2003*.
48. Howard, P. (1973) *Operational Aspects of Agent CS*. USATECOM Deseret Test Center technical report DTC-FR-S700M, April 1973. Cited in: Meselson, M. and Perry Robinson, J. (2003) op. cit.

49. Stockholm International Peace Research Institute (1971) op. cit., p. 212.
50. Furmanski, M. (2005) op. cit., p. 17.
51. Coates, J. (1972) op. cit.
52. Applegate, R. (1969) op. cit., p. 128.
53. National Advisory Commission on Civil Disorders (1969) *Report of the National Advisory Commission on Civil Disorders.* New York: Bantam Books. Cited in: Applegate, R. (1969) op. cit., p. 165.
54. Ibid.
55. Furmanski, M. (2005) op. cit., p. 17.
56. Listman, J. (2000) Kent's other casualties. *National Guard*, May 2000.
57. Ackroyd, C., Margolis, K., Rosenhead, J., and Shallice, T. (1980) op. cit., pp. 212–23.
58. Himsworth, H. (1971) *Report of the Enquiry Into the Medical and Toxicological Aspects of CS (Orthochlorobenzylulene Malononitrile), II: Enquiry Into Toxicological Aspects of CS and Its Use for Civil Purposes.* London: HMSO.
59. Sidell, F. (1997) op. cit.
60. Spellar, J. (1999) *House of Commons Hansard Written Answers for 11 January 1999.* London: HMSO. Accessed December 2006 at: http://www.publications.parliament.uk/.
61. Morrison, C. and Bright, M. (2005) Secret gas was issued for IRA prison riots. *The Observer*, 23 January 2005.
62. US Army Chemical School (2005) Military Chemical Compounds and Their Properties. In: US Army Chemical School, *FM 3-11.9 Potential Military Chemical/Biological Agents and Compounds.* Fort Monroe, VA: US Army Training and Doctrine Command, pp. III–1 and III–24.
63. Olajos E. and Salem, H. (2001) Riot Control Agents: Pharmacology, Toxicology, Biochemistry and Chemistry. *Journal of Applied Toxicology*, pp. 355–91; Sidell, F. (1997) op. cit.
64. Stockholm International Peace Research Institute (1971) op. cit., p. 64.
65. Witten, B. (1968) *Nonlethal Agents in Crime and Riot Control.* Edgewood Arsenal Technical Memorandum EATM 133-1. Chemical Research Laboratory, Edgewood Arsenal, US Army, p. 7.
66. Applegate, R. (1969) op. cit., pp. 126–211; Egner, D. (1977) The *Evaluation of Less-Lethal Weapons, Technical Memorandum 37-77.* Aberdeen Proving Ground, MD: US Army Human Engineering Laboratory, pp. 65–7.
67. Egner, D. (1977) op. cit., pp. 65–7.
68. Stockholm International Peace Research Institute (1971) op. cit., p. 109; Stockholm International Peace Research Institute (1973) op. cit., p. 45.
69. Coates, J. (1972) op. cit.
70. Applegate, R. (1969) op. cit., pp. 196–204; Coates, J. (1972) op. cit.
71. Egner, D. (1977) op. cit., p. 66.
72. Applegate, R. (1969) op. cit., pp. 196–204.
73. Ackroyd, C., Margolis, K., Rosenhead, J., and Shallice, T. (1980) op. cit., pp. 205–12.
74. Seaskate, Inc. (1998) op. cit., p. 40; Ackroyd, C., Margolis, K., Rosenhead, J., and Shallice, T. (1980) op. cit., pp. 205–12.
75. Lumsden, M. (1978) *Anti-Personnel Weapons*, Stockholm International Peace Research Institute. London: Taylor and Francis, p. 108.
76. Millar, R., Rutherford, W., Johnston, S., and Malhotra V. (1975) Injuries caused by rubber bullets: a report on 90 patients. *British Journal of Surgery*, Vol. 62, pp. 480–6.

77. Ackroyd, C., Margolis, K., Rosenhead, J., and Shallice, T. (1980) op. cit., pp. 26–31; Barzilay, D. (1973) *The British Army in Ulster*, Vol. 1. Belfast: Century, pp. 69–81.
78. Ackroyd, C., Margolis, K., Rosenhead, J., and Shallice, T. (1980) op. cit., pp. 205–12; Millar, R., Rutherford, W., Johnston, S., and Malhotra V. (1975) op. cit.; Lumsden, M. (1978) op. cit.
79. Rosenhead, J. (1976) A new look at less 'less lethal' weapons. *New Scientist*, 16 December, pp. 672–4; Lumsden, M. (1978) op. cit., p. 109.
80. Applegate, R. (1971) op. cit.
81. Lumsden, M. (1978) op. cit., p. 109.
82. Egner, D. (1977) op. cit., p. 79; National Institute of Justice (1998) NIJ Takes the RAP. *TECHbeat*, Washington, DC: National Institute of Justice, National Law Enforcement and Corrections Technology Center, p. 3; Flatau, A. (2000) Ring Airfoil Grenade: A Less-Than Lethal Configuration for the Delivery of Selected Chemical Agents. *Presentation to the Non-Lethal Defense IV Conference, Tysons Corner, VA, 21–2 March 2000.*
83. Rosenhead, J. (1976) op. cit.; Security Planning Corporation (1972) op. cit., pp. 25–6.
84. Egner, D. (1977) op. cit., p. 9.
85. Rosenhead, J. (1976) op. cit.
86. Lumsden, M. (1978) op. cit., p. 110.
87. Rejali, D. (2001) Electric Torture: A Global History of a Torture Technology. *Connect: art.politics.theory.practice*, June, pp. 101–9; also see Rejali, D. (2008) *Torture and Democracy*. Princeton, NJ: Princeton University Press.
88. Ibid.
89. Ibid.
90. Security Planning Corporation (1972) op. cit., Appendix A.
91. Applegate, R. (1969) op. cit., p. 233.
92. Ibid., p. 255.
93. Rappert, B. (2003) Shock Tactics. *New Scientist*, Vol. 177, No. 2382, pp. 34–7; Lewer, N. and Davison, N. (2006) *Electrical stun weapons: alternative to lethal force or a compliance tool?* Bradford: University of Bradford.
94. Coates, J. (1970) op. cit.; Security Planning Corporation (1972) op. cit.
95. Egner, D. (1977) op. cit., p. 75.
96. Ibid.
97. Applegate, R. (1969) op. cit., p. 253.
98. Rejali, D. (2001) op. cit.
99. Lumsden, M. (1978) op. cit., p. 203.
100. Laur, D. (1999) *Independent Evaluation Report of TASER and Air TASER Conducted Energy Weapons*. Victoria: Victoria Police Department.
101. US Patent Office (1974) *Weapon for Immobilization and Capture, Patent No. 3,803,463*, 9 April 1974. (Filed in 1972).
102. Ibid.
103. Bleetman, A., Steyn, R., and Lee, C. (2004) Introduction of the Taser into British policing. Implications for UK emergency departments: an overview of electronic weaponry. *Emergency Medicine Journal*, Vol. 21, pp. 136–40.
104. Laur, D. (1999) op. cit.
105. Ibid.; Lumsden, M. (1978) op. cit., p. 203.
106. Bleetman, A. and Steyn, R. (2003) *The Advanced Taser: a Medical Review*. Scottsdale: Taser International, Inc., p. 5.
107. Laur, D. (1999) op. cit.; Lumsden, M. (1978) op. cit., p. 203.

228 *Notes*

108. Ackroyd, C., Margolis, K., Rosenhead, J., and Shallice, T. (1980) op. cit., p. 223.
109. Applegate, R. (1969) op. cit.; Coates, J. (1970) op. cit.; Security Planning Corporation (1972) op. cit.; Coates, J. (1972) op. cit.; Lumsden, M. (1978) op. cit.; R. Bunker (ed.) (1997) *Nonlethal Weapons: Terms and References.* INSS Occasional Paper 15. Colorado: USAF Institute for National Security Studies.
110. Dando, M. and Furmanski, M. (2006) Midspectrum Incapacitant Programs. In: M. Wheelis, L. Rózsa, and M. Dando (eds). *Deadly Cultures: Biological Weapons Since 1945.* Cambridge: Harvard University Press, pp. 236–51.
111. Stockholm International Peace Research Institute (1973) op. cit., pp. 35–6.
112. Ibid., p. 298.
113. Ketchum, J. and Sidell, F. (1997) Incapacitating Agents. In: F. Sidell, E. Takafuji, and D. Franz (eds) *Textbook of Military Medicine: Medical Aspects of Chemical and Biological Warfare.* Washington DC: Borden Institute, Walter Reed Army Medical Center, pp. 287–305.
114. Ibid.
115. Stockholm International Peace Research Institute (1971) op. cit., p. 75.
116. Dando, M. and Furmanski, M. (2006) op. cit.
117. Applegate, R. (1969) op. cit.; Security Planning Corporation (1972) op. cit., p. 27.
118. Witten, B. (1968) op. cit., p. 3.
119. Ibid.
120. van Courtland Moon, J. (2006) The US Biological Weapons Program. In: M. Wheelis, L. Rózsa, and M. Dando (eds). *Deadly Cultures: Biological Weapons Since 1945.* Cambridge: Harvard University Press, pp. 9–46.
121. Stockholm International Peace Research Institute (1973) op. cit., pp. 123–4.
122. Furmanski, M. (2005) op. cit.
123. Coates, J. (1970) op. cit., p. 107.
124. Stockholm International Peace Research Institute (1973) op. cit., pp. 185–6.
125. Urbanetti, J. (1997) Toxic Inhalational Injury. In: F. Sidell, E. Takafuji, and D. Franz (eds) *Textbook of Military Medicine: Medical Aspects of Chemical and Biological Warfare.* Washington DC: Borden Institute, Walter Reed Army Medical Center, pp. 247–70.
126. Applegate, R. (1969) op. cit., p. 188.
127. Security Planning Corporation (1972) op. cit., p. 27.
128. Applegate, R. (1969) op. cit., p. 188.
129. Board on Environmental Studies and Toxicology (1997) *Toxicity of Military Smokes and Obscurants, Volume 1.* Washington, DC: National Academy Press, p. 133.
130. Applegate, R. (1969) op. cit., p. 293; Collins, K., Mathis, R., and Mallow, W. (2000) Non-Lethal Applications of Slippery Substances. *Presentation to the Non-Lethal Defense IV Conference, Tysons Corner, VA, 21–2 March 2000.*
131. Security Planning Corporation (1972) op. cit., p. 28; Applegate, R. (1969) op. cit., 292–3.
132. Applegate, R. (1969) op. cit., p. 293.
133. Ibid.
134. Sunshine Project (2001) *Non-Lethal Weapons Research in the US: Calmatives and Malodorants.* Backgrounder Series No. 8, July 2001. Austin: The Sunshine Project. Accessed December 2006 at: http://www.sunshine-project.org/; Bickford, L., Bowie, D., Collins, K., Salem, H., and Dalton, P. (2000) Odorous Substances for Non-Lethal Applications. *Presentation to the Non-Lethal Defense IV Conference, Tysons Corner, VA, 21–2 March 2000.*

135. Kahn, J. (2001) Aroma Therapy: In The Military, It's Known As 'Nonlethal Weapons Development'. *SFgate.com*, 22 May 2001. Accessed December 2006 at: http://www.sfgate.com; Pain, S. (2001) Stench Warfare. *New Scientist*, Vol. 171, No. 2298, pp. 42–5; Bickford, L., Bowie, D., Collins, K., Salem, H., and Dalton, P. (2000) op. cit.
136. Bickford, L., Bowie, D., Collins, K., Salem, H., and Dalton, P. (2000) op. cit.
137. Bunker, R. (ed.) (1997) op. cit., p. 11.
138. The Sunshine Project (2001) *Non-Lethal Weapons Research in the US: Calmatives and Malodorants*. Backgrounder Series No. 8, July 2001. Austin: The Sunshine Project. Accessed December 2006 at: http://www.sunshine-project.org/.
139. Security Planning Corporation (1972) op. cit., Appendix A.
140. Lumsden, M. (1978) op. cit., p. 202.
141. Ibid., p. 209.
142. Ibid., p. 209.
143. Ibid., pp. 205–6.
144. Bunker, R. (ed.) (1997) op. cit., p. 18.
145. Applegate, R. (1969) op. cit., p. 301.
146. Lumsden, M. (1978) op. cit., p. 210, note 2.
147. Security Planning Corporation (1972) op. cit., p. 28.
148. Anon (1973) Anti-crowd weapons works by causing fits. *New Scientist*, Vol. 57, No. 839, p. 726.
149. Ronson, J. (2004) *The Men Who Stare at Goats*. London: Picador; R. Bunker (ed.) (1997) op. cit., p. 16.
150. Lumsden, M. (1978) op. cit., p. 206; Ackroyd, C., Margolis, K., Rosenhead, J., and Shallice, T. (1980) op. cit., pp. 225–6.
151. Lumsden, M. (1978) op. cit., pp. 203–5; Ackroyd, C., Margolis, K., Rosenhead, J., and Shallice, T. (1980) op. cit., pp. 224–5.
152. Rodwell, R. (1973) 'Squawk box' technology. *New Scientist*, Vol. 59, No. 864, pp. 667–8; Anon (1973) Army tests new riot weapon. *New Scientist*, Vol. 59, No. 864, p. 684; Rodwell, R. (1973) How dangerous is the Army's squawk box? *New Scientist*, Vol. 59, No. 865, p. 730.
153. Coates, J. (1970) op. cit., p. 110.
154. Lumsden, M. (1978) op. cit., pp. 206–9.
155. Human Rights Watch (1995) *U.S. Blinding Laser Weapons*. Human Rights Watch Arms Project, Vol. 7, No. 5. New York: Human Rights Watch, p. 4.
156. Lumsden, M. (1978) op. cit., pp. 206–9.
157. Ibid., p. 110.
158. Security Planning Corporation (1972) op. cit., Appendix A.
159. League of Nations (1925) *Protocol for The Prohibition of The Use In War of Asphyxiating, Poisonous or Other Gases, and of Bacteriological Methods Of Warfare*, Geneva, 1925.
160. Simms, N. (2006) Legal Constraints on Biological Weapons. In: M. Wheelis, L. Rózsa, and M. Dando (eds). *Deadly Cultures: Biological Weapons Since 1945*. Cambridge: Harvard University Press, pp. 329–54.
161. Stockholm International Peace Research Institute (1971) op. cit., pp. 142–52.
162. Furmanski, M. (2005) op. cit.
163. Stockholm International Peace Research Institute (1971) op. cit., pp. 332–5.
164. Stock, T. (1996) *History of the Negotiations on the CWC – short overview*. Stockholm: Stockholm International Peace Research Institute, p. 7.
165. Furmanski, M. (2005) op. cit., p. 16.
166. Ibid., p. 15.

167. Stock, T. (1996) op. cit., pp. 7–8; US State Department (2002) *Protocol for the Prohibition of the Use in War of Asphyxiating, Poisonous or Other Gases, and of Bacteriological Methods of Warfare – Narrative*. Washington, DC: State Department, Bureau of Verification, Compliance, and Implementation. Accessed December 2006 at: http://www.state.gov/.
168. Ibid.
169. Stockholm International Peace Research Institute (1973) op. cit., pp. 185–6.
170. Furmanski, M. (2005) op. cit., pp. 17–18.
171. United States (1975) *Executive Order 11850 – Renunciation of certain uses in war of chemical herbicides and riot control agents, 8 April 1975*. 40 FR 16187, 3 CFR, 1971–5 Comp., p. 980.
172. Furmanski, M. (2005) op. cit., p. 18.
173. United Nations (1972) *Convention on the Prohibition of the Development, Production and Stockpiling of Bacteriological (Biological) and Toxin Weapons and on Their Destruction*. Geneva: United Nations, 10 April 1972.
174. Stockholm International Peace Research Institute (1975) *SIPRI Yearbook 1975, World Armaments and Disarmaments*. Stockholm: Almqvist & Wiksell, pp. 55–6.
175. United Nations (1977) *Protocol Additional to the Geneva Conventions of 12 August 1949, and relating to the Protection of Victims of International Armed Conflicts (Protocol 1)*. Geneva: United Nations, 8 June 1977; Coupland, R. and Loye, D. (2000) International Humanitarian Law and the Lethality or Non-Lethality of Weapons. In: M. Dando (ed) *Non-Lethal Weapons: Technological and Operational Prospects*. London: Jane's Publishing, pp. 60–6.
176. US Supreme Court (1985) *Tennessee v. Garner, 471 U.S. 1*.
177. US Supreme Court (1985) op. cit.
178. Hart, S. (2002) *Statement Before The Subcommittee on Aviation, Committee on Transportation And Infrastructure, U.S. House of Representatives*. Washington DC: House of Representatives.
179. National Institute of Justice (1994) *25 Years of Criminal Justice Research*. Washington, DC: Department of Justice, p. 37, note 1.
180. Sweetman, S. (1987) *Report on the Attorney General's Conference on Less Than Lethal Weapons*. National Institute of Justice. Washington, DC: US Government Printing Office.
181. Ibid., p. iii.
182. Ibid., p. 4.
183. Ibid., p. 11.
184. Ibid., pp. 11–20.
185. Ibid., p. 20.
186. Hart, S. (2002) op. cit.
187. Northam, G. (1988) *Shooting in the Dark*. London: Faber and Faber, pp. 29–64.
188. Turner, J. (1985) *Arms in the 80s*. Stockholm International Peace Research Institute. London: Taylor and Francis.
189. Lewer, N. and Schofield, S. (1997) *Non-Lethal Weapons. A Fatal Attraction? Military Strategies and Technologies for 21st Century Conflict*. London: Zed Books, pp. 34–5.
190. Sweetman, S. (1987) op. cit., p. 25.
191. Williams, P. (1987) Emerging Technology, exotic technology and arms control. In: C. Jacobsen (ed.) *The Uncertain Course. New Weapons Strategies and Mind-Sets*. Stockholm International Peace Research Institute. Oxford: Oxford University Press, pp. 279–93.
192. Human Rights Watch (1995) *U.S. Blinding Laser Weapons*. op. cit., p. 4.

193. Alexander, J. (1999) *Future War: Non-Lethal Weapons in Modern Warfare*. New York: St. Martin's Press, p. 13.
194. Alexander, J (1989) Antimateriel Technology. *Military Review*, Vol. 69, No. 10, October, pp. 29–41.
195. Sweetman, S. (1987) op. cit.
196. Alexander, J (1989) op. cit.
197. Alexander, J. (1999) op. cit., p. 13.
198. Sweetman, S. (1987) op. cit., pp. 4–5.
199. Laur, D. (2000) Taser *Technology Research Paper, Technical Report TR-01-2000*. Canadian Police Research Centre.
200. Laur, D. (2000) *Tasertron TE-95HP Subject Testing 2000-04-07*. Taser International, Inc. Accessed December 2006 at: http://www.taser.com/.
201. Sweetman, S. (1987) op. cit., pp. 4–5.
202. Kornblum, R. and Reddy, S. (1991) Effects of the Taser in fatalities involving police confrontation. *Journal of Forensic Science*, Vol. 36, No. 2, pp. 434–8.
203. Sweetman, S. (1987) op. cit., pp. 4–5 and 16.
204. Ibid., pp. 4–5.
205. Riordan, T. (2003) New Taser Finds Unexpected Home in Hands of Police. *New York Times*, 17 November.
206. Donnelly, T., Douse, K., Gardner, M., and Wilkinson, D. (2002) *PSDB Evaluation of Taser Devices. Publication No. 9/02*. London: UK Home Office, Police Scientific Development Branch, p. 6.
207. Ibid., p. 43.
208. Sweetman, S. (1987) op. cit., pp. 4–5.
209. Ibid., pp. 26–7.
210. Ibid., p. 26.
211. Ibid., p. 5.
212. Bleetman, A. and Steyn, R. (2003) op. cit.
213. Kornblum, R. and Reddy, S. (1991) op. cit.
214. Allen, T. (1992) Discussion of 'Effects of the Taser in Fatalities Involving Police Confrontation'. *Journal of Forensic Science*, Vol. 37, No. 4, pp. 956–8.
215. Amnesty International (1997) *Arming the Torturers: Electro-shock Torture and the Spread of Stun Technology*. ACT 40/001/1997. New York: Amnesty International.
216. Sweetman, S. (1987) op. cit., pp. 8–9.
217. Ibid., p. 19.
218. Ibid., p. 7
219. Hu, H., Fine, J., Epstein, P., Kelsey, K., Reynolds, P., and Walker, B. (1989) Tear Gas – Harassing Agent or Toxic Chemical Weapon? *Journal of the American Medical Association*, Vol. 262, No. 5, pp. 660–3.
220. Sweetman, S. (1987) op. cit., p. 19.
221. Dando, M. and Furmanski, M. (2006) op. cit.
222. Perry Robinson, J. (1994) Developments in 'Non-Lethal Weapons' involving Chemicals. In: International Committee of the Red Cross. *Report of the Expert Meeting on Certain Weapon Systems and on Implementation Mechanisms in International Law, Geneva, 30 May – 1 June 1994*, pp. 92–7.
223. Dando, M. and Furmanski, M. (2006) op. cit.
224. Perry Robinson, J. (2003) *Disabling Chemical Weapons: A Documented Chronology of Events, 1945–2003*. Harvard-Sussex Program, University of Sussex, unpublished version dated 8 October 2003, pp. 76–9.
225. Seaskate, Inc. (1998) op. cit., p. 44; National Institute of Justice (1994) op. cit., p. 51; Pilant, L. (1993) Less-than-Lethal Weapons: New Solutions for Law Enforcement.

Science and Technology, Washington, DC: International Association of Chiefs of Police.

226. Sweetman, S. (1987) op. cit., p. 17.
227. Ibid., p. 17.
228. Ibid., pp. 17–18.
229. Human Rights Watch (1995) *Blinding Laser Weapons: The Need to Ban a Cruel and Inhumane Weapon*. Washington, DC: Human Rights Watch, p. 23
230. Human Rights Watch (1995) *U.S. Blinding Laser Weapons*. op. cit., p. 4.
231. Madsen, E. (1987) Defending Against Battlefield Laser Weapons. *Military Review*, May, pp. 28–33.
232. Ibid.
233. Human Rights Watch (1995) *Blinding Laser Weapons: The Need to Ban a Cruel and Inhumane Weapon*. op. cit., p. 7.
234. Applied Research Laboratories, University of Texas at Austin (2002) *Non-Lethal Swimmer Neutralization Study*. Technical Document 3138. San Diego: SPAWAR Systems Center San Diego, p. 23.
235. United Nations (1980) *Convention on Prohibitions or Restrictions on the Use of Certain Conventional Weapons Which May be Deemed to be Excessively Injurious or to Have Indiscriminate Effects*. Geneva: United Nations, 10 October 1980.
236. International Committee of the Red Cross (1994) Report of the ICRC for the review conference of the 1980 UN convention on Prohibitions or restrictions on the use of certain conventional weapons which may be deemed to be excessively injurious or to have indiscriminate effects. *International Review of the Red Cross*, No. 299, pp. 123–82.
237. Doswald-Beck (1996) New Protocol on Blinding Laser Weapons. *International Review of the Red Cross*, No. 312, pp. 272–99.
238. Ibid.

3　'Non-Lethal' Weapons in the 1990s

1. Hart, S. (2002) *Statement before The Subcommittee on Aviation, Committee on Transportation and Infrastructure*. Washington, DC: House of Representatives.
2. Pilant, L. (1993) Less-than-Lethal Weapons: New Solutions for Law Enforcement. *Science and Technology*, Washington, DC: International Association of Chiefs of Police.
3. Pilant, L. (1993).
4. National Institute of Justice (1995) *NIJ Awards in Fiscal Year 1994*. Washington DC: Department of Justice.
5. Office of Technology Assessment (1991) *Technology Against Terrorism: The Federal Effort*, OTA-ISC-487. Washington DC: Government Printing Office, pp. 95–6.
6. Pilant, L. (1993) op. cit.
7. Andresen, B. and Grant, P. (1997) *Dose Safety Margin Enhancement for Chemical Incapacitation and Less-than-Lethal Targeting, NIJ Final Report and Recommendations*. Livermore, CA: Lawrence Livermore National Laboratory, Forensic Science Center R-Division; Perry Robinson, J. (2003) *Disabling Chemical Weapons: A Documented Chronology of Events, 1945–2003*. Harvard-Sussex Program, University of Sussex, unpublished version dated 8 October 2003, p. 93.
8. Scott, S. (1997) Sticky foam as a less-than-lethal technology. *Proceedings of SPIE*, Volume 2934, pp. 96–103; Goolsby, T. (1997) Aqueous foam as a less-than-lethal technology for prison applications. *Proceedings of SPIE*, Volume 2934, pp. 86–95.

9. Office of Technology Assessment (1991) op. cit., p. 96.
10. Ibid., pp. 141–2.
11. Lewer, N. (1997) *Bradford Non-Lethal Weapons Research Project*, Research Report No. 1. Bradford: University of Bradford.
12. Seaskate, Inc. (1998) The *Evolution and Development of Police Technology*. Washington, DC: National Institute of Justice, p. 46.
13. Pilant, L. (1993) op. cit.
14. Ibid.
15. National Institute of Justice (1994) *25 Years of Criminal Justice Research*. Washington DC: Department of Justice, p. 52.
16. National Institute of Justice (1997) *Department of Justice and Department of Defense Joint Technology Program: Second Anniversary Report*. Washington DC: Department of Justice.
17. Department of Defense, Department of Justice (1994) *Memorandum of Understanding between Department of Defense and Department Of Justice On Operations Other Than War and Law Enforcement*, 20 April 1994. Accessed March 2007 at: http://www.namebase.org/.
18. Between 1993 and 1996 the agency was referred to as the Advanced Research Projects Agency (ARPA).
19. National Institute of Justice (1997) *Department of Justice and Department of Defense Joint Technology Program: Second Anniversary Report*, op. cit.
20. Seaskate, Inc. (1998) op. cit., p. 37.
21. US Supreme Court (1996) *Koon* v. *United States (94–1664), 518 U.S. 81*; Rappert, B. (2004) MORALIZING VIOLENCE: Debating the Acceptability of Electrical Weapons. *Science as Culture*, Vol. 13, No. 1, pp. 3–35; Rejali, D (2003) *Violence You Can't See*. Reed College editorial. Accessed March 2007 at: http://www.collegenews.org/.
22. Pilant, L. (1993) op. cit.
23. Rappert, B. (2004) op. cit.
24. Wood, D. (2002) L.A.'s darkest days. *Christian Science Monitor*, 29 April 2002.
25. Mendel, W. (1996) *Combat in Cities: The LA Riots and Operation Rio*. Foreign Military Studies Office, Fort Leavenworth, KS, July 1996; Rasmussen, M. (1999) *The Military Role in Internal Defense and Security: Some Problems*. Occasional Paper No. 6, The Center for Civil-Military Relations, Naval Postgraduate School, Monterey, CA.
26. Pilant, L. (1994) Adding Less-than-Lethal Weapons to the Crime-Fighting Arsenal. *The Journal*, Autumn 1994.
27. Seaskate, Inc. (1998) op. cit., p. 37.
28. Department of Justice (1993) *Report to the Deputy Attorney General on the Events at Waco, Texas, 28 February to 19 April 1993*. Washington, DC: Department of Justice. Part XIII. The Aftermath of the April 19 Fire. Accessed March 2007 at: http://www.justice.gov/.
29. Ibid., Part XI. Planning and Decision-making Between 23 March and 19 April 1993.
30. Ibid., Part XII. The Events of 19 April 1993.
31. Walsh, E. (1999) FBI Releases Second Waco Videotape. *The Washington Post*, 4 September 1999.
32. Department of Justice (1993) *Report to the Deputy Attorney General on the Events at Waco, Texas, 28 February to 19 April 1993*, op. cit.
33. Koplow, D. (2005) Tangled up in Khaki and Blue: Lethal and Non-Lethal Weapons in Recent Confrontations. *Georgetown Journal of International Law*, Vol. 36, No. 3, p. 761.

34. Tapscott, M. (1993) DOD, Intel Agencies Look at Russian Mind Control Technology, Claims FBI Considered Testing on Koresh. *Defense Electronics*, July 1993; Ronson, J. (2004) *The Men Who Stare at Goats*. Oxford: Picador, pp. 189–206.
35. Pilant, L. (1993) op. cit.; Seaskate, Inc. (1998) op. cit., p. 37.
36. Koplow, D. (2005) op. cit., pp. 703–808; Koplow, D. (2006) *Non-lethal weapons: the law and policy for the military and law enforcement.* Cambridge: Cambridge University Press, pp. 53–66.
37. Rappert, B. (2003) *Non-Lethal Weapons as Legitimizing Forces?: Technology, Politics and the Management of Conflict.* London: Frank Cass, pp. 72–3.
38. Oleoresin capsicum (OC) is actually a biological toxin, not a synthetic chemical but has come to be grouped with CS and other sensory irritant chemical weapons as a riot control agent (RCA).
39. National Institute of Justice (1994) *25 Years of Criminal Justice Research*, op. cit., p. 52.
40. Seaskate, Inc. (1998) op. cit., p. 86.
41. National Institute of Justice (1997) *Department of Justice and Department of Defense Joint Technology Program: Second Anniversary Report*, op. cit.
42. Seaskate, Inc. (1998) op. cit., pp. 87–9.
43. Ibid., p. 87.
44. Ibid., p. 87.
45. Hart, S. (2002) op. cit.; This figure is for all 'non-lethal' weapons funding and includes anti-vehicle weapons.
46. National Institute of Justice (1995) *NIJ Awards in Fiscal Year 1994.* Washington, DC: Department of Justice; National Institute of Justice (1996) *NIJ Awards in Fiscal Year 1995.* Washington, DC: Department of Justice; National Institute of Justice (1997) *NIJ Awards in Fiscal Year 1996.* Washington, DC: Department of Justice; National Institute of Justice (1998) *NIJ Awards in Fiscal Year 1997.* Washington, DC: Department of Justice; National Institute of Justice (1999) *NIJ Awards in Fiscal Year 1998.* Washington, DC: Department of Justice; National Institute of Justice (2000) *NIJ Awards in Fiscal Year 1999.* Washington, DC: Department of Justice.
47. National Institute of Justice (1997) *Department of Justice and Department of Defense Joint Technology Program: Second Anniversary Report*, op. cit.
48. McEwen, T. and Leahy, F. (1994) *Less Than Lethal Force Technologies in Law Enforcement and Correctional Agencies.* A Final Summary Report Presented to the National Institute of Justice. Washington DC: Department of Justice, p. 80.
49. Ibid., p. 82.
50. Ibid., p. 83.
51. National Institute of Justice (1999) *National Institute of Justice 1998 Annual Report to Congress.* Washington, DC: Department of Justice.
52. Now the Home Office Scientific Development Branch (HOSDB).
53. *Partnerships with Other Countries*, National Institute of Justice website. Accessed March 2007 at: http://www.ojp.usdoj.gov/.
54. Northern Ireland Office (2001) *Patten Report Recommendations 69 and 70 Relating to Public Order Equipment: A Paper prepared by the Steering Group led by the Northern Ireland Office.* Belfast: Northern Ireland Office.
55. National Institute of Justice (1997) *NIJ Annual Report to Congress 1996.* Washington, DC: Department of Justice.
56. Burrows, C. (2001) Operationalizing Non-lethality: a Northern Ireland Perspective. *Medicine, Conflict and Survival*, pp. 260–71; Rappert, B. (2003) op. cit., pp. 139–43; Northern Ireland Office (2001) op. cit.

57. Independent Commission on Policing in Northern Ireland (1999) *A New Beginning: Policing in Northern Ireland. The Report of the Independent Commission on Policing for Northern Ireland.* Belfast: Independent Commission on Policing in Northern Ireland, p. 54.
58. Ibid., p. 113.
59. Kock, E. and Rix, B. (1996) A review of police trials of the CS aerosol incapacitant. *Police Research Series.* London: Home Office; Rappert, B. (2003) op. cit., pp. 175–201.
60. Lewer, N. and Schofield, S. (1997) *Non-Lethal Weapons. A Fatal Attraction?* London: Zed Books, p. 34.
61. Dando, M. (1996) *A New Form of Warfare: The Rise of Non-Lethal Weapons.* London: Brasseys, pp. 23–6.
62. Morris, C. and Morris, J. (1991) *Nonlethality: A Global Strategy White Paper.* Washington, DC: US Global Strategy Council, p. 1.
63. Wolfowitz, P. (1991) *Memorandum for the Secretary of Defense, Deputy Secretary of Defense. Do we Need a Nonlethal Defense Initiative?* Washington, DC: Department of Defense.
64. Lovelace, D. and Metz, S. (1998) *Nonlethality and American Land Power: Strategic Context and Operational Concepts.* Carlisle: Strategic Studies Institute, US Army War College, p. 2.
65. Lewer, N. and Schofield, S. (1997) op. cit., pp. 17–20.
66. Mazarr, M. (1993) *The Military Technical Revolution: A Structural Framework. Final Report of the CSIS Study Group on the MTR.* Washington, DC: Center for Strategic and International Studies, p. 43.
67. Dando, M. (1996) op. cit., pp. 24–5; Kokoski, R. (1994) Non-lethal weapons: a case study of new technology developments. In: Stockholm International Peace Research Institute *SIPRI Yearbook 1994.* Oxford: Oxford University Press, pp. 367–86; Lewer, N. and Schofield, S. (1997) op. cit., p. 34.
68. Alexander, J. (1992) *Rethinking National Security Requirements & The Need for Non-Lethal Weapons Options.* Submitted to President-Elect Clinton's Transition Team. LA-UR-92-3773. Los Alamos: Los Alamos National Laboratory.
69. Alexander, J (1989) Antimateriel Technology. *Military Review,* Vol. 69, No. 10, October, pp. 29–41.
70. Alexander, J. (1992) op. cit.
71. Council on Foreign Relations (1995) *Non-Lethal Technologies: Military Options and Implications. Report of an Independent Task Force.* New York: Council on Foreign Relations.
72. Lewer, N. and Schofield, S. (1997) op. cit., p. 33.
73. Ibid., p. 42.
74. National Research Council (2003) *An Assessment of Non-Lethal Weapons Science and Technology.* Washington, DC: National Academies Press, pp. 63–4.
75. Army Armament Research, Development and Engineering Center (ARDEC) (1992) ARDEC exploring less-than-lethal munitions; to give Army greater flexibility in future conflicts. *ARDEC News Release,* 9 October 1992.
76. Ibid.; Tapscott, M. and Atwal, K. (1993) New Weapons That Win Without Killing on DOD's Horizon. *Defense Electronics,* February 1993, pp. 41–6.
77. Harvard Sussex Program (1992) *Chemical Weapons Convention Bulletin.* Issue No. 18, December 1992, p. 12.
78. US Army (1996) *Concept for Nonlethal Capabilities in Army Operations,* TRADOC Pamphlet 525–73. Fort Monroe: Training and Doctrine Command (TRADOC).

79. Army Armament Research, Development and Engineering Center (ARDEC) (1992) op. cit.
80. Lewer, N. and Schofield, S. (1997) op. cit., p. 42.
81. Thomas, M. (1998) *Non-Lethal Weaponry: A Framework for Future Integration.* Air Command and Staff College, Air University, Maxwell Air Force Base, Alabama, p. 7.
82. Advanced Research Projects Agency (ARPA) (1995) Limited Effects Technologies (LET) SOL BAA 95-28. *Commerce Business Daily*, 2 May 1995. Accessed March 2007 at: http://www.fbodaily.com/.
83. Lorenz, F. (1996) Non-Lethal Force: The Slippery Slope to War? *Parameters*, Autumn 1996, pp. 52–62.
84. National Institute of Justice (1997) *Department of Justice and Department of Defense Joint Technology Program: Second Anniversary Report*, op. cit.
85. Ibid.
86. Dando, M. (1996) op. cit., pp. 1–8.
87. National Research Council (2003) op. cit., p. 53; Council on Foreign Relations (1995) op. cit.
88. National Research Council (2003) op. cit., p. 63.
89. Lorenz, F. (1995) 'Less-Lethal' Force in Operation United Shield. *Marine Corps Gazette*, September 1995, pp. 69–77.
90. Ireland, R. (1997) Tactical deployments of laser systems into low-intensity conflicts. *Proceedings of SPIE*, Vol. 2934, pp. 70–4.
91. Ibid.
92. National Research Council (2003) op. cit., p. 15.
93. Harvard Sussex Program (1992) *Chemical Weapons Convention Bulletin*. Issue No. 22, December 1993, p. 25.
94. Lewer, N. and Schofield, S. (1997) op. cit., p. 36.
95. Ibid., p. 36 and p. 46; Black, S. (1993) *Non-Lethal Weapons Systems: The potential impact of new technologies on Low Intensity Conflicts*. Ridgeway Viewpoints, Matthew B. Ridgeway Center for International Security Studies, No. 93–9, p. 4.
96. Council on Foreign Relations (1995) op. cit.; Lewer, N. and Schofield, S. (1997) op. cit., p. 35.
97. Swett, C. (1994) *Draft Policy for Non-Lethal Weapons*. Washington, DC: Office of the Assistant Secretary of Defense, Special Operations/Low Intensity Conflict, Policy Planning. Cited in: Bunker, R. (ed.) (1997) *Nonlethal Weapons: Terms and References*. INSS Occasional Paper 15. Colorado: USAF Institute for National Security Studies.
98. National Research Council (2003) op. cit., p. 69.
99. Council on Foreign Relations (1995) op. cit.
100. US Department of Defense (1996) *Policy for Non-Lethal Weapons*, Directive 3000.3, 9 July 1996. Washington, DC: Office of the Assistant Secretary of Defense, Special Operations/Low Intensity Conflict.
101. Ibid.
102. Ibid.
103. Ibid.
104. Coates, J. (1970) *Nonlethal and Nondestructive Combat in Cities Overseas*. Paper P-569. Arlington, VA: Institute for Defense Analyses, Science and Technology Division.
105. For further discussion of the organisational structure of the JNLWP see: Feakin, T. (2005) *Non-lethal weapons: technology for lowering casualties?* Ph.D. thesis, Department of Peace Studies, University of Bradford.

106. National Research Council (2003) op. cit., p. 41.
107. Alexander, J. (1999) *Future War: Non-Lethal Weapons in Twenty-First-Century Warfare.* New York: St. Martin's Press. Appendix C, pp. 226–7; Joint Non-Lethal Weapons Directorate (1998) *Joint Non-Lethal Weapons Program (JNLWP) Annual Report 1997.* Quantico, VA: JNLWD; Joint Non-Lethal Weapons Directorate (2000) *Joint Non-Lethal Weapons Program (JNLWP) Annual Report 1999.* Quantico, VA: JNLWD; National Research Council (2003) op. cit.; Feakin, T. (2005) op. cit.
108. Garwin, R. (1999) *Nonlethal Technologies: Progress and Prospects. Report of an Independent Task Force.* New York: Council on Foreign Relations.
109. Joint Non-Lethal Weapons Directorate (1998) *Joint Non-Lethal Weapons Program (JNLWP) Annual Report 1997.*
110. Joint Non-Lethal Weapons Directorate (2000) op. cit.
111. Ibid.
112. National Research Council (2003) op. cit., p. 58; Also see website of the Emerald Express 99-1 Small Wars Conference, May 1999 Accessed March 2007 at: http://www.smallwars.quantico.usmc.mil/.
113. National Research Council (2003) op. cit., pp. 63–4.
114. Perry Robinson, J. (2003) op. cit.
115. ERDEC changed its name in 1998, becoming Edgewood Chemical Biological Center (ECBC).
116. Joint Non-Lethal Weapons Directorate (1998) op. cit.
117. National Research Council (2003) op. cit., p. 126.
118. Marine Corps (1998) *Joint Concept for Non-Lethal Weapons.* Commandant of the Marine Corps, 5 January 1998.
119. National Research Council (2003) op. cit., p. 13.
120. Department of Defense (1999) *Fiscal Year 2000 RDT&E Budget Item Justification Sheet, 0603851M Non-Lethal Warfare DEM/VAL.* February 1999.
121. Department of Defense (1999) *Fiscal Year 2000 RDT&E Budget Item Justification Sheet, 0603605F Advanced Weapons Technology.* February 1999; Department of Defense (1999) *Fiscal Year 2000 RDT&E Budget Item Justification Sheet, 0602202F Human Effectiveness Applied Research.* February 1999; Department of Defense (1999) *Fiscal Year 2000 RDT&E Budget Item Justification Sheet, 0603228D8Z Physical Security Equipment.* February 1999.
122. Marine Corps System Command (1998) Research and Development for Non-Lethal Technologies SOL BAA-98-R-0016. *Commerce Business Daily,* 12 May 1998. Accessed March 2007 at: http://www.fbodaily.com/.
123. Joint Non-Lethal Weapons Directorate (2000) op. cit.; Joint Non-Lethal Weapons Directorate (1998) *Joint NLW Directorate News,* Vol. 2, No. 1, November 1998; Joint Non-Lethal Weapons Directorate (1999) *Joint Non Lethal Weapons Program News,* Vol. 2, No. 2, February 1999.
124. Feakin, T. (2005) op. cit., pp. 162–6.
125. Joint Non-Lethal Weapons Directorate (1998) *Joint NLW Directorate News,* op. cit.
126. Brill, A. (2001) The MCRU/Penn State Connection, *Sea Power,* April 2001.
127. Shwaery, G. (2002) JNLWD (Joint Non-lethal Weapons Directorate) and NTIC (Non-lethal Technology Innovation Center) Missions. *Presentation to the National Defense Industrial Association (NDIA) conference, Non-Lethal Defense V: Non-Lethal Weapons: Now, More Than Ever, 26–8 March 2002.*
128. Ibid.; Joint Non-Lethal Weapons Directorate (2000) op. cit.
129. Feakin, T. (2005) op. cit., p. 165.
130. Allison, G., Kelley, P., and Garwin, R. (2004). *Nonlethal Weapons and Capabilities. Report of an Independent Task Force.* New York: Council on Foreign Relations, p. 16.

238   *Notes*

. National Research Council (2003) op. cit., pp. 70–1.
132. Garwin, R. (1999) op. cit.
133. Ibid.
134. Feakin, T. (2005) op. cit., pp. 168–75.
135. NATO (2006) *The Human Effects of Non-Lethal Technologies. The Final Report of NATO, RTO HFM-073*. Brussels: NATO, RTO, Chapter 1.
136. Parent, C. (1995) Methods for deterring enemy aircraft eyed. *Inside the Pentagon*, 27 July 1995.
137. NATO (1997) *Minimizing Collateral Damage during Peace Support Operations. Volume 1: Executive Summary. AGARD Advisory Report 347, Aerospace Applications Study 43*. Brussels: NATO.
138. Lewer, N. (2001) op. cit.
139. Ibid.
140. NATO (1997) op. cit.
141. NATO (1999) *NATO Policy on Non-Lethal Weapons*, 13 October 1999. Brussels: NATO.
142. Joint Non-Lethal Weapons Directorate (2000) op. cit., p. 11.
143. Ibid.
144. House of Commons (1999) *House of Commons Hansard Written Answers for 10 Apr 2001 (pt 9)*. Accessed March 2007 at: http://www.publications.parliament.uk/.
145. Joint Non-Lethal Weapons Directorate (2000) op. cit., p. 11.
146. Rappert, B. (2003) op. cit., pp. 91–121.
147. Pilant, L. (1993) op. cit.; Seaskate, Inc. (1998) op. cit., p. 43.
148. Lee, R., Yolton, R., Yolton, D., Schnider, C., and Janin, M. L. (1996) Personal Defense Sprays: Effects and Management of Exposure. *Journal of the American Optometry Association*. Vol. 67, No. 9, pp. 548–60.
149. Ibid.; Rappert, B. (2003) op. cit., pp. 91–121.
150. Seaskate, Inc. (1998) op. cit., p. 43.
151. Rappert, B. (2003) op. cit., pp. 91–121.
152. Ibid., pp. 102–13.
153. Ibid., p. 104.
154. Ibid., pp. 107–8; Zamorra, J. (1996) Pepper spray study is tainted. *The Examiner*, 20 May 1996.
155. Aerospace Corp. (2001) *Final Report. National law Enforcement and Corrections Technology Center-Western Region*. Washington, DC: National Institute of Justice, pp. 17–18; Stockholm International Peace Research Institute (1973) *The Problem of Chemical and Biological Warfare. Volume II: CB Weapons Today*. Stockholm: Almqvist & Wiksell, p. 306; Olajos, E. and Salem, H. (2001) Riot Control Agents: Pharmacology, Toxicology, Biochemistry and Chemistry. *Journal of Applied Toxicology*, Vol. 21, pp. 355–91.
156. Donnelly, T., Douse, K., Gardner, M., and Wilkinson, D. (2002) *PSDB Evaluation of Taser Devices. Publication No 9/02*. St. Albans: Police Scientific Development Branch (PSDB), pp. 43–4; Laur, D. (1999) *Independent Evaluation Report of TASER and Air TASER Conducted Energy Weapons*. Victoria: Victoria Police Department. Accessed March 2007 at: http://www.taser.com/; *Taser International Corporate Background* website. Accessed March 2007 at: http://www.taser.com/.
157. Smith, R. (1996) Reducing violence: an analytical and technical approach. *Proceedings of SPIE*, Vol. 2934, pp. 27–36.
158. Ibid.
159. Greenberg, I. (1999) Prodding Car Thieves to Reform. *Wired News*, 23 July 1998.

160. Donnelly, T., Douse, K., Gardner, M., and Wilkinson, D. (2002) op. cit., pp. 43–4.
161. Laur, D. (2000) *Taser Technology Research Paper, Technical Report TR-01-2000*. Ottawa: Canadian Police Research Service.
162. Laur, D. (1999) op. cit.
163. *Taser International Corporate Background* website. Accessed March 2007 at: http://www.taser.com/.
164. Laur, D. (1999) op. cit.
165. McNulty, J. (2000) Non-Lethal, Taser Remote Controlled Sentinel Weapon. *Presentation to the National Defense Industrial Association (NDIA) conference, Non-Lethal Defense IV, 20–2 March 2000*.
166. Vasel, E., Bryars, J., Coakley, P., Mallon, C., Millard, J., Niederhaus, G., and Nunan, S. (1997) Sticky Shocker. *Proceedings of SPIE*, Vol. 2934, pp. 10–14.
167. Kenny, J., Murray, W., Sebastianelli, W., Kraemer, W., Fish, R., Mauger, D., and Jones, T. (1999) *Human Effects Advisory Panel. Report of Findings: Sticky Shocker Assessment*. State College, PA: Pennsylvania State University.
168. Amnesty International (1997) *Arming the Torturers. Electro-shock Torture and the Spread of Stun Technology*. ACT 40/001/1997. New York: Amnesty International.
169. Flatau, A. (2000) Ring Airfoil Grenade: A Less-Than Lethal Configuration for the Delivery of Selected Chemical Agents. *Presentation to the National Defense Industrial Association (NDIA) conference, Non-Lethal Defense IV, 20–2 March 2000*; Aerospace Corp. (2001) op. cit., p. 17.
170. Burrows, C. (2001) op. cit.
171. Scott, S. (1997) op. cit.
172. National Research Council (2003) op. cit., p. 127.
173. Scott, S. (1997) op. cit.
174. Goolsby, T. (1997) op. cit.
175. Mathis, R. (2000) Non-Lethal Applications of Slippery Substances. *Presentation to the National Defense Industrial Association (NDIA) conference, Non-Lethal Defense IV, 20–2 March 2000*; Collins, K. (2000) Non-Lethal Applications of Slippery Substances. *Presentation to the National Defense Industrial Association (NDIA) conference, Non-Lethal Defense IV, 20–2 March 2000*.
176. Army (1997) *Odorous Substances*. Research Proposal, July 1997. Edgewood, MD: Edgewood Research, Development, and Engineering Center.
177. Bickford, L. (2000) Odorous Substances for Non-Lethal Applications. *Presentation to the National Defense Industrial Association (NDIA) conference, Non-Lethal Defense IV, 20–2 March 2000*.
178. Dando, M. (1996) op. cit., pp. 136–68.
179. Andresen, B. and Grant, P. (1997) op. cit.
180. Air Force (1994) *Harassing, Annoying, and 'Bad Guy' Identifying Chemicals*. Research proposal, June 1994. Wright-Patterson Air Force Base, OH: Air Force; *BBC News* (2004) US military pondered 'love not war', *BBC News*, 15 January 2004; Plante, H. (2007) Pentagon Confirms It Sought To Build A 'Gay Bomb'. *cbs5.com*, 8 June 2007.
181. Joint Non-Lethal Weapons Directorate (2000) op. cit.
182. Moore, H. (2000) Aversive Audible Acoustic Devices. *Presentation to the National Defense Industrial Association (NDIA) conference, Non-Lethal Defense IV, 20–2 March 2000*; Boesch, H. and Reiff, C. (2000) A Prototype High-Intensity Infrasonic Test Chamber (HILF 1). *Presentation to the National Defense Industrial Association (NDIA) conference, Non-Lethal Defense IV, 20–2 March 2000*.

183. Wes, J. (2000) Man-tossable Acoustic Distraction Device. *Presentation to the National Defense Industrial Association (NDIA) conference, Non-Lethal Defense IV, 20–2 March 2000.*

184. Knoth, A. (1994) Disabling Technologies. A Critical Assessment. *International Defense Review*, No. 7, July 1994, pp. 33–9.

185. Adler, D. (2000) Anti-Personnel Laser Illuminators: Effectiveness Testing of HALT and Dissuader. *Presentation to the National Defense Industrial Association (NDIA) conference, Non-Lethal Defense IV, 20–2 March 2000*; National Research Council (2003) op. cit., p. 28.

186. Adler, D. (2000) op. cit.

187. Hewish, M. (2000) Beam weapons revolution – Directed-energy weapons point the way for battlefield technology. *International Defense Review*, 1 August 2000.

188. Abaie, M. (1998) Unmanned Aerial Vehicle (UAV) Non-Lethal (NL) Payload Delivery System. *Presentation to Non-Lethal Defense III, National Defense Industrial Association (NDIA) conference, US, 25–6 February 1998.*

189. Murphy, D. and Cycon, J. (1999) Applications for mini VTOL UAV for law enforcement. *Proceedings of SPIE*, Vol. 3577, pp. 35–43.

190. Kelly, R. (2000) PepperBall Non-Lethal Weapon Compliance Technology. An Alternative to Lethal Force. *Presentation to the National Defense Industrial Association (NDIA) conference, Non-Lethal Defense IV, 20–2 March 2000.*

191. Doswald-Beck, L. (1996) New Protocol on Blinding Laser Weapons. *International Review of the Red Cross*, No. 312, pp. 272–99.

192. Human Rights Watch (1995) *United States: US Blinding Laser Weapons*. New York: Human Rights Watch; Human Rights Watch (1995) *Blinding Laser Weapons: The Need to Ban a Cruel and Inhumane Weapon*, op. cit.

193. Doswald-Beck, L. (1996) op. cit.; Department of Defense (1995) DOD Announces Policy On Blinding Lasers. *DOD News Release*, No. 482–95, 1 September 1995.

194. United Nations (1995) *Additional Protocol to the Convention on Prohibitions or Restrictions on the Use of Certain Conventional Weapons which may be Deemed to be Excessively Injurious or to have Indiscriminate Effects. Article 1: Additional Protocol: Protocol on Blinding Laser Weapons (Protocol IV)*. CCW/CONF.I/7, 12 October 1995.

195. Ibid.

196. Stock, T. (1996) *History of the Negotiations on the CWC – short overview*. Stockholm: Stockholm International Peace Research Institute.

197. United Nations (1993) *Convention on the Prohibition of the Development, Production, Stockpiling and Use of Chemical Weapons and on their Destruction*, 13 January 1993, Article I.

198. Perry Robinson, J. and Meselson, M. (1994) New Technologies and the Loophole in the Convention. *Chemical Weapons Convention Bulletin*, Issue No. 23, March 1994, pp. 1–2.

199. Dando, M. (1996) op. cit., p. 185.

200. United Nations (1993) op. cit.

201. Ibid., Article II 9(d).

202. Dando, M. (1996) op. cit., p. 185.

203. Perry Robinson, J. and Meselson, M. (1994) op. cit.

204. US Navy (1997) *Preliminary Legal Review of Proposed Chemical-Based Nonlethal Weapons*. Department of the Navy, Office of the Judge Advocate General, International & Operational Law Division.

205. US Senate (1997) *U.S. Senate's Executive Resolution on Ratification of the CWC*, 105th Congress, 1st Session, S. Exec. Res. 75.

206. Fidler, D. (2005) The meaning of Moscow: "Non-lethal" weapons an international law in the early 21st century. *International Review of the Red Cross*, Vol. 87, No. 859, September 2005, pp. 525–52.
207. US Navy (1997) op. cit.
208. Ibid., pp. 21–2.
209. United Nations (1997) *Convention on the Prohibition of the Use, Stockpiling, Production and Transfer of Anti-Personnel Mines and on their Destruction, 18 September 1997.*
210. Arms Control Association (2005) *The Ottawa Convention at a Glance.* Arms Control Association Fact Sheet, December 2005.
211. Joint Non-Lethal Weapons Directorate (1997) *Joint NLW Directorate News*, Vol. 1, No. 3, December 1997.
212. United Nations (1990) *Basic Principles on the Use of Force and Firearms by Law Enforcement Officials.* Geneva: Office of the United Nations High Commissioner for Human Rights.
213. Ibid.

4 The Contemporary Development of 'Non-Lethal' Weapons

1. National Institute of Justice (2001) *National Institute of Justice 2000 Annual Report to Congress.* Washington, DC: Department of Justice, p. 10.
2. Office of Justice Programs (2001) *A Resource Guide to Law Enforcement, Corrections, and Forensic Technologies.* Washington, DC: Department of Justice, p. 12.
3. Kenny, J., Heal, C., and Grossman, M. (2001) *The Attribute-Based Evaluation (ABE) of Less-Than-Lethal, Extended-Range, Impact Munitions.* State College, PA: Pennsylvania State University; Hughes, E., Kenny, J., Heal, C., and Kaufman, P. (2007) *An Attribute Based Evaluation II (ABE-2) of Less-Lethal Impact Munitions.* State College, PA: Pennsylvania State University.
4. NIJ Research Portfolio. Accessed December 2006 at: http://nij.ncjrs.org/portfolio/. [Note: March 2007: This resource in no longer publicly available, it is now password protected].
5. National Institute of Justice (2003) *National Institute of Justice 2002 Annual Report.* Washington, DC: Department of Justice, pp. 5–6.
6. US Government (2001) *Aviation and Transportation Security Act, Public Law 107–71, 19 November 2001, Section 126 (a).*
7. Hart, S. (2002) *Statement before The Subcommittee on Aviation, Committee on Transportation and Infrastructure, U.S. House of Representatives.* Washington, DC: House of Representatives.
8. Ibid.
9. National Commission on Terrorist Attacks upon the United States (2004) *The 9/11 Commission Report: Final Report of the National Commission on Terrorist Attacks Upon the United States*, pp. 5–7.
10. Government Accountability Office (2006) *Aviation Security: Further Study of Safety and Effectiveness and Better Management Controls Needed If Air Carriers Resume Interest in Deploying Less-than-Lethal Weapons*, GAO-06-475. Washington, DC: Government Accountability Office.
11. Hart, S. (2002) op. cit.
12. DePersia, T. and Cecconi, J. (2001) Less-Than-Lethal Program. *Presentation to the Non-lethal Technology and Academic Research Symposium III*, Portsmouth, NH, 7–9 November 2001.

13. Ibid.; Also see, Cecconi, J. (2005) Less Lethal Program. *Presentation to Non-Lethal Defense VI: 'Non-Lethal Weapon Options in the Global Fight Against Terrorism', National Defense Industrial Association (NDIA)*, Reston, VA, 14–16 March 2005.
14. Boyd, D. (2000) The Search for Low Hanging Fruit: Recent Developments in Non-Lethal Technologies. In: M. Dando (ed.) *Non-Lethal Weapons: Technological and Operational Prospects*. Coulsdon: Jane's, pp. 43–50.
15. National Institute of Justice (2002) *NIJ Less-Than-Lethal Technology Solicitation, Fiscal Year 2002*. Washington, DC: Department of Justice.
16. Cecconi, J. (2002) Less Than Lethal Program. *Presentation to Non-Lethal Defense V: Non-Lethal Weapons: Now, More Than Ever, National Defense Industrial Association (NDIA)*, US, 26–8 March 2002.
17. E-LABS, Inc. (2003) *Performance Characterization Study: Noise Flash Diversionary Devices (NFDDs), Final Report*. Washington, DC: National Institute of Justice.
18. Truesdell, A. (2004) Airport Security Measures and the Role of Less-Lethal Technologies. *Presentation to the 2004 National Institute of Justice Annual Technology Conference*.
19. Sandia National Laboratories, Law Enforcement Technologies, Inc., and Martin Electronics, Inc. (2002) *Final Report to the National Institute of Justice on Grant Number 2000LTBXK004, Variable Range Less-Than-Lethal Ballistic*. Washington, DC: National Institute of Justice; Lewis, B. (2003) NIJ's Less-Than-Lethal Flash-Bang Round Project. *Corrections Today*, Vol. 65, No. 5.
20. National Institute of Justice (2001) *NIJ Awards in Fiscal Year 2000*. Washington, DC: Department of Justice; National Institute of Justice (2002) *NIJ Awards in Fiscal Year 2001*. Washington, DC: Department of Justice; National Institute of Justice (2003) *NIJ Awards in Fiscal Year 2002*. Washington, DC: Department of Justice; National Institute of Justice (2004) *NIJ Awards in Fiscal Year 2003*. Washington, DC: Department of Justice; National Institute of Justice (2005) *NIJ Awards in Fiscal Year 2004*. Washington, DC: Department of Justice; National Institute of Justice (2006) *NIJ Awards in Fiscal Year 2005*. Washington, DC: Department of Justice; National Institute of Justice (2007) *NIJ Awards in Fiscal Year 2006*. Washington, DC: Department of Justice; NIJ List of Awards website Accessed February 2009 at: http://www.ojp.usdoj.gov/nij/awards.
21. National Institute of Justice (2004) *Solicitation. Less-Lethal Technologies, Fiscal Year 2004*. SL 000638. Washington, DC: Department of Justice, p. 2.
22. National Institute of Justice (2005) *NIJ Awards in Fiscal Year 2004*. Washington, DC: Department of Justice.
23. National Institute of Justice (2005) *2004 Annual Report to Congress*. Washington, DC: Department of Justice, p. 51; Hambling, D. (2005) Police toy with 'less lethal' weapons. *New Scientist*, 2 May 2005.
24. Marine Corps (2004) Award: A – Technology Investment Program Non-lethal Weapons Study (Ref: M67854-04-R-6007). *FBO Daily*, 3 July 2004.
25. Hambling, D. (2005) op. cit.
26. Air Force Research Laboratory (2005) *AFRL Builds Portable Laser Weapon*. DE-S-06-01. Wright-Patterson AFB, OH: Air Force Research Laboratory.
27. Hambling, D. (2005) op. cit.; Knight, W. (2005) US military sets laser PHASR's to stun. *New Scientist*, 7 November 2005; Air Force Research Laboratory (2005) *AFRL Builds Portable Laser Weapon*, op. cit.
28. National Institute of Justice (2005) *2004 Annual Report to Congress*. op. cit., p. 51.
29. National Institute of Justice (2004) *Solicitation. Less-Lethal Technologies, Fiscal Year 2004*, p. 2.

30. Projects entitled *Verifying Reported Effectiveness of EMDT Devices in Reducing Deaths and Injuries* and *Review of Less-lethal Technology Operational Needs*, running from 1 September 2004 to 31 October 2008. Accessed March 2007 at: http://www.ojp. usdoj.gov/.

31. Mazzara, A. (2005) Less-Lethal Technologies: Today and Tomorrow. *Presentation to the Technologies for Public Safety in Critical Incident Response Conference and Exhibition 2005, 31 October–2 November 2005*, San Diego, CA.

32. National Institute of Justice (2004) *Solicitation for Concept Papers. Less-Lethal and Pursuit Management Technologies*, SL 000689. Washington, DC: Department of Justice, p. 2.

33. National Institute of Justice (2005) *Solicitation for Concept Papers. Outcomes of Police Use of Force*, SL 000695. Washington, DC: Department of Justice, pp. 1–2.

34. National Institute of Justice (2005) *Solicitation for Concept Papers: Less Lethal Technologies*, SL 000728. Washington, DC: Department of Justice.

35. National Institute of Justice (2005) *Solicitation for Concept Papers: School Safety Technologies*, SL 000718. Washington, DC: Department of Justice.

36. Air Force Research Laboratory (2005) *AFRL Builds Portable Laser Weapon*, op. cit.

37. National Institute of Justice (2008) *Study of Deaths Following Electro Muscular Disruption: Interim Report*. Washington, DC: NIJ.

38. National Institute of Justice (2006) *Solicitation: Less-Lethal Technologies*, SL# 000754. Washington, DC: Department of Justice; National Institute of Justice (2007) *Solicitation: Less-Lethal Technologies*, SL# 000810. Washington, DC: Department of Justice.

39. Weiss, D. (2007) Calming Down: Could Sedative Drugs Be a Less-Lethal Option? *NIJ Journal*, No. 261, pp. 42–6.

40. Hart, S. (2002) op. cit.

41. National Research Council (2003) An Assessment of Non-Lethal Weapons Science and Technology. Washington, DC: *National Academies Press*, p. 69.

42. Homeland Security Advanced Research Projects Agency (2005) *Innovative Less-Lethal Devices for Law Enforcement Technology Areas: State and Local*. HSARPA SBIR Fiscal Year 2005.1, Topic H-SB05.1-005.

43. Homeland Security Advanced Research Projects Agency (2005) *Abstracts of Fiscal Year 2005.1 Phase I Awards*; Homeland Security Advanced Research Projects Agency (2006) *Abstracts of Fiscal Year 2005.1 Phase II/Phase II Fast Track Award*. Accessed May 2007 at: https://www.sbir.dhs.gov/.

44. Ibid.

45. Northern Ireland Office (2001) *Patten Report Recommendations 69 and 70 Relating to Public Order Equipment: A Paper prepared by the Steering Group led by the Northern Ireland Office*. Belfast: Northern Ireland Office.

46. Donnelly, T. (2001) *Less Lethal Technologies. Initial Prioritisation and Evaluation. Publication No. 12/01*. St. Albans: Police Scientific Development Branch.

47. Burrows, C. (2001) Operationalizing Non-lethality: a Northern Ireland Perspective. *Medicine, Conflict and Survival*, pp. 260–71.

48. Northern Ireland Office (2001) *Patten Report Recommendations 69 and 70 Relating to Public Order Equipment. A Research Programme into Alternative Policing Approaches Towards the Management of Conflict*. Second Report. Belfast: Northern Ireland Office.

49. Northern Ireland Office (2002) *Patten Report Recommendations 69 and 70 Relating to Public Order Equipment. A Research Programme into Alternative Policing Approaches Towards the Management of Conflict*. Third Report. Belfast: Northern Ireland Office.

50. Ibid.; Donnelly, T., Douse, K., and Gardner, M. (2002) *PSDB Evaluation of Taser Devices. Publication No. 9/02.* St. Albans: Police Scientific Development Branch.
51. Northern Ireland Office (2004) *Patten Report Recommendations 69 and 70 Relating to Public Order Equipment. A Research Programme Into Alternative Policing Approaches Towards The Management of Conflict.* Fourth Report. Belfast: Northern Ireland Office.
52. BBC News (2004) Police offered stun guns option. *BBC News,* 15 September 2004. Accessed March 2007 at: http://news.bbc.co.uk/.
53. Wilkinson, D. (2005) *Police Scientific Development Branch Further Evaluation of Taser Devices. Publication No. 19/05.* St Albans: Police Scientific Development Branch; DSAC Sub-Committee on the Medical Implications of Less-Lethal Weapons (DOMILL) (2005) *Statement on the comparative medical implications of the use of the X26 Taser and the M26 Advanced Taser.* Dstl/BSC/BTP/DOC/803, 7 March 2005; Reuters (2007) Reid to expand use of Taser stun guns. *Reuters UK,* 15 May 2007.
54. Home Office (2008) *Funding for more Police Tasers.* Press Release, 24 November 2008. Accessed November 2008 at: http://press.homeoffice.gov.uk/.
55. Metropolitan Police Authority (2008) *MPS Use of Tasers.* Press Release, November 2008. Accessed November 2008 at: http://www.mpa.gov.uk/.
56. House of Commons (2005) *House of Commons Hansard Written Ministerial Statements for 4 Apr 2005 (pt 4).* London: HMSO.
57. Northern Ireland Office (2006) *Patten Report Recommendations 69 and 70 Relating To Public Order Equipment. A Research Programme Into Alternative Policing Approaches Towards The Management of Conflict.* Fifth Report. Belfast: Northern Ireland Office.
58. Reports of these meetings. Accessed May 2007 at: http://nldt2.arl.psu.edu/.
59. National Security Research, Inc. (2004) *Department of Defense Nonlethal Weapons and Equipment Review: A Research Guide for Civil Law Enforcement and Corrections.* Washington, DC: National Institute of Justice, p. 55.
60. National Research Council (2003) op. cit., p. 24.
61. Ibid., pp. ix–xi.
62. Ibid., pp. 4, 10–11.
63. Ibid., pp. 106–7.
64. Ibid., pp. 107–9.
65. Ibid., p. 11.
66. Ibid., pp. 107–9.
67. Ibid., p. 109.
68. Ibid., p. 101.
69. Ibid., p. 47.
70. Ibid., p. 102.
71. Ibid., pp. 74–7.
72. Ibid., pp. 43–4.
73. Ibid., pp. 104–6.
74. Klauenberg, J. (2002) *Non-Lethal Weapons Human Effects.* HE-02-09. Brooks AFB, TX: Air Force Research Laboratory.
75. Davison, N. and Lewer, N. (2005) *Bradford Non-Lethal Weapons Research Project Research Report No. 7.* Bradford: University of Bradford, p. 28.
76. Ibid., p. 22.
77. National Research Council (2003) op. cit., pp. 21–2.
78. Ibid., p. 73.
79. MacKenzie, D. (2002) US non-lethal weapon reports suppressed. *New Scientist,* 9 May 2002; The Sunshine Project (2002) US Military Operating a Secret Chemical Weapons Program. News Release, 24 September 2002.

80. National Research Council (2003) op. cit., Preface.

81. MacKenzie, D. (2002) op. cit.

82. National Research Council (2003) op. cit., Prologue.

83. Allison, G., Kelley, P., and Garwin, R. (2004) *Nonlethal Weapons and Capabilities: Report of an Independent Task Force Sponsored by the Council on Foreign Relations*. New York: Council on Foreign Relations, pp. 7–8.

84. Ibid., p. 1.

85. Ibid., p. 8.

86. Ibid., p. 4.

87. Ibid., Executive Summary.

88. Department of Defense (2006) *RDT&E Budget Item Justification. 0603851M Non-Lethal Warfare, Demonstration and Validation*, DOD Fiscal Year 2007 Budget.

89. Sherman, J. (2006) DoD: Spend More on Non-Lethal Weapons. *InsideDefense. com*, 24 May 2006. Accessed March 2007 at: http://www.military.com/.

90. Army Project Manager Close Combat Systems website. Accessed March 2007 at: http://ccsweb.pica.army.mil/.

91. Allison, G., Kelley, P., and Garwin, R. (2004) op. cit., p. 1.

92. Joint Non-Lethal Weapons Program (2006) *Individual Serviceman Non-Lethal System (ISNLS) Fact Sheet*. Quantico, VA: JNLWD.

93. Feakin, T. (2005) *Non-lethal weapons: technology for lowering casualties?* Ph.D. Thesis. Bradford: University of Bradford, p. 181.

94. Allison, G., Kelley, P., and Garwin, R. (2004) op. cit.

95. Davison, N. and Lewer, N. (2005) op. cit., pp. 22–4.

96. National Security Research, Inc. (2004) op. cit.; Allison, G., Kelley, P., and Garwin, R. (2004) op. cit., pp. 49–50; Joint Non-Lethal Weapons Program (2006) *Individual Serviceman Non-Lethal System (ISNLS) Fact Sheet*. op. cit.; Joint Non-Lethal Weapons Program (2006) *Non-Lethal Optical Distractors Fact Sheet*. Quantico, VA: JNLWD; Jackson, R. and Hutchinson, J. (2006) Lasers are Lawful Non-Lethal Weapons. *The Army Lawyer*, August 2006, pp. 12–18; Davison, N. and Lewer, N. (2003) *Bradford Non-Lethal Weapons Research Project Research Report No. 4*. Bradford: University of Bradford; Davison, N. and Lewer, N. (2004) *Bradford Non-Lethal Weapons Research Project Research Report No. 5*. Bradford: University of Bradford; Davison, N. and Lewer, N. (2004) *Bradford Non-Lethal Weapons Research Project Research Report No. 6*. Bradford: University of Bradford; Davison, N. and Lewer, N. (2005) op. cit.; Davison, N. and Lewer, N. (2006) *Bradford Non-Lethal Weapons Research Project Research Report No. 8*. Bradford: University of Bradford.

97. Joint Non-Lethal Weapons Program (2007) *Active Denial System (ADS) Fact Sheet*. Quantico, VA: JNLWD; Joint Non-Lethal Weapons Program (2008) *Active Denial System (ADS) Fact Sheet*. Quantico, VA: JNLWD; Joint Non-Lethal Weapons Program (2006) *Acoustic Hailing Devices (AHD) Fact Sheet*. Quantico, VA: JNLWD; Joint Non-Lethal Weapons Program (2006) *Airburst Non-Lethal Munition (ANLM) Fact Sheet*. Quantico, VA: JNLWD; Joint Non-Lethal Weapons Program (2006) *Joint Non-Lethal Warning Munition (JNLWM) Fact Sheet*. Quantico, VA: JNLWD; Joint Non-Lethal Weapons Program (2008) *Joint Non-Lethal Warning Munition (JNLWM) Fact Sheet*. Quantico, VA: JNLWD; Joint Non-Lethal Weapons Program (2006) *Mission Payload Module–Non-Lethal Weapon System (MPM-NLWS) Fact Sheet*. Quantico, VA: JNLWD; Joint Non-Lethal Weapons Program (2006) *Mk19 Non-Lethal Munition (NLM) Fact Sheet*. Quantico, VA: JNLWD; Joint Non-Lethal Weapons Program (2008) *Mk19 Non-Lethal Munition (NLM) Fact Sheet*. Quantico, VA: JNLWD; Air Force Research Laboratory (2006) *Personnel Halting and Stimulation Response (PHaSR) Fact Sheet*.

Kirtland AFB, NM: Air Force Research Laboratory, April 2006; Department of Defense (2005) *RDT&E Budget Item Justification. 0603851M Non-Lethal Warfare, Demonstration and Validation*, DOD Fiscal Year 2006 Budget; Department of Defense (2006) *RDT&E Budget Item Justification. 0603851M Non-Lethal Warfare, Demonstration and Validation*, DOD Fiscal Year 2007 Budget; US Army Picatinny Arsenal website Accessed March 2007 at: http://www.pica.army.mil/; Fulghum, D. (2006) op. cit.; Davison, N. and Lewer, N. (2003) op. cit.; Davison, N. and Lewer, N. (2004) *Bradford Non-Lethal Weapons Research Project Research Report No. 5*, op. cit.; Davison, N. and Lewer, N. (2004) *Bradford Non-Lethal Weapons Research Project Research Report No. 6*, op. cit.; Davison, N. and Lewer, N. (2005) op. cit.; Davison, N. and Lewer, N. (2006) op.cit.; DARPA, Defense Sciences Office, Polymer Ice Program website. Accessed July 2008 at: http://www.darpa. mil/; National Institute of Justice, Active Denial System website. Accessed July 2008 at: http://www.ojp.usdoj.gov/.

98. Acronyms: Joint Non-Lethal Weapons Directorate (JNLWD); Army Research, Development and Engineering Center (ARDEC); Air Force Research Laboratory (AFRL); Naval Surface Warfare Center, Crane Division (NSWC Crane); Edgewood Chemical Biological Center (ECBC); Defense Advanced Research Projects Agency (DARPA); Department of Justice (DOJ); Office of Force Transformation (OFT); and Department of Energy (DOE).

99. Fulghum, D. (2006) Silent Launch. *Aviation Week & Space Technology*. Vol. 165, Issue 4, 24 July 2006, p. 66.

100. Davison, N. and Lewer, N. (2005) op. cit., p. 26.

101. Allison, G., Kelley, P., and Garwin, R. (2004) op. cit., pp. 58–63.

102. Institute for Non-Lethal Defense Technologies (INLDT) website. Accessed March 2007 at: http://nldt2.arl.psu.edu/.

103. Non-lethal Technology Innovation Center (NTIC) website. Accessed March 2007 at: http://www.unh.edu/ntic/.

104. Lamb, T. (2003) Army nonlethal weapons/scalable-effects program: a think piece. *Military Police*, PB-19-03-1, April 2003; Galvan, J. and Kang, T. (2006) The Future of the Army Nonlethal Scalable Effects Center. *Military Police*, PB-19-06-1, April 2006; Army ARDEC website. Accessed March 2007 at: http://www.pica.army.mil/.

105. Armament Research, Development and Engineering Center (ARDEC) (undated) *Target Behavioral Response Laboratory (TBRL) Fact Sheet*. Picatinny, NJ: ARDEC.

106. Stress and Motivated Behavior Institute (SMBI) website. Accessed March 2007 at: http://www.umdnj.edu/smbiweb/.

107. Ibid.

108. Army Research Laboratory, Research and Analysis Programs – Lethality, website. Accessed March 2007 at: http://www.arl.army.mil/.

109. Army Research Laboratory, Research and Analysis Programs – Power & Energy, website. Accessed March 2007 at: http://www.arl.army.mil/.

110. Edgewood Chemical Biological Center (ECBC) website. Accessed March 2007 at: http://www.ecbc.army.mil/.

111. Air Force Research Laboratory, Directed Energy Directorate website. Accessed March 2007 at: http://www.de.afrl.af.mil/.

112. Air Force Research Laboratory (2005) *Research in support of the Directed Energy Bioeffects Division of the Human Effectiveness Directorate. Broad Agency Announcement Number: BAA 05-05 HE*. Brooks AFB, TX: AFRL.

113. Davison, N. and Lewer, N. (2004) *Bradford Non-Lethal Weapons Research Project Research Report No. 5*, op. cit., pp. 13–14.

114. Joint Non-Lethal Weapons Directorate (2006) *JNLWP Fiscal Year 2006–7 Technology Broad Area Announcement. Non-Lethal Weapons Technology Fiscal Year 2006–7 Applied Research And Development Efforts.*

115. Ibid.

116. Ibid.

117. Joint Non-Lethal Weapons Directorate (2008) *JNLWP FY09 Technology Broad Area Announcement. Non-Lethal Weapons FY09 Applied Research Efforts.* Also see Joint Non-Lethal Weapons Directorate (2008) *DOD Non-Lethal Weapons Program. Annual Report 2008.* Quantico, VA: JNLWD.

118. Also see similar announcements for Fiscal Year 2008 and Fiscal Year 2009.

119. Davison, N. and Lewer, N. (2005) op. cit., pp. 24–5.

120. Air Force Research Laboratory (2005) *Research in support of the Directed Energy Bioeffects Division of the Human Effectiveness Directorate,* op. cit.; Davison, N. and Lewer, N. (2005) op. cit., p. 28.

121. Defense Science Board (2004) *Defense Science Board Task Force on Future Strategic Strike Forces.* Washington, DC: Department of Defense, pp. 7–18.

122. Department of Defense (2005) *Strategy for Homeland Defense and Civil Support.* Washington, DC: Department of Defense, pp. 42–4.

123. Department of Defense (2006) *Quadrennial Defense Review Report.* Washington, DC: Department of Defense, p. 35.

124. NATO (2002) *The NATO Handbook. Chapter 2: The Transformation of the Alliance.* Brussels: NATO. Accessed March 2007 at: http://www.nato.int/.

125. Murphy, M. (2005) NATO Studies on Non-Lethal Weapons (NLWs): Effectiveness, Human Effects, and Future Technologies. *Proceedings of the 3rd European Symposium on Non-Lethal Weapons, Ettlingen, Germany, 10–12 May 2005.* V20. Pfinztal: Fraunhofer ICT.

126. NATO Research and Technology Organisation (RTO) website. Accessed March 2007 at: http://www.rta.nato.int/.

127. NATO (2004) *Non-Lethal Weapons and Future Peace Enforcement Operations,* RTO-TR-SAS-040. Brussels: NATO, RTO.

128. Ibid.

129. Ibid., Chapter 5, p. 2.

130. NATO (2006) *The Human Effects of Non-Lethal Technologies.* RTO-TR-HFM-073. Brussels: NATO, RTO.

131. RTO-EN-HFM-145 – Human Effects of Non-Lethal Technologies, project summary website. Accessed July 2008 at: http://www.rta.nato.int/.

132. Davison, N. and Lewer, N. (2004) *Bradford Non-Lethal Weapons Research Project Research Report No. 6,* op. cit. pp. 34–8.

133. Smith, G., Macfarlane, M., and Crockett, J. (2004) *Comparison of CS and PAVA. Operational and toxicological aspects.* Publication No. 88/04. St. Albans: Police Scientific Development Branch.

134. Davison, N. and Lewer, N. (2005) op. cit., p. 26.

135. Euripidou, E., MacLehose, R., and Fletcher, A. (2004) An investigation into the short term and medium term health impacts of personal incapacitant sprays. A follow up of patients reported to the National Poisons Information Service (London). *Emergency Medicine Journal,* Vol. 21, pp. 548–52.

136. Rappert, B. (2003) *Non-Lethal Weapons as Legitimizing Forces?: Technology, Politics and the Management of Conflict.* London: Frank Cass, p. 104

137. National Institute of Justice (2004) *Impact Munitions Use: Types, Targets, Effects.* Washington, DC: Department of Justice.

138. Kenny, J., Heal, S., and Grossman, M. (2001) *The Attribute-Based Evaluation (ABE) of Less-Than-Lethal, Extended-Range, Impact Munitions.* State College, PA: Pennsylvania State University.
139. Northern Ireland Office (2002) op. cit.
140. National Research Council (2003) op. cit., p. 25.
141. National Institute of Justice (2004) *Impact Munitions Use: Types, Targets, Effects,* op. cit.
142. Burrows, C. (2001) op. cit.
143. Omega Foundation (2003) *Baton Rounds: A Review of the human rights implications of the introduction and use of the L21A1 baton round in Northern Ireland and proposed alternatives to the baton round.* Belfast: Northern Ireland Human Rights Commission.
144. Northern Ireland Office (2006) op. cit.
145. Starmer, K. and Gordon, J. (2005) *Report on the Policing of the Ardoyne and Whiterock Parades 2005.* Belfast: Northern Ireland Policing Board.
146. Maguire, K., Hughes, D., Fitzpatrick, M., Dunn, F., Rocke, L., and Baird, C. (2006) Injuries caused by the attenuated energy projectile: the latest less lethal option. *Emergency Medicine Journal,* Vol. 24, No. 71, pp. 103–5.
147. Taser International, Inc., Statistics website. Accessed December 2006 at: http://www.taser.com/.
148. Taser International, Inc., Taser Cartridges website. Accessed May 2007 at: http://www2.taser.com/.
149. Taser International, Inc., Taser C2 website. Accessed May 2007 at: http://www2.taser.com/.
150. Bloomberg (2007) Newest Taser stuns US police. *New Zealand Herald,* 26 April 2007; Davis, R. (2007) Taser sells small version for wider use. *USA Today,* 8 January 2007.
151. Davison, N. and Lewer, N. (2004) *Bradford Non-Lethal Weapons Research Project Research Report No. 6,* op cit., pp. 5–8.
152. Business Journal of Phoenix (2004) Taser unveils rifle-mounting system. *Business Journal of Phoenix,* 29 October 2004.
153. Taser International, Inc. (2006) *TASER International Announces Formation of Senior Executive Advisory Board.* Press Release, 16 August 2006.
154. Stinger Systems, Inc. website. Accessed March 2007 at: http://www.stingersystems.com/.
155. Council of the European Union (2005) COUNCIL REGULATION (EC) No 1236/2005 of 27 June 2005 concerning trade in certain goods which could be used for capital punishment, torture or other cruel, inhuman or degrading treatment or punishment. *Official Journal of the European Union,* L200/1–L200/19. Brussels: Council of the European Union.
156. Davison, N. and Lewer, N. (2004) *Bradford Non-Lethal Weapons Research Project Research Report No. 6,* op. cit.; Davison, N. and Lewer, N. (2005) op. cit.; Davison, N. and Lewer, N. (2006) op. cit.
157. Lewer, N. and Davison, N. (2006) *Electrical stun weapons: alternative to lethal force or a compliance tool?* Bradford: University of Bradford.
158. Taser International, Inc. (2005) *TASER International Successfully Demonstrates Wireless TASER(R) eXtended Range Electro-muscular Projectile to Military Officials.* Press Release, 14 February 2006.
159. Previously this was under development with Tasertron and General Dynamics.
160. Taser International, Inc., TASER Remote Area Denial (TRAD) website. Accessed May 2007 at: http://www2.taser.com/.

161. Taser International, Inc., TASER Shockwave website. Accessed July 2008 at: http://www.taser.com/.
162. iRobot Corp. (2007) *iRobot and TASER Team to Deliver New Robot Capabilities for Military, Law Enforcement*. Press release, 28 June 2007; *New Scientist* (2007) Armed autonomous robots cause concern. *NewScientist.com*, 7 July 2007.
163. Sandia National Laboratories, Law Enforcement Technologies, Inc., and Martin Electronics, Inc. (2002) *Variable Range Less-Than-Lethal Ballistic, Final Report*. NCJ 199046. Washington, DC: Department of Justice; Grubelich, M. and Cooper, P. (2005) Diversionary Device History and Revolutionary Advancements. *Proceedings of the 3rd European Symposium on Non-Lethal Weapons, Ettlingen, Germany, 10–12 May 2005*. P56. Pfinztal: Fraunhofer ICT.
164. Joint Non-Lethal Weapons Program (2008) *Improved Flash Bang Grenade (IFBG) Fact Sheet*. Quantico, VA: JNLWD.
165. Fenton, G. and Nelson, J. (2003) Multi-Sensory Incapacitation. *Presentation to Jane's Less Lethal Weapons Conference, 2–3 October 2003, UK*.
166. Department of Defense (2006) *RDT&E Budget Item Justification. 0603651M Joint Non-Lethal Weapons Technology Development*. DOD Fiscal Year 2007 Budget.
167. United States Patent Office (2003) *Less lethal multi-sensory distraction grenade, United States Patent 6,543,364, 8 April 2003*; Scientific Applications & Research Associates Inc. (2003) Multi-Sensory Grenade website. Accessed November 2003 at: http://www.sara.com/.
168. Lewis, B. (2003) NIJ's Less-Than-Lethal Flash-Bang Round Project. *Corrections Today*, Vol. 65, No. 5; National Law Enforcement and Corrections Technology Center (2003) *Technology Project: Multi-Sensor Grenade and Field Evaluation*. Accessed November 2003 at: http://www.nlectc.org/.
169. Swenson, K. (2002) Joint Non-Lethal Weapons Program (JNLWP) Update. *Presentation to The 2002 International Infantry & Joint Services Small Arms Systems Section Symposium, Exhibition & Firing Demonstration, National Defense Industrial Association (NDIA), US, 13–16 May 2002*.
170. Tiron, R (2002) Stopping Intruders Can Be a Sticky Mess. *National Defense Magazine*, March 2002.
171. DARPA, Defense Sciences Office, Polymer Ice Program website, op. cit.
172. Anderson, C., Dimonie, V., Daniels, E., and EL-Aasser, M. (2003) Development of Particle-Based Slippery Material Technologies for Non-Lethal Weapons Applications. *Abstract of presentation to the Non-lethal Technology and Academic Research Symposium V, 5–6 November 2003, VA, US*.
173. Shwaery, G. (2003) Leveraging Non-Lethal Technology Research In Academia. *Proceedings of the 2nd European Symposium on Non-Lethal Weapons, Ettlingen, Germany, 13–14 May 2003*. P50. Pfinztal: Fraunhofer ICT.
174. National Research Council (2003) op. cit., pp. 26–7.
175. Ibid., p. 81.
176. Omega Foundation (2003) op. cit.
177. Allison, G., Kelley, P., and Garwin, R. (2004) op. cit., p. 56.
178. Joint Non-Lethal Weapons Directorate (2001) *JNLWD Newsletter, 2nd Quarter 2001*. Quantico, VA: JNLWD.
179. Lakoski, J., Bosseau Murray, W., and Kenny, J. (2000) *The Advantages and Limitations of Calmatives for Use as a Non-Lethal Technique*. State College, PA: Pennsylvania State University.
180. National Research Council (2003) op. cit., pp. 124–5.
181. Klochikhin, V., Lushnikov, A., Zagaynov, V., Putilov, A., Selivanov, V., and Zatevakhin, M. (2005) Principles of Modelling of the Scenario of Calmative

Application in a Building with Deterred Hostages. *Proceedings of the 3rd European Symposium on Non-Lethal Weapons, Ettlingen, Germany, 10–12 May 2005.* V17. Pfinztal: Fraunhofer ICT.

182. Stanley, T. (2003) Human immobilization: is the experience in Moscow just the beginning? *European Journal of Anaesthesiology.* Vol. 20, pp. 427–8.

183. Paton Walsh, N. (2003) Families claim death toll from gas in Moscow siege kept secret. *The Guardian,* 18 October 2003.

184. Hess, L., Schreiberova, J., and Fusek, J. (2005) Pharmacological Non-Lethal Weapons. *Proceedings of the 3rd European Symposium on Non-Lethal Weapons, Ettlingen, Germany, 10–12 May 2005.* V23. Pfinztal: Fraunhofer ICT.

185. American Technology Corp., Long Range Acoustic Device (LRAD) website. Accessed May 2007 at: http://www.atcsd.com/.

186. Altmann, J. (2005) Acoustic NLW Working in the Audio Range. *Proceedings of the 3rd European Symposium on Non-Lethal Weapons, Ettlingen, Germany, 10–12 May 2005.* P38. Pfinztal: Fraunhofer ICT; Altmann, J. (2005) Assessing New Types of LLW. *Presentation to Jane's 8th Annual Less-Lethal Weapons Conference, Leeds, UK, 26–7 October 2005.*

187. American Technology Corporation (2005) *Long Range Acoustic Device.* Presentation provided by the company, September 2005.

188. DefenseTech.org (2005) L.A. Cops' Super Sonic Blaster. *DefenceTech.org,* 11 August 2005. Available March 2007 at: http://www.defensetech.org/.

189. Magnuson, S. (2006) Lasers Seen as Solution To Checkpoint Safety. *National Defense,* February 2006; Joint Non-Lethal Weapons Program (2006) *Acoustic Hailing Devices (AHD) Fact Sheet,* op. cit.

190. Department of Defense (2006) *Department of Defense Annual Report on Cooperative Agreements and Other Transactions Entered into During Fiscal Year 2005 Under 10 USC 2371.* Washington, DC: Department of Defense, p. 118.

191. Joint Non-Lethal Weapons Program (2008) *Distributed Sound and Light Array (DSLA) Fact Sheet.* Quantico, VA: JNLWD.

192. Edwards, J. A. (2003) Initial Simulations Of A Single Shot Vortex Gun. *Proceedings of the 2nd European Symposium on Non-Lethal Weapons, Ettlingen, Germany, 13–14 May 2003.* V31. Pfinztal: Fraunhofer ICT; Backhaus, J., Deimling, L., Blanc, A., Schweitzer, S., and Thiel, K.-D. (2003) Impulse Transport by propagating Vortex Rings. *Proceedings of the 2nd European Symposium on Non-Lethal Weapons, Ettlingen, Germany, 13–14 May 2003.* V23. Pfinztal: Fraunhofer ICT; Scientific Applications & Research Associates Inc. (2003) Law Enforcement Applications (Non-lethals). SARA website. Accessed November 2003 at: http://www.sara.com/; Havermann, M. (2005) Influence of Physical and Geometrical Parameters on Vortex Rings Generated by a Shock Tube. *Proceedings of the 3rd European Symposium on Non-Lethal Weapons, Ettlingen, Germany, 10–12 May 2005.* V24. Pfinztal: Fraunhofer ICT; Levin, D. and Selivanov, V. (2005) Engineering Method to Calculate Vortex Generators Parameters – Physical Capabilities Modeling of Vortex Ring and its Spreading Parameters. *Proceedings of the 3rd European Symposium on Non-Lethal Weapons, Ettlingen, Germany, 10–12 May 2005.* P41. Pfinztal: Fraunhofer ICT.

193. Komarow, S. (2005) Energy beam Weapon may lower Iraq civilian deaths. *USA Today,* 24 July 2005; Komarow, S. (2005) Pentagon deploys array of non-lethal weapons. *USA Today,* 24 July 2005.

194. New Scientist (2007) US aims to use heat-beam weapon by 2010. *NewScientist. com,* 25 January 2007; Joint Non-Lethal Weapons Program (2007) *Active Denial System (ADS) Fact Sheet,* op. cit.

195. National Research Council (2003) op. cit., p. 30.
196. Air Force Research Laboratory (2006) *Personnel Halting and Stimulation Response (PHaSR) Fact Sheet*, April 2006, op. cit.; Air Force Research Laboratory (2006) *Personnel Halting and Stimulation Response (PHaSR) Fact Sheet*. Kirtland AFB, NM: Air Force Research Laboratory, May 2006.
197. US Navy (2005) Award: A – AZ13 – LASER INDUCED PLASMA CHANNEL WEAPONIZATION. *FBO Daily*, 27 January 2006.
198. Joint Non-Lethal Weapons Program (2006) *Individual Serviceman Non-Lethal System (ISNLS) Fact Sheet*, op. cit.
199. Northern Ireland Office (2002) op. cit.; Northern Ireland Office (2006) op. cit.
200. Davison, N. and Lewer, N. (2003) op. cit.; Davison, N. and Lewer, N. (2004) *Bradford Non-Lethal Weapons Research Project Research Report No. 5*, op. cit.; Davison, N. and Lewer, N. (2004) *Bradford Non-Lethal Weapons Research Project Research Report No. 6*, op. cit.; Davison, N. and Lewer, N. (2005) op. cit.; Davison, N. and Lewer, N. (2006) op. cit.
201. Fidler, D. (2005) The meaning of Moscow: "Non-lethal" weapons an international law in the early 21st century. *International Review of the Red Cross*, Vol. 87, No. 859, September 2005, pp. 525–52.
202. Fidler, D. (2001) 'Non-lethal' Weapons and International Law: Three Perspectives on the Future. *Medicine, Conflict and Survival*, Vol. 17, No. 3, pp. 194–206.
203. Fidler, D. (2005) op. cit.
204. Kelle, A. (2003) CWC Report: The CWC After Its First Review Conference: Is the Glass Half Full or Half Empty? *Disarmament Diplomacy*, Issue No. 71, June–July 2003.
205. Meier, O. (2008) CWC Review Conference Avoids Difficult Issues. *Arms Control Today*, May 2008.
206. Chevrier, M. and Leonard, J. (2005) Biochemicals and the Biological and Toxin Weapons Convention. *Symposium on Incapacitating Biochemical Weapons: Scientific, Military Legal and Policy Perspectives and Prospects, Geneva, Switzerland, 11 June 2005*. Washington, DC: Center for Arms Control and Non-Proliferation.
207. Fidler, D. (2005) op. cit.
208. Harvard Sussex Program (2003) *The CBW Conventions Bulletin*, Issue No. 61, September 2003, pp. 1–2.
209. McGlinchey, D. (2003) United States: Rumsfeld Says Pentagon Wants Use of Nonlethal Gas. *Global Security Newswire*, 6 February 2003. Accessed March 2007 at: http://www.nti.org/; Hay, A. (2003) Out of the straitjacket. *The Guardian*, 12 March 2003.
210. United Nations (1993) *Convention On The Prohibition Of The Development, Production, Stockpiling And Use Of Chemical Weapons And On Their Destruction*, 13 January 1993.
211. Ministry of Defence (2003) *Defence Secretary and the Chief of the Defence Staff: Press Conference at the Ministry of Defence*, London, 27 March 2003. Accessed March 2007 at: http://www.operations.mod.uk/.
212. National Research Council (2003) op. cit., Preface. The original section 2.10 on 'Legal Considerations' is included in the prepublication copy of the report, Chapter 2, pp. 36–7.
213. Center for Arms Control and Non-Proliferation (2005) *Ensign Amendment 1374 on the Use of Riot Control Agents*. Press Release, 7 November 2005; Gaffney Jr., F. (2005) CWC fog at Foggy Bottom. *The Washington Times*, 11 October 2005; Garamone, J. (2006) DoD Officials Urge Use of Non-lethal Weapons in Terror War. *American Forces Press Service*, 27 September 2006.

214. Davison, N. and Lewer, N. (2005) op. cit., p. 27; US Navy (1997) *Preliminary Legal Review of Proposed Chemical-Based Nonlethal Weapons*. Department of the Navy, Office of the Judge Advocate General, International & Operational Law Division.
215. Allison, G., Kelley, P., and Garwin, R. (2004) op. cit., p. 56.
216. NATO (2004) op. cit., Chapter 5, p. 4.
217. Jontz, S. (2004) Marines in Iraq trying out controversial new hailing and warning device. *Stars and Stripes*, 25 March 2004.
218. International Committee of the Red Cross (2006) *A Guide to the Legal Review of New Weapons Means and Methods of Warfare*. Measures to Implement Article 36 of Additional Protocol I of 1977. Geneva: ICRC.

5   Chemical and Biochemical Weapons

1. Cooper, G. and Rice, P. (eds) (2002) Chemical Casualties: Centrally acting inca-pacitants. *Journal of the Royal Army Medical Corps*, Vol. 148, No. 4, pp. 388–91; Also see: Stockholm International Peace Research Institute (1973) *The Problem of Chemical and Biological Warfare. Volume II: CB Weapons Today*. Stockholm: Almqvist & Wiksell, pp. 302–3; US Army (1996) Part III, Chapter 6: Incapacitants. In: *FM 8–9: NATO Handbook on the Medical Aspects of NBC Defensive Operations. AmedP-6(B)*. Washington, DC: US Army.
2. Ibid.
3. Lakoski, J., Bosseau Murray, W., and Kenny, J. (2000) *The Advantages and Limitations of Calmatives for Use as a Non-Lethal Technique*. State College, PA: Pennsylvania State University, pp. 5–7.
4. Kelle, A., Nixdorf, K., and Dando, M. (2006) *Controlling Biochemical Weapons: Adapting Multilateral Arms Control for the 21st Century*. New York: Palgrave Macmillan; The terms 'incapacitating chemical' and 'incapacitating biochemi-cal' are used interchangeably in this Chapter.
5. Dando, M. (2002) Scientific and technological change and the future of the CWC: the problem of non-lethal weapons. *Disarmament Forum*, No. 4, pp. 33–44; Wheelis, M. and Dando, M. (2005) Neurobiology: A case study of the imminent militarization of biology. *International Review of the Red Cross*, No. 859, pp. 553–72.
6. Adapted from: Pearson, G. (2002) Relevant Scientific And Technological Developments For The First CWC Review Conference: The BTWC Review Conference Experience. *CWC Review Conference Paper No. 1*. Bradford: University of Bradford.
7. Department of Defense (1996) *Advances in Biotechnology and Genetic Engineering: Implications for the Development of New Biological Warfare Agents*. Washington, DC: Office of the Deputy Assistant Secretary of Defense for Chemical and Biological Defense, p. 4.
8. Kagan, E. (2001) Bioregulators as Instruments of Terror. *Clinics in Laboratory Medicine*. Vol. 21, No. 3. pp. 607–18.
9. Stockholm International Peace Research Institute (1973) op. cit., p. 303; Petro, J., Plasse, T., and McNulty, J. (2003) Biotechnology: Impact on Biological Warfare and Biodefense. *Biosecurity and Bioterrorism*, Vol. 1, No. 3, pp. 161–8.
10. Stockholm International Peace Research Institute (1973) op. cit., pp. 298–306; Lakoski, J., Bosseau Murray, W., and Kenny, J. (2000).
11. Lakoski, J., Bosseau Murray, W., and Kenny, J. (2000).
12. Ketchum, J. and Sidell, F. (1997) Incapacitants. In: F., Sidell, E., Takafuji, and D., Franz (eds) *Textbook of Military Medicine: Medical Aspects of Chemical and*

Biological Warfare. Washington DC: Borden Institute, pp. 287–305; Kirby, R. (2006) Paradise Lost: The Psycho Agents. *The CBW Conventions Bulletin*, No. 71, pp. 1–5.

13. Stockholm International Peace Research Institute (1971) *The Problem of Chemical and Biological Warfare. Volume I: The Rise of CB Weapons.* Stockholm: Almqvist & Wiksell, pp. 75–7.
14. The CIA programmes, such as MKULTRA, are not covered here. For more information see for example: Marks, J. (1980) *The Search for the Manchurian Candidate: The CIA and Mind Control.* New York: McGraw-Hill.
15. Stockholm International Peace Research Institute (1971), p. 75.
16. Dando, M. and Furmanski, M. (2006) Midspectrum Incapacitant Programs. In: M., Wheelis, L., Rózsa, and M. Dando (eds). *Deadly Cultures: Biological Weapons Since 1945.* Cambridge: Harvard University Press, pp. 236–51.
17. Stockholm International Peace Research Institute (1971) op. cit., p. 76.
18. Ibid., pp. 198–9.
19. Dando, M. and Furmanski, M. (2006) op. cit.
20. Stockholm International Peace Research Institute (1973) op. cit., pp. 298–300.
21. Perry Robinson, J. (1967) Chemical Warfare. *Science Journal*, No. 4, pp. 33–40; Kirby, R. (2006) op. cit.
22. Furmanski, M. (2005) Military Interest in Low-lethality Biochemical Agents: The Historical Interaction of Advocates, Experts, Pragmatists and Politicians. *Symposium on Incapacitating Biochemical Weapons: Scientific, Military Legal and Policy Perspectives and Prospects, Geneva, Switzerland, 11 June 2005.* Washington, DC: Center for Arms Control and Non-Proliferation; Stockholm International Peace Research Institute (1973) op. cit., p. 301.
23. Dando, M. (1996) *A New Form of Warfare: The Rise of Non-Lethal Weapons.* London: Brasseys, pp. 87–8.
24. Dando, M. and Furmanski, M. (2006) op. cit.
25. Ibid.
26. Stockholm International Peace Research Institute (1973) op. cit., p. 301.
27. Stockholm International Peace Research Institute (1971) op. cit., p. 77.
28. Dando, M. and Furmanski, M. (2006) op. cit.; Kirby, R. (2006) op. cit.
29. Ketchum, J. and Sidell, F. (1997) op. cit.
30. Dando, M. and Furmanski, M. (2006) op. cit.; Kirby, R. (2006) op. cit.; Since this section was written a book has been published that recounts relevant research at Edgewood Arsenal during the 1960s: Ketchum, J. (2007) *Chemical Warfare: Secrets Almost Forgotten.* James S. Ketchum.
31. Kirby, R. (2006) op. cit.
32. Dando, M. and Furmanski, M. (2006) op. cit.
33. Kirby, R. (2006) op. cit.
34. Pfizer and Co., Inc. (1964) *Research on New Chemical Incapacitating Agents. Army CRDC contract No. DA18-108-AMC-240(A). Annual Report No. 1. June 28, 1963 – 30 June 1964. Part I.* Groton, CT: Pfizer and Co., Inc.
35. Witten, B. (1968) *Nonlethal Agents in Crime and Riot Control.* Edgewood Arsenal Technical Memorandum EATM 133-1. Chemical Research Laboratory, Edgewood Arsenal, US Army.
36. In pharmacology an agonist is defined as a drug that binds to a cell receptor to elicit certain effects. An antagonist is a drug that blocks the action of an agonist by binding to the same cell receptor.
37. Witten, B. (1968) op. cit.; Perry Robinson, J. (1994) Developments in 'Non-Lethal Weapons' involving chemicals. In: *Report of the Expert Meeting on Certain Weapon*

Systems and on Implementation Mechanisms in International Law, Geneva, 30 May – 1 June 1994. Geneva: International Committee of the Red Cross, pp. 92–7.

38. Dando, M. and Furmanski, M. (2006) op. cit.
39. Ibid.
40. Dando, M. (2006) *The UK's Search for an Incapacitating ('Non-Lethal') Chemical Agent in the 1960s.* Bradford Science and Technology Paper No. 6. Bradford: University of Bradford.
41. Dando, M. and Furmanski, M. (2006) op. cit.
42. Ibid., p. 243.
43. Dando, M. (1996) op. cit., p. 147.
44. Ibid., p. 149.
45. Perry Robinson, J. (2003) *Disabling Chemical Weapons: A Documented Chronology of Events, 1945–2003.* Harvard Sussex Program, University of Sussex, unpublished version dated 8 October 2003, p. 68; Kirby, R. (2006) op. cit.
46. Dando, M. (1996) op. cit., pp. 136–68.
47. Ibid.
48. Dando, M. and Furmanski, M. (2006) op. cit.
49. Dando, M. (1996) op. cit., p. 140.
50. Perry Robinson, J. (2003) op. cit., pp. 71–2.
51. Ibid., p. 73.
52. Dando, M. (1996) op. cit., pp. 136–68.
53. Perry Robinson, J. (1994) op. cit.
54. Dando, M. and Furmanski, M. (2006) op. cit.; Kirby, R. (2006) op. cit.
55. Ibid.
56. Dando, M. (1996) op. cit., p. 147.
57. Ibid., pp. 136–68; Perry Robinson, J. (2003) op. cit., pp. 75–6.
58. Harvard Sussex Program (2003) Editorial: 'Non-Lethal' Weapons, the CWC and the BWC. *The CBW Conventions Bulletin*, No. 61, pp. 1–2.
59. Schulz, W. (2005) Top Pharmaceuticals: Fentanyl. *Chemical and Engineering News.* Special Issue, Vol. 83, Issue 25.
60. Perry Robinson, J. (2003) op. cit., p. 92.
61. CRDEC was renamed Edgewood Research, Development, and Engineering Center (ERDEC) in the early 1990s.
62. Mears, K. (1999) *Nonlethal Chemical Incapacitants.* Thesis, CSC. Quantico, VA: Marine Corps University.
63. Stanley, T. (2003) Human immobilization: is the experience in Moscow just the beginning? *European Journal of Anaesthesiology.* Vol. 20, No. 6, pp. 427–8.
64. Dando, M. (1996) op. cit., pp. 136–68.
65. Hart, S. (2002) *Statement before The Subcommittee on Aviation, Committee on Transportation and Infrastructure, U.S. House of Representatives.* Washington, DC: House of Representatives.
66. Pilant, L. (1993) Less-than-Lethal Weapons: New Solutions for Law Enforcement. *Science and Technology*, Washington DC: International Association of Chiefs of Police; Seaskate Inc. (1998) The *Evolution and Development of Police Technology.* Washington, DC: National Institute of Justice, p. 44.
67. Hart, S. (2002) op. cit.
68. Pilant, L. (1993) op. cit.; Seaskate, Inc. (1998) op. cit., p. 44.
69. Also at this time the Office of Technological Assessment was mandated by the US Senate to investigate scientific and technical responses to terrorism. Their 1991 report noted ongoing research and development of incapacitating biochemical

agents and raised the question of their utility in hostage scenarios: Office of Technology Assessment (1991) *Technology Against Terrorism: The Federal Effort*, OTA-ISC-487. Washington DC: Government Printing Office, pp. 58–9.

70. Ferguson, C. (1994) *Antipersonnel Chemical Immobilizers: Synthetic Opioids.* Research proposal, 27 April 1994. Aberdeen Proving Ground, MD: US Army ERDEC; Dando, M. (1996) op. cit., pp. 136–68.

71. Dando, M. (1996) op. cit., pp. 136–68.

72. Perry Robinson, J. (1994) op. cit.

73. Perry Robinson, J. (2003) op. cit., p. 17.

74. Dando, M. (1996) op. cit., pp. 136–68.

75. Perry Robinson, J. (2003) op. cit., p. 84.

76. Dando, M. (1996) op. cit., pp. 136–68; Perry Robinson, J. (2003) op. cit., pp. 84–5.

77. Perry Robinson, J. (2003) op. cit., p. 95.

78. Pearce, H. (1994) *Demonstration of Chemical Immobilizers.* Research proposal, 27 April 1994. Aberdeen Proving Ground, MD: US Army ERDEC.

79. United Nations (1993) *Convention on the Prohibition of the Development, Production, Stockpiling and Use of Chemical Weapons and on their Destruction,* 13 January 1993.

80. Dando, M. (1996) op. cit., pp. 136–68.

81. Perry Robinson, J. (2003) op. cit., p. 92.

82. Ibid., p. 78; Dando, M. (1996) op. cit., pp. 160–3.

83. Dando, M. (1996) op. cit., pp. 136–68; Vainio, O. (1989) Introduction to the clinical pharmacology of medetomidine. *Acta Veterinaria Scandinavica*, Supplement, Vol. 85, pp. 85–8.

84. Dando, M. (1996) op. cit., pp. 136–68.

85. Edgewood ERDEC (1989–94) Scientific Conference on Chemical and Biological Defense Research: Abstract Digest. Aberdeen Proving Ground, MD: US Army Chemical and Biological Defense Command. Quoted in: Dando, M. (1996) op. cit., p. 162.

86. Defined by the DOD as programmes to 'exploit mature and maturing technologies to solve important military problems'. See DOD website. Accessed March 2007 at: http://www.acq.osd.mil/.

87. Pearce, H. (1994) op. cit.

88. Ibid.

89. Ferguson, C. (1994) *Antipersonnel Chemical Immobilizers: Synthetic Opioids.* op. cit.

90. Ferguson, C. (1994) *Antipersonnel Chemical Immobilizers: Sedatives.* Research proposal, 27 April 1994. Aberdeen Proving Ground, MD: US Army ERDEC.

91. Ferguson, C. (1994) *Antipersonnel Chemical Immobilizers: Synthetic Opioids.* op. cit.

92. United States Patent Office (1998) *Opiate analgesic formulation with improved safety, United States Patent 5,834,477, 10 November 1998*; Perry Robinson, J. (2003) op. cit., p. 105.

93. Pearson, A. (2006) Incapacitating Biochemical Weapons: Science, Technology, and Policy for the 21st Century. *The Nonproliferation Review*, Vol. 13, No. 2, July 2006, pp. 151–88; Stanley, T. (2000) Anesthesia for the 21st century. *Proceedings of Baylor University Medical Center*, Vol. 13, No. 1, pp. 7–10.

94. Ferguson, C. (1994) *Antipersonnel Chemical Immobilizers: Synthetic Opioids.* op. cit.

95. Ferguson, C. (1994) *Antipersonnel Chemical Immobilizers: Sedatives.* op. cit.

96. Ibid.

97. Ferguson, C. (1994) *Antipersonnel Calmative Agents.* Research proposal, 27 April 1994. Aberdeen Proving Ground, MD: US Army ERDEC.

98. Ferguson still holds this view, however, in recent years the term 'calmative' has been used by weapons developers as a catch-all description for incapacitating agents. See: Davison, N. and Lewer, N. (2004) *Bradford Non-Lethal Weapons Research Project Research Report No. 5*. Bradford: University of Bradford, pp. 39–41.
99. Ferguson, C. (1994) *Antipersonnel Calmative Agents*. op. cit.
100. Perry Robinson, J. (2003) op. cit., p. 108.
101. Ibid., p. 93.
102. Pilant, L. (1993) op. cit.
103. Andresen, B. and Grant, P. (1997) *Dose Safety Margin Enhancement for Chemical Incapacitation and Less-than-Lethal Targeting. NIJ Final Report and Recommendations*. Livermore, CA: Lawrence Livermore National Laboratory, Forensic Science Center R-Division.
104. Ibid., p. 2
105. These data are from the Livermore researchers literature review and are taken from: Andresen, B. and Grant, P. (1997) op. cit.
106. Ibid., p. 11.
107. Ibid., p. 14.
108. Ibid., p. 6.
109. Ibid., p. 14.
110. Ibid., p. 18.
111. Ibid., pp. 20–1.
112. Ibid., pp. 24–7.
113. US Navy (1997) *Preliminary Legal Review of Proposed Chemical-Based Nonlethal Weapons*. Department of the Navy, Office of the Judge Advocate General, International & Operational Law Division.
114. Department of Defense (1999) *Chemical and Biological Defense Program. Topic No.: CBD00-108: Chemical Immobilizing Agents for Non-Lethal Applications. Small Business Innovation Research Solicitation, Fiscal Year 2000*. Washington, DC: Department of Defense. Accessed March 2007 at: http://www.acq.osd.mil/.
115. Ibid.
116. Edgewood Chemical Biological Center (2000) *CB Quarterly*, Issue No. 21, March 2000. Aberdeen Proving Ground, MD: US Army, ECBC, p. 19; Edgewood Chemical Biological Center (2000) *CB Quarterly*, Issue No. 22, June 2000. Aberdeen Proving Ground, MD: US Army ECBC, pp. 24–5; Also see the OptiMetrics, Inc. website. Accessed March 2007 at: http://optimetrics.org/.
117. Department of Defense (1999) *Chemical and Biological Defense Program. Topic No.: CBD00-108: Chemical Immobilizing Agents for Non-Lethal Applications. Small Business Innovation Research, Phase I Selections from the 00.1 Solicitation, Fiscal Year 2000*. Washington, DC: Department of Defense. Accessed March 2007 at: http://www.dodsbir.net/.
118. Considerably less than the $1.25 million requested for the Phase I research in 1994.
119. Regan, M. (2004) Marines Get Site to Pull Knockout Gas Info. *Associated Press*, 17 July 2004.
120. Ruppe, D. (2002) United States: U.S. Military Studying Nonlethal Chemicals. *Global Security Newswire*, 4 November 2002. Accessed March 2007 at: http://www.nti.org/.
121. Lakoski, J., Bosseau Murray, W., and Kenny, J. (2000) op. cit.; Although this document is not classified it was only made publicly available when it was obtained

under a Freedom of Information Act request by The Sunshine Project in mid-2002. The INLDT subsequently published the document on their website a few months later with a minor adjustment to the front cover, removing a diagram of the fentanyl molecule and adding a preface to the report.
122. Ibid., p. 5.
123. Ibid., p. 7.
124. Allison, G., Kelley, P., and Garwin, R. (2004) *Nonlethal Weapons and Capabilities: Report of an Independent Task Force Sponsored by the Council on Foreign Relations.* New York: Council on Foreign Relations, p. 2.
125. Ibid., p. 10.
126. Ibid., p. 10.
127. Ibid., p. 10.
128. Listed in the order agents are considered in the report. It is not clear whether this has any significance in terms of priorities.
129. Another characteristic noted in the report is that carfentanil has a long duration of action.
130. Mears, K. (1999) *Nonlethal Chemical Incapacitants.* op. cit.
131. Lakoski, J., Bosseau Murray, W., and Kenny, J. (2000) op. cit., p. 17.
132. Ibid., p. 18.
133. Ibid., pp. 20–1; Gertler, R., Brown, H. C., Mitchell, D., and Silvius, E. (2001) Dexmedetomidine: a novel sedative-analgesic agent. *Proceedings of Baylor University Medical Center,* Vol. 14, No. 1, pp. 13–21.
134. Lakoski, J., Bosseau Murray, W., and Kenny, J. (2000) op. cit., p. 21.
135. One effect of dexmedetomidine is to increase the individuals' susceptibility to electric shock. The report points to the possibility of using this drug in association with electrical or electromagnetic 'non-lethal' weapons.
136. Ibid., p. 37.
137. Ibid., pp. 47–8.
138. Ibid., p. 38.
139. Ibid., p. 38.
140. Ibid., pp. 21–5.
141. Ibid., pp. 26–8.
142. Ibid., p. 30.
143. Ibid., pp. 39–42.
144. Ibid., pp. 42–5.
145. Ibid., pp. 46–9.
146. Lakoski, J., Bosseau Murray, W., and Kenny, J. (2000) op. cit., Preface.
147. The Sunshine Project (2002) *The MCRU Calmatives Study and JNLWD: A Summary of (Public) Facts.* The Sunshine Project, 19 September 2002. Accessed March 2007 at: http://www.sunshine-project.org/.
148. Joint Non-Lethal Weapons Directorate (2001) *JNLWD Newsletter, 2nd Quarter 2001.* Quantico, VA: JNLWD.
149. National Research Council (2003) *An Assessment of Non-Lethal Weapons Science and Technology.* Washington, DC: National Academies Press, pp. 43–4.
150. Copeland, R. (2002) Joint Non-Lethal Weapons Program. *Presentation to the 2002 Mines, Demolition and Non-Lethal Conference & Exhibition, National Defense Industrial Association (NDIA), US, 3–5 June 2002.*
151. Joint Non-Lethal Weapons Directorate (2003) *Front End Analysis for Non-Lethal Chemicals.* Accessed March 2007 at: http://www.sunshine-project.org/.

152. National Research Council (2003) op. cit., pp. 124–5.
153. Ibid., pp. 106–7.
154. United States/United Kingdom (2001) *US/UK Non-Lethal Weapons (NLW)/Urban Operations Executive Seminar, 30 November 2000, London. Assessment Report.* ONR-NLW-038.
155. *National Institute of Justice Grant No. 2001-RD-CX-K002.* Details from NIJ Research Portfolio. Accessed December 2006 at: http://nij.ncjrs.org/portfolio/ [Note: March 2007: This resource in no longer publicly available, it is now password protected].
156. Cecconi, J. (2003) Less-Than-Lethal Program. *Presentation to the 2003 National Institute of Justice Annual Technology Conference.*
157. Ibid.
158. Fenton, G. (2001) *Presentation for Airline Pilot Association, October 2001.* Quantico, VA: JNLWD.
159. Birch, D. (2006) Some of Edgewood's most secret work involves weapons that aren't supposed to kill. *Baltimore Sun,* 10 December 2006.
160. Carrell, S. and Lean, G. (2003) US Prepares to Use Toxic Gases in Iraq. *The Independent on Sunday,* 2 March 2003; Knickerbocker, B. (2003) The fuzzy ethics of nonlethal weapons. *The Christian Science Monitor,* 14 February 2003.
161. Joint Non-Lethal Weapons Directorate (2006) *JNLWP Fiscal Year 2006–7 Technology Broad Area Announcement. Non-Lethal Weapons Technology Fiscal Year 2006–7 Applied Research And Development Efforts.* Accessed March 2007 at: https://www.jnlwp.com/.
162. Weiss, D. (2007) Calming Down: Could Sedative Drugs Be a Less-Lethal Option? *NIJ Journal,* No. 261, pp. 42–6; Also see: National Institute of Justice (2008) *Community Acceptance Panel – Riot Control Agents, 30 April 2007.* Accessed February 2009 at: http://www.ojp.usdoj.gov/nij/.
163. BBC News (2002) How special forces ended siege. *BBC News,* 29 October 2002. Accessed March 2007 at: http://news.bbc.co.uk/; BBC Television (2003) *Horizon: The Moscow Theatre Siege. Transcript.* Available March 2007 at: http://www.bbc.co.uk/science/ (the Horizon programme suggested the agent was released an hour before Special Forces entered the building); Perry Robinson, J. (2003) op. cit., pp. 138–41.
164. Paton Walsh, N. (2003) Families claim death toll from gas in Moscow siege kept secret. *The Guardian,* 18 October 2003. In 2006 a book was published by an organisation representing the survivors of the siege, Burban, L., Gubareva, S., Karpova, N., Karpov, V., Kurbatov, D., Milovidov, P., and Finogenov, P. (2006) *'Nord-Ost' Investigation Unfinished ... Events, facts, conclusions.* Moscow: Regional Public Organization for Support of Victims of Terrorist Attacks. Details accessed June 2007 at: http://www.pravdabeslana.ru/.
165. BBC News (2002) Gas 'killed Moscow hostages'. *BBC News,* 27 October 2002. Accessed March 2007 at: http://news.bbc.co.uk/.
166. BBC News (2002) Russia names Moscow siege gas. *BBC News,* 31 October 2002. Accessed February 2004, from: http://news.bbc.co.uk/; BBC Television (2003) *Horizon: The Moscow Theatre Siege.* op. cit.
167. BBC Television (2003) *Horizon: The Moscow Theatre Siege.* op. cit.; Wax, P., Becker, C., and Curry, S. (2003) Unexpected 'Gas' Casualties in Moscow: A Medical Toxicology Perspective. *Annals of Emergency Medicine.* Vol. 41, No. 5, pp. 700–5; the effects of opioid agonists such as the fentanyls can be reversed by the non-selective opioid antagonist naloxone.

168. Wax, P., Becker, C., and Curry, S. (2003) op. cit.
169. Chemical and Biological Weapons Nonproliferation Program (2002) *The Moscow Theater Hostage Crisis: Incapacitants and Chemical Warfare*. Center for Nonproliferation Studies, 4 November 2002. Accessed March 2007 at: http://www.cns.miis.edu/; Stanley, T. (2003) op. cit.; Brown, D. and Baker, P. (2002) Moscow Gas Likely A Potent Narcotic: Drug Normally Used to Subdue Big Game. *Washington Post*, 9 November 2002.
170. Stanley, T. (2003) op. cit.; Brown, D. and Baker, P. (2002) op. cit.
171. Davison, N. and Lewer, N. (2004) *Bradford Non-Lethal Weapons Research Project Research Report No. 5*. Bradford: University of Bradford, p. 40; Significant research was carried out by the Army Edgewood Chemical Biological Center on carfentanil in the 1980s, which included experiments with carfentanil aerosols on primates, carried out by Ferguson and Stanley but not published, see: Stanley, T. (2003) op. cit.; Carfentanil, which is a licensed in veterinary practice for immobilising large animals (trade name Wildnil) and is not approved for use in humans, is the most potent fentanyl derivative. It also has a wider therapeutic index than fentanyl itself or alfentanil, although lower than that of sufentanil and remifentanil.
172. However he said that M99 contained fentanyl: Alexander, J. (2003) Less-Lethal Weapons in the War against Terrorism. *Proceedings of the 2nd European Symposium on Non-Lethal Weapons, Ettlingen, Germany, May 13–14 2003*. V5. Pfinztal: Fraunhofer ICT. This claim was repeated in: Selivanov, V., Alexander, J., Cole, D., Klochikhin, V., and Rams, O. (2005) Current and Emerging Non-Lethal Technologies. Report of the Virtual Working Group. *Proceedings of the 3rd European Symposium on Non-Lethal Weapons, Ettlingen, Germany, 10–12 May 2005*. V3, p. 33. Pfinztal: Fraunhofer ICT.
173. MosNews (2005) Secret Antidote May Have Killed Beslan Children – Nord-Ost Survivor. *MosNews*, 26 October 2005. Accessed March 2007 at: http://www.mosnews.com/.
174. Harvard Sussex Program (2005) News Chronology. *The CBW Conventions Bulletin*. No. 69 and 70, p. 60; Paton Walsh, N. (2005) Russian troops root out militants after days of fighting leave 100 dead. *The Guardian*, 15 October 2005; Osborn, A. (2005) Troops crush Chechen 'bandits' as Putin promises no mercy. *The Independent*, 15 October 2005; *Associated Press* (2005) Russia says rebel assault over; toll tops 100. *Associated Press*, 14 October 2005; Eckel, M. and Tlisova, F. (2005) Hostage in Russia Attacks Recalls Ordeal. *Associated Press*, 15 October 2005; Holley, D. (2005) Russian Forces Crush Rebels After Two Days of Fighting. *Los Angeles Times*, 15 October 2005.
175. Klochikhin, V., Pirumov, V., Putilov, A., and Selivanov, V. (2003) The Complex Forecast of Perspectives of NLW for European Application. *Proceedings of the 2nd European Symposium on Non-Lethal Weapons, Ettlingen, Germany, May 13–14 2003*. V16. Pfinztal: Fraunhofer ICT.
176. Klochikhin, V., Lushnikov, A., Zagaynov, V., Putilov, A., Selivanov, V., and Zatevakhin, M. (2005) Principles of Modelling of the Scenario of Calmative Application in a Building with Deterred Hostages. *Proceedings of the 3rd European Symposium on Non-Lethal Weapons, Ettlingen, Germany, 10–12 May 2005*. V17. Pfinztal: Fraunhofer ICT.
177. Hess, L., Schreiberova, J., and Fusek, J. (2005) Pharmacological Non-Lethal Weapons. *Proceedings of the 3rd European Symposium on Non-Lethal Weapons, Ettlingen, Germany, 10–12 May 2005*. V23. Pfinztal: Fraunhofer ICT; Shreiberova,

J., Hess, L., Marcus, M., and Joostens, E. (2005) A search for safe and rapid method of immobilization. A study in macaque monkeys. *European Journal of Anaesthesiology*. Volume 22, Supplement S34, May 2005, A-694; Shreiberova, J. (2005) Pharmacological Non-Lethal Weapons. *Presentation to the Jane's 8th Annual Less-Lethal Weapons Conference, Leeds, UK, 26–7 October 2005.*

178. Jane's Information Group (2005) *Speaker Biographies, Jane's 8th Annual Less-Lethal Weapons Conference.* Accessed March 2007 at: http://www.janes.com/; Hess, L., Schreiberova, J., and Fusek, J. (2003) Zbrane, které nezabíjejí. *Vesmír*, 82, pp. 156–8. [In Czech].

179. Purkyne Military Medical Academy (2002) *Vyrocni Zprava. Za akademicky rok 2000–1. A vycvikovy rok 2001* [In Czech]. Hradec Kralove: Purkyne Military Medical Academy, p. 24. Accessed March 2007 at: http://www.pmfhk.cz/; Purkyne Military Medical Academy (2003) *Vyrocni Zprava. Za akademicky rok 2001–2. A vycvikovy rok 2002* [In Czech]. Hradec Kralove: Purkyne Military Medical Academy, p. 24. Accessed March 2007 at: http://www.pmfhk.cz/.

180. Hess, L., Schreiberova, J., and Fusek, J. (2005) op. cit.

181. Lakoski, J., Bosseau Murray, W., and Kenny, J. (2000) op. cit.

182. Hess, L., Schreiberova, J., and Fusek, J. (2005) op. cit.

183. Conversation with the author at the 3rd European Symposium on Non-Lethal Weapons, Ettlingen, Germany, 10–12 May 2005.

184. Hess, L., Schreiberova, J., and Fusek, J. (2005) op. cit.

185. Plant, L. (1994) Adding Less-than-Lethal Weapons to the Crime-Fighting Arsenal. *The Journal*, Autumn 1994.

186. Andresen, B. and Grant, P. (1997) op. cit.

187. NATO (2006) *The Human Effects of Non-Lethal Technologies*, RTO-TR-HFM-073. Brussels: NATO, RTO, pp. M1–M14.

188. Comments made during the presentation of the following paper: Murphy, M. (2005) NATO Studies on Non-Lethal Weapons: Effectiveness, Human Effects, and Future Technologies. *Proceedings of the 3rd European Symposium on Non-Lethal Weapons, Ettlingen, Germany, 10–12 May 2005.* V20. Pfinztal: Fraunhofer ICT.

189. Hess, L., Schreiberova, J., and Fusek, J. (2005) op. cit.; Patocka, J. and Fusek, J. (2004) Chemical Agents and Chemical Terrorism. *Central European Journal of Public Health*, Vol. 12, Supplement, pp. S75–S77; Streda, L. and Patocka, J. (2004) Neletální Chemické Zbrane a Úmluva o Zákazu Chemickych Zbraní [Non-lethal Chemical Weapons and the Convention on Prohibition of Chemical Weapons], *Vojenske Zdra Votnicke Listy*, Vol. LXXIII, c. 5–6; Patocka, J., Bajgar, J., Cabal, J., Fusek, J., and Streda, L. (2004) Neletální chemické zbrane [Non-Lethal Chemical Weapons], *Kontakt*, Vol. 6, No. 2; Hess, L., Schreiberova, J., Malek, J., Votava, M., and Fusek, J. (2007) Drug-induced loss of aggressiveness in the Macaque Rhesus. *Proceedings of the 4th European Symposium on Non-Lethal Weapons, Ettlingen, Germany, 21–3 May 2007.* V15. Pfinztal: Fraunhofer ICT.

190. The Sunshine Project (2004) French Non-Lethal Chemical Weapons In: *Sunshine Project Country Study No. 2: A Survey of Biological and Biochemical Weapons Related Research Activities in France*, 16 November 2004. pp. 26–32. Accessed March 2007 at: http://www.sunshine-project.org/.

191. Bismuth, C. and Barriot, P. (2003) De destruction massive ou conventionnelles, les armes tuent les civils. *Le Monde Diplomatique*, May 2003. Accessed March 2007 at: http://www.monde-diplomatique.fr/.

192. Bismuth, C., Borron, S., Baud, F., and Barriot, P. (2004) Chemical Weapons: documented use and compounds on the horizon. *Toxicology Letters*, Vol. 149, No. 1–3, pp. 11–18.

193. Northern Ireland Office (2004) *Patten Report Recommendations 69 and 70 Relating to Public Order Equipment. A Research Programme Into Alternative Policing Approaches Towards The Management of Conflict.* Fourth Report. Belfast: Northern Ireland Office.
194. Ibid., p. 129.
195. Ibid., p. 129.
196. House of Commons (2001) *Non-lethal weapons, House of Commons Hansard Written Answers for 10 Apr 2001 (pt 9).* London: HMSO.
197. United States/United Kingdom (2001) op. cit.
198. Allison, G., Kelley, P., and Garwin, R. (2004) op. cit., p. 26.
199. National Research Council (2003) op. cit., p. 107.
200. The Sunshine Project (2002) op. cit.
201. US Army (1998) *Mobile Non-Lethal Disseminator* [redacted]. Research proposal. Aberdeen Proving Ground, MD: US Army.
202. Davison, N. and Lewer, N. (2003) *Bradford Non-Lethal Weapons Research Project Research Report No. 4.* Bradford: University of Bradford.
203. Joint Non-Lethal Weapons Program (2006) *Individual Serviceman Non-Lethal System (ISNLS) Fact Sheet.* Quantico, VA: JNLWD.
204. Vanek Prototype Co. (2002) *Proposal for Multi-Shot Launcher with Advanced Less-Than-Lethal Ring Airfoil Projectiles.* Submitted by Vanek Prototype Co. to the US National Institute of Justice, 25 March 2002.
205. Vanek Prototype Co. (2004) *Statement of Work to Support Rapid Development of an LTL System Based on a Multishot RAP Launcher and Advanced Segmented Projectile.* National Institute of Justice, Grant No.: 2004-IJ-CX-K054.
206. Cecconi, J. (2004) Research Opportunities – Civilian Less Lethal Program. *Presentation to the Non-lethal Technology and Academic Research Symposium VI (NTAR VI), Winston-Salem, NC, US, 15–17 November 2004.*
207. Joint Non-Lethal Weapons Directorate (1999) *Joint Non Lethal Weapons Program News,* Vol. 2, No. 2, February 1999.
208. Primex Aerospace Company (2000) *Overhead Liquid Dispersal System (OLDS) Non-Lethal Demonstration Program. DAAE30-99-C-1072. Final Report.* Redmond, WA: Primex Aerospace Company.
209. US Army (2001) *Liquid Payload Dispensing Concept Studies Techniques for the 81 mm Non-Lethal Mortar Cartridge.* US Army Contract No. DAAE-30-01-M-1444, September 2001.
210. Hegarty, R. (2003) Joint Non-Lethal Weapons Program: Non-Lethal Mortar Cartridge (NLMC). *Presentation to the 2003 Picatinny Chapter/PEO Mortars Conference, National Defense Industrial Association (NDIA), US, 1–3 October 2003.*
211. Joint Non-Lethal Weapons Directorate (1998) *Joint NLW Directorate News,* Vol. 2, No.1, November 1998; Lyon, D., Johnson, R., and Domanico, J. (2000) Design and Development of an 81 mm Non-Lethal Mortar Cartridge. *Presentation to Non-Lethal Defense IV, National Defense Industrial Association (NDIA), US, 20–2 March 2000.* US Army (2000) *Joint Non-Lethal Weapons Directorate 1Q Fiscal Year 2001 Director's Reviews. Joint RDT&E Pre-Milestone 0 & Concept Exploration Program: 81 mm Non-Lethal Mortar.* 20 November 2000. Picatinny Arsenal, NJ: US Army TACOM/ARDEC-PSAC Center; US Army (2001) *81 mm Frangible Case Cartridge.* US Army Contract No. DAAE-30-01-C-1077, June 2001.
212. US Marine Corps (2002) *A Technical Assessment of the 81 mm Non-Lethal Mortar Munition (81NLMM).* US Marine Corps Contract No. M67004-99-D-0037, January 2002.

213. Evangelisti, M. (2002) Delivery of Non-Lethal Mortar Payloads by Mortar Systems, Joint RDT&E Pre-Milestone A Program. *Presentation to the 2002 International Infantry & Joint Services Small Arms Systems Section Symposium, National Defense Industrial Association (NDIA), US, 13–16 May 2002.*
214. Garner, J. and Lyon, D. (2003) Proof-of-Principle for an 81 mm Non-Lethal Mortar Cartridge. *Proceedings of the 2nd European Symposium on Non-Lethal Weapons Ettlingen, Germany, 13–14 May 2003.* V10. Pfinztal: Fraunhofer ICT.
215. Mihm, S. (2004) The Quest for the Nonkiller App. *The New York Times*, 25 July 2004; Sanchez, C. (2002) OICW Non-Lethal Munition. *Presentation to the 2002 International Infantry & Joint Services Small Arms Systems Section Symposium, National Defense Industrial Association (NDIA), US, 13–16 May 2002.*
216. Sanchez, C. (2001) Non-Lethal Airburst Munitions for Objective Individual Combat Weapon. *Presentation to the 2001 Joint Services Small Arms Symposium, Exhibition & Firing Demonstration, National Defense Industrial Association (NDIA), US, 13–16 August 2001*; National Research Council (2003) op. cit., p. 63.
217. Sanchez, C. (2002) op. cit.; Pennsylvania State University (2002) *Independent Technology Assessment: The Objective Individual Combat Weapon Non-Lethal Munition, Pennsylvania State University Applied Research Lab (USMC Contract M67004-99-D-0037-0050), October 2002.*
218. Ibid., p. 20.
219. US Army (2004) *Airburst Non-Lethal Munition (ANLM) Design Improvements.* Solicitation No. W15QKN-04-Q-0416. US Army TACOM-ARDEC, July 2004.
220. Joint Non-Lethal Weapons Program (2006) *Airburst Non-Lethal Munition (ANLM) Fact Sheet.* Quantico, VA: JNLWD; Joint Non-Lethal Weapons Program (2008) *Airburst Non-Lethal Munition (ANLM) Fact Sheet.* Quantico, VA: JNLWD
221. US Army ARDEC (2004) Solicitation (Modification) R – 155 mm XM1063 Non-Lethal Artillery Engineering Support Contract (Ref: W15QKN-04-X-0819). *FBO Daily*, 30 September 2004.
222. For details of the M864 see global security website. Accessed March 2007 at: http://www.globalsecurity.org/.
223. McCormick, J. (2006) 155 mm XM1063 Non-Lethal Personnel Suppression Projectile. *Presentation to the 41st Annual Armament Systems: Guns and Missile Systems, Conference & Exhibition, National Defense Industrial Association (NDIA), US, 27–30 March 2006.*
224. US Army (2005) *NLOS-C Non-Lethal Personnel Suppression.* US Army ARDEC brochure.
225. McCormick, J. (2006) op. cit.
226. US Army ARDEC (2004) op. cit.; McCormick, J. (2006) op. cit.; A 'vehicle area denial payload' comprising nanoparticles is also planned.
227. US Army ARDEC (2004) op. cit.
228. Whether this is CS, PAVA or a malodorant, observers have questioned the suitability of such a large, long-range munition for 'law enforcement purposes', which is the only exemption permitted for the use of RCAs under the Chemical Weapons Convention. One potential liquid payload (anti-personnel or anti-materiel) that would not fall under the CWC would anti-traction materials, that is, slippery substances.
229. US Army (2004) *Non-Lethal Artillery Structural Firing (Fiscal Year 2004) Purchase Order Contract In Support of the Fiscal Year 2004 155 MM Non-Lethal Artillery Projectile Program (Solicitation W15QKN-04-M-0328)*, September 2004. Picatinny Arsenal, NJ: US Army.

230. US Army ARDEC (2006) XM1063 155 MM Non-Lethal. *Commerce Business Daily*, 18 August 2006.
231. McCormick, J. (2007) 155 mm XM1063 Non-Lethal Personnel Suppression Projectile. *Presentation to the 42nd Annual Armament Systems: Guns and Missile Systems, Conference & Exhibition, National Defense Industrial Association (NDIA), US, 23–6 April 2007*.
232. Hambling, D. (2008) US weapons research is raising a stink. *The Guardian*, 10 July 2008.
233. United States Patent Office (2003) *Rifle-launched non-lethal cargo dispenser, United States Patent 6,523,478, 25 February 2003*.
234. The Sunshine Project (2003) *US Army Patents Biological Weapons Delivery System, Violates Bioweapons Convention*. Sunshine Project News Release, 8 May 2003.
235. United States Patent Office (2004) *Rifle-launched non-lethal cargo dispenser, United States Patent 6,688,032, 10 February 2004*.
236. United States Patent Office (2004) *Particle aerosol belt, United States Patent 6,802,172, 12 October 2004*.
237. Department of Defense (2002) *Unmanned Aerial Vehicles Roadmap*. Washington, DC: Office of the Secretary of Defense.
238. Department of Defense (2005) *Unmanned Aircraft Systems Roadmap 2005–30*. August 2005. Washington, DC: Office of the Secretary of Defense.
239. Abaie, M. (1998) Unmanned Aerial Vehicle (UAV) Non-Lethal (NL) Payload Delivery System. *Presentation to Non-Lethal Defense III, the National Defense Industrial Association (NDIA), US, 25–6 February 1998*; Also see video of JNLWD testing, accessed March 2007 at: http://www.sunshine-project.org/; Tests were also conducted in the late 1990s with Cypher UAVs delivering smoke munitions for law enforcement applications, see: Murphy, D. and Cycon, J. (1999) Applications for mini VTOL UAV for law enforcement. *Proceedings of SPIE*, Vol. 3577, pp. 35–43; A 1994 Army document proposed a 200lb liquid payload: US Army ARDEC (1994). *Liquid/Aerosol Dispersant Module for Short Range UAV Plaform*. Research Proposal, ONR-NLW-098.
240. Southwest Research Institute (2000) *Automation, Bioengineering, Avionics, and Training Systems*. SwRI Annual Report 2000.
241. EX-171 ERGM Extended-Range Guided Munition. See global security website. Accessed March 2007 at: http://www.globalsecurity.org/.
242. National Research Council (2003) op. cit., p. 43; Joint Non-Lethal Weapons Directorate (2001) *The US Department of Defense Joint Non-Lethal Weapons Program: Program Overview*. Presentation, April 2001; Copeland, R. (2002) op. cit.
243. National Research Council (2003) op. cit., p. 109.
244. Durant, Y. (1999) Use of Encapsulation Technology for NLW. *Presentation to the Non-Lethal Technology and Academic Research Symposium I (NTAR I), Quantico, VA, US, 5 May 1999*.
245. Durant, Y. (2000) Encapsulation technologies for Non-lethal weapons. *Presentation to the Non-Lethal Technology and Academic Research Symposium II (NTAR II), NH, US, 15–17 November 2000*; Durant, Y. (1999) op. cit.
246. Advanced Polymer Laboratory (2003) *Current Projects*. APL, University of New Hampshire website. Accessed November 2003 at: http://www.unh.edu/apl/; US Army (1997) *Odorous Substances* [redacted]. Research Proposal, July 1997. Aberdeen Proving Ground, MD: US Army ERDEC.
247. National Research Council (2003) op. cit., p. 107.

248. Dando, M. and Furmanski, M. (2006) op. cit., p. 250.
249. Furthermore proponents argued that better medical attention would have decreased the mortality rate.
250. Dando, M. (2002) Scientific and technological change and the future of the CWC: the problem of non-lethal weapons. *Disarmament Forum*. No. 4, pp. 33–44.
251. Dando, M. (2003) *The Danger to the Chemical Weapons Convention from Incapacitating Chemicals*. CWC Review Conference Paper No. 4. Bradford: University of Bradford.
252. Lakoski, J., Bosseau Murray, W., and Kenny, J. (2000) op. cit.
253. Wheelis, M. (2002) Biotechnology and Biochemical Weapons. *The Nonproliferation Review*. Vol. 9, No. 1, pp. 48–53; United Nations (2006) *Background Information Document on New Scientific and Technological Developments Relevant to the Convention*. BWC/CONF.VI/INF.4, 28 September 2006.
254. Dando, M. (2002) op. cit.
255. Davison, N. and Lewer, N. (2004) op. cit., p. 40.
256. Klotz, L., Furmanski, M., and Wheelis, M. (2003) *Beware the Siren's Song: Why "Non-Lethal" Incapacitating Chemical Agents are Lethal*. Washington, DC: Federation of American Scientists; In Moscow the fatality rate was over 15 per cent.
257. Ruppe, D. (2002) United States I: New Research Offers Safer Incapacitating Chemicals. *Global Security Newswire*, 6 November 2002. Accessed March 2007 at: http://www.nti.org/.
258. This problem was recognised early on, as discussed earlier in this Chapter.
259. Davison, N. and Lewer, N. (2004) op. cit., pp. 35–8.
260. Mears, K. (1999) op. cit.
261. British Medical Association (2007) *The use of drugs as weapons. The concerns and responsibilities of healthcare Professionals*. London: British Medical Association, Board of Science. May 2007. pp. 14–15.
262. Federation of American Scientists (2003) *Position Paper: Chemical Incapacitating Weapons Are Not Non-Lethal*. Washington, DC: Federation of American Scientists.
263. British Medical Association (2007) op. cit., p. 25.
264. Mears, K. (1999) op. cit.
265. Lakoski, J., Bosseau Murray, W., and Kenny, J. (2000) op. cit.
266. Stanley, T. (2003) op. cit.
267. Klotz, L., Furmanski, M., and Wheelis, M. (2003) op. cit.
268. National Research Council (2003) op. cit., pp. 63–4.
269. United Nations (1993) op. cit.
270. US Senate (1997) *U.S. Senate's Executive Resolution on Ratification of the CWC*, 105th Congress, 1st Session, S. Exec. Res. 75.
271. Boyd, K. (2003) Rumsfeld Wants to Use Riot Control Agents in Combat. *Arms Control Today*, March 2003; Hay, A. (2003) Out of the straitjacket. *The Guardian*, 12 March 2003; Garamone, J. (2006) DoD Officials Urge Use of Non-lethal Weapons in Terror War. *American Forces Press Service*, 27 September 2006.
272. United States/United Kingdom (2001) op. cit.; US Navy (1997) op. cit.; Riot control agents are defined in the Chemical Weapons Convention as those agents that 'can produce rapidly in humans sensory irritation or disabling physical effects which disappear within a short time following termination of exposure'.
273. Perry Robinson, J. (2006) *Development of the Governance Regime for Biological and Chemical Weapons*. Brighton: University of Sussex. Item 456, version of 10 December 2006.
274. Northern Ireland Office (2002) *Patten Report Recommendations 69 and 70 Relating to Public Order Equipment. A Research Programme into Alternative Policing*

Approaches Towards the Management of Conflict. Third Report. Belfast: Northern Ireland Office, p. 110.
275. United States/United Kingdom (2001) op. cit.
276. Ibid.
277. National Research Council (2003) op. cit., p. 6.
278. Harvard Sussex Program (1994) Editorial: New Technologies and the Loophole in the Convention. *The CBW Conventions Bulletin*, No. 23, pp. 1–2.
279. Dando, M. (2002) op. cit.
280. Krutzsch, W. (2005) 'Never Under Any Circumstances': The CWC Three Years after its First Review Conference. *The CBW Conventions Bulletin*, No. 68, pp. 1 and 6–12.
281. Harvard Sussex Program (2004) *Open Forum on the Chemical Weapons Convention: Challenges to the Chemical Weapons Ban*, 1 May 2003. Brighton: University of Sussex, pp. 27–36; Fidler, D. (2005) The meaning of Moscow: "Non-lethal" weapons an international law in the early 21st century. *International Review of the Red Cross*, Vol. 87, No. 859, September 2005, pp. 525–52.
282. Fidler, D. (2005) op. cit.; Davison, N. and Lewer, N. (2004) op. cit., pp. 39–41.
283. NATO (2006) op. cit., pp. M1–M14; Stanley, T. (2003) op. cit.
284. Pearson, A. (2006) op. cit.
285. Perry Robinson, J. (2007) The Governance Regime for Biological and Chemical Weapons, and the Review Conferences of 2006 and 2008. *Swiss Pugwash Association.* Accessed March 2007 at: http://www.pugwash.ch/; Perry Robinson, J. (2006) op. cit.
286. Harvard Sussex Program (2003) op. cit.
287. Wheelis, M. and Dando, M. (2005) op. cit.; This militarisation has even been espoused by some authors, Guo Ji-wei and Xue-sen Yang (2005) Ultramicro, Nonlethal, and Reversible: Looking Ahead to Military Biotechnology. *Military Review*, July–August 2005, pp. 75–8.
288. Kelle, A. (2003) CWC Report: The CWC After Its First Review Conference: Is the Glass Half Full or Half Empty? *Disarmament Diplomacy*, Issue No. 71, June–July 2003.
289. Meier, O. (2008) CWC Review Conference Avoids Difficult Issues. *Arms Control Today*, May 2008.
290. Example, The Center for Arms Control and Non-Proliferation held a *Symposium on Incapacitating Biochemical Weapons: Scientific, Military Legal and Policy Perspectives and Prospects* in Geneva, Switzerland on 11 June 2005 immediately prior to Biological Weapons Convention Meeting of Experts.
291. Wheelis, M. (2002) op. cit.; Chevrier, M. and Leonard, J. (2005) Biochemicals and the Biological and Toxin Weapons Convention. *Symposium on Incapacitating Biochemical Weapons: Scientific, Military Legal and Policy Perspectives and Prospects, Geneva, Switzerland, 11 June 2005.* Washington, DC: Center for Arms Control and Non-Proliferation; Kelle, A., Nixdorf, K., and Dando, M. (2006) op. cit.
292. Although, unlike the CWC, the BWC lacks any mechanism for verification of compliance.
293. Wheelis, M. (2002) op. cit.
294. Lakoski, J., Bosseau Murray, W., and Kenny, J. (2000) op. cit.
295. Petro, J., Plasse, T., and McNulty, J. (2003) op. cit.
296. Davis, C. (1999) Nuclear Blindness: An Overview of the Biological Weapons Programs of the Former Soviet Union and Iraq. *Emerging Infectious Diseases.* Vol. 5, No. 4. pp. 509–12.

297. National Research Council (2006) *Globalization, Biosecurity, and the Future of the Life Sciences*. Committee on Advances in Technology and the Prevention of their Application to Next Generation Washington, DC: National Academies Press, p. 188.

298. Furmanski, M. (2005) Military Interest in Low-lethality Biochemical Agents: The Historical Interaction of Advocates, Experts, Pragmatists and Politicians. *Symposium on Incapacitating Biochemical Weapons: Scientific, Military Legal and Policy Perspectives and Prospects, Geneva, Switzerland, 11 June 2005*. Washington, DC: Center for Arms Control and Non-Proliferation.

299. Council on Foreign Relations (1995) *Non-Lethal Technologies: Military Options and Implications. Report of an Independent Task Force*. New York: Council on Foreign Relations.

300. Garwin, R. (1999) *Nonlethal Technologies: Progress and Prospects. Report of an Independent Task Force*. New York: Council on Foreign Relations.

301. Fidler, D. (2005) op. cit.

302. Allison, G., Kelley, P., and Garwin, R. (2004) op. cit., p. 32.

303. Ibid., p. 31.

304. National Research Council (2006) op. cit., p. xiii.

305. Defense Science Board (1994) *Report of the Defense Science Board Task Force on Military Operations in Built-Up Areas (MOBA)*. Washington, DC: Department of Defense, pp. 33–4.

306. Defense Science Board (2004) *Report of the Defense Science Board Task Force on Future Strategic Strike Forces*. Washington, DC: Department of Defense, Chapter 7, p. 18.

307. Ibid., Chapter 7, p. 12.

308. NATO (2004) *Non-Lethal Weapons and Future Peace Enforcement Operations*, RTO-TR-SAS-040. Brussels: NATO, RTO; The report seemingly justifies this interest on the basis of the law enforcement exemption in Chemical Weapons Convention.

309. Davison, N. and Lewer, N. (2005) *Bradford Non-Lethal Weapons Research Project Research Report No. 7*. Bradford: University of Bradford, p. 26.

310. Whitbred IV, G. (2006) *Offensive Use of Chemical Technologies by US Special Operations Forces in the Global War on Terrorism: The Nonlethal Option*. Maxwell Paper No. 37. Maxwell Air Force Base, AL: Air University Press.

311. Harvard Sussex Program (2003) op. cit.

312. Stanley, T. (2003) op. cit.

313. Wax, P., Becker, C., and Curry, S. (2003) op. cit.

314. Hess, L., Schreiberova, J., and Fusek, J. (2005) op. cit.

315. Moreno, J. (2004) Medical Ethics and Non-Lethal Weapons. *The American Journal of Bioethics*. Vol. 4., No. 4, W1.

316. Coupland, R. (2003) Incapacitating chemical weapons: a year after the Moscow theatre siege. *The Lancet*, Vol. 362, Issue 9393, p. 1346.

317. British Medical Association (2007) op. cit.

318. Furmanski, M. (2005) op. cit.

319. The Soctsman (2002) No safe solution says Tony Blair. *The Scotsman*, 29 October 2002; BBC News (2002) Moscow siege gas 'not illegal'. *BBC News*, 29 October 2002. Accessed March 2007 at: http://news.bbc.co.uk/.

320. Pearson, A. (2006) op. cit.; for additional discussion of the issues surrounding the development of these weapons see, A., Pearson, M., Chevrier, and M. Wheelis, (eds) (2007) *Incapacitating Biochemical Weapons: Promise or Peril?* Lanham, MD: Lexington Books.

321. Fidler, D. (2005) op. cit.; Pearson has observed that 'all that is really needed for a biochemical incapacitant to be used and to gain traction is for it to be viewed as being "good enough" – and what is considered "good enough" can change from one time and place to another'. Pearson, A. (2006) op. cit.

6   Directed Energy Weapons

1. Department of Defense (2007) *Joint Publication 1-02: Department of Defense Dictionary of Military and Associated Terms 12 April 2001 (As Amended Through 13 June 2007)*. Washington, DC: Department of Defense.
2. Laser is an acronym for Light Amplification by Stimulated Emission of Radiation.
3. Frequencies/wavelengths given are approximate. Key: ELF = Extremely Low Frequency, VF = Voice Frequency, VLF = Very Low Frequency, LF = Low Frequency, UV = Ultraviolet; Adapted from: Ulaby, F. (2006) *Fundamentals of Applied Electromagnetics*. Upper Saddle River, NJ: Pearson Prentice Hall, pp. 26–8.
4. Hecht, J. (1984) *Beam Weapons: The Next Arms Race*. New York: Plenum Press; Anderberg, B. and Wolbarsht, M. (1992) *Laser Weapons: The Dawn of a New Military Age*. New York: Plenum Press; Hewish, M. (2000) Beam Weapons Revolution: Directed-Energy Weapons Point the Way for Battlefield Technology. *Jane's International Defense Review*, Vol. 33, August 2000, pp. 34–41; Lincoln, T. (2004) *Directed Energy Weapons: Do We Have a Game Plan?* Monograph, AY 03–04. Fort Leavenworth, KA: Army Command and General Staff College; Beason, D. (2005) *The E-bomb: How America's New Directed Energy Weapons Will Change the Way Future Wars Will Be Fought*. Cambridge, MA: Da Capo Press.
5. Rogers, P. (2002) Directed energy: a new kind of weapon. *openDemocracy*, 31 July 2002. Accessed March 2007 at: http://www.opendemocracy.net/.
6. Karcher, D. and Wertheim, E. (not dated) Safeguarding Peace, Safeguarding Life: How Non-Lethal Directed Energy Weapons Promise Both. *Homeland Defense Journal Online*. Accessed March 2007 at: http://www.homelanddefensejournal.com/; Allison, G., Kelley, P., and Garwin, R. (2004) *Nonlethal Weapons and Capabilities: Report of an Independent Task Force Sponsored by the Council on Foreign Relations*. New York: Council on Foreign Relations; NATO (2004) *Non-Lethal Weapons and Future Peace Enforcement Operations*. RTO-TR-SAS-040. Brussels: NATO, RTO.
7. Marine Corps (1998) *Joint Concept for Non-Lethal Weapons*. Commandant of the Marine Corps, 5 January 1998.
8. Allison, G., Kelley, P., and Garwin, R. (2004) op. cit., p. 12.
9. Karcher, D. and Wertheim, E. (not dated) op. cit.
10. National Research Council (2003) *An Assessment of Non-Lethal Weapons Science and Technology*. Washington, DC: National Academies Press, pp. 28–31
11. Dennis, R., Hamson, J., Mitchell, W., Apsey, D., Cora, S., and Williams , J. (2001) *Visual Effects Assessment of the Green Laser-Baton Illuminator (GLBI) (Revised Edition)*. AFRL-HE-BR-TR-2001-0095. Brooks Air Force Base, TX: Air Force Research Laboratory, p. 7.
12. Even they can cause eye damage with long exposure or viewed through magnifying optics.
13. Health Protection Agency (2007) *Information Sheet: Laser Pointers*. May 2006 (revised January 2007). Health Protection Agency, UK. Accessed March 2007 at: http://www.hpa.org.uk/.

14. Zimet, E. (2002) High-Energy Lasers: Technical, Operational, and Policy Issues. *Defense Horizons*, No. 18, October 2002.
15. Anderberg, B. and Wolbarsht, M. (1992) op. cit., p. 92.
16. Ibid., pp. 11–42; Beason, D. (2005) op. cit., pp. 197–205.
17. Hecht, J. (1984) op. cit., pp. 161–73; Giri, D. (2004) *High-power Electromagnetic Radiators: Nonlethal Weapons and Other Applications.* Cambridge, MA: Harvard University Press.
18. Giri, D. (2004) op. cit., p. 68; Thuery, J. (1992) *Microwaves: industrial, scientific, and medical applications.* London: Artech House, pp. 443–552.
19. Geis II, J. (2003) *Directed Energy Weapons on the Battlefield: A New Vision for 2025.* Occasional Paper No. 32, April 2003. Maxwell Air Force Base, AL: Air University; Also see Thuery, J. (1992) op. cit., pp. 443–552.
20. Giri, D. (2004) op. cit., p. 68; Thuery, J. (1992) op. cit., pp. 443–552.
21. NATO (2004) op. cit., Chapter 3, pp. 8–10; NATO (2006) *The Human Effects of Non-Lethal Technologies.* RTO-TR-HFM-073. Brussels: NATO, RTO, Annex J.
22. See for example: Weinberger, S. (2007) Mind Games. *Washington Post,* 14 January 2007.
23. Hecht, J. (1984) op. cit., p. 25; Anderberg, B. and Wolbarsht, M. (1992) op. cit., pp. 43–63.
24. Anderberg, B. and Wolbarsht, M. (1992) op. cit., pp. 141–2.
25. Bacon, D. (1980) Battlefield Lasers: A New Problem with an Old Cure. *Military Review,* October, pp. 33–9.
26. Hecht, J. (1984) op. cit., pp. 265–93.
27. Anderberg, B. and Wolbarsht, M. (1992) op. cit., pp. 98–9.
28. Madsen, E. (1987) Defending Against Battlefield Laser Weapons. *Military Review,* May, pp. 28–33.
29. Ibid.
30. Anon (1990) Royal Navy Laser Range 5 km. *Flight International,* 17–23 January 1990; Anderberg, B. and Wolbarsht, M. (1992) op. cit., p. 155.
31. Anderberg, B. and Wolbarsht, M. (1992) op. cit., p. 144.
32. Alexander, J (1989) Antimateriel Technology. *Military Review,* Vol. 69, No. 10, October, pp. 29–41.
33. Knoth, A. (1994) Disabling Technologies. A Critical Assessment. *International Defense Review,* No. 7, July 1994, pp. 33–9.
34. Human Rights Watch (1995) *United States: US Blinding Laser Weapons.* New York: Human Rights Watch, Vol. 7, No. 5, May 1995, p. 4.
35. Anderberg, B. and Wolbarsht, M. (1992) op. cit., pp. 156–60.
36. Alexander, J. (1989) op. cit.
37. Human Rights Watch (1995) *United States: US Blinding Laser Weapons.* op. cit., p. 12.
38. Quoted In: Human Rights Watch (1995) *United States: US Blinding Laser Weapons.* op. cit., p. 12.
39. Anderberg, B. and Wolbarsht, M. (1992) op. cit., p. 161.
40. Human Rights Watch (1995) *United States: US Blinding Laser Weapons.* op. cit., p. 13; Anderberg, B. and Wolbarsht, M. (1992) op. cit., pp. 160–1.
41. Human Rights Watch (1995) *United States: US Blinding Laser Weapons.* op. cit., pp. 13–14.
42. Munro, N. (1990) Army tests hand-held laser rifles. *Defense News,* 5 March 1990; Anderberg, B. and Wolbarsht, M. (1992) op. cit., p. 153.
43. Ibid., pp. 161–3.

44. Human Rights Watch (1995) *United States: US Blinding Laser Weapons*. op. cit., pp. 10–11.
45. Anderberg, B. and Wolbarsht, M. (1992) op. cit., pp. 163–4.
46. Human Rights Watch (1995) *United States: US Blinding Laser Weapons*. op. cit., pp. 8–9; Doswald-Beck, L. (1996) New Protocol on Blinding Laser Weapons. *International Review of the Red Cross*, No. 312, pp. 272–99.
47. Department of Defense (1995) *Contracts for Thursday, August 31, 1995. No. 478-95*. Accessed March 2007 at: http://www.defenselink.mil/.
48. United Nations (1995) *Protocol on Blinding Laser Weapons* (Protocol IV of the 1980 Convention on Certain Conventional Weapons), 13 October 1995.
49. Department of Defense (1995) *DoD News Briefing: Mr. Kenneth H. Bacon, ATSD (PA)*. 12 October 1995. Accessed March 2007 at: http://www.defenselink.mil/.
50. Doswald-Beck, L. (ed.) (1993) *Blinding Weapons: Reports of the meetings of experts convened by the International Committee of the Red Cross on battlefield laser weapons 1989–91*. Geneva: ICRC.
51. Human Rights Watch (1995) *United States: US Blinding Laser Weapons*. op. cit.; Human Rights Watch (1995) *Blinding Laser Weapons: The Need to Ban a Cruel and Inhumane Weapon*. New York: Human Rights Watch, Vo. 7, No. 1, September 1995.
52. For example the LCMS programme continued as TLOS: Gourley, S. (2000) Making Light. *Jane's Defence Weekly*, 24 May 2000, pp. 22–6.
53. Marshall, J. (1997) Blinding laser weapons: Still Available on the Battlefield. *British Medical Journal*. Vol. 315, p. 1392.
54. Doswald-Beck, L. (1996) op. cit.
55. Sometimes referred to as 'illuminators'.
56. Kehoe, J. and Nelson, R. (1997) Nonlethal laser baton. *Proceedings of SPIE*, Vol. 2934, pp. 6–9; Ireland, R. (1997) Tactical deployments of laser systems into low-intensity conflicts. *Proceedings of SPIE*, Vol. 2934, pp. 70–4; Human Rights Watch (1998) *HRW Questions U.S. Laser Programs As Blinding Laser Weapon Ban Becomes International Law*. Press release, 29 July 1998. New York: Human Rights Watch.
57. Human Rights Watch (1995) *Blinding Laser Weapons: The Need to Ban a Cruel and Inhumane Weapon*. op. cit., p. 23.
58. Anderberg, B. and Wolbarsht, M. (1992) op. cit., p. 153.
59. German, J. D., and Cramer, E. (1998) Eye-Safe Laser Illuminators as Non-Lethal Weapons. *Presentation to Non-Lethal Defense III, National Defense Industrial Association (NDIA), US, 25–6 February 1998*.
60. Gavron, V., Taylor, H., Howe III, J., Hughes, R., Stevens, D., Swalm, T., Hilmas, D., and Fuchs, R. (1998) *Report on United States Air Force Expeditionary Forces. Volume 3: Appendix I*. SAB-TR-97-01, February 1998. Washington, DC: US Air Force Scientific Advisory Board, p. 57.
61. Human Rights Watch (1995) *United States: US Blinding Laser Weapons*. op. cit.; Gourley, S. (2000) op. cit.
62. Ireland, R. (1997) op. cit.; Lorenz noted trips to Sandia National Laboratories and the Air Force Philips Laboratory but did not mention laser weapons, see: Lorenz. F. (1995) 'Less-Lethal' Force in Operation United Shield. *Marine Corps Gazette*, September 1995, pp. 69–77.
63. Ireland, R. (1997) op. cit.
64. Department of Defense (1999) *Fiscal Year 2000 Research, Development, Test & Evaluation, Defense-Wide, Budget Activity 4. Physical Security Equipment, PE 0603228D8Z*. Washington, DC: Department of Defense; Adler, D. (1998) *U.S. Air Force Laser Illuminators*. Billerica, MA: Horizons Technology.
65. Adler, D. (1998) op. cit.

66. Adler, D. (2000) Anti-Personnel Laser Illuminators: Effectiveness Testing of HALT and Dissuader. *Presentation to Non-Lethal Defense IV, National Defense Industrial Association (NDIA), US, 20–2 March 2000.*
67. German, J. D., and Cramer, E. (1998) op. cit.; United States Patent Office (1997) *Eye safe laser security device, United States Patent 5,685,636,* 11 November 1997.
68. Adler, D. (2000) op. cit.; Adler, D. (1998) op. cit.
69. Adler, D. (2000) op. cit.; Hambling, D. (2002) A gleam in the eye. *The Guardian,* 31 October 2002; Department of Defense (2000) *Fiscal Year 2001 Research, Development, Test & Evaluation, Defense-Wide, Budget Activity 4. Physical Security Equipment, PE 0603228D8Z.* Washington, DC: Department of Defense.
70. Adler, D. (1998) op. cit.; Adler, D. (2000) op. cit.; Gourley, S. (2000) op. cit.
71. National Security Research, Inc. (2002) *Department of Defense Nonlethal Weapons and Equipment Review: A Research Guide for Civil Law Enforcement and Corrections.* Washington, DC: National Institute of Justice; National Security Research, Inc. (2004) *Department of Defense Nonlethal Weapons and Equipment Review: A Research Guide for Civil Law Enforcement and Corrections.* Washington, DC: National Institute of Justice.
72. In late 2005 Apogen became a subsidiary of the UK defence company, QinetiQ.
73. Apogen Technologies website. Accessed March 2007 at: http://www.apogentech. com/.
74. Department of Defense (1999) *Fiscal Year 2000 Research, Development, Test & Evaluation, Defense-Wide, Budget Activity 4. Physical Security Equipment, PE 0603228D8Z.* op. cit.
75. Department of Defense (2000) *Fiscal Year 2001 Research, Development, Test & Evaluation, Defense-Wide, Budget Activity 4. Physical Security Equipment, PE 0603228D8Z.* op. cit.
76. Department of Defense (2001) *Fiscal Year 2002 Research, Development, Test & Evaluation, Defense-Wide, Budget Activity 4. Physical Security Equipment, PE 0603228D8Z;* Washington, DC: Department of Defense; Department of Defense (2002) *Fiscal Year 2003 Research, Development, Test & Evaluation, Defense-Wide, Budget Activity 4. Physical Security Equipment, PE 0603228D8Z.* Washington, DC: Department of Defense.
77. National Research Council (2003) op. cit., p. 28.
78. Cooley, W., Davis, T., and Kelly, J. (1998) Battlefield Optical Surveillance System (BOSS) – A HMMWV Mounted System for Non-Lethal Point Defense. *Presentation to Non-Lethal Defense III, National Defense Industrial Association (NDIA), US, 25–6 February 1998;* Latham, W. (2000) *Industry and Government Applications of the High-Power Semiconductor Lasers Technology Program. DE-99-01,* June 2000. Kirtland Air Force Base, NM: Air Force Research Laboratory.
79. National Institute of Justice (1997) *Department of Justice and Department of Defense Joint Technology Program: Second Anniversary Report,* NCJ 164268. Washington DC: National Institute of Justice.
80. Kehoe, J. and Nelson, R. (1997) op. cit.; Ireland, R. (1997) op. cit.
81. German, J. D., and Cramer, E. (1998) op. cit.
82. Dennis, R., et al. (2001) op. cit.
83. Ibid., pp. 12–14.
84. LE Systems Laser Dazzler website. Accessed March 2007 at: http://www.laserdazzler.net/; United States Patent Office (1997) *Compact high power laser dazzling device, United States Patent Application 20060233215,* 19 October 2006.
85. Jackson, R. and Hutchinson, J. (2006) Lasers are Lawful Non-Lethal Weapons. *The Army Lawyer,* August 2006, pp. 12–18.

86. LE Systems (2005) *Laser Dazzler. May 2005 Status.* Accessed March 2007 at: http://www.laserdazzler.net/. Also see the safety section of the LE Systems website.
87. Lardner, R. (2007) Marines In Iraq Decry Lack Of Laser System. *Tampa Tribune*, 31 January 2007.
88. Simpson, J. (2005) US must learn from Calipari. *BBC News*, 5 May 2005. Accessed March 2007 at: http://news.bbc.co.uk/1/hi/world/.
89. Gordon, C. (2005) Checkpoint safety under scrutiny. *Newsday.com*, 2 May 2005. Accessed March 2007 at: http://www.newsday.com/; and Hess, P. (2005) U.S. still grapples with traffic tactics. *UPI International*, 2 May 2005.
90. Magnuson, S. (2006) Lasers Seen as Solution To Checkpoint Safety. *National Defense*, February 2006.
91. US Army (2006) Rapid Equipping Force helps Soldiers with a bright idea: laser pointers. *US Army News Release*, 3 February 2006.
92. Jackson, R. and Hutchinson, J. (2006) op. cit.
93. Department of Defense (2006) *DoD News Briefing with Lt. Gen. Chiarelli from Iraq.* 19 May 2006. Washington, DC: Department of Defense.
94. XADS website. Accessed March 2007 at: http://www.xtremeads.com/.
95. Ackerman, R. (2006) A Brighter Future for Battlefield Vision. *SIGNAL Magazine*, April 2006.
96. Lardner, R. (2007) op. cit.
97. Knight, W. (2006) Lasers to dazzle drivers at Iraqi checkpoints. *New Scientist*, 19 May 2006; BE Meyers website, Green and Visible Lasers. Accessed March 2007 at: http://www.bemeyers.com/; B. E. Meyers (2004) *Operator's Manual. GBD III Green Beam Designator. Model #532-A1*, June 2004. Accessed March 2007 at: http://www.bemeyers.com/.
98. Rainey, J. (2006) A Safer Weapon, With Risks. *Los Angeles Times*, 18 May 2006; Knight, W. (2006) op. cit.
99. Joint Non-Lethal Weapons Program (2006) *Non-Lethal Optical Distractors Fact Sheet.* Quantico, VA: JNLWD.
100. Hambling, D. (2005) Dazzle gun will protect US helicopters. *New Scientist*, 24 December 2005.
101. United Nations (2006) *Proposal For A Mandate To Study Laser Systems. Presented by Germany and Switzerland.* CCW/CONF.III/WP.2*.
102. Human Rights Watch (2006) *Statement during the General Exchange of Views, Third Review Conference of the Convention on Conventional Weapons. Geneva, Switzerland, 8 November 2006.*
103. United States (2006) *Statement of United States Delegation on Mandate to Study Laser Systems, 9 November 2006.* Accessed March 2007 at: http://www.ccwtreaty.com/.
104. Hambling, D. (2005) Police toy with 'less lethal' weapons. *New Scientist*, 2 May 2005; Air Force Research Laboratory (2005) *AFRL Builds Portable Laser Weapon.* DE-S-06-01. Wright-Patterson Air Force Base, OH: Air Force Research Laboratory.
105. Blaylock, E. (2005) *Non-Lethal Laser Weapon Halts Aggressors.* Air Force Research Laboratory, Public Affairs, 1 November 2005; Knight, W. (2005) US military sets laser PHASRs to stun. *New Scientist*, 7 November 2005.
106. Air Force Research Laboratory (2005) *AFRL Builds Portable Laser Weapon.* DE-S-06-01. op. cit.; Knight, W. (2005) op. cit.; Burgess, L. (2005) PHaSRs May Soon Make 'Trek' to Battle. *Stars and Stripes*, 11 November 2005.
107. Hambling, D. (2005) Police toy with 'less lethal' weapons. op. cit.

108. Air Force Research Laboratory (2006) *Personnel Halting and Stimulation Response (PHaSR) Fact Sheet*, May 2006. Kirtland Air Force Base, NM: Air Force Research Laboratory.
109. Ibid.
110. NATO (2004) op. cit., pp. 3–9.
111. Burgess, L. (2005) op. cit.
112. Air Force Research Laboratory (2005) *AFRL Builds Portable Laser Weapon*. DE-S-06-01. op. cit.; Air Force Research Laboratory (2006) *Personnel Halting and Stimulation Response (PHaSR) Fact Sheet*, May 2006. op. cit.; Blaylock, E. (2005) op. cit.
113. Air Force Research Laboratory (2006) *Personnel Halting and Stimulation Response (PHaSR) Fact Sheet*, April 2006. Kirtland Air Force Base, NM: Air Force Research Laboratory.
114. Air Force Research Laboratory (2005) *AFRL Develops Aircraft Countermeasures Laser System*. DE-S-06-02. Wright-Patterson Air Force Base, OH: Air Force Research Laboratory; Hambling, D. (2005) Dazzle gun will protect US helicopters. op. cit.
115. National Research Council (2003) op. cit., p. 28.
116. Zuclich, J., Glickman, R., and Menendez, A. (1992) In situ measurements of lens fluorescence and its interference with visual function. *Investigative Ophthalmology & Visual Science*, Vol. 33, pp. 410–15.
117. Joint Non-Lethal Weapons Directorate (2001) *JNLWD Newsletter, 2nd Quarter 2001*. Quantico, VA: JNWLD.
118. Copeland, R. (2002) Joint Non-Lethal Weapons Program. *Presentation to the 2002 Mines, Demolition and Non-Lethal Conference & Exhibition, National Defense Industrial Association (NDIA), US, 3–5 June 2002*.
119. Hambling, D (2002) 'Safe' laser weapon comes under fire. *New Scientist*, 8 September 2002; Hambling, D. (2002) A gleam in the eye. op. cit.
120. National Research Council (2003) op. cit., p. 29.
121. Previc, F., McLin, L., Novar, B., and Kosnik, W. (2005) Comparison of violet versus red laser exposures on visual search performance in humans. *Journal of Biomedical Optics*, Vol. 10, Issue 3, p. 034003; Zuclich, J., Previc, F., Novar, B., and Edsall, P. (2005) Near-UV/blue light-induced fluorescence in the human lens: potential interference with visual function. *Journal of Biomedical Optics*, Vol. 10, Issue 4, p. 44021; Smith, P., McLin, L., Kee, D., Novar, B., and Garcia, P. (2005) Laser induced fluorescence in the human lens. *Journal of Vision*, Vol. 5, No. 8, Abstract 462, p. 462a; Smith, P., Martinsen, G., Kee, D., and Garcia, P. (2006) The dependence of laser-induced lens fluorescence on laser irradiance. *Journal of Vision*, Vol. 6, No. 6., Abstract 699, p. 699a.
122. SARA, Inc. Laser Dazzlers website. Accessed March 2007 at: http://www.sara.com/.
123. Northeast Photosciences website. Accessed March 2007 at: http://npidazzle.com/.
124. Stress and Motivated Behavior Institute website. Accessed March 2007 at: http://www.umdnj.edu/smbiweb/.
125. ARDED Homeland Defense Technologies website. Accessed March 2007 at: http://www.pica.army.mil/HLD/.
126. Stress and Motivated Behavior Institute website, Military Applications section. Accessed March 2007 at: http://www.umdnj.edu/smbiweb/.
127. National Institute of Justice (2005) *NIJ Awards in Fiscal Year 2004*. Washington, DC: National Institute of Justice.
128. Watt, D. (2004) Adaptive Retro-Reflection and Sensor Localization. *Presentation to the Non-lethal Technology and Academic Research Symposium VI (NTAR VI), Winston-Salem, NC, US, 15–17 November 2004*; Upton, T., Ludman, J., and Watt, D. (2004) Smart

white-light dazzler. *Proceedings of SPIE*, Vol. 5403, pp. 493–501; Watt, D. (2003) Smart Laser Dazzler. *Abstract of presentation to the Non-lethal Technology and Academic Research Symposium V (NTAR V), VA, US, 5–6 November 2003.*

129. Donne, A., Hauck, J., Ludman, J., Moldow, R., Servatius, R. and Yagrich, K. (2006) Multi-wavelength optical dazzler for personnel and sensor incapacitation. *Proceedings of SPIE*, Vol. 6219, p. 621902.

130. Ibid.

131. NATO (2004) op. cit., Chapter 3, p. 14.

132. NATO (2006) op. cit., p. G-2.

133. Department of Defense (2002) *DoD SBIR Fiscal Year 2002.2 – Solicitation Selections w/Abstracts. Phase I Selections from the 02.2 Solicitation.* Accessed March 2007 at: http://www.dodsbir.net/.

134. HSARPA (2005) *SBIR Past Awards Fiscal Year 2005.1 Phase I.* Accessed May 2007 at: https://www.sbir.dhs.gov/; HSARPA (2006) *SBIR Past Awards Fiscal Year 2005.1 Phase II/Phase II Fast Track.* Accessed May 2007 at: https://www.sbir.dhs.gov/.

135. HSARPA (2006) *Abstracts of Fiscal Year 2005.1 Phase II/Phase II Fast Track Awards.* Accessed May 2007 at: https://www.sbir.dhs.gov/.

136. La Franchi, P. (2007) US Army to demonstrate UAV-mounted strobe Searchlight for non-lethal crowd control. *Flighglobal.com*, 15 February 2007; Hambling (2008) How flickering light could replace rubber bullets. *New Scientist*, No. 2655, 7 May 2008.

137. US Air Force (2003) *Airborne Laser (YAL-1A). Fact Sheet.* Kirtland Air Force Base, NM: Air Force Research Laboratory; Missile Defense Agency (2007) *The Airborne Laser. Fact Sheet.* Washington, DC: Missile Defense Agency.

138. Beason, D. (2005) op. cit., pp. 171–2.

139. National Research Council (2003) op. cit., p. 29.

140. Ibid., pp. 29–30; Air Force Research Laboratory (2006) *Advanced Tactical Laser.* Kirtland Air Force Base, NM: Air Force Research Laboratory; Boeing Corp. (1999) *Boeing Completes Testing of Tactical High Energy Laser.* News Release, 21 April 1999. Accessed March 2007 at: http://www.boeing.com/.

141. Karcher, D. and Wertheim, E. (not dated) op. cit.

142. National Research Council (2003) op. cit., p. 30.

143. Tillman, A. (1994) Weapons for the 21st Century Soldier. *International Defense Review*, No. 27, January 1994, pp. 34–8; Tapscott, M. and Atwal, K. (1993) New Weapons That Win Without Killing op. cit.; Kokoski, R. (1994) Non-lethal weapons: a case study of new technology developments. In: Stockholm International Peace Research Institute *SIPRI Yearbook 1994.* Oxford: Oxford University Press, pp. 367–86.

144. National Research Council (2003) op. cit., pp. 63–4.

145. Army Armament Research, Development and Engineering Center (1992) ARDEC exploring less-than-lethal munitions; to give Army greater flexibility in future conflicts. *ARDEC News Release*, 9 October 1992.

146. Moore, H. (2000) Laser Technology Update: Pulsed Impulsive Kill Laser (PIKL). *Presentation to the 2000 Joint Services Small Arms Symposium, Exhibition and Firing Demonstration, National Defense Industrial Association (NDIA), US, 28–31 August 2000.*

147. Moore, H. (2000) op. cit.

148. Farrer, D. (2002) Health Effects and Laser Induced Plasma. *Presentation to the Non-lethal Technology and Academic Research Symposium IV (NTAR IV), La Jolla, CA, US, 19–21 November 2002.*

149. Moore, H. (2000) op. cit.

150. Anderberg, B. and Wolbarsht, M. (1992) op. cit., p. 118.
151. Moore, H. (2000) op. cit.
152. Joint Non-Lethal Weapons Directorate (1998) *Joint NLW Directorate News*, Vol. 2, No. 1, November 1998.
153. National Research Council (2003) op. cit., p. 30.
154. Ibid., p. 83.
155. Hambling, D. (2005) *Weapons Grade: Revealing the links between modern warfare and our high-tech world*. London: Constable, pp. 233–4.
156. National Research Council (2003) op. cit., pp. 82–3.
157. Ibid., p. 109.
158. Moore, H. (2000) op. cit.
159. Department of Defense (2003) *RDT&E Project Justification. 0603851M Non-Lethal Warfare, Demonstration and Validation*, DOD Fiscal Year 2004 Budget, February 2003; Department of Defense (2004) *RDT&E Project Justification. 0603851M Non-Lethal Warfare, Demonstration and Validation*, DOD Fiscal Year 2005 Budget, February 2004; Department of Defense (2005) *RDT&E Project Justification. 0603851M Non-Lethal Warfare, Demonstration and Validation*, DOD Fiscal Year 2006 Budget, February 2005; Department of Defense (2006) *RDT&E Project Justification. 0603851M Non-Lethal Warfare, Demonstration and Validation*, DOD Fiscal Year 2007 Budget, February 2006; Department of Defense (2007) *RDT&E Project Justification. 0603851M Non-Lethal Warfare, Demonstration and Validation*, DOD Fiscal Year 2008 Budget, February 2007.
160. Department of Defense (2007) *RDT&E Project Justification. 0603851M Non-Lethal Warfare, Demonstration and Validation*, DOD Fiscal Year 2008 Budget, February 2007.
161. Office of Naval Research/University of Florida (2004) *Sensory consequences of electromagnetic pulses emitted by laser induced plasmas. Contract No. M67854-04-C-5074*.
162. University of Florida College of Dentistry (2004) *UFCD ACTIVE AWARDS 2004–5*. Accessed March 2007 at: http://www.dental.ufl.edu/.
163. University of Central Florida (2004) *Sensory Consequences of Electromagnetic Pulses Emitted by Laser Induced Plasmas*. Office of Research and Commercialization. Accessed March 2007 at: https://argis.research.ucf.edu/.
164. Office of Naval Research/University of Florida (2004) op. cit.
165. Defintion of 'nociceptor' from *Dorlands Medical Dictionary*: 'a receptor for pain caused by injury to body tissues; the injury may be from physical stimuli such as mechanical, thermal, or electrical stimuli, or from chemical stimuli such as the presence of a toxin or an excess of a nontoxic substance. Most nociceptors are in either the skin or the walls of viscera [internal organs]'. Accessed March 2007 at: http://www.mercksource.com/.
166. Cooper, B. (2004) Transduction and Encoding of Pain by Nociceptors. *Presentation to the Non-lethal Technology and Academic Research Symposium VI (NTAR VI), Winston-Salem, NC, US, 15–17 November 2004*; Richardson, M. (2004) Propagation and Interaction Effects of High Intensity Femtosecond Laser Beams in the Atmosphere. *Presentation to the Non-lethal Technology and Academic Research Symposium VI (NTAR VI), Winston-Salem, NC, US, 15–17 November 2004*.
167. Shwaery, G., Blitch, J., and Land, C. (eds) (2006) Enabling Technologies and Design of Nonlethal Weapons. *Proceedings of SPIE*, Vol. 6219, May 2006; Nene, D., Jiang, N., Rau, K., Richardson, M., and Cooper, B. (2006) Nociceptor activation

and damage by pulsed E-fields. *Proceedings of SPIE*, Vol. 6219, p. 621904; Aspiotis, J., Barbieri, N., Bernath, R., Brown, C., and Richardson, M. (2006) Detection and analysis of RF emission generated by laser-matter interactions. *Proceedings of SPIE*, Vol. 6219, p. 621908.

168. Hambling, D. (2008) Pain Laser Finds New Special Forces Role. *Wired.com*, 18 September 2008. Accessed September 2008 at: http://blog.wired.com/.

169. US Marine Corps (2004) Award: A – Technology Investment Program Non-lethal Weapons Study (Ref: M67854-04-R-6007). *FBO Daily*, 3 July 2004; National Institute of Justice (2005) *NIJ Awards in Fiscal Year 2004*. Washington, DC: National Institute of Justice.

170. Email communication with the author of Hambling, D. (2005) Police toy with 'less lethal' weapons.

171. Department of Defense (2002) *DoD SBIR Fiscal Year 2002.2 – Solicitation Selections w/Abstracts. Phase I Selections from the 02.2 Solicitation*; Reichert, D. (2006) *Reichert Secures $17 Million for Local DOD Projects. 28 September 2006*. Accessed March 2007 at: http://www.house.gov/; Hambling, D. (2007) Plasma shield may stun and disorientate enemies. *NewScientist.com*, 26 April 2007.

172. Beason, D. (2005) op. cit., p. 211.

173. Owen, G. (1997) Directed energy weapons: A historical perspective. *Journal of Defence Science*, Vol. 2, No. 1, pp. 89–93.

174. Khan, N., Mariun, N., Aris, I., and Yeak, J. (2002) Laser-triggered lightning discharge. *New Journal of Physics*. Vol. 4, pp. 61.1–61.20; Kozma, M. (1994) *A Brief History of Laser Guided Lightning Discharge Models and Experiments*. Hanscom Air Force Base, MA: Air Force Research Laboratory; Natural Sciences and Engineering Council of Canada (2005) *Bringing Down Thunderbolts With Lasers*. News Release, 6 October 2005. Accessed March 2007 at: http://www.nserc.gc.ca/.

175. Schneider, D. (2005) To Boldly Go (Again). *American Scientist*, July–August 2005.

176. Hambling, D. (2004) Sweeping stun guns to target crowds. *New Scientist*, 16 June 2004, p. 24.

177. US Air Force (2004) *Research Agreement Signed*. Press Release, Air Force Research Laboratory, 14 January 2004. Accessed March 2007 at: http://www.de.afrl.af.mil/.

178. Dearmin, T. (2005) Ionatron, Inc. *Presentation to Roth Capital Partners Conference, 22 February 2005*.

179. Ionatron, Inc. (2006) *Form 10-Q for IONATRON, INC. Quarterly Report*. 9 November 2006. Accessed March 2007 at: http://biz.yahoo.com/.

180. US Navy (2005) Solicitation: A – AZ13 – LASER INDUCED PLASMA CHANNEL WEAPONIZATION. *FBO Daily*, 6 November 2005; US Navy (2006) Award: A – AZ13 – LASER INDUCED PLASMA CHANNEL WEAPONIZATION. *FBO Daily*, 27 January 2006.

181. Penano, J. (2004) Ultrashort Laser Pulse Propagation and Induced Discharges. *Presentation to the Non-lethal Technology and Academic Research Symposium VI (NTAR VI), Winston-Salem, NC, US, 15–17 November 2004*. Ting, A., Gordon, D., Hubbard, R., Penano, J., Sprangle, P., and Manka, C. (2003) Filamentation and Propagation of Ultra-Short, Intense Laser Pulses in Air. *NRL Review*.

182. Department of Defense (2007) *Fiscal Year 2008 Research, Development, Test & Evaluation, Navy, Budget Activity 4. Directed Energy and Electric Weapon Systems, PE 0603925N*. Washington, DC: Department of Defense.

183. Department of Defense (2007) *Fiscal Year 2008 Army RDT&E Budget Item Justification (R-2 Exhibit). Budget Activity 2, Applied Research. Weapons and Munitions Technology, PE 0602624A*. Washington, DC: Department of Defense.

184. Department of Defense (2007) *Fiscal Year 2008 Army RDT&E Budget Item Justification (R-2 Exhibit). Budget Activity 3, Advanced Technology Development. Weapons and Munitions Advanced Technology, PE 0603004A*. Washington, DC: Department of Defense.

185. Weinberger, S. (2005) The Shock Jocks. *Aviation Week & Space Technology*, Vol. 163, No. 10, p. 11; Weinberger, S. (2005) Xtreme Defense. *Washington Post*, 28 August 2005, p. W18.

186. Ionatron Inc. (2004) *Ionatron Introduces Portal Denial System*. Press Release, 7 December 2004.

187. Weinberger, S. (2005) Xtreme Defense. op. cit.

188. Ibid.; Hambling, D. (2004) Stun weapons to target crowds, *New Scientist*, 19 June 2004, p. 24.

189. Weinberger, S. (2005) The Shock Jocks. United States Patent Office (1997) *Non-lethal tetanizing weapon, United States Patent 5,675,103;* 7 October 1997.

190. Space and Naval Warfare Systems Command (2005) *SPAWAR – Award Synopsis N66001-05-C-6054 – Non-Lethal Weapon Science and Technology Applied Research and Technology Development Efforts.*

191. Space and Naval Warfare Systems Command (2005) *SSC-San Diego – Award Synopsis N66001-06-C-6003 – Non-Lethal Weapon Science and Technology Applied Research and Technology Development Efforts.*

192. SPIE (2006) *Defense and Security 2006, Technical Program*. SPIE Events, p. 73. Accessed March 2007 at: http://www.spie.org/.

193. Carter, A. and Samson, B. (2005) New technology advances applications for high-power fiber lasers. *Military & Aerospace Electronics*, February 2005; Diefenbach, V. (2006) *Fiber lasers with 2µm emission*. Orlando, FL: University of Central Florida, College of Optics and Photonics; Beason, D. (2005) op. cit., pp. 199–205.

194. Chen, B., Thomsen, S., Thomas, R., Oliver, J., and Welch, A. (2008) Histological and modeling study of skin thermal injury to 2.0 micrometer laser irradiation. *Lasers in Surgery and Medicine*, Vol. 40, Issue 5, pp. 358–70; also see Joint Non-Lethal Weapons Directorate (2008) *DOD Non-Lethal Weapons Program. Annual Report 2008*. Quantico, VA: JNLWD.

195. Hecht, J. (1984) op. cit., p. 163.

196. Owen, G. (1997) op. cit., pp. 89–93.

197. Beason, D. (2005) op. cit., p. 102.

198. Hambling, D. (2005) *Weapons Grade: Revealing the links between modern warfare and our high-tech world*. op. cit. As Hambling notes it was Raytheon Corp. who developed the first microwave oven.

199. Thuery, J. (1992) op. cit., pp. 443–552 and 553–84.

200. Stockholm International Peace Research Institute (1975) *SIPRI Yearbook 1975, World Armaments and Disarmaments*. Stockholm: Almqvist & Wiksell, pp. 55–6.

201. Hecht, J. (1984) op. cit., pp. 161–3.

202. Byron, E. (1966) *Project Pandora (U). Final Report*. Silver Spring, MD: The Johns Hopkins University, Applied Physics Laboratory, November 1966; Weinberger, S. (2007) op. cit.; Guyatt, D. (1996) *Some Aspects of Anti-Personnel Electromagnetic Weapons*. A synopsis prepared for the International Committee of the Red Cross Symposium, 'The Medical Profession and the Effects of Weapons', Montreux, Switzerland, 8–10 March 1996; Kues, H., Mazik, P. and Monahan, J. (1997) Microwave Exposure: Safeguarding Public Health in the Absence of National Standards. *Johns Hopkins APL Technical Digest*, Vol. 18, No. 2.

203. Thuery, J. (1992) op. cit., p. 445.
204. Bushnell, D. (2001) Future Strategic Issues/Future Warfare [Circa 2025]. *Presentation to the 4th Annual Testing and Training for Readiness Symposium & Exhibition: Emerging Challenges, Opportunities and Requirements, National Defense Industrial Association (NDIA), US, 13–16 August 2001*, pp. 49–50; Guyatt, D. (1996) op. cit.
205. US Senate (1976) *Final Report of the Select Committee to Study Governmental Operations with Respect to Intelligence Activities of the United States Senate. Book I: Foreign and Military Intelligence*. Washington, DC: US Senate, 4th Congress, 2nd Session, No. 94–755, pp. 385–422; Advisory Committee on Human Radiation (1994) *Interim Report of the Advisory Committee on Human Radiation Experiments*. Washington, DC: Advisory Committee on Human Radiation, 21 October 1994, Appendix E; Marks, J. (1980) *The Search for the Manchurian Candidate: The CIA and Mind Control*. New York: McGraw-Hill, pp. 195–214.
206. Hecht, J. (1984) op. cit., p. 163.
207. Lumsden, M. (1978) *Anti-Personnel Weapons*, Stockholm International Peace Research Institute. London: Taylor and Francis, p. 209.
208. Hecht, J. (1984) op. cit., pp. 161–73.
209. Beason, D. (2005) op. cit., pp. 95–111; Hecht, J. (1984) op. cit., p. 165.
210. Miller, R., Murphy, M., and Merritt, J. (2002) Radio Frequency Radiation Bioeffects Programs at the U.S. Air Force Research Laboratory. *Proceedings of the 2nd International Workshop on Biological Effects of Electromagnetic Fields, Rhodes, Greece, 7–11 October 2002*, pp. 468–77.
211. AFOSR is part of the Air Force Research Laboratory (AFRL) and manages basic research.
212. Southwest Research Institute (1982) *Final Report On Biotechnology Research Requirements For Aeronautical Systems Through The Year 2000. Volume II Proceedings of Biotechnology Research Requirements Study Session, 4–8 January 1982*. San Antonio, TX: Southwest Research Institute, pp. 176–88.
213. Ibid., p. 183.
214. Ibid.
215. Tyler, P. (1986) The Electromagnetic Spectrum in Low-Intensity Conflict. In: D. Dean (ed.) *Low-Intensity Conflict and Modern Technology*. Maxwell Air Force Base, AL: Air University Press, pp. 249–60.
216. Alexander, J. (1980) The New Mental Battlefield: 'Beam Me Up, Spock'. *Military Review*, Vol. LX, No. 12, December 1980, pp. 47–54.
217. Ronson, J. (2004) *The Men Who Stare at Goats*. London: Picador.
218. Pasternak, D. (1997) Wonder Weapons. *U.S. News and World Report*, 29 June 1997; Guyatt, D. (1996) op. cit.
219. Hecht, J. (1984) op. cit., p. 168.
220. Ibid.
221. Ibid., pp. 169–72.
222. Ibid., pp. 170–71.
223. Sweetman, S. (1987) *Report on the Attorney General's Conference on Less Than Lethal Weapons*. National Institute of Justice. Washington, DC: US Government Printing Office, pp. 17–18.
224. Seaskate Inc. (1998) The *Evolution and Development of Police Technology*. Washington, DC: National Institute of Justice, p. 46; Pilant, L. (1993) Less-than-Lethal Weapons: New Solutions for Law Enforcement. *Science and Technology*, Washington, DC: International Association of Chiefs of Police; Lewer, N. (1997) *Bradford Non-Lethal Weapons Research Project Research Report No. 1*. Bradford: University of Bradford.

225. Knoth, A. (1994) op. cit.; Alexander, J (1989) op. cit., pp. 29–41; Council on Foreign Relations (1995) *Non-Lethal Technologies: Military Options and Implications. Report of an Independent Task Force.* New York: Council on Foreign Relations; Kokoski, R. (1994) op. cit.; O'Connell, E. and Dillaplain, J. (1994) Nonlethal Concepts Implications for Air Force Intelligence. *Air and Space Power Journal*, Winter 1994.
226. Army Armament Research, Development and Engineering Center (1992) op. cit.; Tapscott, M. and Atwal, K. (1993) op. cit.
227. US Army (1998) *Bioeffects of Selected Nonlethal Weapons.* Fort Meade, MD: US Army Intelligence and Security Command. (Addendum to the Nonlethal Technologies Worldwide Study, NGIC-I 147-101-98); Hambling, D. (2008) US Army toyed with telepathic ray gun. *NewScientist.com*, 21 March 2008.
228. Siniscalchi, J. (1998) *Non-Lethal Technologies: Implications for Military Strategy.* Occasional Paper No. 3. Maxwell Air Force Base, AL: Air University, Air War College.
229. Miller, R., Murphy, M., and Merritt, J. (2002) Radio Frequency Radiation Bioeffects Programs at the U.S. Air Force Research Laboratory. *Proceedings of the 2nd International Workshop on Biological Effects of Electromagnetic Fields, Rhodes, Greece, 7–11 October 2002*, pp. 468–77.
230. Hackett, K. (2001) *Active Denial Technology.* DE-01-01. Kirtland Air Force Base, NM: Air Force Research Laboratory; Air Force Research Laboratory (2006) *Active Denial System Fact Sheet.* Kirtland Air Force Base, NM: Air Force Research Laboratory; Joint Non-Lethal Weapons Program (2006) *Frequently Asked Questions Regarding the Active Denial System.* Quantico, VA: JNLWD.
231. Forecast International (1998) *Electronic Systems Forecast. BISS – Archived 7/98.* Newtown, CT: Forecast International. Accessed March 2007 at: http://www.forecastinternational.com/.
232. Office of Technology Assessment (1992) *Technology Against Terrorism: Structuring Security*, OTA-ISC-511. Washington, DC: Government Printing Office. January 1992, pp. 139–40.
233. Forecast International (1998) op. cit.
234. It is unclear whether this document was openly available at the time of publication.
235. Gavron, V., Taylor, H., Howe III, J., Hughes, R., Stevens, D., Swalm, T., Hilmas, D., and Fuchs, R. (1998) *United States Air Force Expeditionary Forces Volume 3: Appendix I.* SAB-TR-97-01, February 1998. Washington, DC: Air Force Scientific Advisory Board, pp. I–34.
236. Hackett, K. (2001) op. cit.; Altmann, J. (2007) Millimetre-Wave and Laser NLW: Physics Analysis and Inferences. *Proceedings of the 4th European Symposium on Non-Lethal Weapons, Ettlingen, Germany, 21–3 May 2007.* P59. Pfinztal: Fraunhofer ICT.
237. Gregorac, L. (2004) ADT/ADS – Weapons of the 21st Century? *Military Technology*, Vol. 5, pp. 40–5.
238. Fuchs, R., McCarthy, J., Corder, J., Rankine, R., Miller, W., and Borky, J. (1998) *United States Air Force Expeditionary Forces Volume 2: Appendices E – H.* SAB-TR-97-01, February 1998. Washington, DC: Air Force Scientific Advisory Board, p. G-7.
239. Hewish, M. (2000) op. cit.
240. Beason, D. (2005) op. cit., pp. 113–25; Hackett, K. (2001) op. cit.
241. Gregorac, L. (2004) op. cit.; Kelkar, A. (1991) FLAPS – Conformal phased reflecting surfaces. *Proceedings of the 1991 IEEE National Radar Conference*,

Los Angeles, CA, 12–13 March 1991. New York: Institute of Electrical and Electronics Engineers, Inc.
242. Communications & Power Industries, Gyrotrons website. Accessed March 2007 at: http://www.cpii.com/; The Active Denial System uses the VGB-8095 model.
243. Joint Non-Lethal Weapons Program (2007) *Active Denial System (ADS) Fact Sheet.* Quantico, VA: JNLWD; Beason, D. (2005) op. cit., pp. 113–25.
244. Beason, D. (2005) op. cit., pp. 113–25.
245. Brinkley, C. M. (2001) The People Zapper. *Marine Corps Times,* 5 March 2001.
246. United States Air Force (2001) *Fact Sheet: Active Denial Technology.* Kirtland Air Force Base, NM: Air Force Research Laboratory.
247. National Research Council (2003) op. cit., p. 55.
248. Ibid., p. 82.
249. Over $50 million was spent during that period on the project as a whole; Air Force Research Laboratory (2005) *Active Denial System Fact Sheet.* Kirtland Air Force Base, NM: Air Force Research Laboratory; Air Force Research Laboratory (2006) *Active Denial System Fact Sheet.* Kirtland Air Force Base, NM: Air Force Research Laboratory.
250. Blick, D., Adair, E., Hurt, W., Sherry, C., Walters, T., and Merritt, J. (1997) Thresholds of microwave-evoked warmth sensations in human skin. *Bioelectromagnetics,* Vol. 18, No. 6, pp. 403–9; Riu, P., Foster, K., Blick, D., and Adair, E. (1997) A thermal model for human thresholds of microwave-evoked warmth sensations. *Bioelectromagnetics,* Vol. 18, No. 8, pp. 578–83; Ryan, K., D'Andrea, J., Jauchem, J., and Mason, P. (2000) Radio Frequency Radiation of Millimeter Wave Length: Potential Occupational Safety Issues Relating to Surface Heating. *Health Physics,* Vol. 78, No. 2, pp. 170–81; Walters, T., Blick, D., Johnson, L., Adair, E., and Foster, K. (2000) Heating and Pain Sensation Produced in Human Skin by Millimeter Waves: Comparison to a Simple Thermal Model. *Health Physics,* Vol. 78, No. 3, pp. 259–67; Nelson, D., Nelson, M., Walters, T., and Mason, P. (2000) Skin heating effects of millimeter-wave irradiation-thermal modeling results. *IEEE Transactions on Microwave Theory and Techniques,* Vol. 48, No. 11, pp. 2111–20; Mason, P., Walters, T., DiGiovanni, J., Beason, C., Jauchem, J., Dick Jr, E., Mahajan, K., Dusch, S., Shields, B., Merritt, J., Murphy, M., and Ryan, K. (2001) Lack of effect of 94 GHz radio frequency radiation exposure in an animal model of skin carcinogenesis. *Carcinogenesis,* Vol. 22, No. 10, pp. 1701–8; Chalfin, S., D'Andrea, J., Comeau, P., Belt, M., and Hatcher, D. (2002) Millimeter Wave Absorption In The Nonhuman Primate Eye at 35 GHz And 94 GHz. *Health Physics,* Vol. 83, No. 1, pp. 83–90; Nelson, D., Walters, T., Ryan, K., Emerton, K., Hurt, W., Ziriax, J., Johnson, L., and Mason, P. (2003) Inter-Species Extrapolation of Skin Heating Resulting from Millimeter Wave Irradiation: Modeling and Experimental Results. *Health Physics,* Vol. 84, No. 5, pp. 608–15; Foster, K., D'Andrea, J., Chalfin, S., and Hatcher, D. (2003) Thermal Modeling of Millimeter Wave Damage to the Primate Cornea at 35 GHz And 94 GHz. *Health Physics,* Vol. 84, No. 6, pp. 764–69; Walters, R., Ryan, K., Nelson, D., Blick, D., and Mason, P. (2004) Effects Of Blood Flow on Skin Heating Induced by Millimeter Wave Irradiation In Humans. *Health Physics,* Vol. 86, No. 2, pp. 115–20.
251. Beason, D. (2005) op. cit., pp. 113–25.
252. Joint Non-Lethal Weapons Program (2006) *Active Denial System (ADS) Fact Sheet.* op. cit.; Department of Defense website, Introduction to ACTD's. Accessed March 2007 at: http://www.acq.osd.mil/jctd/.

253. Bloomberg (2004) Raytheon Completes Prototype of First Nonlethal Energy Weapon. *Bloomberg.com*, 1 December 2004; Apparently two of these prototype systems were built, see: US Air Force (2003) Solicitation Notice – Active Denial System. *FBO Daily*, 8 April 2004, FBO No. 0864.
254. Hambling, D. (2005) Details of US microwave-weapon tests revealed. *NewScientist*, 22 July 2005. Hambling, D. (2006) New Weapon, Human Tests. *Wired.com*, 5 December 2006.
255. Titles of the experimental protocol documents obtained by The Sunshine Project were as follows: Protocol F-WR-2001-0006-H: Perceptual and Thermal Effects of Non-ionizing Radiation; Protocol F-WR-2002-0016-H: Effects of Skin and Environmental Conditions on Sensations Evoked by Millimeter Waves; Protocol F-WR-2002-0023-H: Facial Sensitivity and Eye Aversion Response to Millimeter Waves; Protocol F-WR-2002-0024-H: Effects of Ethanol on Millimeter-Wave-Induced Pain; Protocol F-WR-2002-0046-H: Perceptual and Thermal Effects of Millimeter waves; Protocol F-WR-2003-0028-H: Perceptual and Thermal Effects of Frontal Exposure to Millimeter Wave Energy; Protocol F-WR-2003-0331 -H, Limited Military Utility Assessment of the Active Denial System (ADS); Protocol F-WR-2004-0029-H: Effects of Active Denial System Exposures on the Performance of Military Working Dog Teams; Protocol F-WR-2005-0003-H, Military Utility Assessment of the Active Denial System (ADS); Protocol F-WR-2005-0037-H: Military Utility Assessment of the Active Denial System (ADS) in an Urban Environment; Protocol F-BR-2005-0057-H: Thermal Effects of Exposure to 400 W, 95 GHz, Millimeter Wave Energy; Protocol F-WR-2006-0001-H: Military Utility Assessment of the Active Denial System (ADS) in a Maritime Environment; Protocol F-BR-2006-0018-H: Effects of Exposure to 400-W, 95-GHz Millimeter Wave Energy on Non-Stationary Humans.
256. Joint Non-Lethal Weapons Program (2006) *Active Denial System (ADS) Fact Sheet.* op. cit.; Joint Non-Lethal Weapons Program (2007) *Active Denial System Information Posters.* Quantico, VA: Joint Non-Lethal Weapons Directorate, April 2007.
257. Johnson, R. (2007) Pentagon readies ray gun. *EE Times Online*, 26 January 2007. Accessed March 2007 at: http://www.eetimes.com/; Joint Non-Lethal Weapons Program (2007) *Active Denial System (ADS) Fact Sheet.* op. cit.
258. Magnuson, S. (2006) Non-lethal Weapon Readied for Battlefield. *National Defense*, January 2006.
259. Murphy, M., Merritt, J., Mason, J., D'Andrea, J., Blick, D., and Scholl, D. (2003) Bio-effects Research in support of the Active Denial System (ADS). *Proceedings of the 2nd European Symposium on Non-Lethal Weapons, Ettlingen, Germany, 13–14 May 2003.* V23. Pfinztal: Fraunhofer ICT.
260. Ibid.
261. Joint Non-Lethal Weapons Program (2007) *Active Denial System (ADS) Fact Sheet.* op. cit.
262. Altmann, J. (2007); also see Altmann (2008) *Millimetre Waves, Lasers, Acoustics for Non-Lethal Weapons? Physics Analyses and Inferences.* Osnabrück: Deutsche Stiftung Friedensforschung (DSF).
263. In human experiments volunteers were given a 15 second cooling off period.
264. Altmann, J. (2005) Assessing New Types of LLW. *Presentation to the Jane's 8th Annual Less-Lethal Weapons Conference, October 2005, Leeds, UK.*
265. Altmann, J. (2007) op. cit.
266. Hambling, D. (2006) Say Hello to the Goodbye Weapon. *Wired.com*, 5 December 2006; Osborn, K. (2007) Airman injured in heat-beam test. *Air Force Times*, 7

April 2007; Joint Non-Lethal Weapons Program (2006) *Frequently Asked Questions Regarding the Active Denial System*. Quantico, VA: JNLWD; Joint Non-Lethal Weapons Program (2007) *Frequently Asked Questions Regarding the Active Denial System*. Quantico, VA: JNLWD; Hambling, D. (2007) US military in denial over 'pain ray'. *The Guardian*, 13 December 2007.

267. Hearn, K. (2001) Scientists dispute military 'raygun' claims. *UPI News*, 6 March 2001; Hearn, K. (2005) Rumsfeld's Ray Gun. *AlterNet*, 19 August 2005. Accessed March 2007 at: http://www.alternet.org/; Castelli, C. (2001) Questions Linger About Health Effects of DOD's Non-Lethal Ray. *Inside the Navy*, Vol. 14, No. 12, 26 March 2001.

268. Particularly in Eastern Europe, see for example: Radzievsky, A., Rojavin, M., Cowan, A., and Ziskin, M. (1999) Suppression of Pain Sensation Caused by Millimeter Waves: A Double-Blinded, Cross-Over, Prospective Human Volunteer Study. *Anesthesia & Analgesia*, Vol. 88, pp. 836–40.

269. NATO (2004) op. cit., Chapter 3, p. 9.

270. Mason, P. et al. (2001) op. cit.

271. Joint Non-Lethal Weapons Program (2006) *Active Denial System (ADS) Fact Sheet*. op. cit.; The 7.5 million contract for this was awarded to Raytheon in mid-2005, see: Department of Defense (2005) *Contracts: 29 April 2005*. Washington, DC: Department of Defense, Office of the Assistant Secretary of Defense (Public Affairs). Accessed March 2007 at: http://www.defenselink.mil/; Joint Non-Lethal Weapons Program (2008) *Active Denial System (ADS) Fact Sheet*. Quantico, VA: JNLWD.

272. National Institute of Justice (2005) *NIJ Awards in Fiscal Year 2004*. Washington, DC; National Institute of Justice; Hambling, D. (2005) Police toy with 'less lethal' weapons. op. cit.

273. Cecconi, J. (2005) Less Lethal Program. *Presentation to Non-Lethal Defense VI: Non-Lethal Weapon Options in the Global Fight Against Terrorism, National Defense Industrial Association (NDIA), Reston, VA, US 14–15 March 2005*; Davison, N. and Lewer, N. (2005) *Bradford Non-Lethal Weapons Research Project Research Report No. 7*. Bradford: University of Bradford, pp. 28–9.

274. Steiner, T. (2006) Active Denial System Advanced Concept Technology Demonstration. *Presentation to the Defense Manufacturing Conference*. Accessed March 2007 at: https://www.jnlwp.com/; Joint Non-Lethal Weapons Program (2007) *Active Denial System Information Posters*. op. cit.

275. Alan Fischer, a Raytheon spokesperson, said the company is "working on a number of active denial projects, with various ranges. ADS may some day be miniaturized down to a hand-held device that could be carried in a purse or pocket and used for personal protection instead of something like Mace. The potential for this technology is huge". See: Hearn, K. (2005) op. cit.

276. Gregorac, L. (2004) op. cit.

277. National Institute of Justice (2007) *Active Denial System Deters Subject Without Harm*. 25 October 2007. Accessed December 2007 at: http://www.ojp.usdoj.gov/.

278. Altmann, J. (2007) op. cit.; Joint Non-Lethal Weapons Program (2007) *Active Denial System (ADS) Fact Sheet*. op. cit.; Fulghum, D. (2006) Silent Launch. *Aviation Week & Space Technology*. Vol. 165, Issue 4, 24 July 2006, p. 66; Raytheon, Co. (2006) *Silent Guardian Protection System*. Tuscon, AZ: Raytheon, Co. Missile Systems. Accessed March 2007 at: http://www.raytheon.com/; Hambling, D. (2006) Say Hello to the Goodbye Weapon. op. cit.; Joint Non-Lethal Weapons Program (2006) *Active Denial System (ADS) Fact Sheet*. op. cit.; Sandia National Laboratories (2005) *Team investigates Active Denial System for security applications*.

News Release, 30 June 2005; Air Force Research Laboratory (2004) *Nonlethal Technology Going Airborne*. AFRL Directed Energy Directorate, Press Release, 4 October 2004; Bloomberg (2004) op. cit.

279. Joint Non-Lethal Weapons Program (2006) *Frequently Asked Questions Regarding the Active Denial System*. op. cit.
280. Raytheon, Co. (2006) op. cit.; Sandia National Laboratories (2005) *Team investigates Active Denial System for security applications*. News Release, 30 June 2005.
281. Kerber, R. (2004) Ray gun, sci-fi staple, meets reality. *The Boston Globe*, 24 September 2004.
282. Mihm, S. (2004) The Quest for the Nonkiller App. *The New York Times*, 25 July 2004; Regan, M. (2004) Military embrace of 'non-lethal' energy weapons sparks debate. *Associated Press*, 2 August 2004; Joint Non-Lethal Weapons Directorate (2005) *Joint Non-Lethal Weapons Program Newsletter, Second Quarter, Fiscal Year 2005*. Quantico, VA: JNLWD; Bergstein, B. (2005) Military's energy-beam weapons delayed. *USA Today*, 9 July 2005; Komarow, S. (2005) Energy beam weapon may lower Iraq civilian deaths. *USA Today*, 24 July 2005; Komarow, S. (2005) Pentagon deploys array of non-lethal weapons. *USA Today*, 24 July 2005.
283. Titles of the experimental protocol documents obtained by The Sunshine Project were: Protocol F-WR-2005-0003-H, Military Utility Assessment of the Active Denial System (ADS); Protocol F-WR-2005-0037-H: Military Utility Assessment of the Active Denial System (ADS) in an Urban Environment; Protocol F-WR-2006-0001-H: Military Utility Assessment of the Active Denial System (ADS) in a Maritime Environment.
284. Wood, S. (2007) DoD Shows Off Non-lethal Energy Weapon. *American Forces Press Service*, 26 January 2007.
285. NewScientist.com (2007) US aims to use heat-beam weapon by 2010. *NewScientist. com*, 25 January 2007.
286. InsideDefense.com (2008) Active Denial System Poised For First Iraq Deployment Next Year. *InsideDefense.com*, 1 August 2008.
287. Raytheon, Co. (2006) op. cit.
288. Fulghum, D. (2006) op. cit.
289. Titles of the experimental protocol documents obtained by The Sunshine Project were: Protocol F-BR-2005-0057-H: Thermal Effects of Exposure to 400 W, 95 GHz, Millimeter Wave Energy; Protocol F-BR-2006-0018-H: Effects of Exposure to 400-W, 95-GHz Millimeter Wave Energy on Non-Stationary Humans.
290. Sandia National Laboratories (2005) op. cit.; Bergstein, B. (2005).
291. Inside the Army (2005) Multi-National Corps-Iraq Requests 14 'Project Sheriff' Vehicles. *Inside the Army*, 30 May 2005.
292. Roosvelt, A. (2006) Army Prepares For Stryker ICV-FSEP–Former OFT Project Sheriff. *Defense Daily*, 7 July 2006.
293. Magnuson, S. (2008) Office Seeks to Quickly Field Counter-Terrorism Technologies. *National Defense Magazine*, July 2008.
294. Baker, W., Bednarz, E. and Sierakowski, R. (2004) *Controlled Effects*. DE-04-01, June 2004. Kirtland Air Force Base, NM: Air Force Research Laboratory.
295. National Research Council (2003) op. cit., p. 164.
296. Craviso, G. and Chatterjee, I. (2005) *Sensitivity of Neurotransmitter Release to Radiofrequency Fields*. Final performance report 1 Jun 2002–31 May 2005. Air Force Contract No.: F49620-02-1-0306. 10 August 2005.
297. Craviso, G., Brouse, D., Hagan, T., McPherson, D., and Chatterjee, I. (2005) Use of Cultured Adrenal Chromaffin Cells as an In Vitro Model System to Study

Non-Thermal Effects of RF Radiation on Exocytosis. *Bioelectromagnetics 2005 Abstract Collection.*
298. Craviso, G. and Chatterjee, I. (2006) *Interdisciplinary Research Project to Explore the Potential for Developing Non-Lethal Weapons Based on Radiofrequency/Microwave Bioeffects.* Final performance report 15 Mar 2004–14 Dec 2005. Air Force Contract No.: FA9550-04-1-0194 (Work continued under Contract No.: FA9550-05-1-0308). 31 January 2006; Also see, Yoon, J., Chatterjee, I., McPherson, D., and Craviso, G. (2006) Characterization, and Optimization of a Broadband Mini Exposure Chamber for Studying Catecholamine Release From Chromaffin Cells Exposed to Microwave Radiation: Finite Difference Time-Domain Technique. *IEEE Transactions on Plasma Science,* Vol. 34, No. 4, pp. 1455–69.
299. Craviso, G. and Chatterjee, I. (2006) op. cit.
300. University of Nevada (2005) *Department Of Defense EPSCoR.* Website. Accessed March 2007 at: http://www.nevada.edu/; This research, funded under the DEPSCoR programme is entitled Exploring Non-Thermal Radiofrequency Bioeffects for Novel Military Applications.
301. Chatterjee, I. and Craviso, G. (2004) *Expanding Current Research Capabilities for Investigating RF/Microwave Bioeffects.* Final report 15 Apr 2003–14 Apr 2004. Air Force Contract No.: F49620-03-1-0267. 10 July 2004.
302. University of Nevada (2003) *Dept. of Defense awards $500,000 to study radio frequency radiation.* Press Release, 12 March 2003. Accessed March 2007 at: http://www.unr.edu/.
303. NATO (2006) op. cit., p. G-1.
304. Thuery, J. (1992) op. cit., pp. 478–81; Reppert, B. (1988) Looking at the Moscow Signal, the Zapping of an Embassy 35 years later, The Mystery Lingers. *Associated Press,* 22 May 1988.
305. US Air Force (1994) *Disclosure And Record Of Invention: A Method for Encoding & Transmitting Speech by Means of the Radio Frequency Hearing Phenomena,* 1 November 1994; Weinberger, S. (2007) op. cit.
306. United States Patent Office (2002) *Method and device for implementing the radio frequency hearing effect,* United States Patent 6,470,214, 22 October 2002.
307. United States Patent Office (2003) *Apparatus for audibly communicating speech using the radio frequency hearing effect,* United States Patent 6,587,729, 1 July 2003.
308. US Navy (2003) *Navy SBIR Award: Remote Personnel Incapacitation System.* Contract No.: M67854-04-C-1012. Accessed March 2007 at: http://www.navysbirprogram.com/.
309. US Navy (2004) *Phase I Summary Report: Remote Personnel Incapacitation System.* Contract No.: M67854-04-C-1012. Accessed March 2007 at: http://www.navysbirprogram.com/.
310. Weinberger, S. (2005) Xtreme Defense. op. cit.; Gibbs, G. (2005) Through the Wall Directed Energy Application. *Presentation to Directed Energy Weapons, Institute for Defense and Government Advancement (IDGA), Arlington, VA, US, 28–9 June 2005.*
311. Hambling, D. (2008) Microwave ray gun controls crowds with noise. *NewScientist. com,* 3 July 2008.
312. Heger, M. (2008) Why Microwave Auditory Effect Crowd-Control Gun Won't Work. *IEEE Spectrum,* July 2008.
313. US Navy (2003) *Navy SBIR Award: EPIC (Electromagnetic Personnel Interdiction Control). Contract No.: M67854-04-C-1013.* Accessed March 2007 at: http://www.navysbirprogram.com/.

314. US Navy (2005) *Navy SBIR Award: EPIC (Electromagnetic Personnel Interdiction Control). Contract No.: M67854-04-C-1013.* Accessed March 2007 at: http://www.navysbirprogram.com/; Invocon, Inc. (not dated) *Non-lethal Electromagnetic Stand-off Weapon.* Conroe, TX: Invocon, Inc.
315. Schachtman, N. (2007) Navy Researching Vomit Beam (Updated). *Wired.com,* 6 March 2007. Accessed March 2007 at: http://blog.wired.com/.
316. *Bioelectromagnetics,* Vol. 24, Issue S6, pp. S1–S213, 2003.
317. Air Force Research Laboratory (2005) *Research in support of the Directed Energy Bioeffects Division of the Human Effectiveness Directorate. Broad Agency Announcement Number: BAA 05-05 HE.* Brooks Air Force Base, TX: Air Force Research Laboratory.
318. Joint Non-Lethal Weapons Directorate (2006) *JNLWP Fiscal Year 2006–7 Technology Broad Area Announcement. Non-Lethal Weapons Technology Fiscal Year 2006–Fiscal Year 2007 Applied Research And Development Efforts.* Accessed March 2007 at: https://www.jnlwp.com/.
319. Moreno, J. (2006) *Mind Wars: Brain Research and National Security.* New York: Dana Press.
320. Rose, S. (2006) Brain Gain. In: P. Miller and J. Wilsdon (eds) *Better Humans? The politics of human enhancement and life extension.* London: Demos.
321. Ibid.
322. National Research Council (2008) *Emerging Cognitive Neuroscience and Related Technologies.* Washington, DC: National Academies Press.
323. United States/United Kingdom (2001) *US/UK Non-Lethal Weapons (NLW)/Urban Operations Executive Seminar, 30 November 2000, London. Assessment Report.* ONR-NLW-038. p. 37.
324. Gayl, F. (2008) *Compact High Power Laser Dazzler (CHPLD). Ground Combat Element (GCE) Advocate Science and Technology (S&T) Advisor Case Study.* Quantico, VA: US Marine Corps.
325. Zimet, E. (2002) High-Energy Lasers: Technical, Operational, and Policy Issues. *Defense Horizons,* No. 18, October 2002; Stephens, H. (2006) Toward A New Laser Era. *Air Force Magazine,* Vol. 89, No. 6, June 2006. Hecht, J. (2006) Lasers advance slowly into the battlefield. *New Scientist,* 24 August 2006.
326. Lumsden, M. (1978) op. cit., p. 208.
327. Hecht, J. (2004) Laser weapons go solid state. *Laser Focus World,* Vol. 40, Issue. 61.
328. Sweetman, B. (2006) Directed energy lasers – fact or fiction? *Jane's Defence Weekly,* Vol. 43, Issue 8, February 2006, pp. 24–9.
329. National Research Council (2003) op. cit., p. 82.
330. The Advanced Tactical Laser, not addressed here because of its clearly lethal effects, is a case in point: Karcher, D. and Wertheim, E. (not dated) op. cit.
331. Coupland, R. (2005) Modelling armed violence: a tool for humanitarian dialogue in disarmament and arms control. In: J. Borrie and V. Martin Randin (eds) *Alternative Approaches in Multilateral Decision Making: Disarmament as Humanitarian Action.* Geneva: United Nations Institute for Disarmament Research (UNDIR), May 2005, pp. 39–49.
332. Kochems, A. and Gudgel, A. (2006) *The Viability of Directed-Energy Weapons.* Backgrounder No. 1931, 28 April 2006. Washington, DC: The Heritage Foundation.
333. Karcher, D. and Wertheim, E. (not dated) op. cit.
334. Joint Non-Lethal Weapons Program (2006) *Frequently Asked Questions Regarding the Active Denial System.* op. cit.; Joint Non-Lethal Weapons Program (2007) *Active Denial System Information Posters.* op. cit.

335. NATO (2004) op. cit., Chapter 3, p. 9.
336. National Research Council (2003) op. cit., p. 165.
337. Beason, D. (2005) op. cit., pp. 113–25.
338. Brinkley, C. (2001); Hecht, J. (2001) Microwave beam weapon to disperse crowds. *New Scientist*, 20 October 2001.
339. Baldor, C. (2006) Nonlethal weapons touted for use on U.S. citizens. *Seattle Post-Intelligencer*, 12 September 2006; Wright, S. (2006) Targeting the pain business. *The Guardian*, 5 October 2006.
340. Hambling, D. (2005) Maximum pain is aim of new US weapon. *New Scientist*, 2 March 2005.
341. New Scientist (2005) Editorial: Pain-maximising weapon could be abused. *New Scientist*, 5 March 2005.
342. Wright, S. (2006) op. cit.
343. Altmann, J. (2007) op. cit.
344. Lewer, N. and Davison, N. (2006) *Electrical stun weapons: alternative to lethal force or a compliance tool?* Bradford: University of Bradford.
345. Although the ambiguity of the causal relationship between the deaths and the weapon has limited the impact of this criticism.
346. Hambling, D. (2006) Say Hello to the Goodbye Weapon. op. cit.
347. As opposed to the maximum power capability of the transmitter, which is known.
348. Joint Non-Lethal Weapons Program (2007) *Active Denial System (ADS) Fact Sheet.* op. cit.; Kenny, J., Ziskin, M., Adair, B., Murray, B., Farrer, D., Marks, L., and Bovbjerg, V. (2008) *A Narrative Summary and Independent Assessment of the Active Denial System.* The Human Effects Advisory Panel. State College, PA: Pennsylvania State University.
349. Roque, A. (2005) 'Active Denial System' Sought for Iraq. *InsideDefense.com*, 21 December 2005.
350. Shachtman, N. (2007) Marines Want Pain Ray, ASAP. *Wired.com*. Accessed May 2007 at: http://blog.wired.com/.
351. Defense Science Board (2007) *Task Force on Directed Energy Weapons*. Washington, DC: Department of Defense, pp 38–9.
352. Loye, D. (2003) Non-Lethal Capabilities Facing International Humanitarian Law. *Proceedings of the 2nd European Symposium on Non-Lethal Weapons, Ettlingen, Germany, 13–14 May 2003*. V3. Pfinztal: Fraunhofer ICT.
353. Joint Non-Lethal Weapons Program (2007) *Active Denial System Information Posters*. Quantico, VA: Joint Non-Lethal Weapons Directorate, April 2007.
354. Joint Non-Lethal Weapons Program (2006) *Frequently Asked Questions Regarding the Active Denial System*. Quantico, VA: Joint Non-Lethal Weapons Directorate, October 2006; Roque, A. (2005) DOD To Contract With Industry For Project Sheriff Integration. *Inside the Army*, 1 August 2005; Bender, B. (2005) US testing nonlethal weapons arsenal for use in Iraq. *The Boston Globe*, 5 August 2005.
355. See for example: http://www.mindjustice.org/.
356. See for example: Geis II, J. (2003) op. cit.

7   Acoustic Weapons

1. Taken from: Altmann, J. (2001) Acoustic Weapons – A Prospective Assessment. *Science & Global Security*, Vol. 9, pp. 165–234.

2. Altmann, J. (1999) *Acoustic Weapons – A Prospective Assessment: Sources, Propagation, and Effects of Strong Sound*. Occasional Paper No. 22, May 1999. Ithaca, NY: Cornell University, Peace Studies Program; Altmann, J. (2000) Acoustic Weapons: Myths and Reality. In: M. Dando (ed.) *Non-Lethal Weapons: Technological and Operational Prospects*. Coulsdon: Jane's, pp. 51–9; Altmann, J. (2001) Acoustic Weapons – A Prospective Assessment. *Science & Global Security*, Vol. 9, pp. 165–234.

3. Jauchem, J. and Cook, M. (2007) High-Intensity Acoustics for Military Nonlethal Applications – A Lack of Useful Systems. *Military Medicine*, Vol. 172, No. 2, February 2007, pp. 182–9.

4. Altmann, J. (2001) op. cit.; NATO (2004) *Non-Lethal Weapons and Future Peace Enforcement Operations*, RTO-TR-SAS-040. Brussels: NATO, RTO, Chapter 3, p. 11.

5. National Research Council (2003) *An Assessment of Non-Lethal Weapons Science and Technology*. Washington, DC: National Academies Press, p. 31.

6. Applegate, R. (1969) New Ways with Sound. In: R. Applegate, *Riot Control – Materiel and Techniques*. First edition, Harrisburg, PA: Stackpole Books, pp. 269–73.

7. Ackroyd, C., Margolis, K., Rosenhead, J., and Shallice, T. (1980) *The Technology of Political Control*. Second edition, London: Pluto Press, pp. 223–6.

8. Applegate, R. (1969) op. cit., p. 271.

9. Security Planning Corporation (1972) *Non-Lethal Weapons for Law Enforcement: Research Needs and Priorities. A Report to the National Science Foundation*. Washington, DC: Security Planning Corporation, Appendix A.

10. Gavreau, V. (1968) Infrasound. *Science Journal*, Vol. 4, No. 1, January 1968, pp. 33–7.

11. Leventhall, G. (2005) How the 'mythology' of infrasound and low frequency noise related to wind turbines might have developed. *First International Meeting on Wind Turbine Noise: Perspectives for Control, Berlin, 17–18 October 2005*.

12. Lumsden, M. (1978) *Anti-Personnel Weapons*, Stockholm International Peace Research Institute. London: Taylor and Francis, pp. 203–5; Leventhall, G. (1998) The infrasonic weapon revisited. *Noise and Vibration WorldWide*, May 1998, pp. 22–6; Leventhall, G. (2005) op. cit.

13. Rodwell, R. (1973) 'Squawk box' technology. *New Scientist*, Vol. 59, No. 864, pp. 667–8; Anon (1973) Army tests new riot weapon. *New Scientist*, Vol. 59, No. 864, p. 684; Rodwell, R. (1973) How dangerous is the Army's squawk box? *New Scientist*, Vol. 59, No. 865, p. 730.

14. Altmann, J. (1999) op. cit.; Altmann, J. (2001) op. cit.

15. Broner, N. (1978) The effects of low frequency noise on people – A review. *Journal of Sound and Vibration*, Vol. 58, Issue 4, pp. 483–500.

16. United Nations (1978) *Hungarian People's Republic. Working paper on infrasound weapons*. CCD/575, 14 August 1978. Geneva: United Nations.

17. The DISPERSE programme is described in: University of Texas at Austin (2002) *Non-Lethal Swimmer Neutralization Study*. San Diego, CA: US Navy, pp. 17, 23–4, and 29; Documents cited in this report include: Harry Diamond Laboratories (1975) *DISPERSE: A Survey of Relevant Literature and Research Activities*. Adelphi, MD: US Army Materiel Command; Harry Diamond Laboratories (1975) *DISPERSE: A Survey of Relevant Literature and Research Activities*. Adelphi, MD: US Army Materiel Command; Harry Diamond Laboratories (1975) *DISPERSE: An Assessment of the Utility of Future Effort on 'Aversive Audible Acoustic Stimuli'*. Adelphi, MD: US Army Materiel Command; Harry Diamond Laboratories (1975)

DISPERSE: Considerations for Developing Nonpermanently Damaging Crowd Control Devices. Adelphi, MD: US Army Materiel Command.

18. Harry Diamond Laboratories (1975) *DISPERSE: A Survey of Relevant Literature and Research Activities*. Adelphi, MD: US Army Materiel Command. Quoted In: University of Texas at Austin (2002) op. cit., p. 17.

19. Ibid., p. 17, 23–4, and 29.

20. Coates, J. (1970) *Nonlethal and Nondestructive Combat in Cities Overseas*. Washington, DC: Institute for Defense Analyses, p. 110.

21. As described in: Lucey, G. and Jasper, L. (1998) Vortex Ring Generator. *Presentation to Non-Lethal Defense III, National Defense Industrial Association (NDIA), US, 25–6 February 1998*.

22. Sweetman, S. (1987) *Report on the Attorney General's Conference on Less Than Lethal Weapons*. National Institute of Justice. Washington, DC: US Government Printing Office.

23. Army Armament Research, Development and Engineering Center (1992) ARDEC exploring less-than-lethal munitions; to give Army greater flexibility in future conflicts. *ARDEC News Release*, 9 October 1992.

24. Scientific Applications and Research Associates, Inc. (1996) *Less Than Lethal Acoustic Devices for Law Enforcement and Corrections Applications. Technical Volume Tabs G, H, and I*. GRD-96-003. Huntington Beach, CA: Scientific Applications and Research Associates, Inc.; Arkin, W. (1997) Acoustic Anti-personnel Weapons: An Inhumane Future? *Medicine, Conflict and Survival*, Vol. 14, No. 4, pp. 314–26.

25. Scientific Applications and Research Associates, Inc. (1996) op. cit.; Sherry, C., Cook, M., Brown, C., Jauchem, J., Merritt, J., and Murphy, M. (2000) *An Assessment of the Effects of Four Acoustic Energy Devices on Animal Behavior*. AFRL-HE-BR-TR-2000-0153. Brooks Air Force Base, TX: Air Force Research Laboratory.

26. Scientific Applications and Research Associates, Inc. (1996) op. cit.

27. Ibid.

28. Tapscott, M. and Atwal, K. (1993) New Weapons That Win Without Killing on DOD's Horizon. *Defense Electronics*, February 1993, pp. 41–6; Knoth, A. (1994) Disabling Technologies. A Critical Assessment. *International Defense Review*, No. 7, July 1994, pp. 33–9; Kokoski, R. (1994) Non-lethal weapons: a case study of new technology developments. In: Stockholm International Peace Research Institute *SIPRI Yearbook 1994*. Oxford: Oxford University Press, pp. 367–86; Pasternak, D. (1997) Wonder Weapons. *U.S. News and World Report*, 29 June 1997; Alexander, J. (1999) *Future War: Non-Lethal Weapons in Twenty-First-Century Warfare*. New York: St. Martin's Press, pp. 95–102.

29. Tapscott, M. and Atwal, K. (1993) op. cit.

30. Pasternak, D. (1997) op. cit.

31. Altmann, J. (2000); also see Altmann, J. (2001).

32. Joint Non-Lethal Weapons Directorate (1998) *Joint Non-Lethal Weapons Program (JNLWP) Annual Report 1997*. Quantico, VA: JNLWD.

33. Boesch Jr., E., Benwell, B., and Ellis, V. (1998) A High-Power Electrically Driven Impulsive Acoustic Source for Target Effects Experiments and Area-Denial Applications. *Presentation to Non-Lethal Defense III, National Defense Industrial Association (NDIA), US, 25–26 February 1998*.

34. Gayl, F. (1998) High intensity sound as a nonlethal weapon. *Marine Corps Gazette*, January 1998, p. 29.

35. Sherry, C. et al. (2000) op. cit.

36. Sze, H., Gilmam, C., Lyon, J., Naff, T., Pomeroy, S., and Shaw, R. (1998) An Acoustic Blaster Demonstration Program. *Presentation to Non-Lethal Defense III, National Defense Industrial Association (NDIA), US, 25–26 February 1998.*

37. Moore, H. and Shippell Jr., R. (1996) Directed Energy Technologies: Weaponization and Barrier Applications. *Proceedings of the 30th IEEE Annual International Carnahan Conference on Security Technology, 2–4 October 1996,* pp. 220–5.

38. Murphy, M. (1998) *Biological Effects of Non-Lethal Weapons: Issues and Solutions.* Brooks Air Force Base, TX: Air Force Research Laboratory; Sherry, C. et al. (2000) op. cit.

39. Murphy, M. (1998) op. cit.

40. Lorenz, F. (1996) Non-Lethal Force: The Slippery Slope to War? *Parameters,* Autumn 1996, pp. 52–62; National Institute of Justice (1998) *NIJ Awards in Fiscal Year 1997.* Washington, DC: National Institute of Justice; Murphy, M. (1998) op. cit.

41. National Institute of Justice (1998) *NIJ Awards in Fiscal Year 1997.* Washington, DC: National Institute of Justice.

42. Altmann, J. (2001) op. cit.

43. Murphy, M., Jauchem, J., and Merritt, J. (2001) Acoustic Bioeffects Research for Non-Lethal Applications. *Proceedings of the 1st European Symposium on Non-Lethal Weapons, Ettlingen, Germany, 25–26 September 2001.* V9. Pfinztal: Fraunhofer ICT; Murphy, M. (1998) op. cit.

44. Murphy, M., Jauchem, J., and Merritt, J. (2001) op. cit.

45. Jauchem, J. Sherry, C., Cook, M., Brown, G., Merritt, J., and Murphy, M. (2003) The Potential Use of High Intensity Acoustics for Non-Lethal Applications. *Abstract of presentation to the Non-lethal Technology and Academic Research Symposium V (NTAR V), VA, US, 5–6 November 2003.*

46. *Ibid.*; Also see, Sherry, C. et al. (2000) op. cit.; Jauchem, J. and Cook, M. (2007) op. cit.

47. Sherry, C. et al. (2000) op. cit., p. 3.

48. Ibid., p. 68.

49. Ibid., p. 67.

50. Ibid., pp. 67–8.

51. University of Texas at Austin (2002) op. cit., p. 41; Also see, Sherry, C. et al. (2000) op. cit.

52. Which was conducted between May 1996 and January 1999.

53. Joint Non-Lethal Weapons Directorate (2000) *Joint Non-Lethal Weapons Program (JNLWP) Annual Report 1999.* Quantico, VA: JNLWD.

54. Alker, G. (1996) Acoustic Weapons – A feasibility study. Report No.: DRA/SS(PS)/CR96039/1.0. Farnborough, UK: Defence Evaluation and Research Agency. Cited In: Sherry, C. et al. (2000) op. cit.

55. Altmann, J. (1999) op. cit.

56. Lucey, G. and Jasper, L. (1998) op. cit.

57. Joint Non-Lethal Weapons Directorate (1998) op. cit.

58. National Research Council (2003) op. cit., p. 42.

59. Altmann, J. (2000) op. cit.

60. National Research Council (2003) op. cit., p. 39.

61. Ibid., p. 162.

62. American Technology Corp. website. Accessed March 2007 at: http://www.atcsd.com/; Holosonic Research Labs Inc. website. Accessed March 2007 at: http://www.holosonics.com/.

63. American Technology Corp. (2001) *HSS Technology Introduction* (Rev. F). San Diego, CA: American Technology Corp.; Croft, J. and Norris, J. (2001) *White Paper: Theory, History, and the Advancement of Parametric Loudspeakers* (Abridged edition, Rev. D). San Diego, CA: American Technology Corp.; Anon (1997) Hypersonic Sound: Sound From Thin Air. *Popular Mechanics*, June 1997; United States Patent Office (1999) *Acoustic heterodyne device and method, United States Patent 5,889,870, 30 March 1999;* United States Patent Office (2000) *Resonant tuned, ultrasonic electrostatic emitter, United States Patent 6,044,160, 28 March 2000.*

64. Altmann, J. (2005) Acoustic NLW Working in the Audio Range. *Proceedings of the 3rd European Symposium on Non-Lethal Weapons, Ettlingen, Germany, 10–12 May 2005.* P38. Pfinztal: Fraunhofer ICT.

65. American Technology Corp. (2003) *American Technology Announces Licensing and Sales Agreements with General Dynamics.* Press Release, 20 February 2003.

66. Altmann, J. (2005) op. cit.; Others have suggested that it employs an ultrasonic source: Leventhall, G. (2004) Big Noise in Baghdad. *Noise and Vibration Worldwide*, June 2004, pp. 27–30.

67. BBC News (2005) Cruise lines turn to sonic weapon. *BBC News*, 8 November 2005. Accessed March 2007 at: http://news.bbc.co.uk/.

68. American Technology Corp. website, Product Lines – LRAD. Accessed March 2007 at: http://www.atcsd.com/.

69. American Technology Corp. (2005) *Long Range Acoustic Device.* Powerpoint Presentation, September 2005. San Diego, CA: American Technology Corp.; American Technology Corp. (not dated) *LRAD Technology Backgrounder.* San Diego, CA: American Technology Corp. Accessed March 2007 at: http://www.atcsd.com/.

70. American Technology Corp. (not dated) *LRAD 500 Military Datasheet.* San Diego, CA: American Technology Corp.; American Technology Corp. (not dated) *LRAD 1000 Military Datasheet.* San Diego, CA: American Technology Corp.

71. American Technology Corp. website, Military – LRAD. Accessed September 2008 at: http://www.atcsd.com/.

72. Altmann, J. (2005) op. cit.

73. American Technology Corp. (2005) *Long Range Acoustic Device.* op. cit.; Altmann, J. (2005) op. cit.; American Technology Corp. website, Military – LRAD. Accessed March 2007 at: http://www.atcsd.com/.

74. American Technology Corp. (2005) *Long Range Acoustic Device.* op. cit.; CNN (2004) Troops get high tech noisemaker. *CNN.com*, 3 March 3004; Bostwick, C. (2005) Noise May Help Fight Crime. *Daily News of Los Angeles*, 2 September 2005.

75. Pappalardo, J. (2005) Security Beat. *National Defense*, July 2005.

76. American Technology Corp. (2005) *Long Range Acoustic Device.* op. cit.; Bostwick, C. (2005) op. cit.; American Technology Corp. (2004) *American Technology Reports On Growing Long Range Acoustic Devices (Lrad™) Business.* Press Release, 26 August 2004.

77. McCutcheon, C. (2004) Military's Needs Speed Development of New Non-Lethal Weapons. *Newhouse News Service*, 9 June 2004; Braiker, B. (2004) Master Blaster: A New Noisemaker. *Newsweek*, 12 July 2004.

78. Jardin, X. (2005) Focused Sound 'Laser' for Crowd Control. *NPR*, 21 September 2005. Accessed March 2007 at: http://www.npr.org/templates/.

79. Blenford, A. (2005) Cruise lines turn to sonic weapon. *BBC News*, 8 November 2005. Accessed March 2007 at: http://news.bbc.co.uk/; Ravilious, K. (2005) The secrets of sonic weapons. *The Guardian*, 8 November 2005; Jardin, X. (2005) Sonic 'Lasers' Head to Flood Zone. *Wired News*, 2 September 2005.

80. Shachtman, N. (2007) Georgia Police Turns Sonic Blaster on Demonstrators. *Wired. com*, 15 November 2007. Accessed December 2007 at: http://blog.wired.com/.

81. Hambling, D. (2008) Loudhailer or weapon? *NewScientist.com*, 13 May 2008; Hambling, D. (2008) US 'Sonic Blasters' Sold To China. *Wired.com*, 15 May 2008. Accessed September 2008 at: http://blog.wired.com/.

82. One UK distributor is Audionation UK, website. Accessed September 2008 at: http://www.audionation-uk.com/.

83. Metropolitan Police Authority (2007) *Public order review. Report: 6, 26 April 2007.* Accessed December 2007 at: http://www.mpa.gov.uk/.

84. Joint Non-Lethal Weapons Program (2006) *Acoustic Hailing Devices (AHD) Fact Sheet*. Quantico, VA: JNLWD.

85. Anon (2004) More services using nonlethal Long Range Acoustic Device, says maker. *Military and Aerospace Electronics Online*, 26 August 2004.

86. Occupational Health and Safety Administration (not dated) *Occupational Safety and Health Standards. Standard Number 1910.5: Occupational noise exposure.* Washington, DC: Occupational Health and Safety Administration.

87. National Institute for Occupational Safety and Health (1998) *Criteria for a Recommended Standard: Occupational Noise Exposure.* NIOSH Publication No. 98-126, June 1998. Atlanta, GA: National Institute for Occupational Safety and Health.

88. Email communication with Nicholas Nicholas, Applied Research Laboratory, Pennsylvania State University, 8 March 2006.

89. Grimes, J. (2005) *Modelling Sound As A Non-lethal Weapon in the CombatXXI Simulation Model.* Thesis, June 2005. Monterey, CA: Naval Postgraduate School, p. 12.

90. Altmann, J. (2005) op. cit.

91. Jontz, S. (2004) Marines in Iraq trying out controversial new hailing and warning device. *Stars and Stripes*, 25 March 2004.

92. Sella, M. (2003) The Sound of Things to Come. *New York Times*, 23 March 2003; Telephone conversation with AJ Ballard at American Technology Corp., 22 September 2005; Also see the Pennsylvania State University website for Dr. Tom Frank: 'Human Effects Assessment of the Long Range Acoustic Device (LRAD) (Co Principal Investigator with Nicholas, PI, Senior Research Associate, Institute for Non-Lethal Defense Technologies). The purpose of this research was to: (1) establish safe operating guidelines for the LRAD, and (2) determine the effectiveness of presenting different types of sounds via the LRAD that interfere with communication, create an annoyance, and for crowd control and dispersal. This project was funded by M2 Technologies, Inc.'. Accessed March 2007 at: http://csd.hhdev.psu.edu/.

93. Koplow, D. (2006) *Non-Lethal Weapons: The Law and Policy of Revolutionary Technologies for the Military and Law Enforcement.* Cambridge: Cambridge University Press, pp. 53–66.

94. The 361st Psychological Operations Company in Iraq. Unofficial website. Accessed March 2007 at: http://www.psywarrior.com/361stPsyopIraq.html.

95. See for example: Magnetic Audio Device website. Accessed March 2007 at: http://www.getmad.com/; Power Sonix, Inc. website. Accessed March 2007 at: http://www.powersonix.com/; IML Corp. website, Sound Commander, available March 2007 at: http://www.imlcorp.com/; Wattre Corp. website, Hyperspike. Accessed August 2007 at: http://wattre.com/; Freinberg, T. (2004) Israel to stun rioters into submission with 'shouting' gun. *The Daily Telegraph*, 17 October 2005.

96. Power Sonix website, Military loudspeakers and sirens. Accessed March 2007 at: http://www.powersonix.com/.

97. US Army ARDEC (2006) Special Notice. 99–Acoustic Hailing Devices. *FBO Daily*, 11 January 2006, FBO No. 1507; Joint Non-Lethal Weapons Program (2006) op. cit.

98. Magnuson, S. (2006) Lasers Seen as Solution To Checkpoint Safety. *National Defense*, February 2006.

99. Tiron, R. (2002) Acoustic-Energy Research Hits Sour Note. *National Defense*, March 2002; American Technology Corporation (2003) *American Technology Corporation Shareholder Alert*. Press Release, 23 April 2003.

100. Department of Defense (2006) *Department of Defense Annual Report on Cooperative Agreements and Other Transactions Entered into During Fiscal Year 2005 Under 10 USC 2371*. Washington, DC: Department of Defense, p. 117.

101. SARA, Inc. remains interested in acoustic weapons, see for example: Wes, J. (2000) Man-tossable Acoustic Distraction Device. *Presentation to Non-Lethal Defense IV, National Defense Industrial Association (NDIA), US, 20–2 March 2000*; United States Patent Office (2003) *Less lethal multi-sensory distraction grenade, United States Patent 6,543,364, 8 April 2003*.

102. Sella, M. (2003); Arkin, W. (2004) The Pentagon's Secret Scream. *Los Angeles Times*, 6 March 2004.

103. Moore, H. (2000) Aversive Audible Acoustic Devices. *Presentation to Non-Lethal Defense IV, National Defense Industrial Association (NDIA), US, 20–2 March 2000*; United States Patent Office (2002) *High intensity directed light and sound crowd dispersion device, United States Patent 6,359,835, 19 March 2002*.

104. United States Patent Office (1999) *Directed stick radiator, United States Patent 5,940,347, 17 August 1999*.

105. United States Patent Office (2000) *Directed radiator with modulated ultrasonic sound, United States Patent 6,016,351, 18 January 2000*; Sample, I. (2001) Pentagon considers ear-blasting anti-hijack gun. *New Scientist*, 14 November 2001; Tiron, R. (2002) op. cit.; American Technology Corporation (2003) op. cit.; Eisenreich, N., Thiel, K-D, Herzog, A., and Walschburger, E. (2005) Aspects of the Directed Stick Radiator (DSR). *Proceedings of the 3rd European Symposium on Non-Lethal Weapons, Ettlingen, Germany, 10–12 May 2005*. P40. Pfinztal: Fraunhofer ICT.

106. Kenyon, H. (2002) Noisemakers Called to Arms. *SIGNAL Magazine*, July 2002.

107. US Securities and Exchange Commission (2003) *American Technology Corporation. Form 10-K Annual Report For the fiscal year ended September 30, 2003*. Washington, DC: Securities and Exchange Commission.

108. Jauchem, J. and Cook, M. (2007) op. cit.

109. Altmann, J. (2005) op. cit.

110. Moore, H. (2001) Directed Energy Assessment. *Presentation to the Armaments for the Army Transformation Conference, National Defense Industrial Association (NDIA), US, 18–20 June 1998*.

111. Moore, H. (2002) Multi-Sensory Deprivation 'Land Mine'. *Presentation to the International Infantry & Joint Services Small Arms Systems Section Symposium, Exhibition & Firing Demonstration, National Defense Industrial Association (NDIA), US, 13–16 May 2002*.

112. Armament Research, Development and Engineering Center (not dated) *Target Behavioral Response Laboratory (TBRL) Fact Sheet*. Picatinny, NJ: ARDEC.

113. VanMeenen, K., Short, K., DeMarco, R., Chua, F., Janal, M., and Servatius, R. (1996) Suppression: sound and light interference with targeting. *Proceedings of SPIE*, Vol. 6219, p. 62190J; Yagrich, K. and Crabbe, J. (2003) Target Effects Based Requirements Generation. The Role of the ARDEC Target Behavioral Response

Laboratory. *Presentation to the 2003 Mines, Demolitions, and Non-Lethal Weapons Conference & Exhibition, National Defense Industrial Association (NDIA), New Orleans, LA, US, 9–11 September 2003.*

114. Beck, K., Short, K., VanMeenen, K., and Servatius, R. (2006) Suppression through acoustics. *Proceedings of SPIE*, Vol. 6219, p. 62190I; Yagrich, K. and Crabbe, J. (2003) op. cit.; Stress and Motivated Behavior Institute website, Aversive Acoustic Stimuli section. Accessed March 2007 at: http://www.umdnj.edu/smbiweb/.

115. Boesch, H. and Reiff, C. (2000) A Prototype High-Intensity Infrasonic Test Chamber (HILF 1). *Presentation to Non-Lethal Defense IV, National Defense Industrial Association (NDIA), US, 20–2 March 2000*; This would be called HILF 2. The original HILF 1 was constructed in 1998 and produced sound levels of 143 dB.

116. Stress and Motivated Behavior Institute website, Infrasonic Stimuli section. Accessed March 2007 at: http://www.umdnj.edu/smbiweb/; Armament Research, Development and Engineering Center (not dated) *Target Behavioral Response Laboratory (TBRL) Fact Sheet.* op. cit.; Beck, K., Short, K., VanMeenen, K., and Servatius, R. (2006).

117. Beck, K., Short, K., VanMeenen, K., and Servatius, R. (2006).

118. Ibid.

119. Shawaery, G. (2003) Leveraging Non-Lethal Technology Research In Academia. *Proceedings of the 2nd European Symposium on Non-Lethal Weapons, Ettlingen, Germany, 13–14 May 2003.* P50. Pfinztal: Fraunhofer ICT; Grimm, M., Rang, E., Israel, R., and Lippert, S. (2004) Ultrasonic Properties Of Human Tissues. Constitutive Information for Assessing Effects of Ultrasound Use in Non-Lethal Weapons – A Progress Report. *Presentation to the Non-lethal Technology and Academic Research Symposium VI (NTAR VI), Winston-Salem, NC, US, 15–17 November 2004.*

120. Scientific Applications & Research Associates Inc. (2003) *Law Enforcement Applications (Non-lethals).* SARA website. Accessed November 2003 at: http://www.sara.com/.

121. Edwards, J. (2003) Initial Simulations Of A Single Shot Vortex Gun. *Proceedings of the 2nd European Symposium on Non-Lethal Weapons, Ettlingen, Germany, 13–14 May 2003.* V31. Pfinztal: Fraunhofer ICT; Backhaus, J., Deimling, L., Blanc, A., Schweitzer, S., and Thiel, K-D. (2003) Impulse Transport by propagating Vortex Rings. *Proceedings of the 2nd European Symposium on Non-Lethal Weapons, Ettlingen, Germany, 13–14 May 2003.* V32. Pfinztal: Fraunhofer ICT; Onipko, E. and Selivanov, V. (2003) Application Of Vortex Technologies For Crowd Control. *Proceedings of the 2nd European Symposium on Non-Lethal Weapons, Ettlingen, Germany, 13–14 May 2003.* P37. Pfinztal: Fraunhofer ICT; Havermann, M. (2005) Influence of Physical and Geometrical Parameters on Vortex Rings Generated by a Shock Tube. *Proceedings of the 3rd European Symposium on Non-Lethal Weapons, Ettlingen, Germany, 10–12 May 2005.* V24. Pfinztal: Fraunhofer ICT; Edwards, J. and Kontis, K. (2005) Fluid Dynamic Issues in the Development of a Single Shot Vortex Gun. *Proceedings of the 3rd European Symposium on Non-Lethal Weapons, Ettlingen, Germany, 10–12 May 2005.* V27. Pfinztal: Fraunhofer ICT.

122. Stocker, H., Dick, J., and Berube, G. (2004) *Non-Lethal Weapons: Opportunities for R&D.* Technical Memorandum, DRDC-TM-2004-006, December 2004. Ottawa: Defence R&D Canada. Annex E, p. 6.

123. National Research Council (2003) op. cit., pp. 31–2.

124. University of Texas at Austin (2002) op. cit.; The report noted with regard to audible sound that 'In water, human hearing is 30–40 dB less sensitive on average, which raises the threshold of pain'., p. 26.

125. Ibid., p. 39.

126. Ibid., pp. 47–9.

127. Ibid., pp. 42–4.

128. Ibid., p. 44.

129. Schaefer, R. and Grapperhaus, M. (2006) Non-lethal unfriendly swimmer and pipe defense combining sound and flash pulses using a new sparker. *Proceedings of SPIE*, Vol. 6204, p. 620407.

130. Schaefer, R. and Grapperhaus, M. (2006) Nonlethal combined flash and sound pulse projector for counter-personnel and crowd control. *Proceedings of SPIE*, Vol. 6219, p. 621901.

131. University of Texas at Austin (2002) op. cit., pp. 39–40; Erikson, K (2002) Non-Lethal Denial Of Access to Water-Borne Intruders Using Intense Sound: An Introduction. *Abstract of presentation to the Non-lethal Technology and Academic Research symposium IV (NTAR IV), 19–21 November 2002, La Jolla, CA, US.*

132. e²M, Inc. (2005) *Environmental Assessment of the Installation and Operation of an Integrated Anti-Swimmer System San Pedro, California.* Fairfax, VA: e²M, Inc.

133. US Coast Guard Research and Development Center (2006) *Extended Range Underwater Loudhailer for Port Security Applications.* Report No. CG-D-04-06. Washington, DC: US Coast Guard.

134. Atlesek, P. (2006) *US Coast Guard. Environmental Law Update Course, 28 June 2006.* Powerpoint presentation; Daniel, J. (2006) Leveraging Biomedical Knowledge to Enhance Homeland Defense, Submarine Medicine and Warfighter Performance at Naval Submarine Medical Research Laboratory. *CHIPS Magazine*, January–March 2006; Anderson, M. (2005) Underwater security garners more cash & new technologies. *Government Security News*, May 2005; Lipton, E. (2005) Coast Guard Turns Its Eyes Underwater. *New York Times*, 2 February 2005.

135. US Navy (2008) A – Non-Lethal Surface Swimmer Deterrent System. *FBO Daily*, 8 September 2008.

136. Stocker, H., Dick, J., and Berube, G. (2004) op. cit., Annex E.

137. University of Texas at Austin (2002) op. cit.

138. Jauchem, J. et al. (2003) op. cit.

139. Jauchem, J. and Cook, M. (2007) op. cit.

140. Joint Non-Lethal Weapons Directorate (2006) *JNLWP Fiscal Year 2006-7 Technology Broad Area Announcement. Non-Lethal Weapons Technology Fiscal Year 2006–Fiscal Year 2007 Applied Research And Development Efforts.* Accessed March 2007 at: https://www.jnlwp.com/.

141. Joint Non-Lethal Weapons Program (2008) *Distributed Sound and Light Array (DSLA) Fact Sheet.* Quantico, VA: JNLWD.

142. Lumsden, M. (1978) op. cit., pp. 203–5; Liszka, Z. (1994) Sonic Beam Devices – Principles. In: *Report of the Expert Meeting on Certain Weapon Systems and on Implementation Mechanisms in International Law, Geneva, 30 May–1 June 1994.* Geneva: International Committee of the Red Cross, pp. 89–91; Altmann, J. (1999) op. cit.; Altmann, J. (2001) op. cit.; Arkin, W. (1997) op. cit.

143. Jauchem, J. and Cook, M. (2007) op. cit.

144. Possible exceptions include underwater applications and weapons based on vortex ring concepts. However, the latter may be better defined as delivery systems than acoustic weapons.

8   Conclusion

1. Allison, G., Kelley, P., and Garwin, R. (2004) *Nonlethal Weapons and Capabilities. Report of an Independent Task Force.* New York: Council on Foreign Relations Press, Appendix A: Currently Available (or Nearly Available) Nonlethal Weapons, pp. 49–50; National Institute of Justice (2004) *Department of Defense Nonlethal Weapons and Equipment Review: A Research Guide for Civil Law Enforcement and Corrections.* Washington, DC: National Institute of Justice, US Department of Justice, October 2004; also see Chapters 1, 2, and 3 of this book.
2. Security Planning Corporation (1972) *Non-Lethal Weapons for Law Enforcement: Research Needs and Priorities. A Report to the National Science Foundation.* Washington, DC: Security Planning Corporation, pp. 25–9.
3. Office of the United Nations High Commissioner for Human Rights (1990) *Basic Principles on the Use of Force and Firearms by Law Enforcement Officials.* Adopted by the Eighth United Nations Congress on the Prevention of Crime and the Treatment of Offenders, Havana, Cuba; 27 August to 7 September 1990.
4. Theories of supply side influence on demand in the context of unconventional weapons development and uptake have been put forward by Perry Robinson, see: Perry Robinson, J. (1982) The changing status of chemical and biological warfare: recent technical, military and political developments. In: *World Armaments and Disarmament, SIPRI Yearbook 1982.* London: Taylor and Francis, pp. 317–61; Perry Robinson, J. (1989) Supply, Demand and Assimilation in Chemical-warfare armament. In: H. Brauch (ed.) *Military Technology, Armaments Dynamics and Disarmament.* Basingstoke, UK: Macmillan, pp. 112–23.

Index